デルトラクエスト

Volume 4

Story by Emily Rodda

Illustrated by Makoto Niwano

Translated by Alethea Nibley and Athena Nibley
Lettered by Bobby Timony

KC
KODANSHA
COMICS

Deltora Quest volume 4, is a work of fiction. Names, characters, places, and incidents are the products of the author's imagination or are used fictitiously. Any resemblance to actual events, locales, or persons, living or dead, is entirely coincidental.

Original story by Emily Rodda

A Kodansha Comics Trade Paperback Original

Published in the United States by Kodansha Comics, an imprint of Kodansha USA Publishing, LLC, New York.

Publication rights for this English edition arranged through Kodansha Ltd., Tokyo.

First published in Japan in 2006 by Kodansha Ltd., Tokyo.

ISBN 978-1-935429-31-9

Printed in the United States of America

www.kodanshacomics.com

9 8 7 6 5 4 3 2 1

Translator: Alethea Nibley and Athena Nibley
Lettering: Bobby Timony

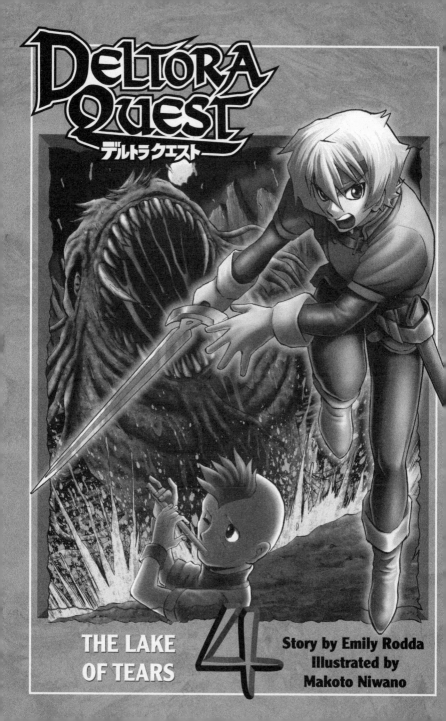

DELTORA QUEST
デルトラ クエスト

THE LAKE
OF TEARS

4

Story by Emily Rodda
Illustrated by
Makoto Niwano

Deltora Quest
デルトラクエスト

Volume 4: Character Introductions

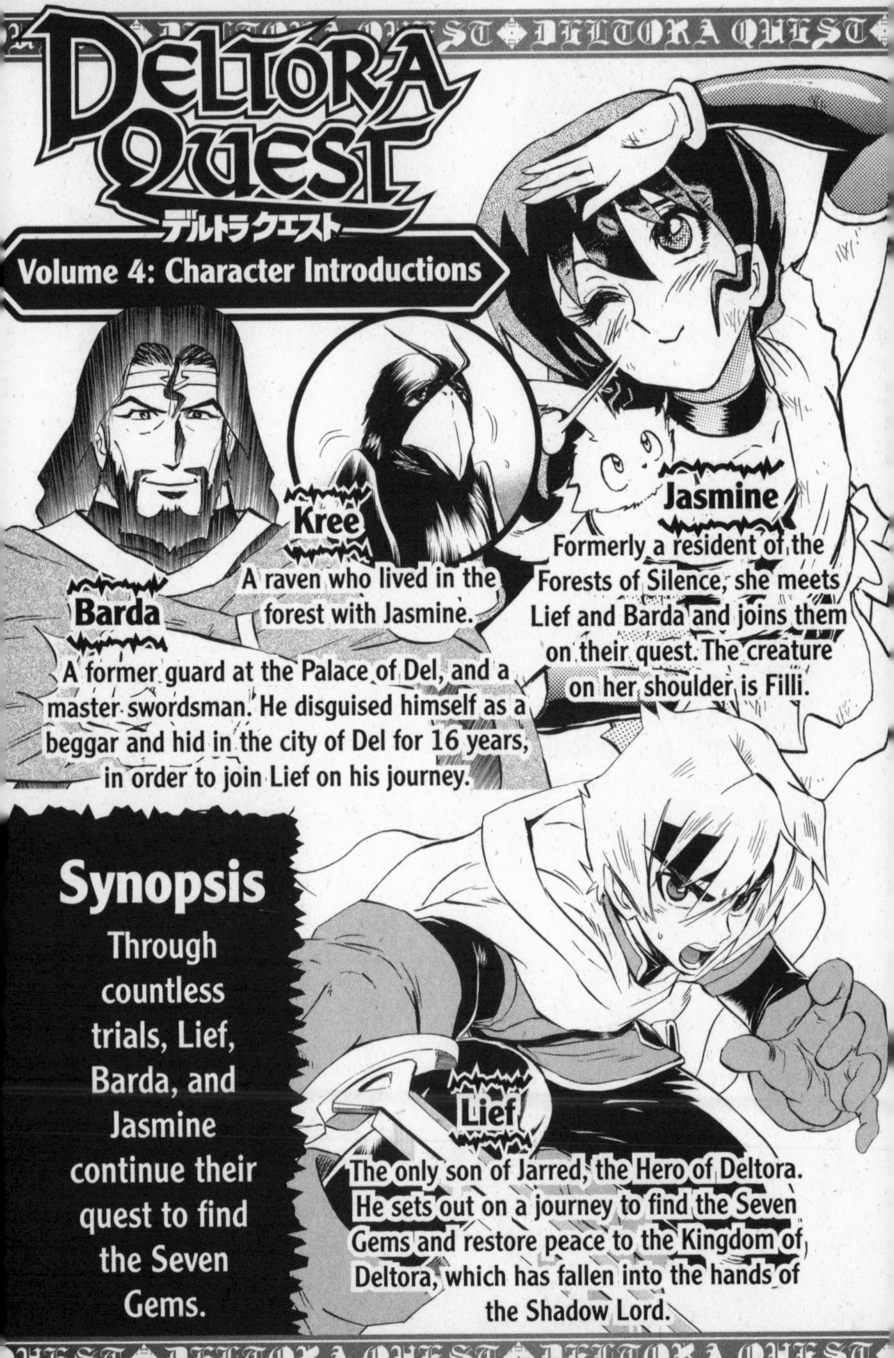

Barda
A former guard at the Palace of Del, and a master swordsman. He disguised himself as a beggar and hid in the city of Del for 16 years, in order to join Lief on his journey.

Kree
A raven who lived in the forest with Jasmine.

Jasmine
Formerly a resident of the Forests of Silence, she meets Lief and Barda and joins them on their quest. The creature on her shoulder is Filli.

Lief
The only son of Jarred, the Hero of Deltora. He sets out on a journey to find the Seven Gems and restore peace to the Kingdom of Deltora, which has fallen into the hands of the Shadow Lord.

Synopsis
Through countless trials, Lief, Barda, and Jasmine continue their quest to find the Seven Gems.

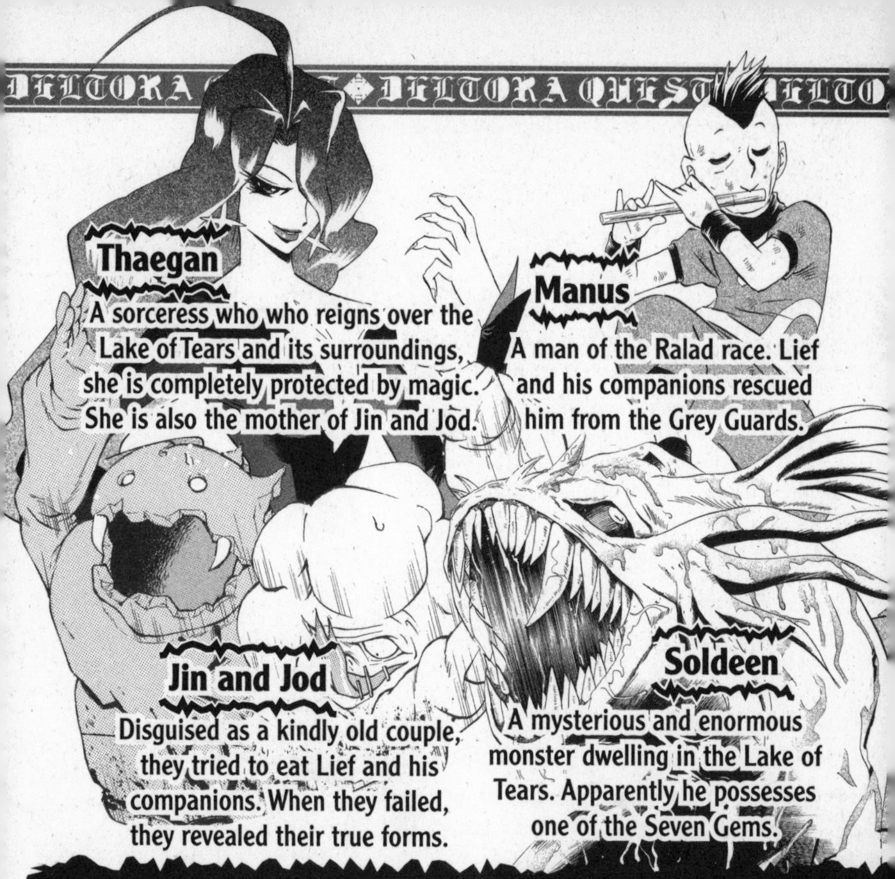
Thaegan
A sorceress who who reigns over the Lake of Tears and its surroundings, she is completely protected by magic. She is also the mother of Jin and Jod.
Manus
A man of the Ralad race. Lief and his companions rescued him from the Grey Guards.
Jin and Jod
Disguised as a kindly old couple, they tried to eat Lief and his companions. When they failed, they revealed their true forms.
Soldeen
A mysterious and enormous monster dwelling in the Lake of Tears. Apparently he possesses one of the Seven Gems.

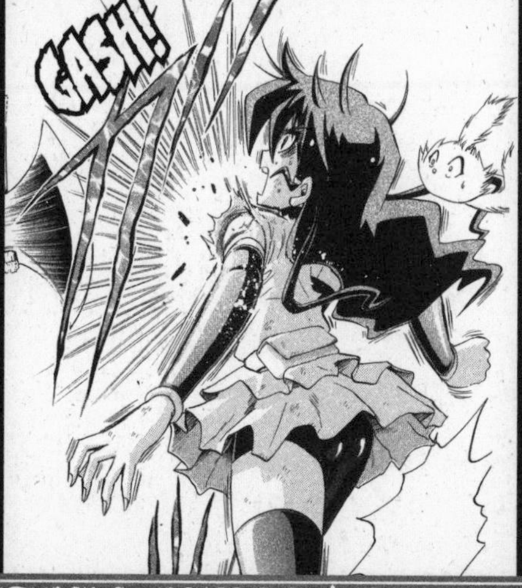
GASH!

Jin and Jod attack; after a fierce battle, Lief and his friends make them strike each other down. However, just when the party thinks the two are dead, Jin and Jod merge and revive as a giant monster. As they try to escape, Jasmine falls behind and is hit by a flying axe.

DELTORA QUEST

デルトラクエスト

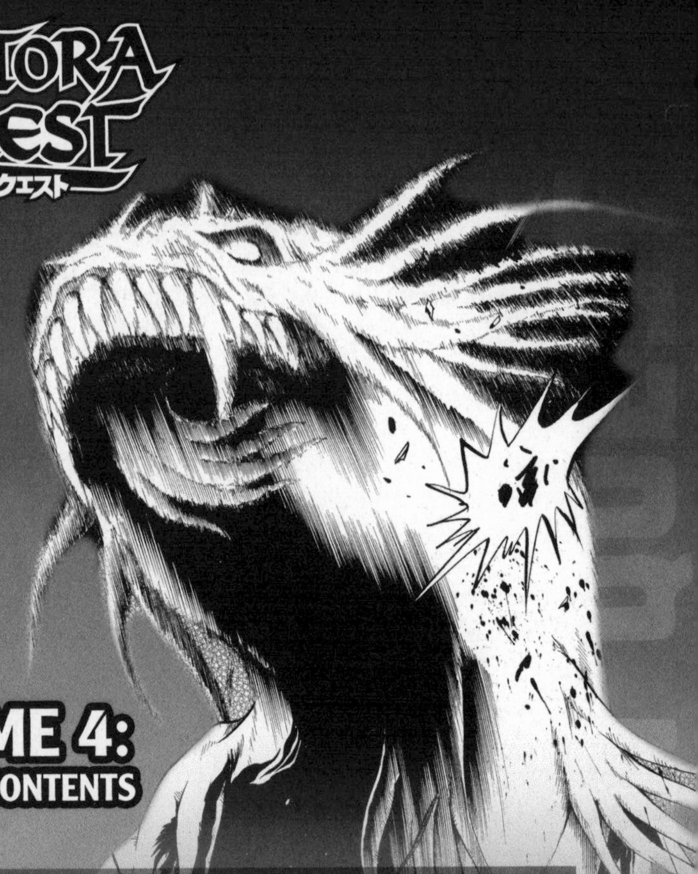

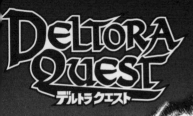

VOLUME 4:
TABLE OF CONTENTS

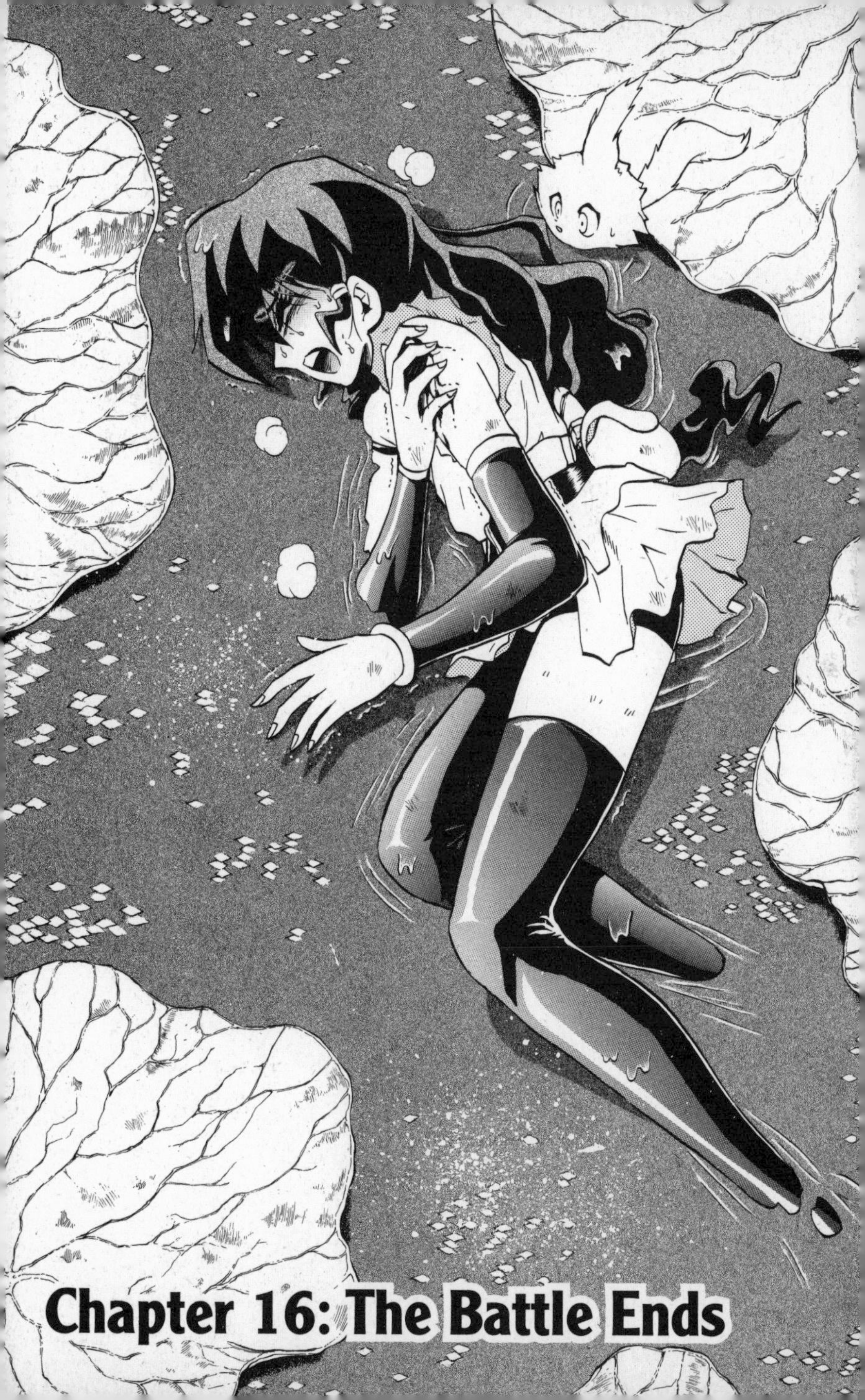

Chapter 16: The Battle Ends

SPLASH

S-

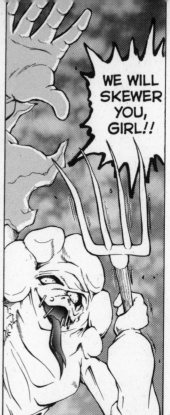

WE WILL SKEWER YOU, GIRL!!

STOP !!

CAW !!

FWOOSH

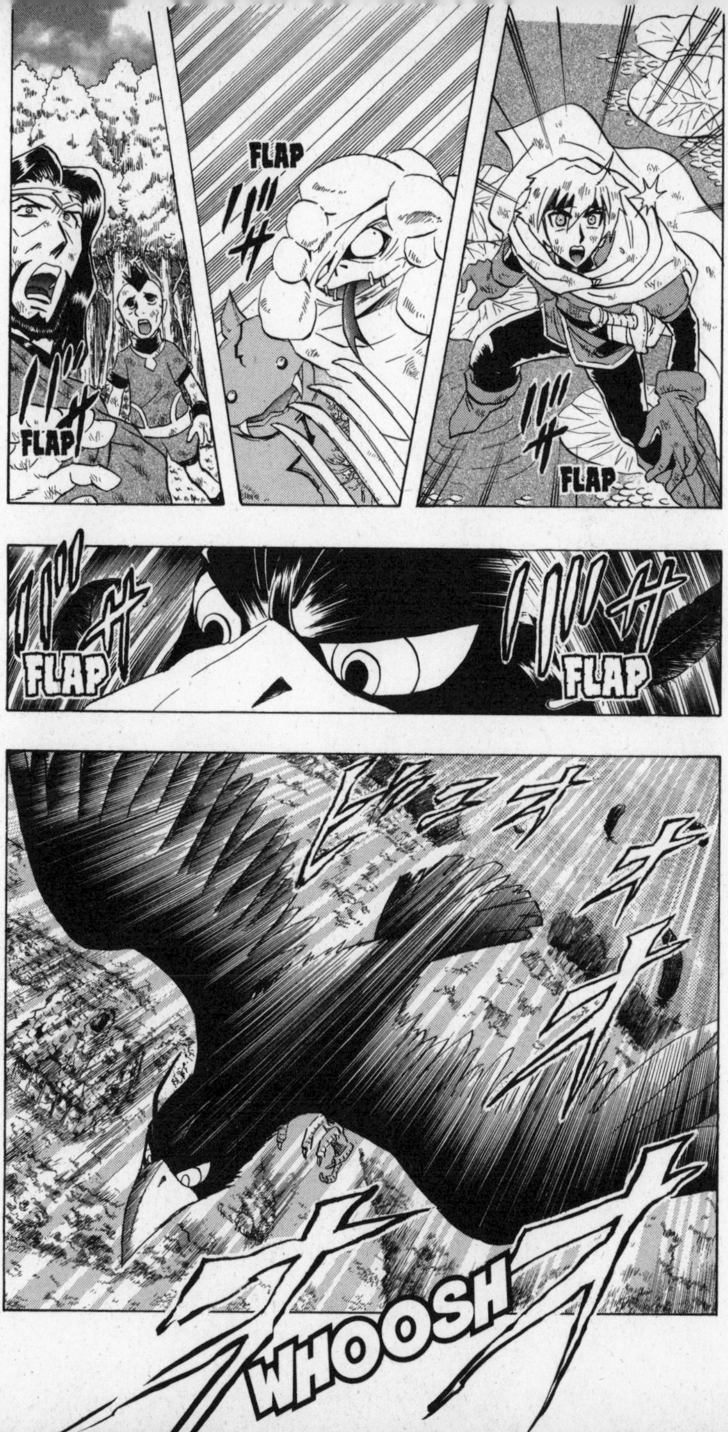

FLAP
FLAP
FLAP
FLAP
FLAP
WHOOSH

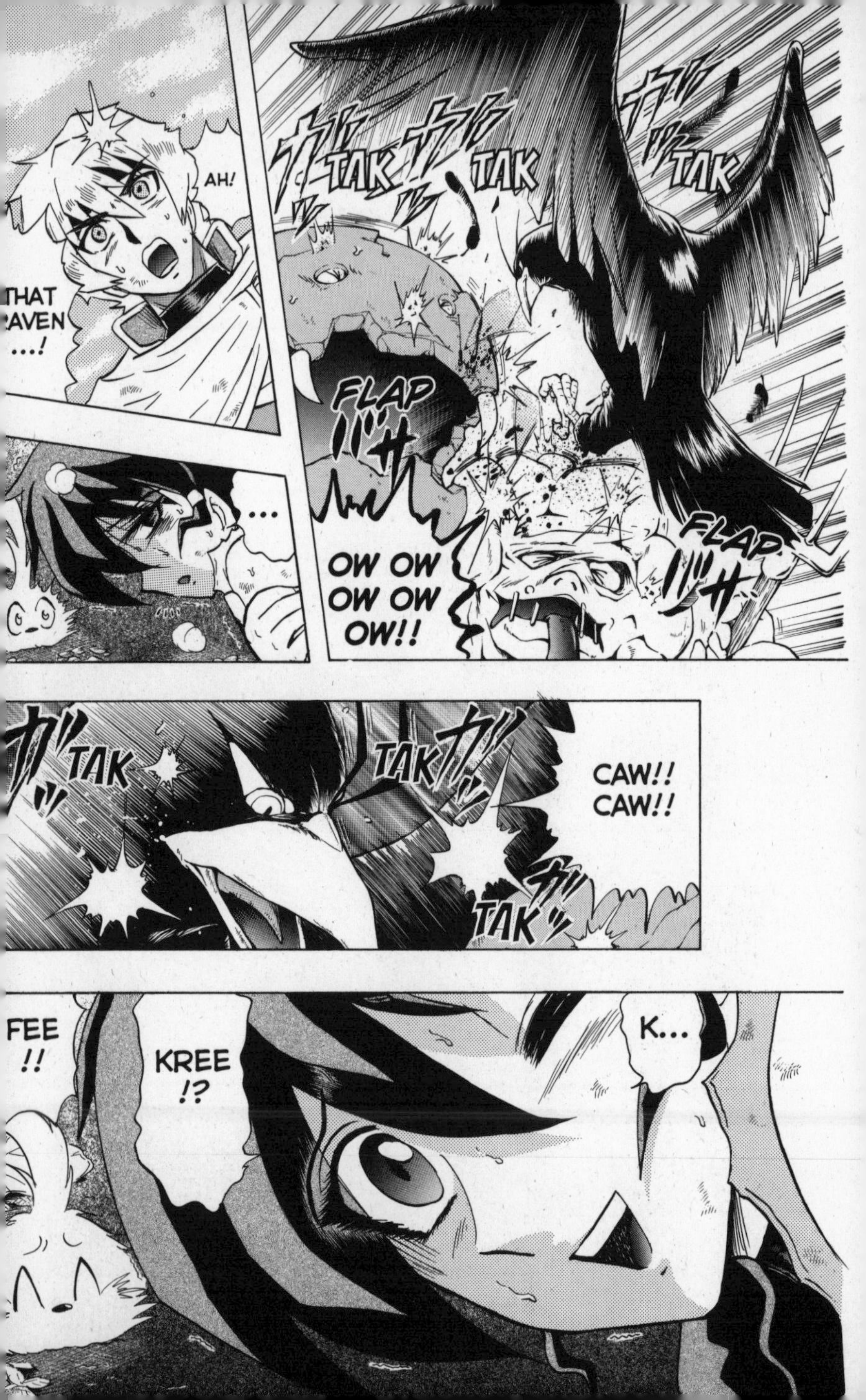
TAK
TAK
TAK
FLAP
FLAP
OW OW OW OW OW!!
AH!
THAT AVEN ...!
...
CAW!! CAW!!
TAK
TAK
TAK
K...
KREE !?
FEE !!

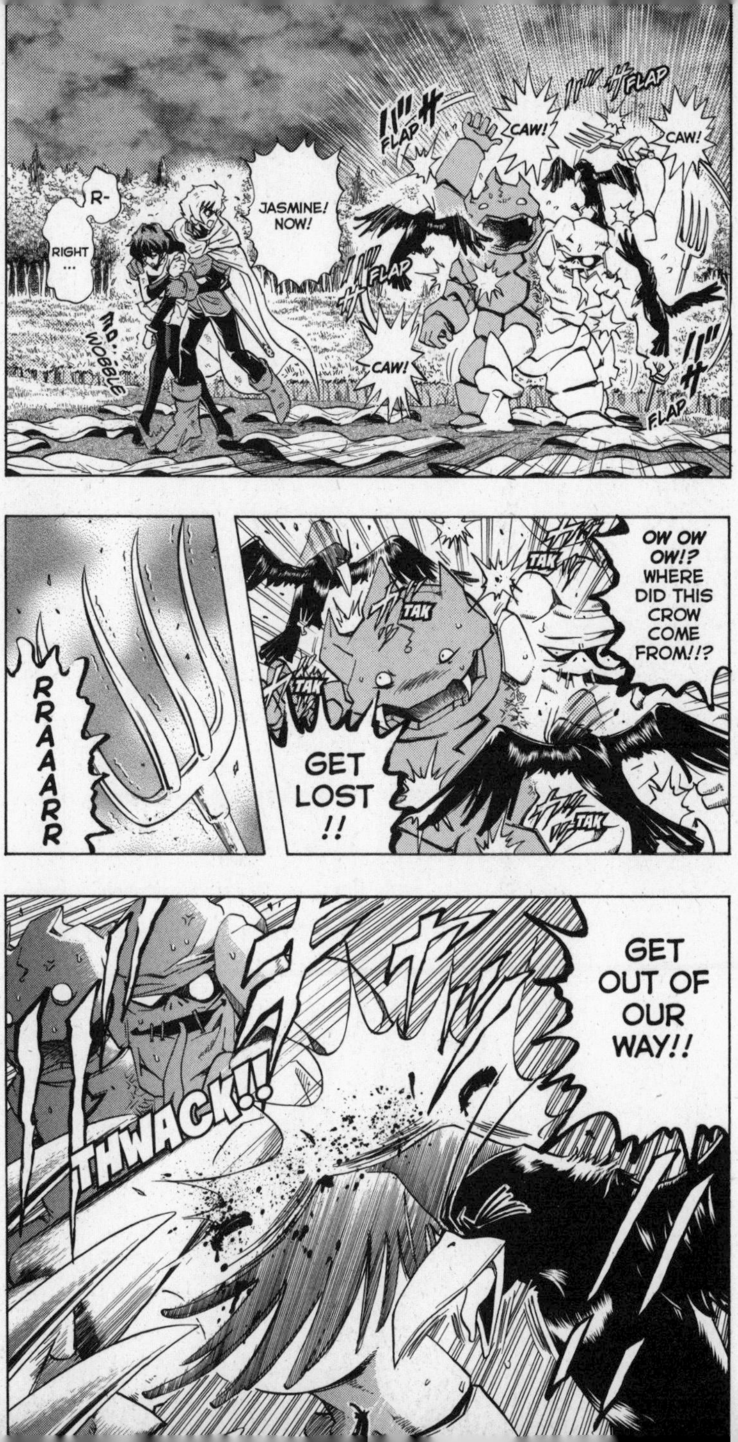
FLAP
CAW!
CAW!
FLAP
JASMINE! NOW!
R-
RIGHT ...
FLAP
FLAP
CAW!
WOBBLE
OW OW OW!? WHERE DID THIS CROW COME FROM!!?
TAK
TAK
TAK
GET LOST !!
TAK
RRAAAARR
GET OUT OF OUR WAY!!
THWACK!!

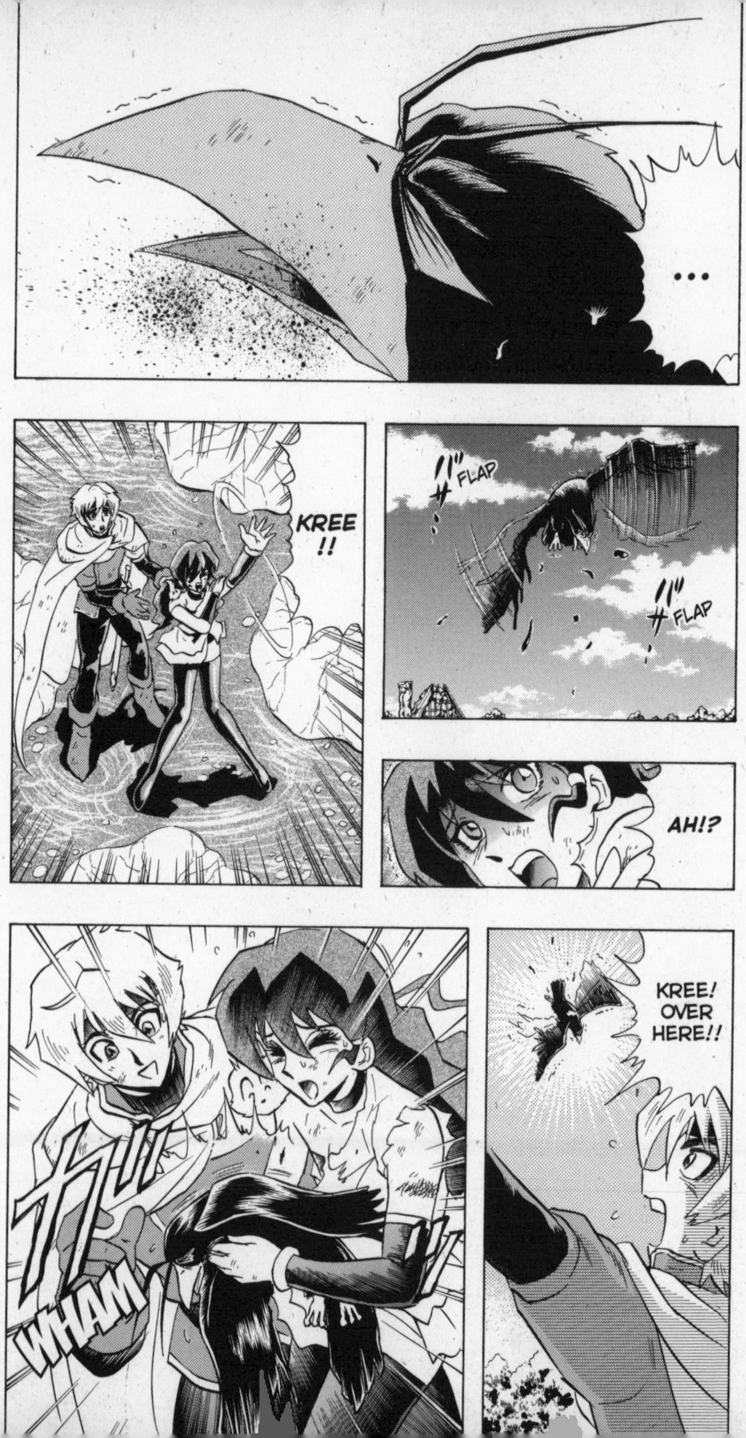
...
FLAP
FLAP
AH!?
KREE !!
KREE! OVER HERE!!
WHAM

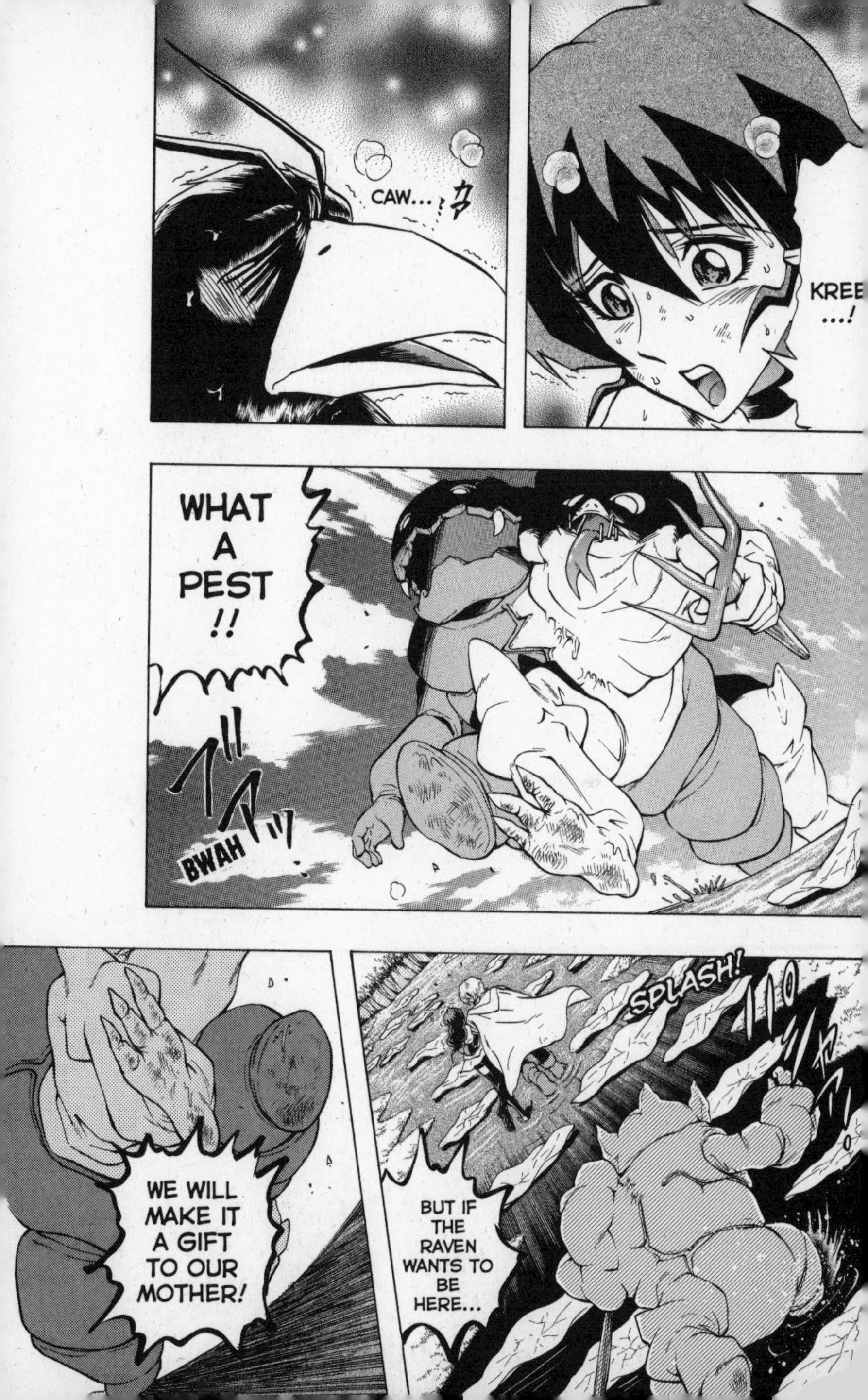
KREE ...!
CAW...
カ
WHAT A PEST !!
バァッ
BWAH
SPLASH!
シュ
BUT IF THE RAVEN WANTS TO BE HERE...
WE WILL MAKE IT A GIFT TO OUR MOTHER!

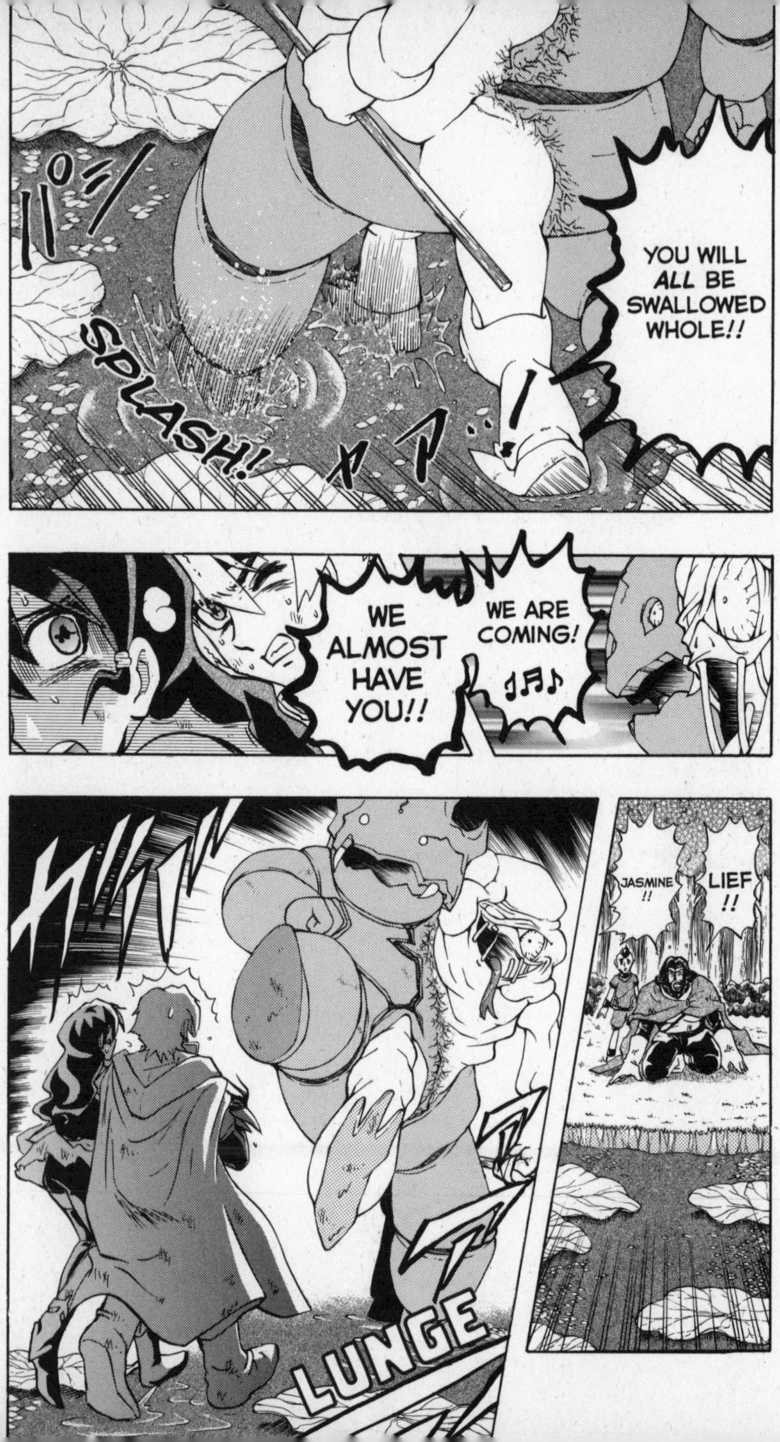
YOU WILL ALL BE SWALLOWED WHOLE!!
SPLASH!
WE ARE COMING! ♪♬♪
WE ALMOST HAVE YOU!!
LIEF!!
JASMINE!!
LUNGE

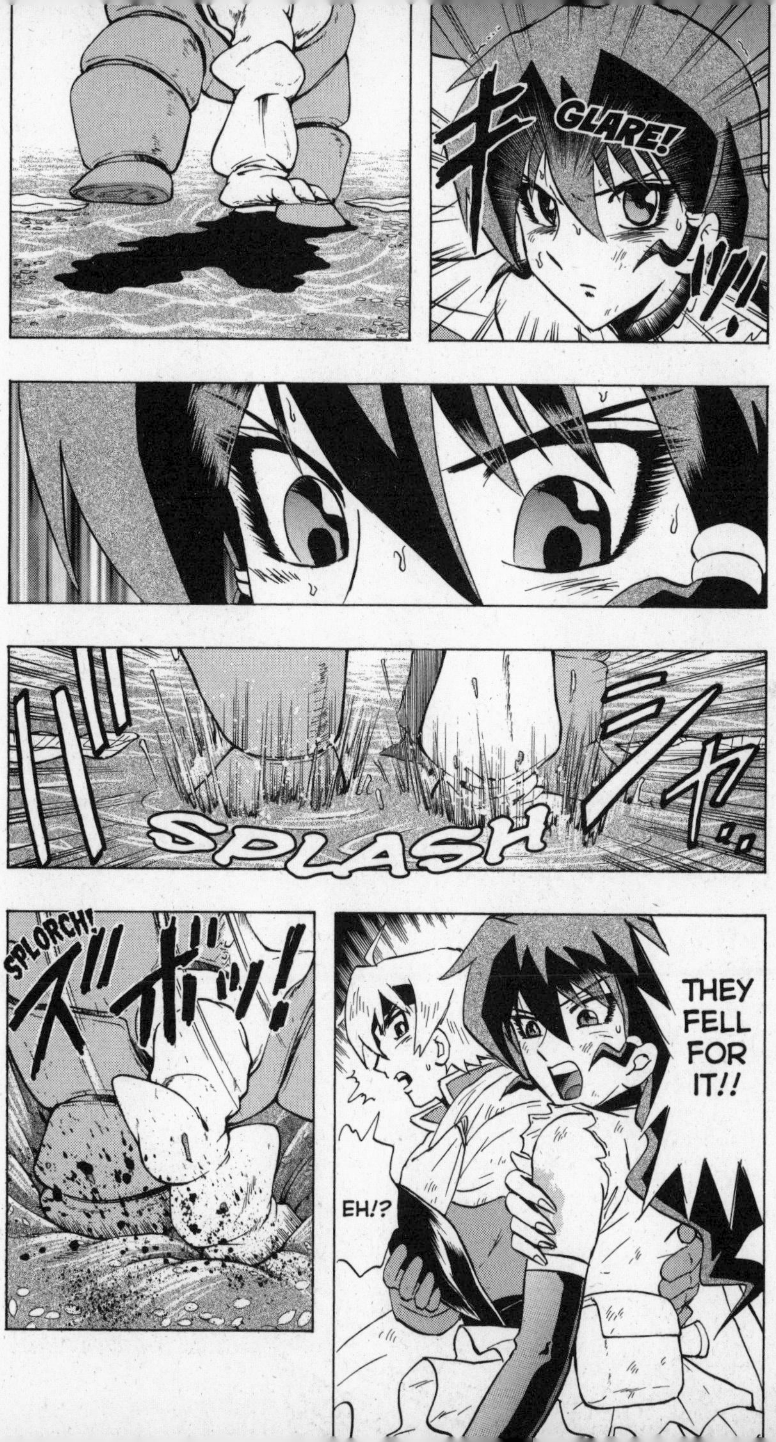
GLARE!
SPLASH
THEY FELL FOR IT!!
EH!?
SPLORCH!

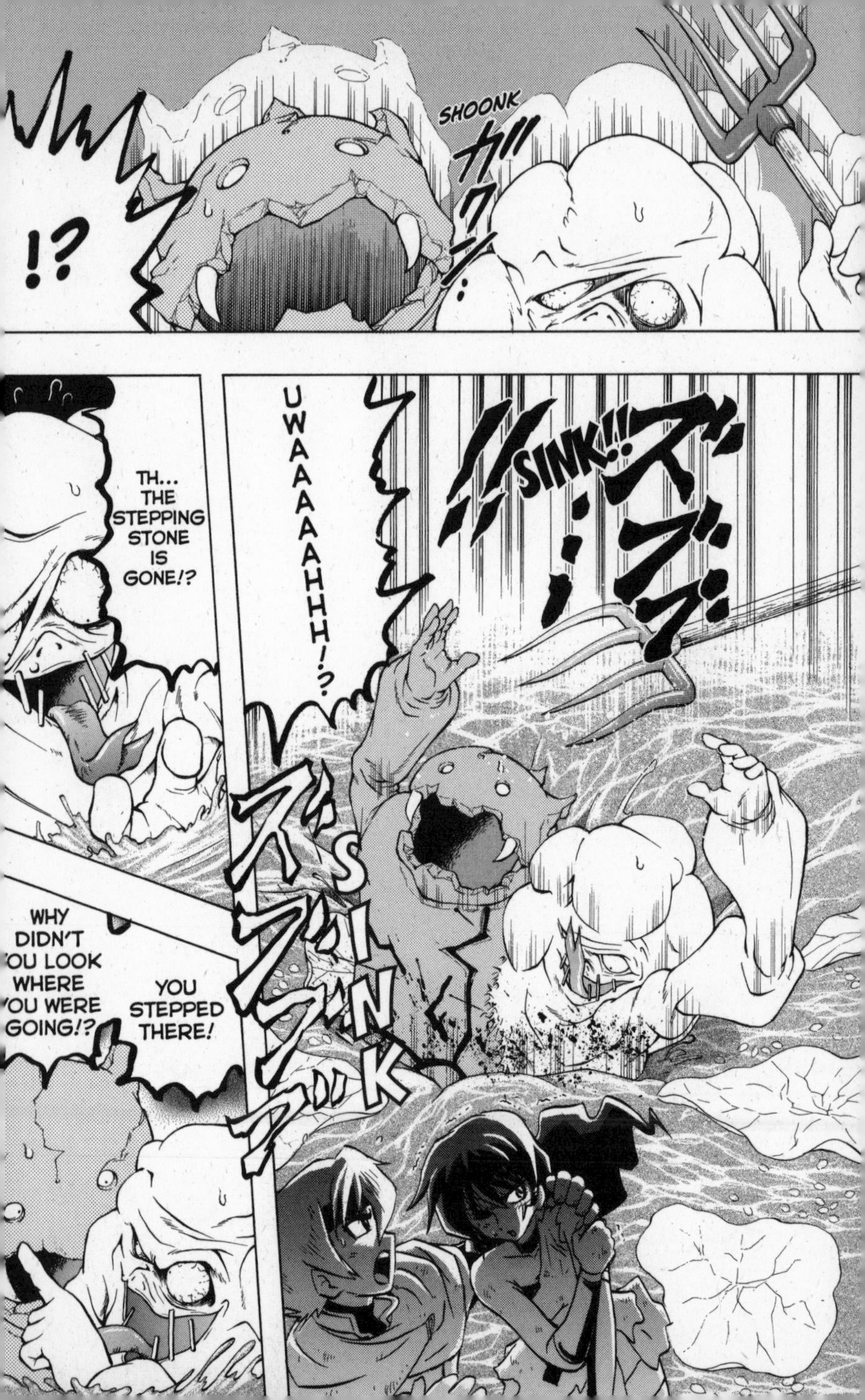
SHOONK
!?
SINK!!
UWAAAAAAHHH!?
SINK
TH... THE STEPPING STONE IS GONE!?
YOU STEPPED THERE!
WHY DIDN'T OU LOOK WHERE OU WERE GOING!?

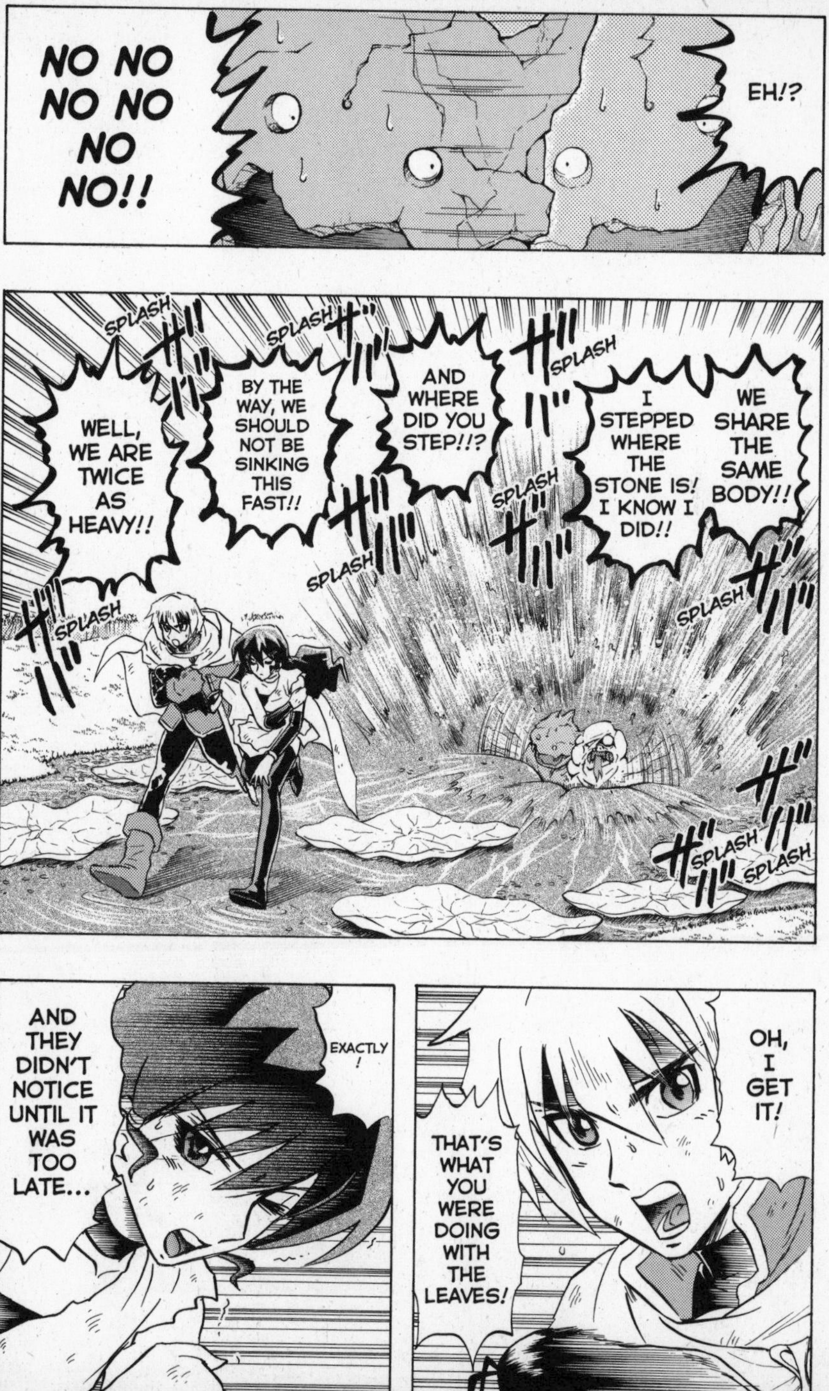
EH!?
NO NO NO NO NO NO!!
SPLASH
SPLASH
WE SHARE THE SAME BODY!!
I STEPPED WHERE THE STONE IS! I KNOW I DID!!
SPLASH
AND WHERE DID YOU STEP!!?
SPLASH
BY THE WAY, WE SHOULD NOT BE SINKING THIS FAST!!
SPLASH
WELL, WE ARE TWICE AS HEAVY!!
SPLASH
SPLASH
SPLASH
SPLASH
OH, I GET IT!
THAT'S WHAT YOU WERE DOING WITH THE LEAVES!
EXACTLY!
AND THEY DIDN'T NOTICE UNTIL IT WAS TOO LATE...

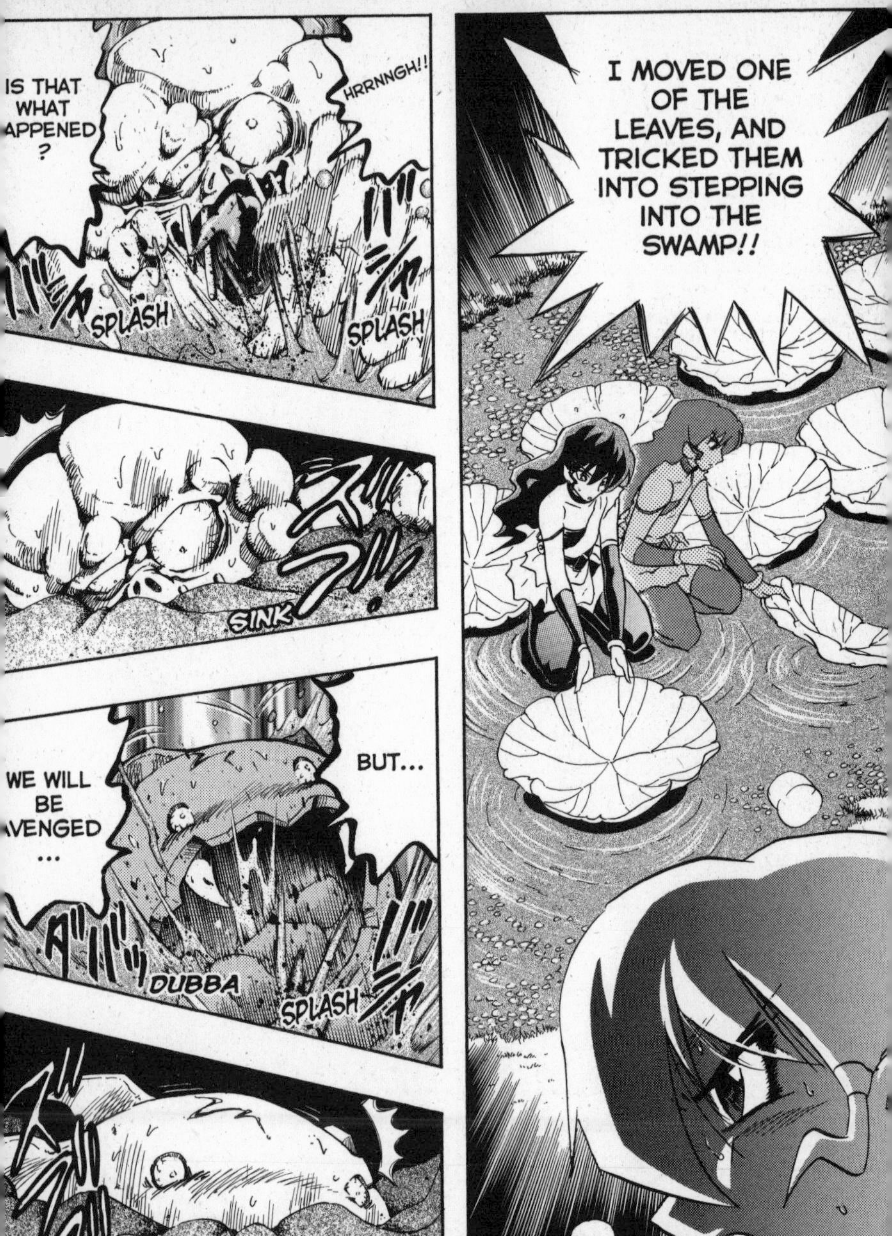
I MOVED ONE OF THE LEAVES, AND TRICKED THEM INTO STEPPING INTO THE SWAMP!!
HRRNNGH!!
IS THAT WHAT APPENED ?
SPLASH
SPLASH
SINK
BUT...
WE WILL BE AVENGED ...
SPLASH
DUBBA
SINNNK

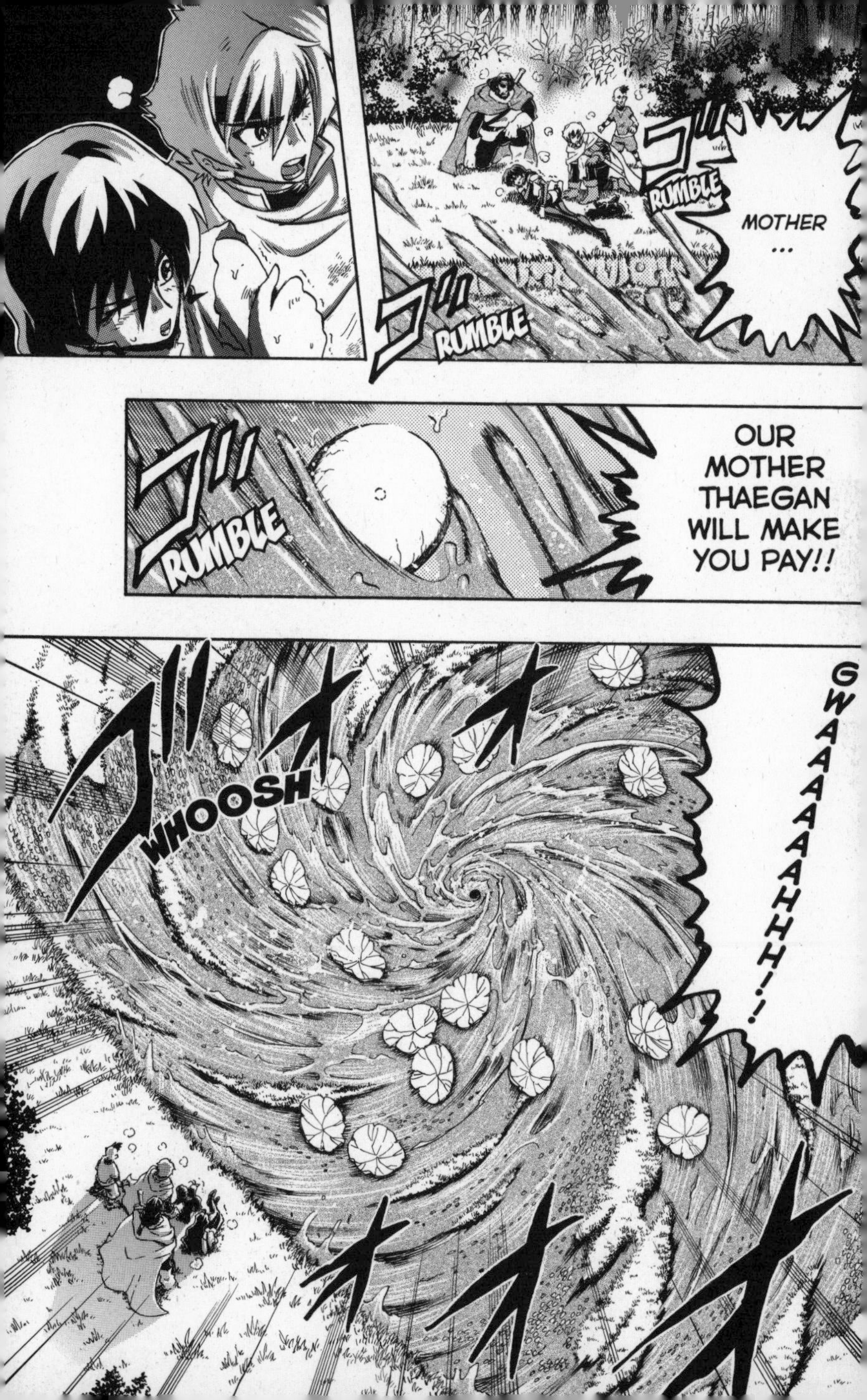
RUMBLE
MOTHER ...
RUMBLE
OUR MOTHER THAEGAN WILL MAKE YOU PAY!!
RUMBLE
GWAAAAAAHHH!!!
WHOOSH

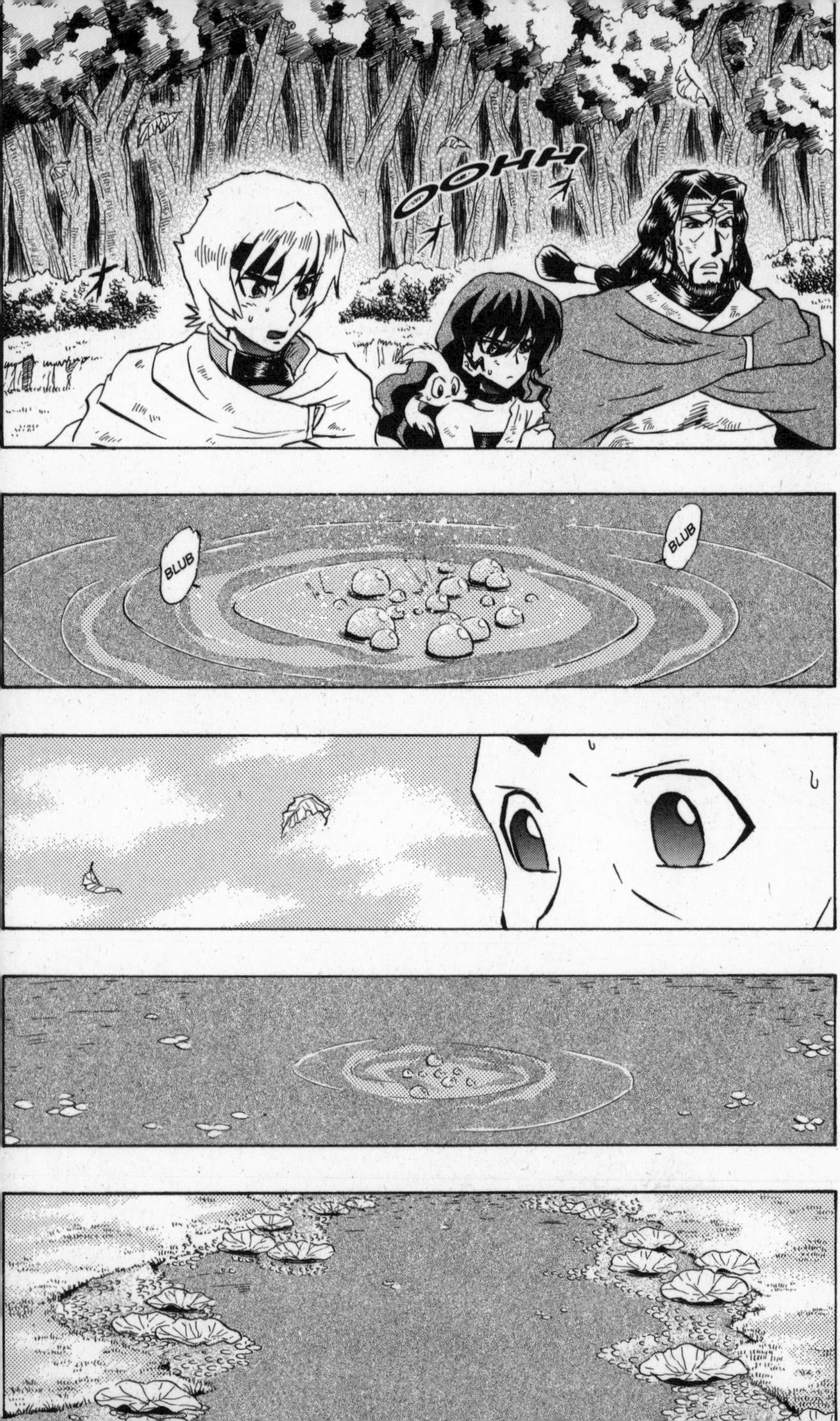
OOHH
BLUB
BLUB

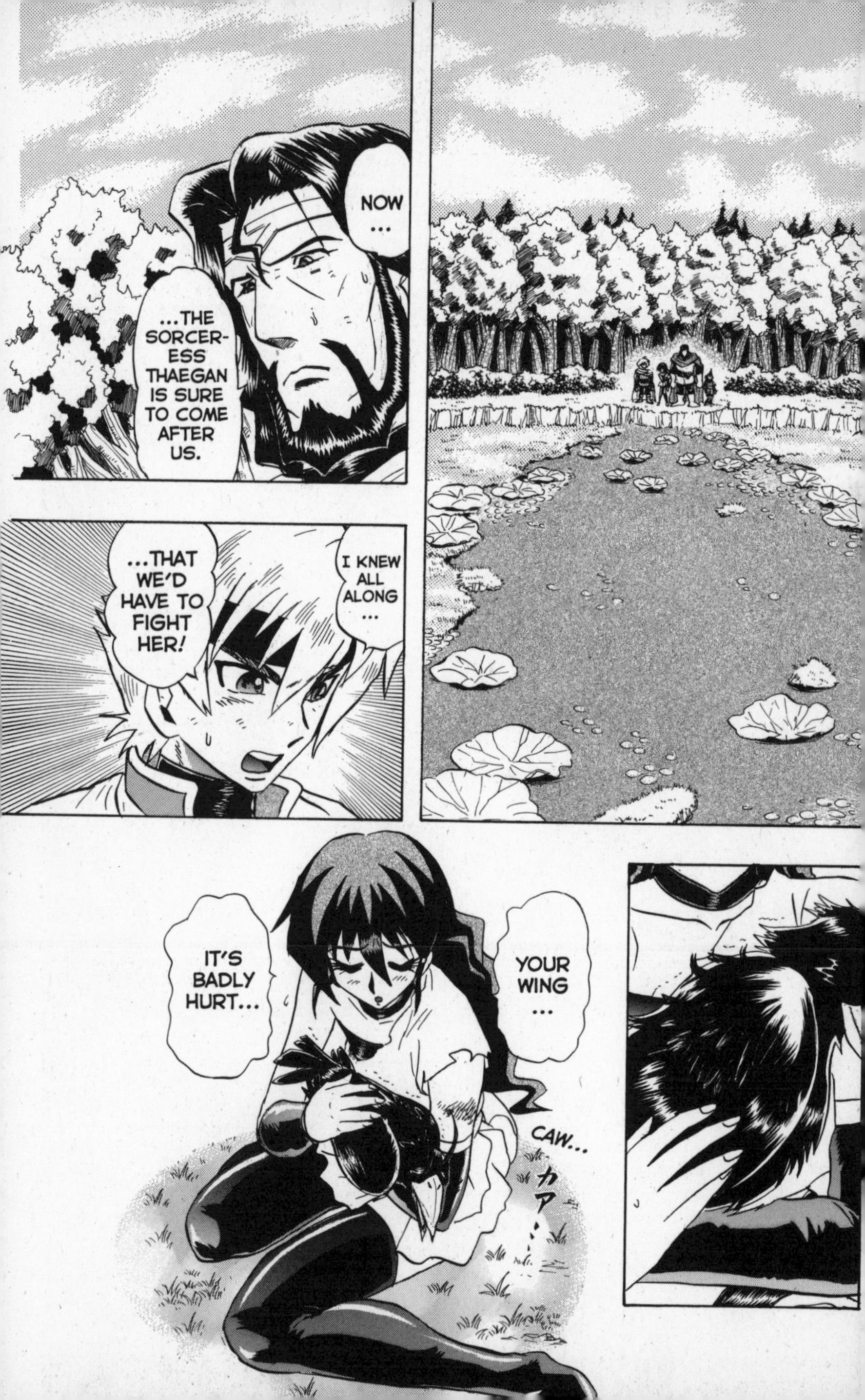
NOW ...
...THE SORCERESS THAEGAN IS SURE TO COME AFTER US.
I KNEW ALL ALONG ...
...THAT WE'D HAVE TO FIGHT HER!
YOUR WING ...
IT'S BADLY HURT...
CAW...
カア...

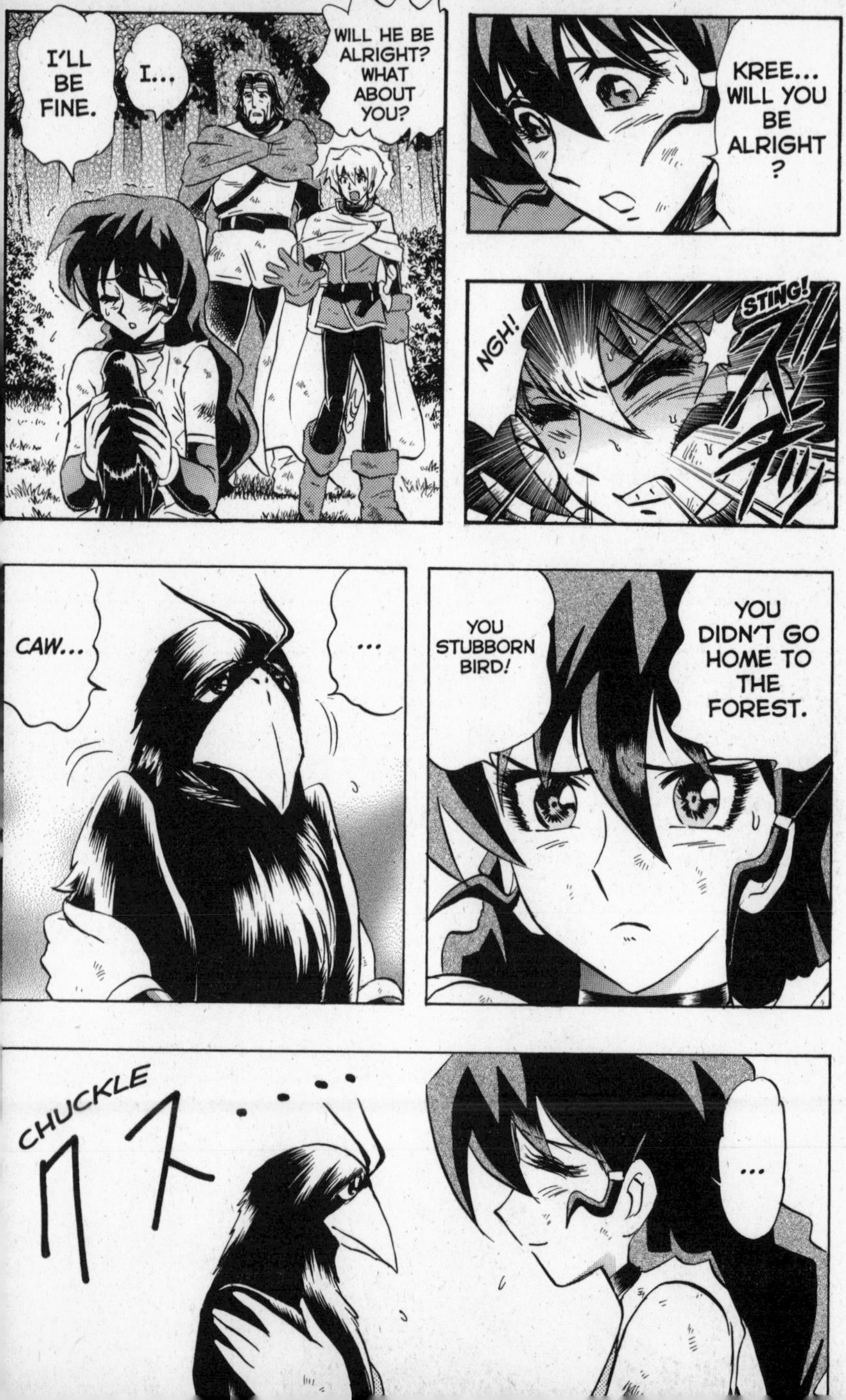
KREE... WILL YOU BE ALRIGHT?
STING!
NGH!
WILL HE BE ALRIGHT? WHAT ABOUT YOU?
I...
I'LL BE FINE.
YOU DIDN'T GO HOME TO THE FOREST.
YOU STUBBORN BIRD!
...
CAW...
...
CHUCKLE

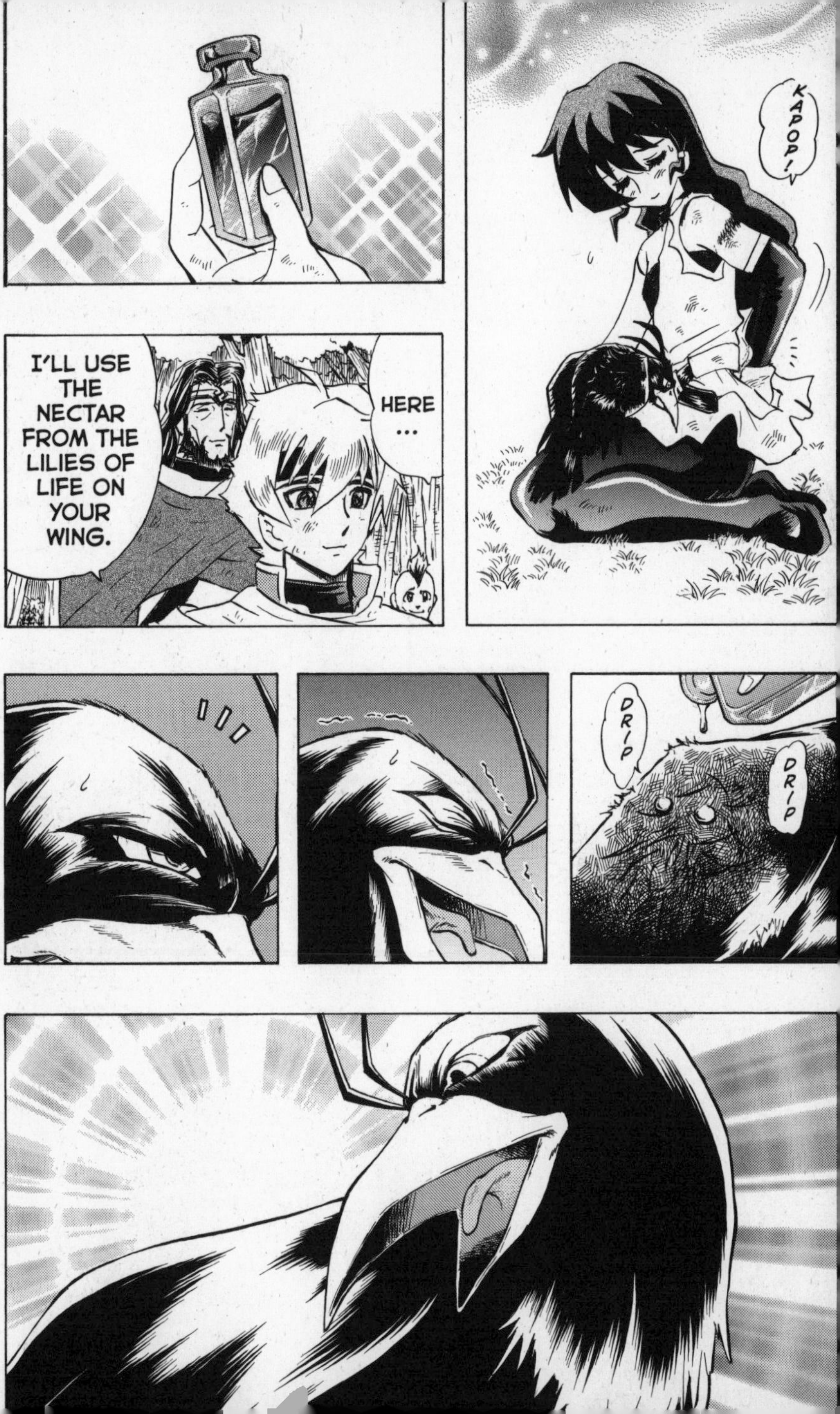
KAPOP!
HERE...
I'LL USE THE NECTAR FROM THE LILIES OF LIFE ON YOUR WING.
DRIP
DRIP

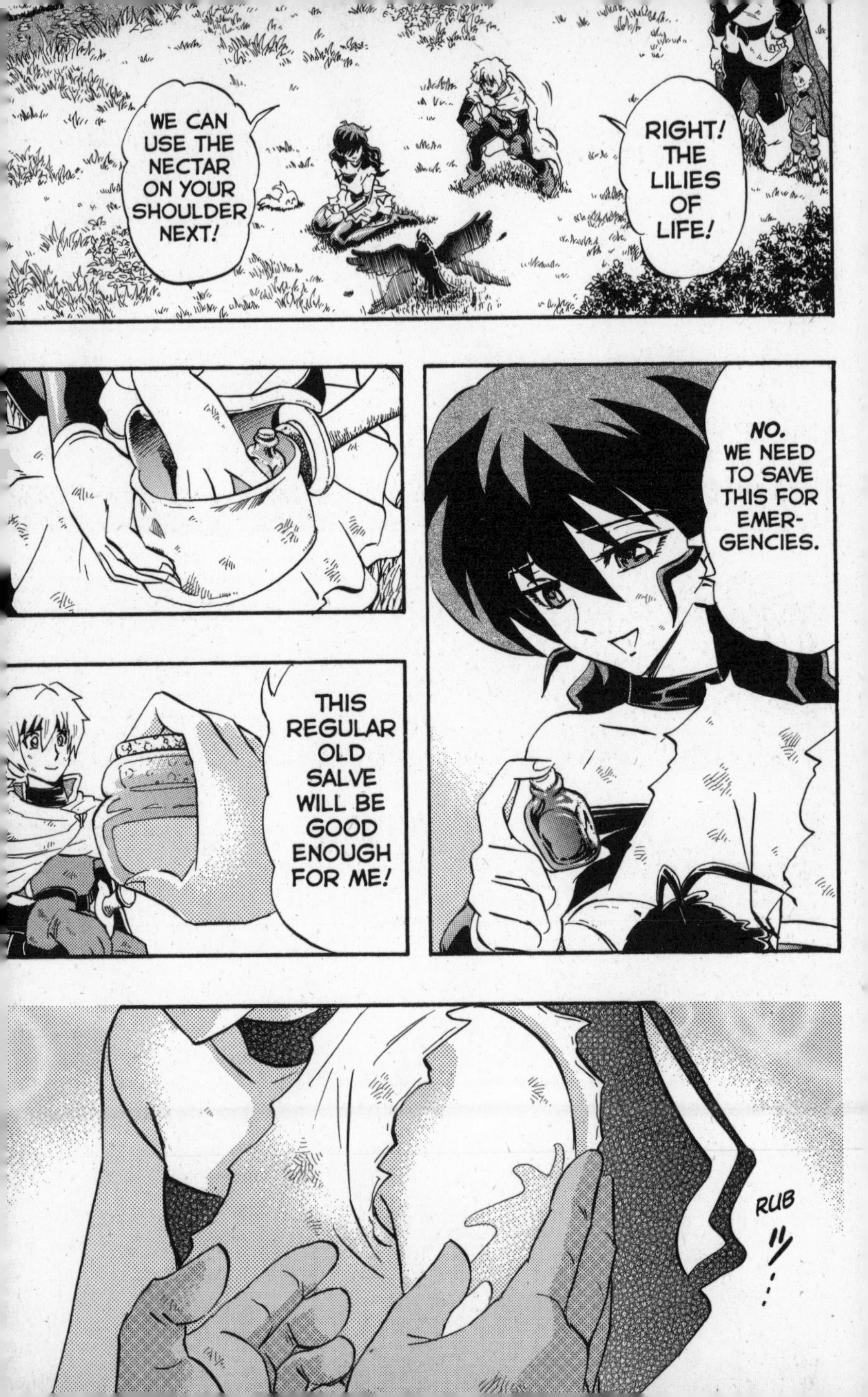
RIGHT! THE LILIES OF LIFE!
WE CAN USE THE NECTAR ON YOUR SHOULDER NEXT!
NO. WE NEED TO SAVE THIS FOR EMER-GENCIES.
THIS REGULAR OLD SALVE WILL BE GOOD ENOUGH FOR ME!
RUB

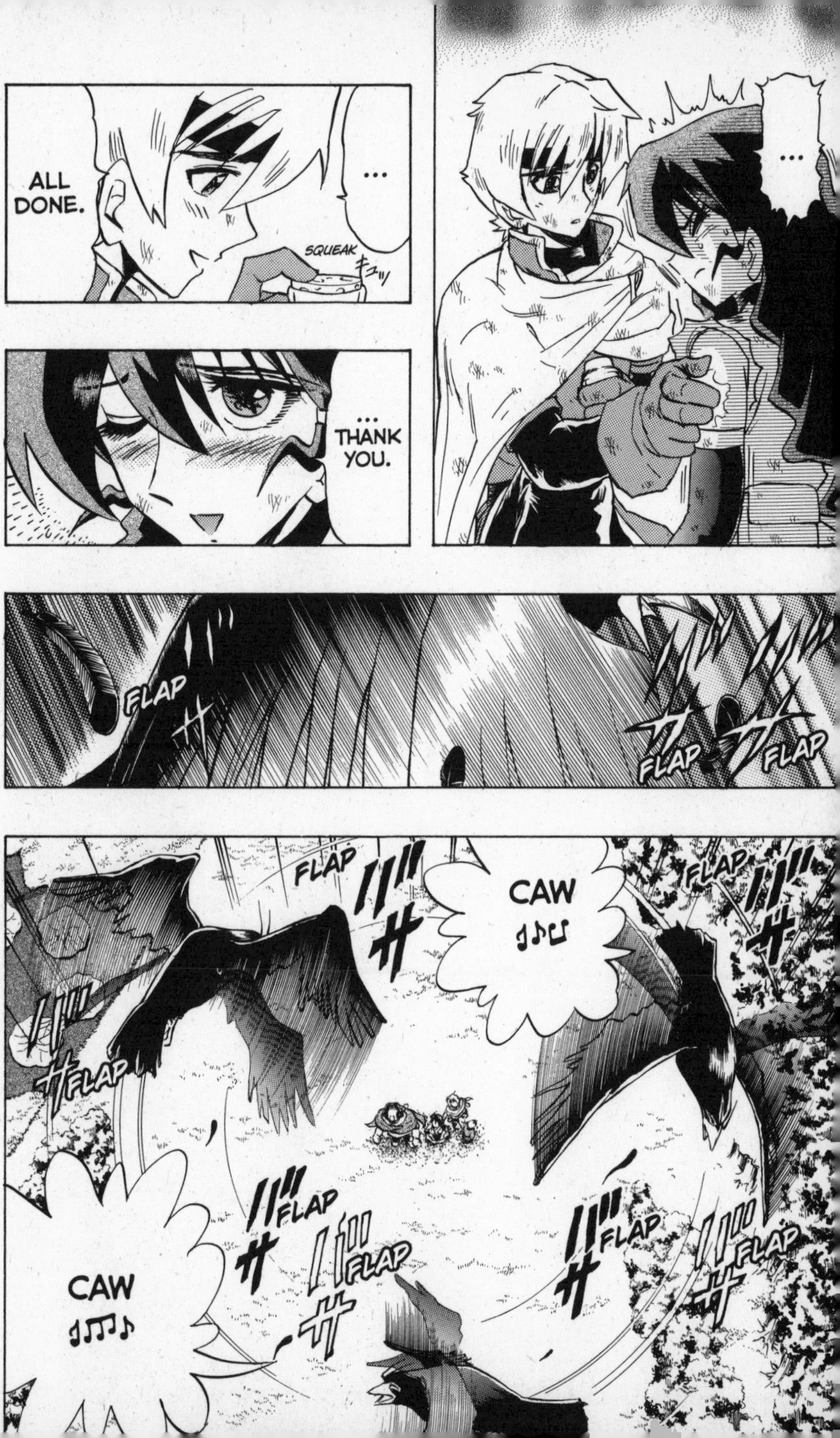
...
...
ALL DONE.
SQUEAK
... THANK YOU.
FLAP
FLAP
FLAP
FLAP
CAW
FLAP
FLAP
FLAP
FLAP
FLAP
FLAP
CAW

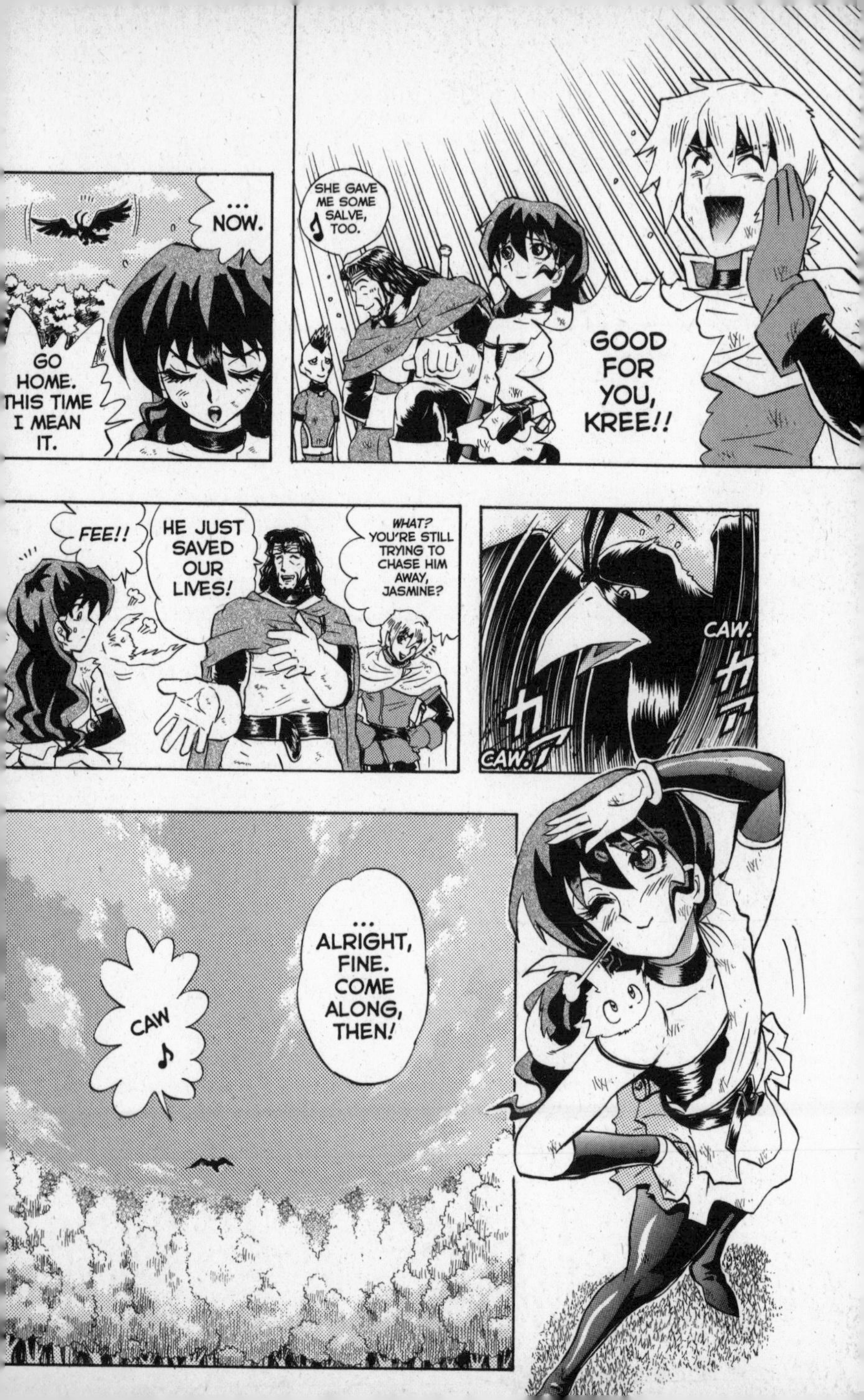

SHE GAVE ME SOME SALVE, TOO. ♪
GOOD FOR YOU, KREE!!
... NOW.
GO HOME. THIS TIME I MEAN IT.
CAW.
カァ
カァ
CAW.
WHAT? YOU'RE STILL TRYING TO CHASE HIM AWAY, JASMINE?
HE JUST SAVED OUR LIVES!
FEE!!
... ALRIGHT, FINE. COME ALONG, THEN!
CAW ♪

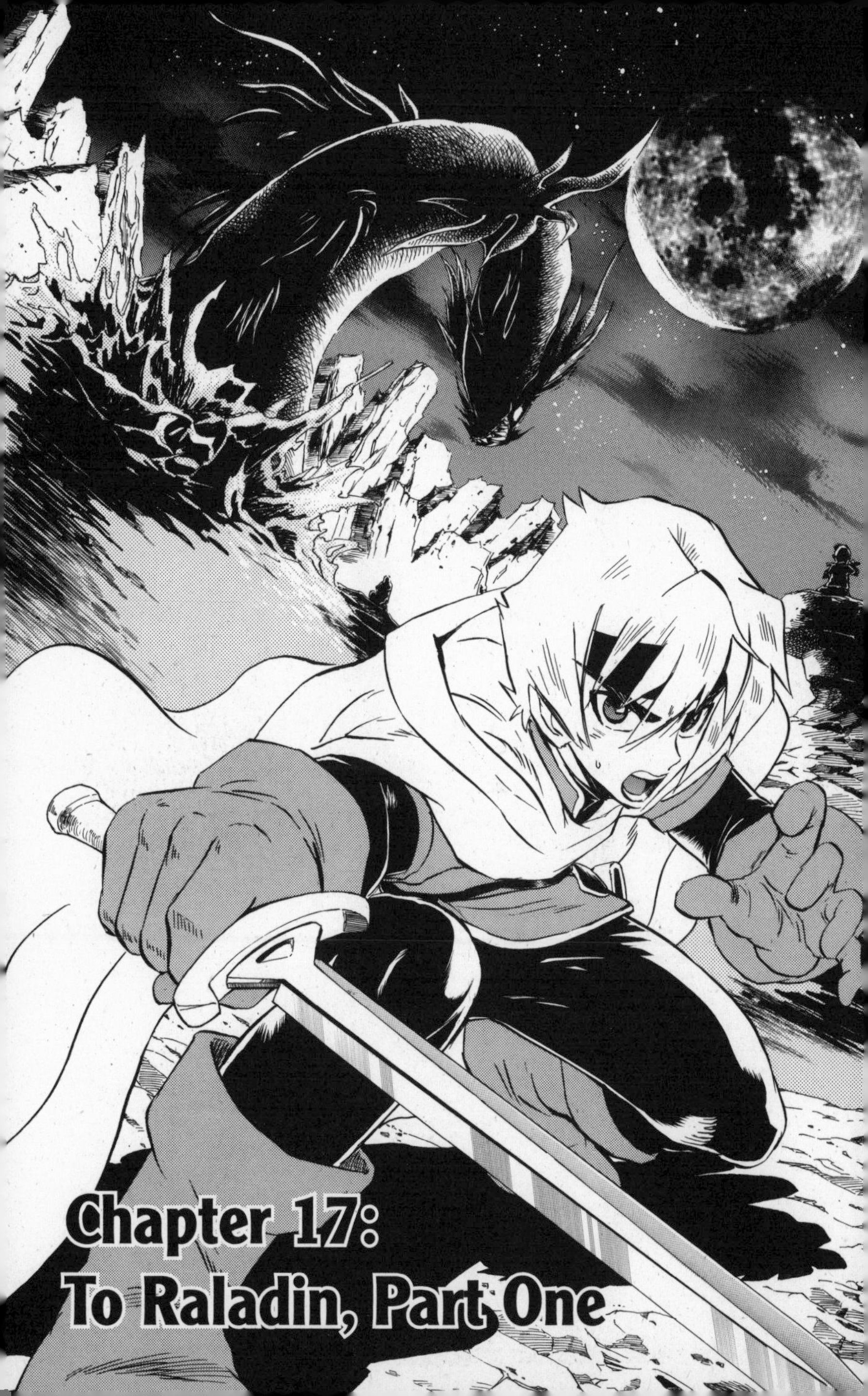
Chapter 17:
To Raladin, Part One

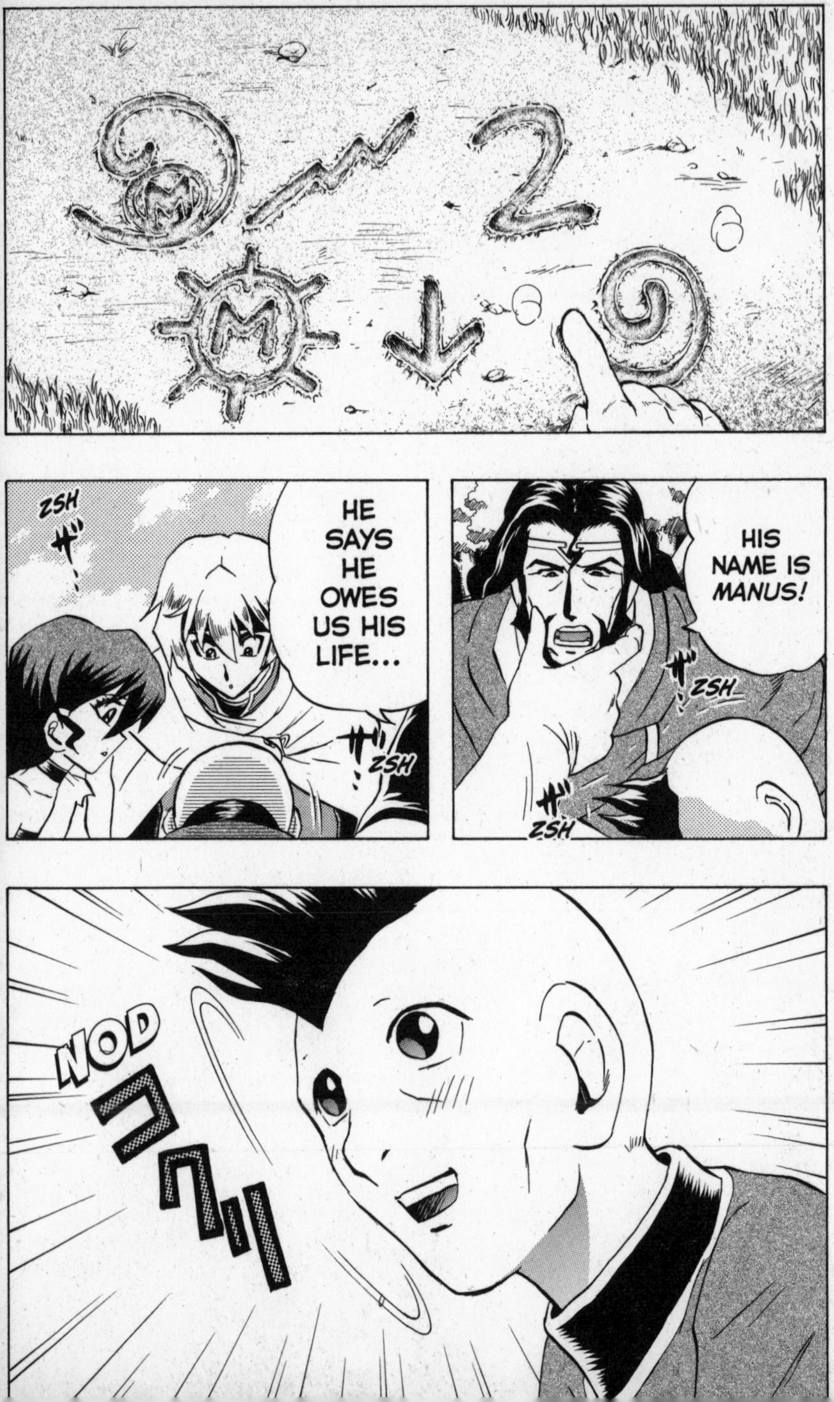
HIS NAME IS MANUS!
ZSH
ZSH
HE SAYS HE OWES US HIS LIFE...
ZSH
ZSH
NOD
コクッ

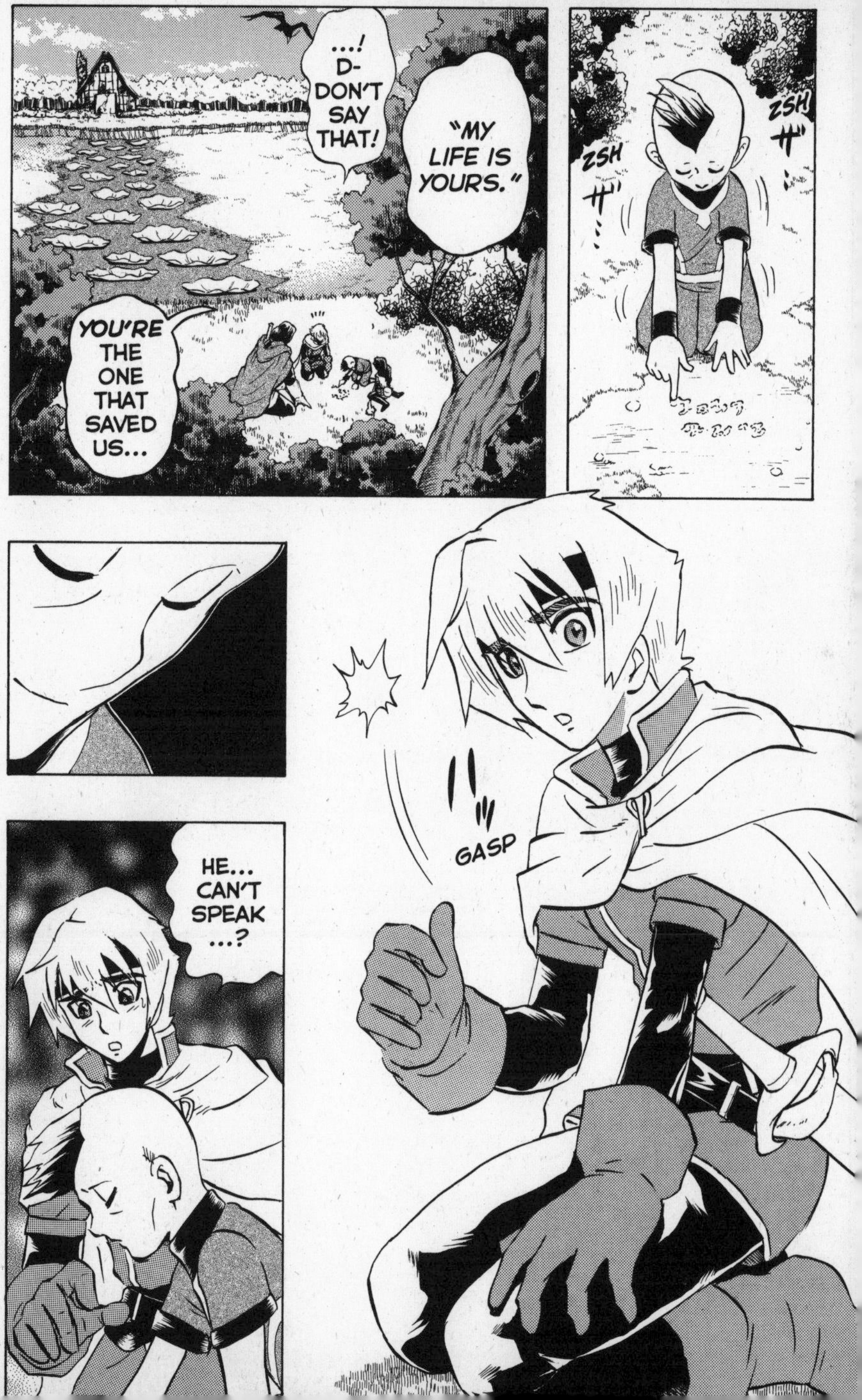
ZSH
ザ
ZSH
ザ
"MY LIFE IS YOURS."
...! D-DON'T SAY THAT!
YOU'RE THE ONE THAT SAVED US...
GASP
HE... CAN'T SPEAK ...?

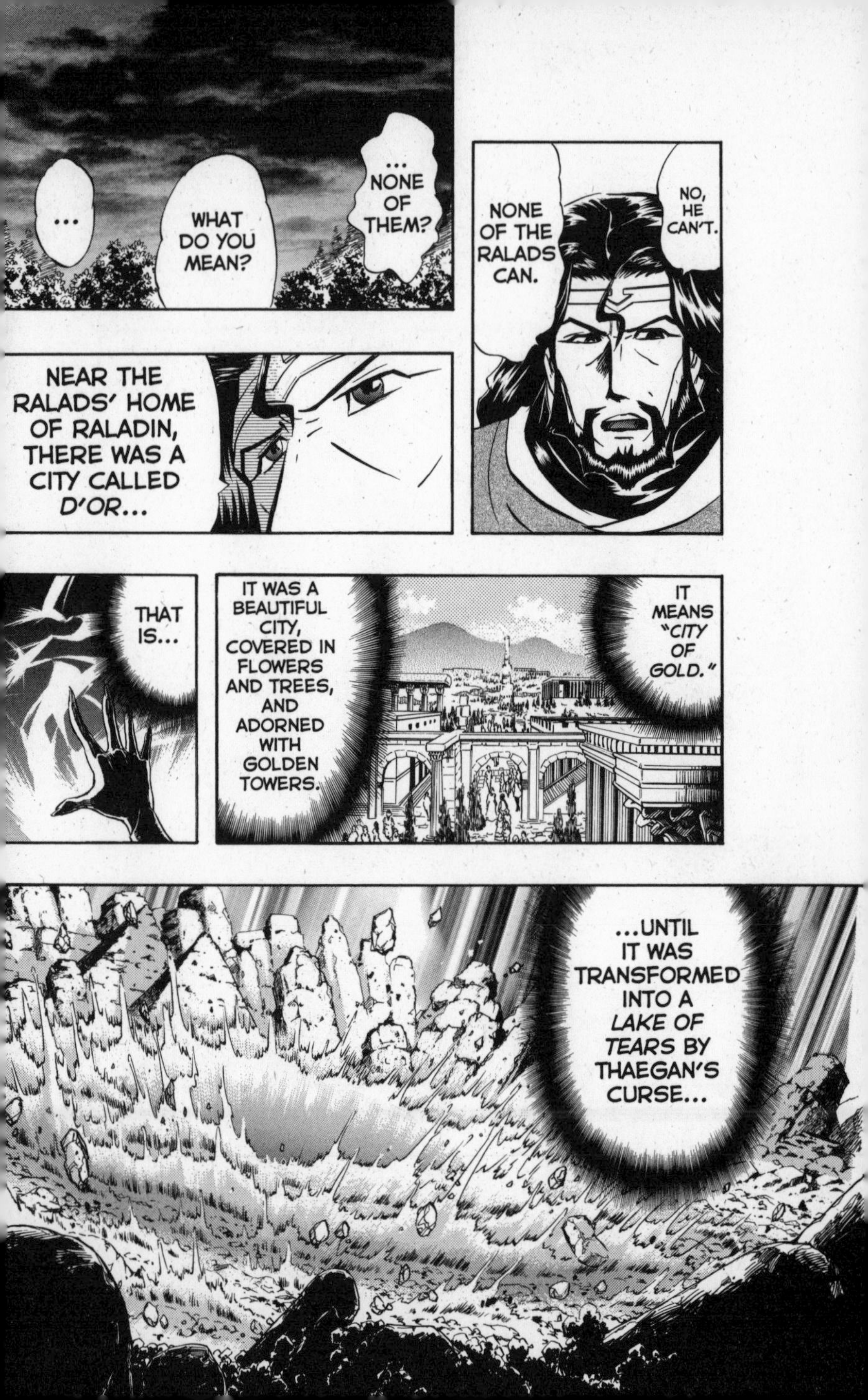
NO, HE CAN'T.
NONE OF THE RALADS CAN.
... NONE OF THEM?
WHAT DO YOU MEAN?
...
NEAR THE RALADS' HOME OF RALADIN, THERE WAS A CITY CALLED *D'OR*...
IT MEANS *"CITY OF GOLD."*
IT WAS A BEAUTIFUL CITY, COVERED IN FLOWERS AND TREES, AND ADORNED WITH GOLDEN TOWERS.
THAT IS...
...UNTIL IT WAS TRANSFORMED INTO A *LAKE OF TEARS* BY THAEGAN'S CURSE...

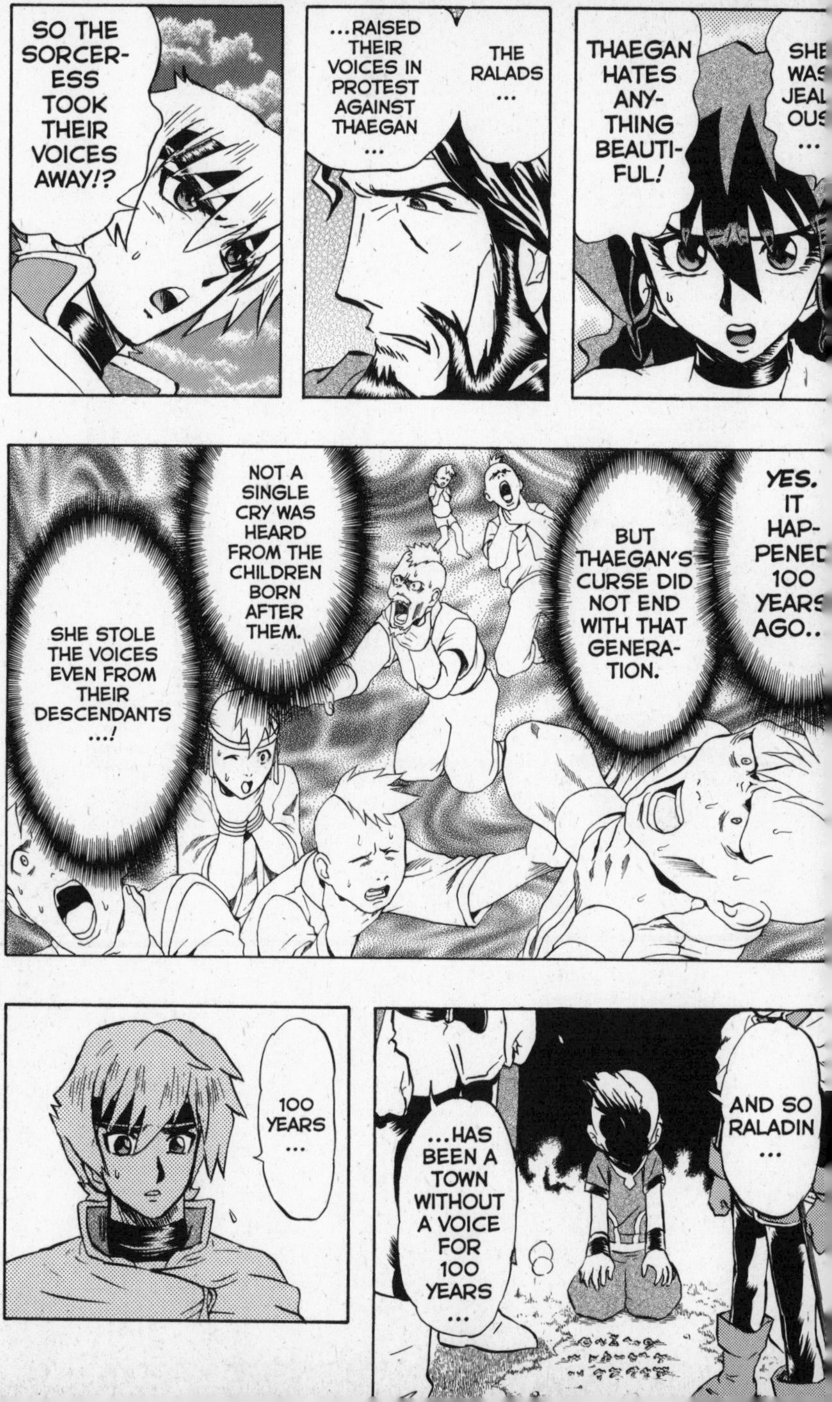
SHE WAS JEAL-OUS …
THAEGAN HATES ANYTHING BEAUTIFUL!
THE RALADS …
…RAISED THEIR VOICES IN PROTEST AGAINST THAEGAN …
SO THE SORCERESS TOOK THEIR VOICES AWAY!?
YES. IT HAPPENED 100 YEARS AGO…
BUT THAEGAN'S CURSE DID NOT END WITH THAT GENERATION.
NOT A SINGLE CRY WAS HEARD FROM THE CHILDREN BORN AFTER THEM.
SHE STOLE THE VOICES EVEN FROM THEIR DESCENDANTS …!
AND SO RALADIN …
…HAS BEEN A TOWN WITHOUT A VOICE FOR 100 YEARS …
100 YEARS …

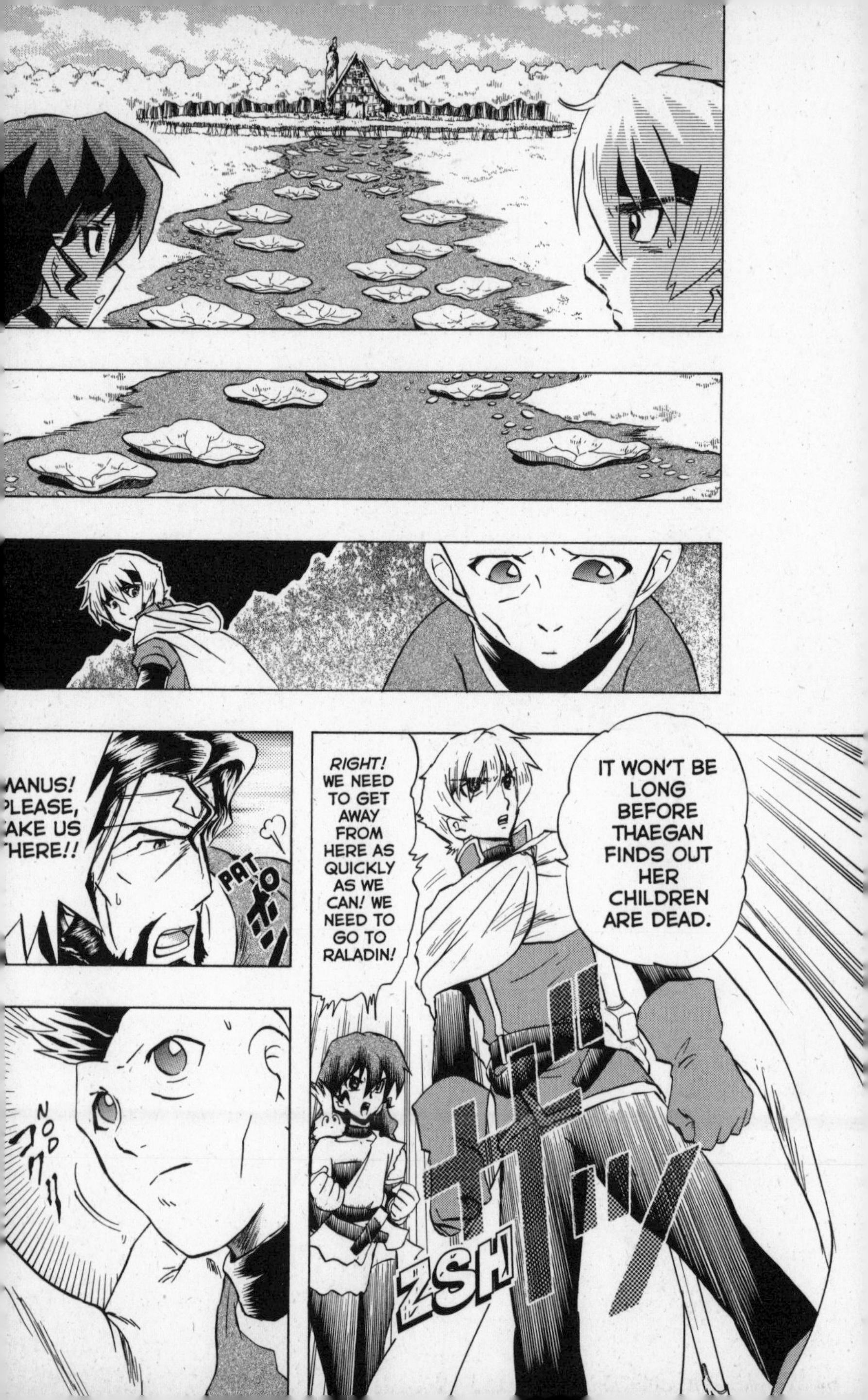
IT WON'T BE LONG BEFORE THAEGAN FINDS OUT HER CHILDREN ARE DEAD.
RIGHT! WE NEED TO GET AWAY FROM HERE AS QUICKLY AS WE CAN! WE NEED TO GO TO RALADIN!
ZSH
MANUS! PLEASE, TAKE US THERE!!
PAT
NOD

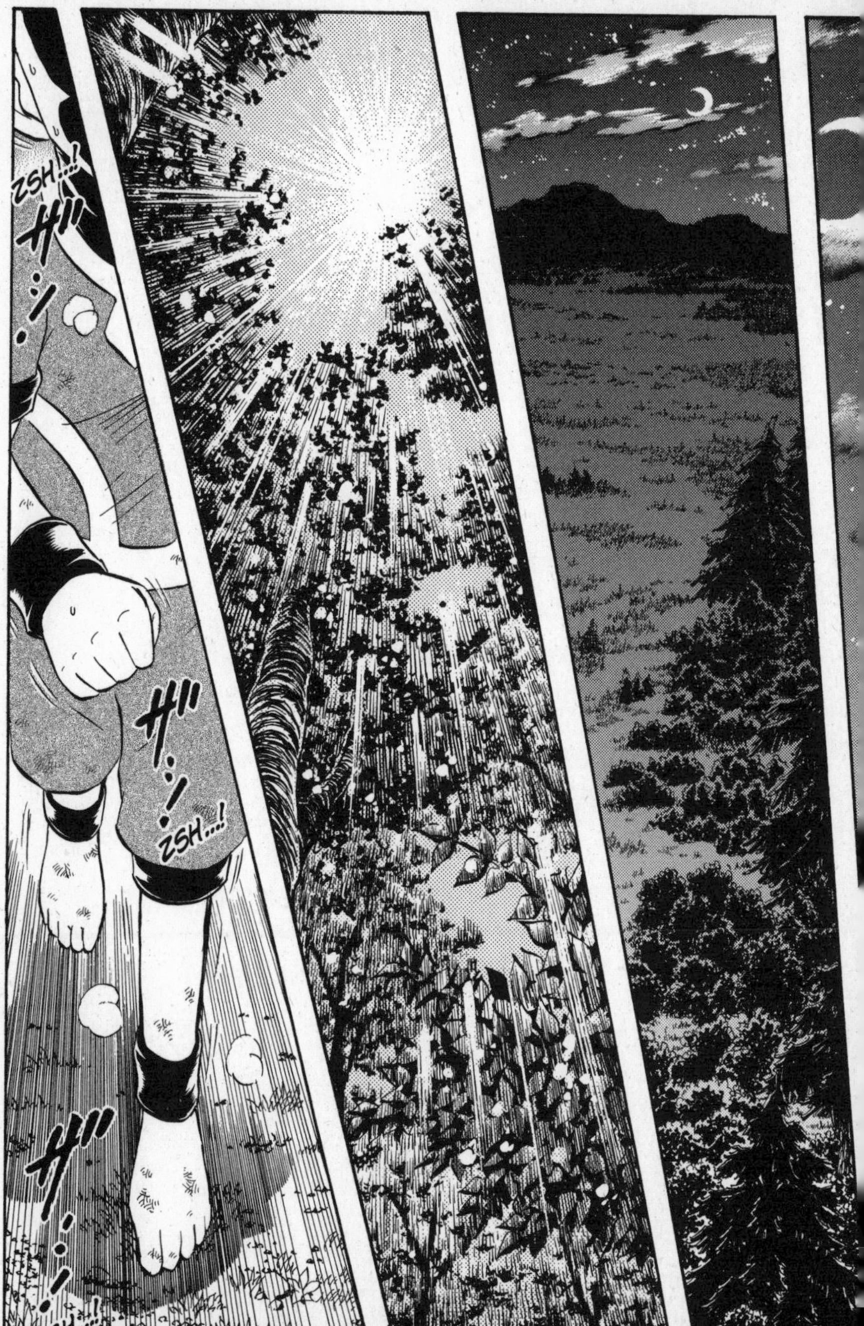
ZSH...!
ZSH...!
ZSH....!

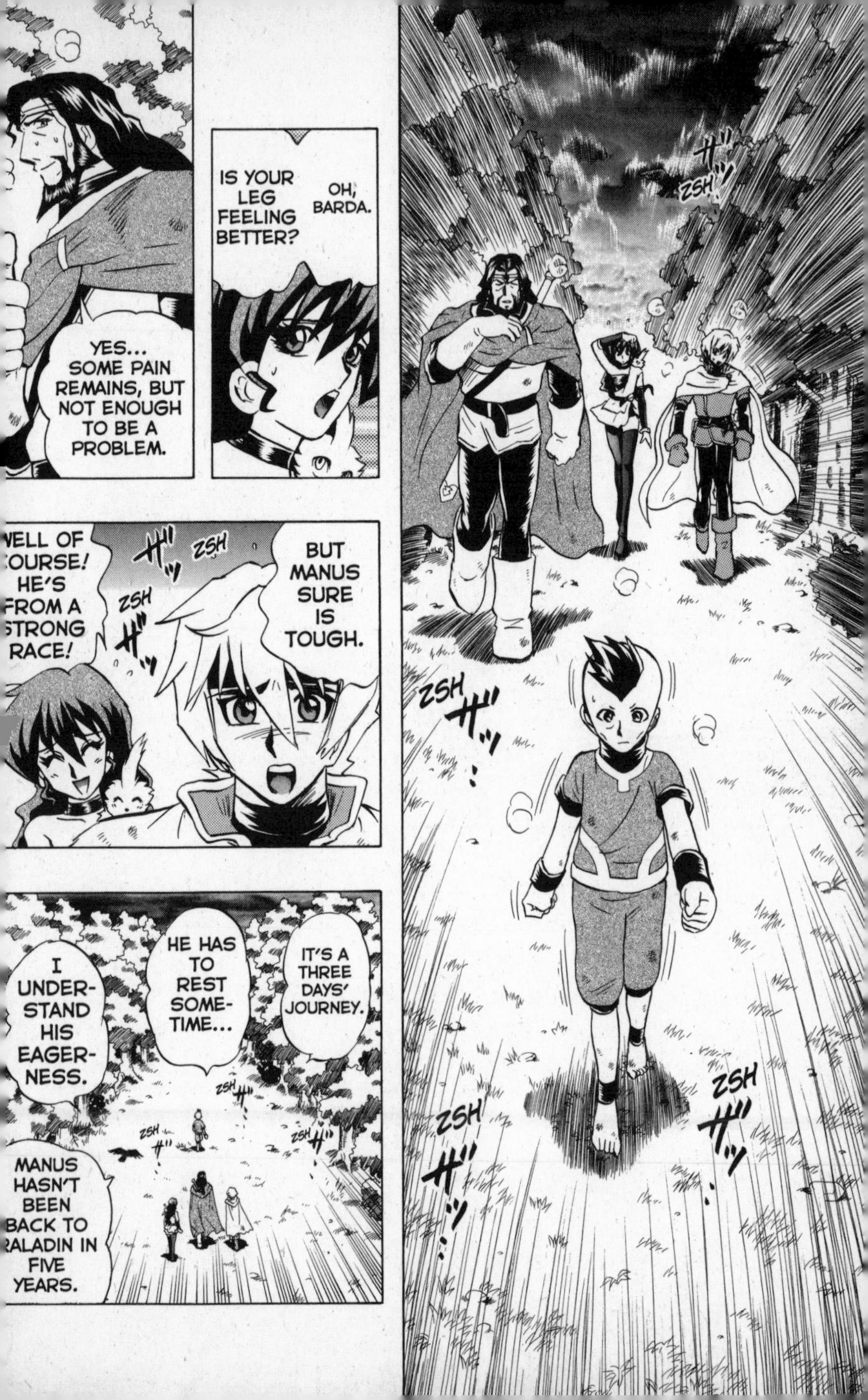
ZSH
ZSH
ZSH
ZSH
OH, BARDA.
IS YOUR LEG FEELING BETTER?
YES... SOME PAIN REMAINS, BUT NOT ENOUGH TO BE A PROBLEM.
BUT MANUS SURE IS TOUGH.
ZSH
ZSH
WELL OF COURSE! HE'S FROM A STRONG RACE!
IT'S A THREE DAYS' JOURNEY.
HE HAS TO REST SOMETIME...
I UNDERSTAND HIS EAGERNESS.
ZSH
ZSH
ZSH
MANUS HASN'T BEEN BACK TO RALADIN IN FIVE YEARS.

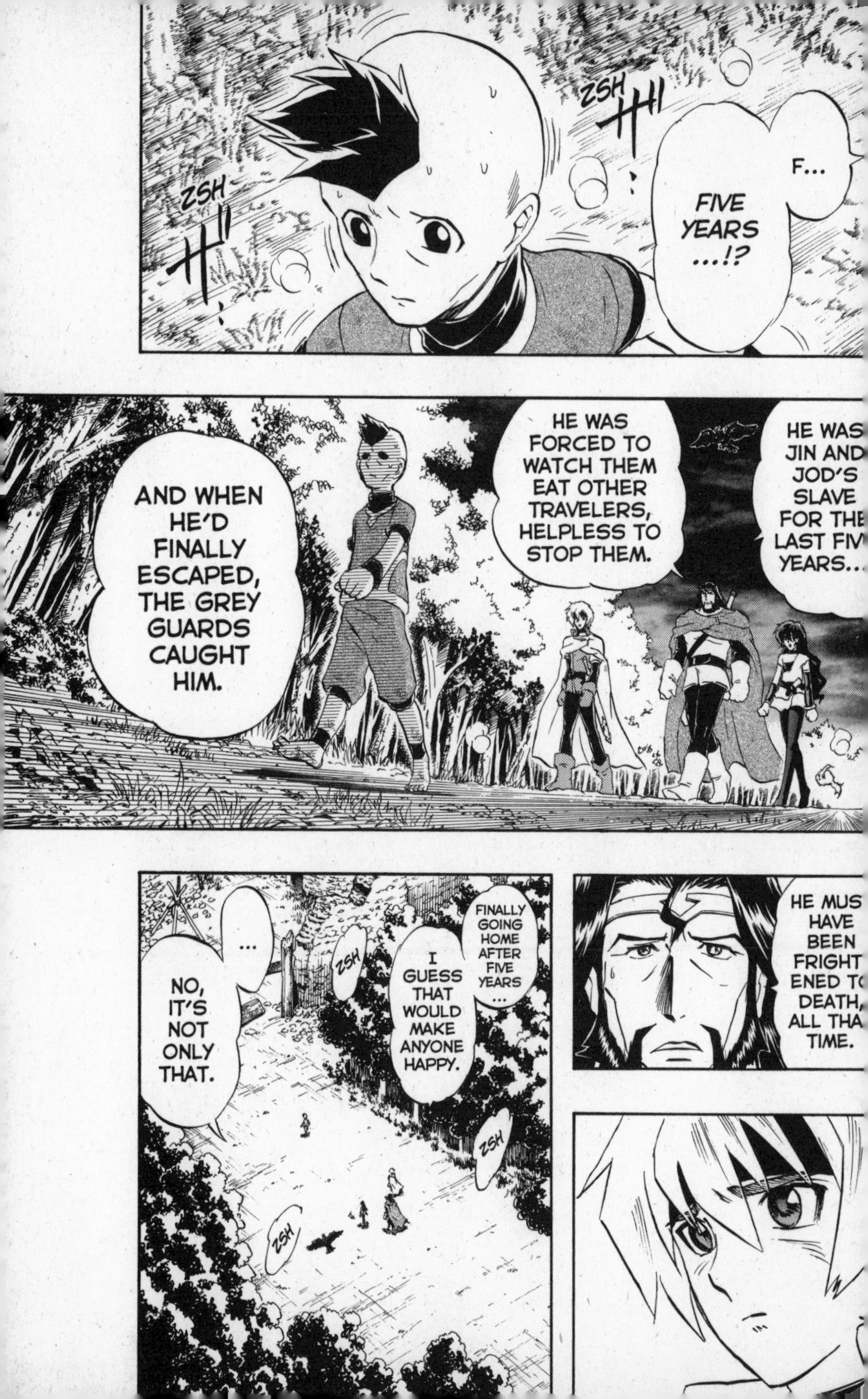
ZSH
ZSH
F...
FIVE YEARS ...!?
HE WAS JIN AND JOD'S SLAVE FOR THE LAST FIV YEARS...
HE WAS FORCED TO WATCH THEM EAT OTHER TRAVELERS, HELPLESS TO STOP THEM.
AND WHEN HE'D FINALLY ESCAPED, THE GREY GUARDS CAUGHT HIM.
HE MUS HAVE BEEN FRIGHT ENED T DEATH, ALL THA TIME.
FINALLY GOING HOME AFTER FIVE YEARS ...
I GUESS THAT WOULD MAKE ANYONE HAPPY.
ZSH
ZSH
ZSH
...
NO, IT'S NOT ONLY THAT.

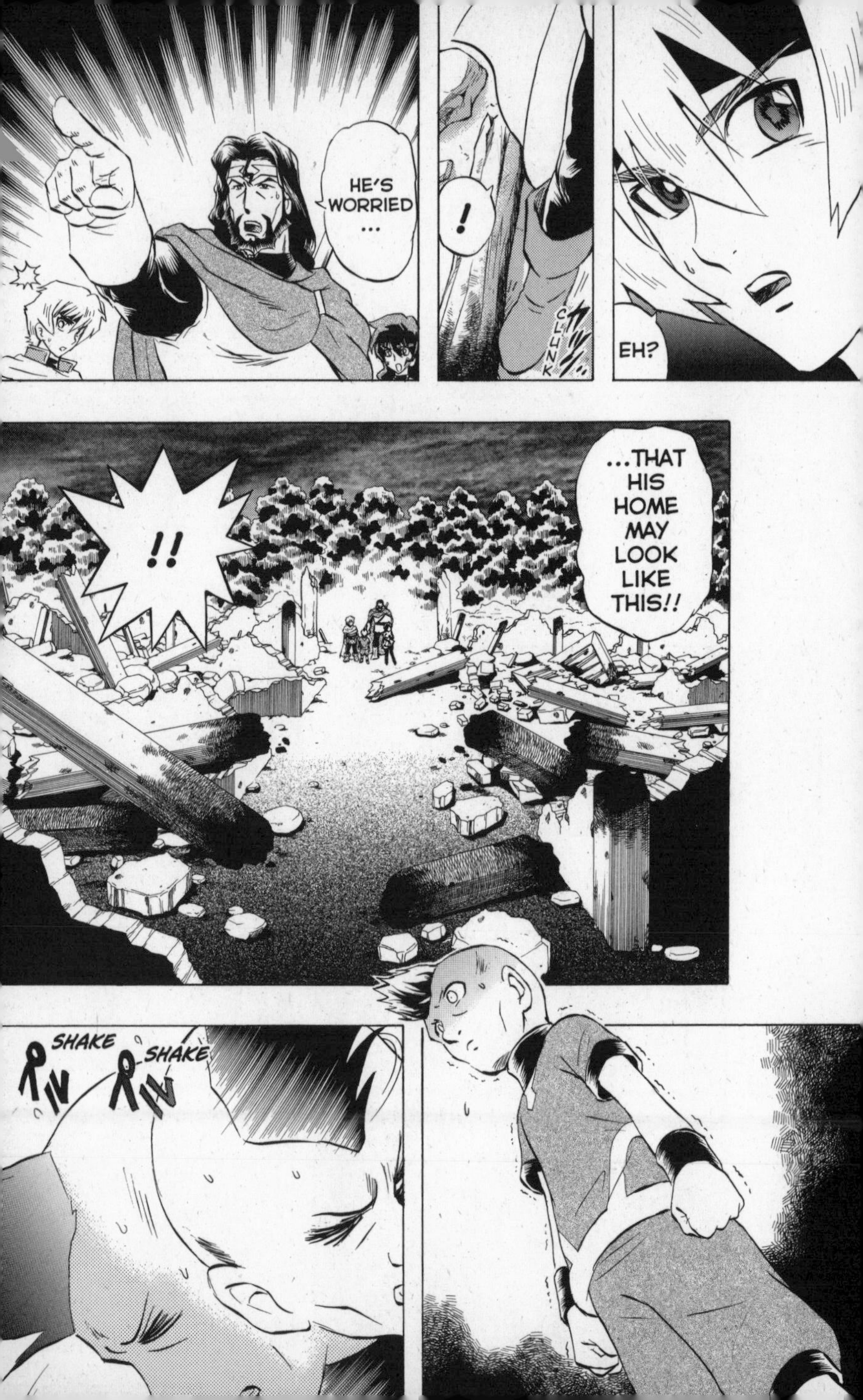
EH?
!
CLUNK
HE'S WORRIED ...
...THAT HIS HOME MAY LOOK LIKE THIS!!
!!
SHAKE
SHAKE

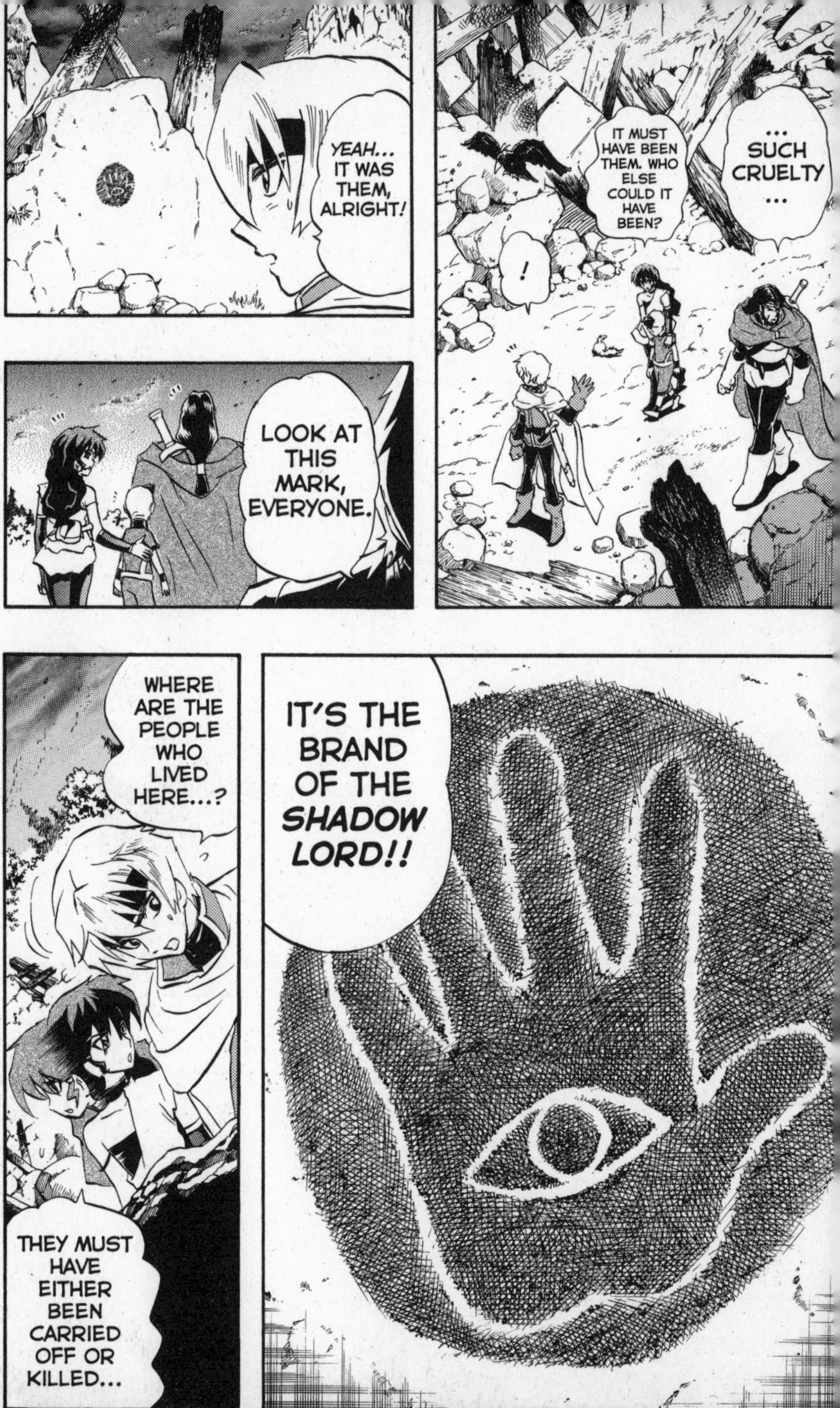
...SUCH CRUELTY...
IT MUST HAVE BEEN THEM. WHO ELSE COULD IT HAVE BEEN?
!
YEAH... IT WAS THEM, ALRIGHT!
LOOK AT THIS MARK, EVERYONE.
IT'S THE BRAND OF THE SHADOW LORD!!
WHERE ARE THE PEOPLE WHO LIVED HERE...?
THEY MUST HAVE EITHER BEEN CARRIED OFF OR KILLED...

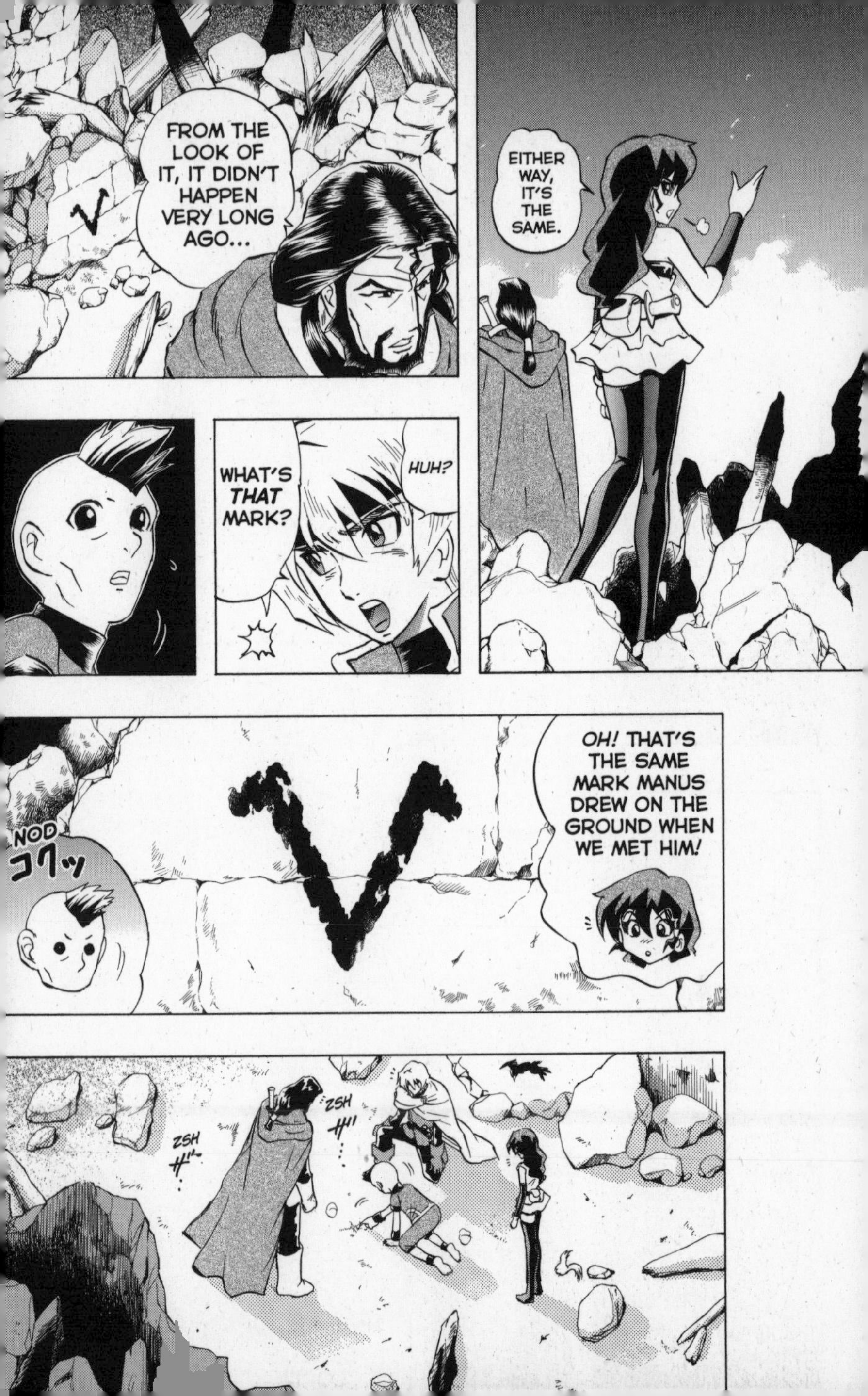
EITHER WAY, IT'S THE SAME.
FROM THE LOOK OF IT, IT DIDN'T HAPPEN VERY LONG AGO...
HUH?
WHAT'S *THAT* MARK?
OH! THAT'S THE SAME MARK MANUS DREW ON THE GROUND WHEN WE MET HIM!
NOD
コクッ
ZSH
ZSH

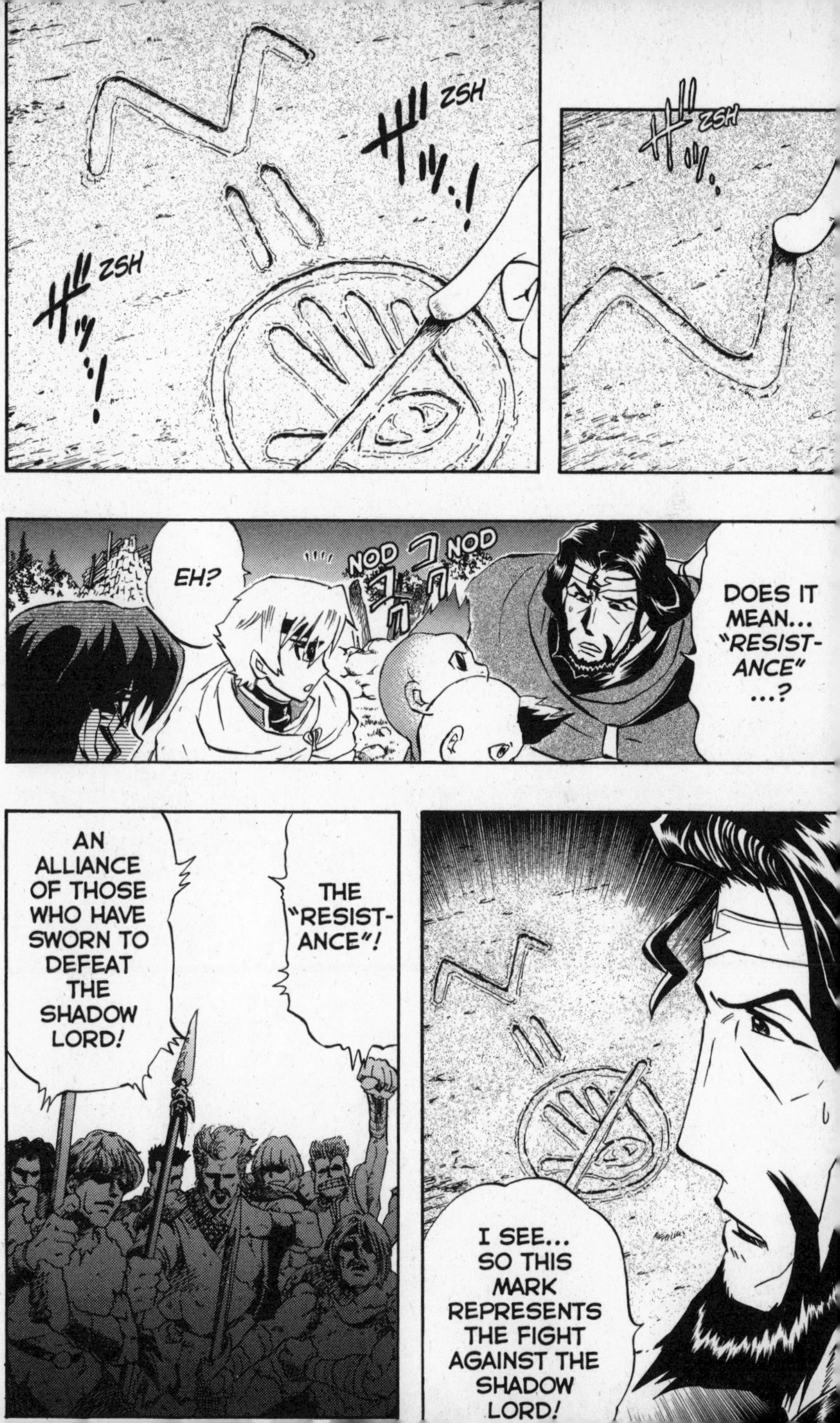
ZSH
ZSH
ZSH
DOES IT MEAN... "RESIST-ANCE" ...?
NOD NOD
EH?
I SEE... SO THIS MARK REPRESENTS THE FIGHT AGAINST THE SHADOW LORD!
THE "RESIST-ANCE"!
AN ALLIANCE OF THOSE WHO HAVE SWORN TO DEFEAT THE SHADOW LORD!

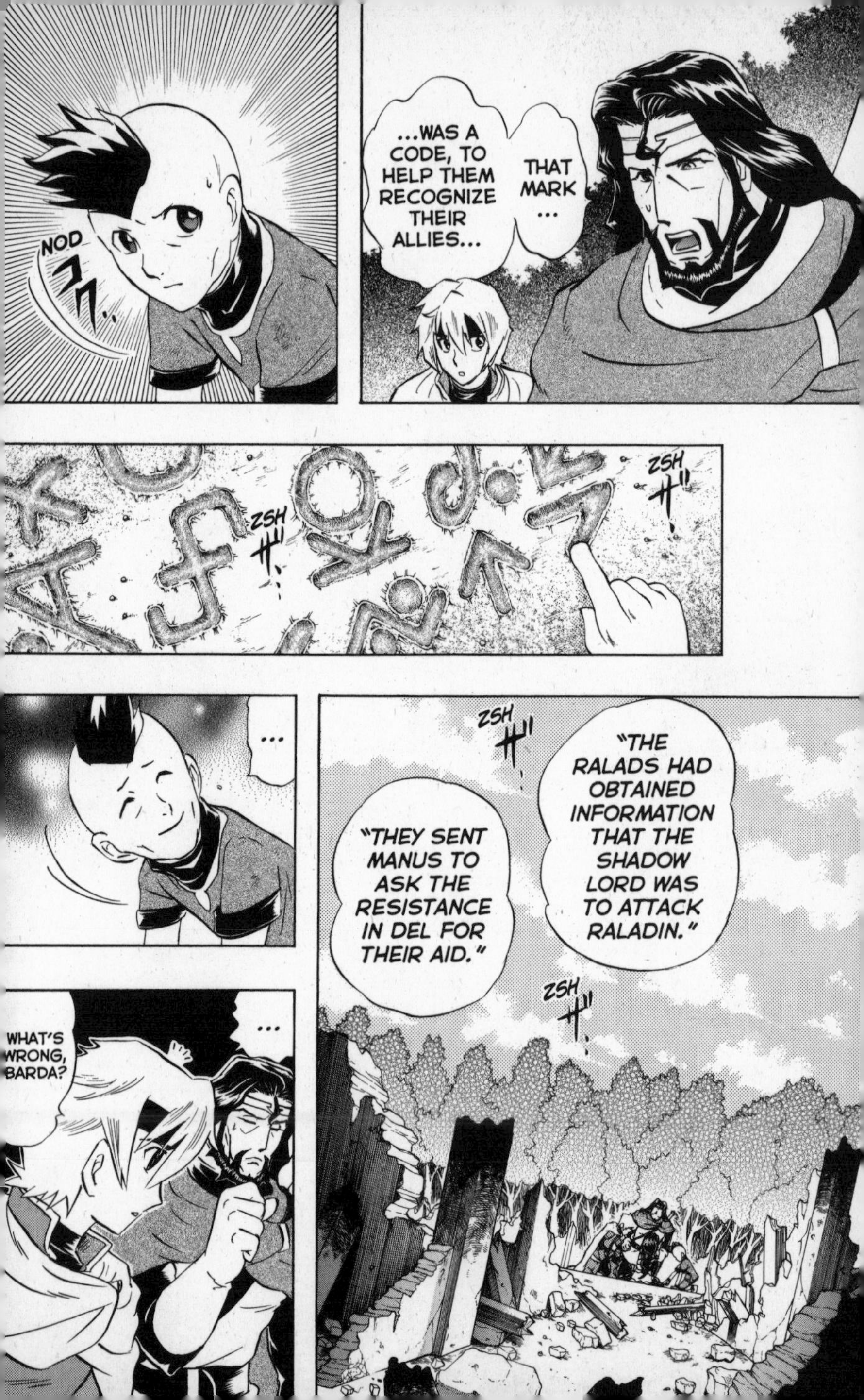
THAT MARK ...
...WAS A CODE, TO HELP THEM RECOGNIZE THEIR ALLIES...
NOD
ZSH
ZSH
ZSH
"THE RALADS HAD OBTAINED INFORMATION THAT THE SHADOW LORD WAS TO ATTACK RALADIN."
"THEY SENT MANUS TO ASK THE RESISTANCE IN DEL FOR THEIR AID."
ZSH
...
...
WHAT'S WRONG, BARDA?

THE RESISTANCE IN DEL...

I'M SORRY, MANUS.

...WAS *ANNIHILATED* ...A LONG TIME AGO.

LET'S HURRY TO RALADIN!!

ZÀM

・・・

A
DEAD
END...

SHH

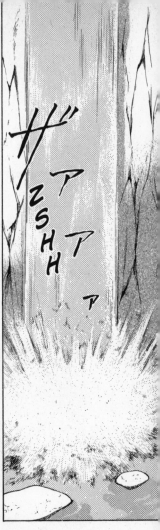

RUSHH

・・・

H-HEY! MANUS
!?

SPLASH

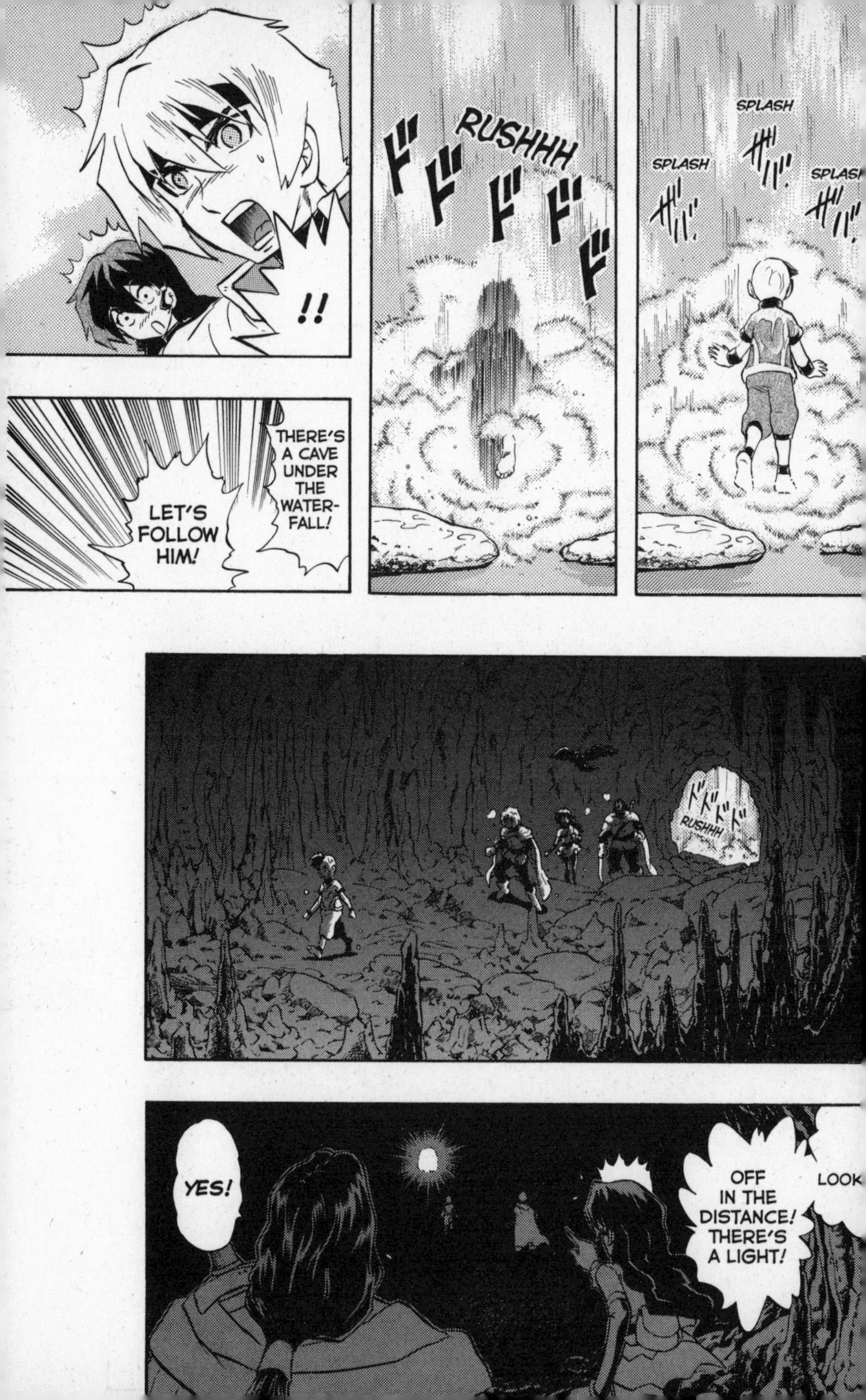
SPLASH
SPLASH
SPLASH
RUSHHH
ドドドドド
!!
THERE'S A CAVE UNDER THE WATER-FALL!
LET'S FOLLOW HIM!
ドドドド
RUSHHH
LOOK
OFF IN THE DISTANCE! THERE'S A LIGHT!
YES!

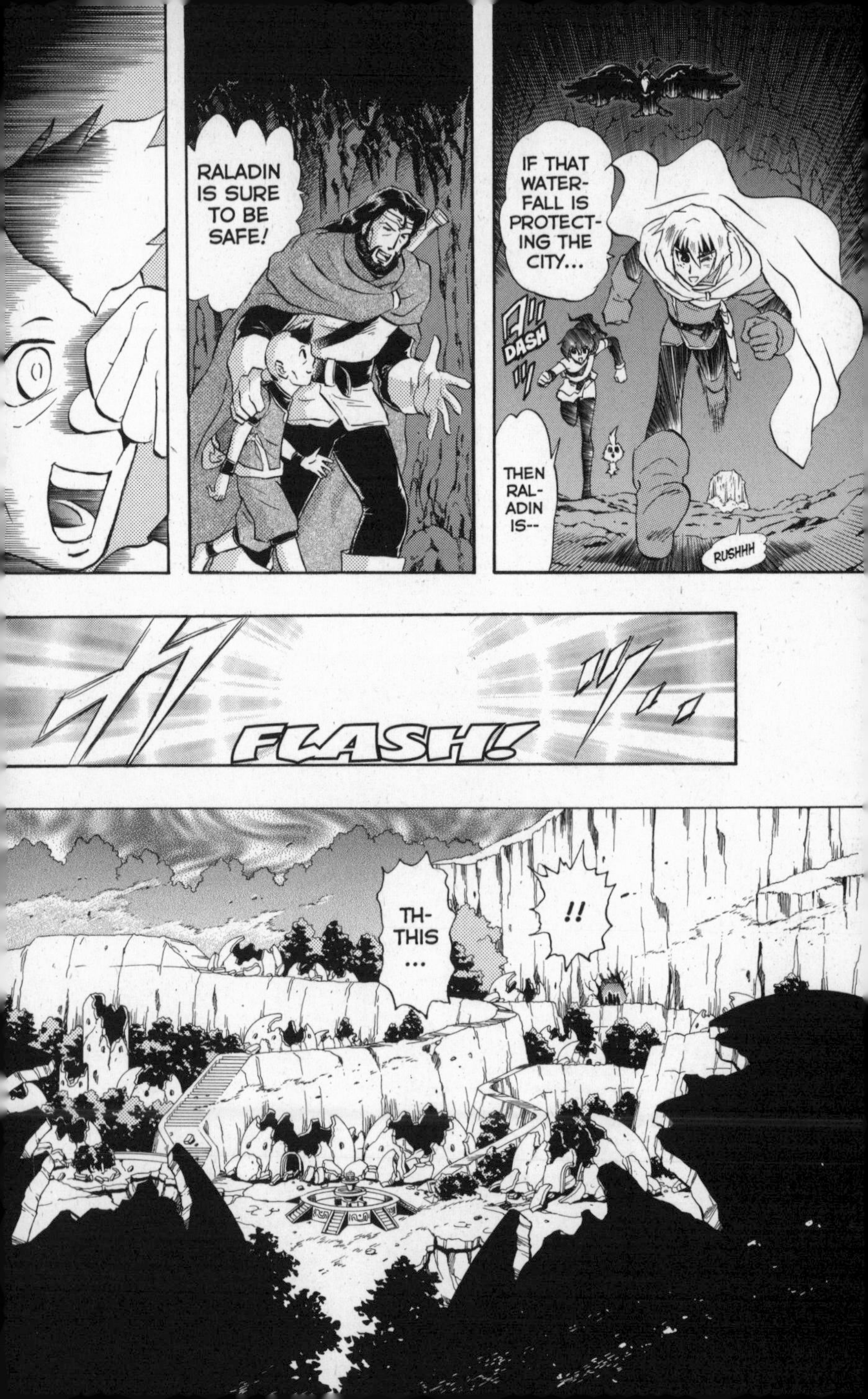
IF THAT WATERFALL IS PROTECTING THE CITY...
DASH
THEN RALADIN IS--
RUSHHH
RALADIN IS SURE TO BE SAFE!
FLASH!
!!
TH-THIS ...

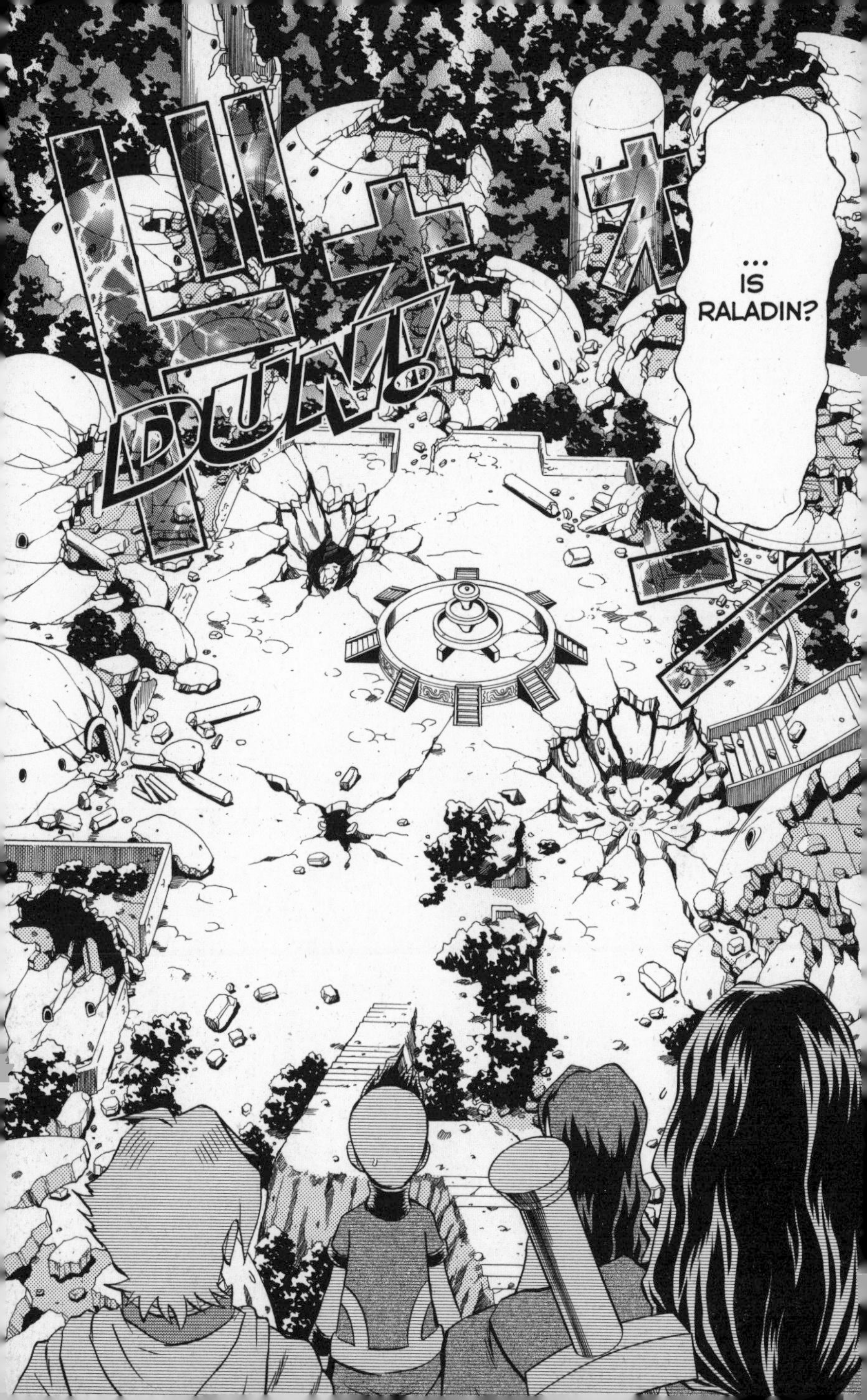
DUN!
... IS RALADIN?

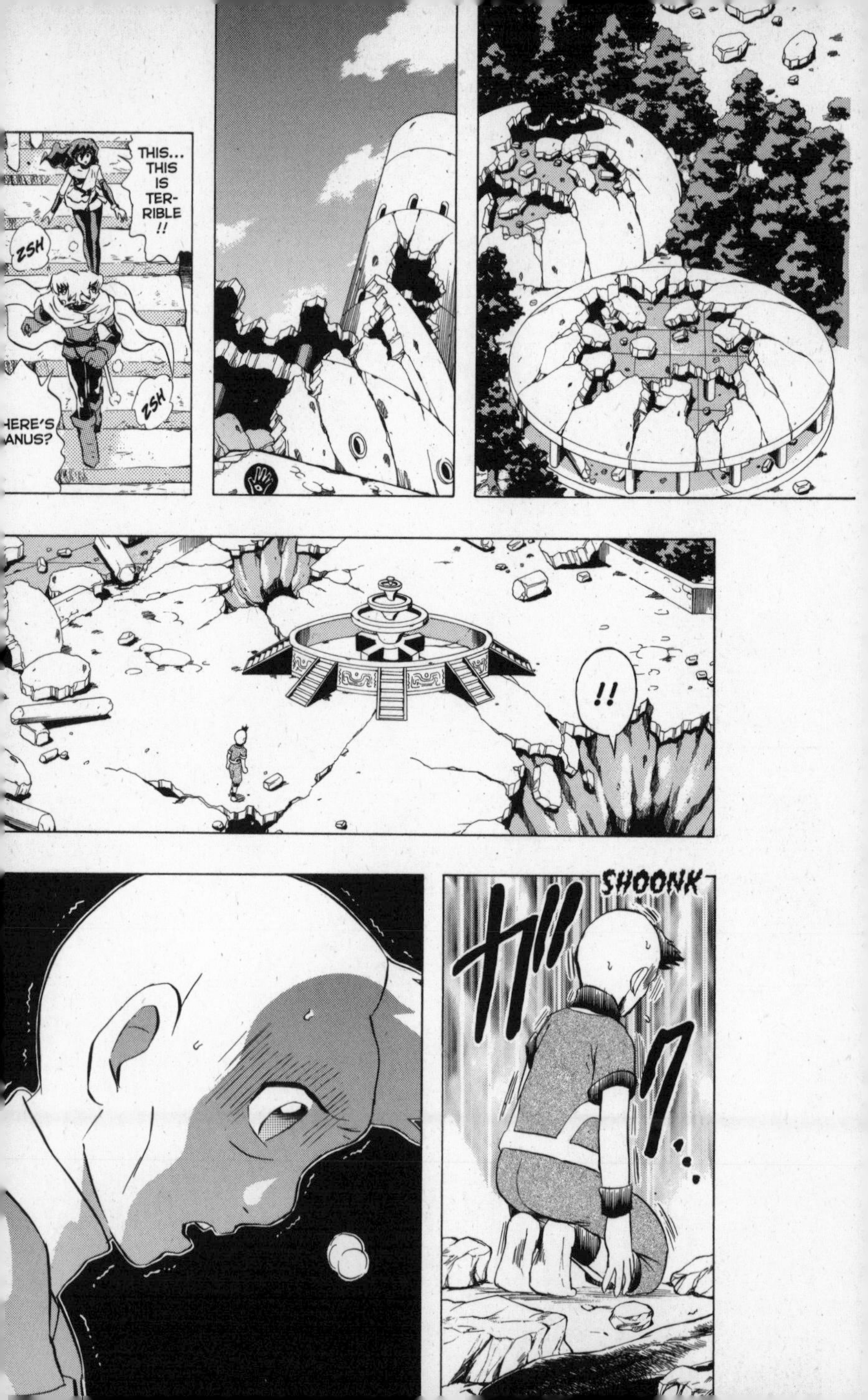
THIS... THIS IS TER-RIBLE!!
ZSH
ZSH
HERE'S ANUS?
!!
SHOONK

LOOK!

AH!

MANUS...

THE... THE GREY GUARDS!!

NO... WE WERE TOO LATE!!

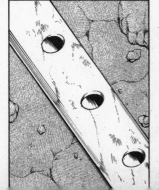

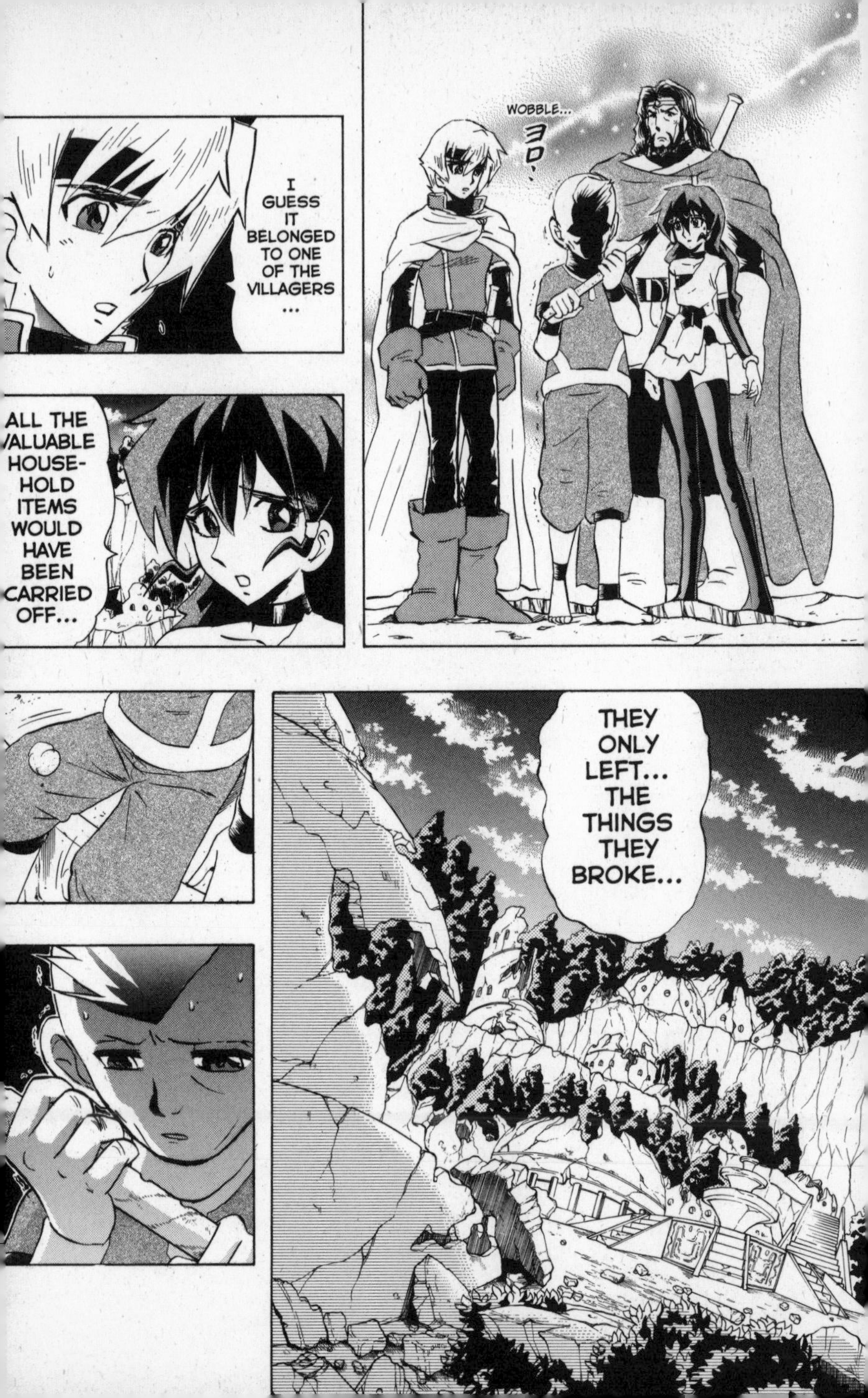
WOBBLE...
ヨロ
I GUESS IT BELONGED TO ONE OF THE VILLAGERS ...
ALL THE VALUABLE HOUSE-HOLD ITEMS WOULD HAVE BEEN CARRIED OFF...
THEY ONLY LEFT... THE THINGS THEY BROKE...

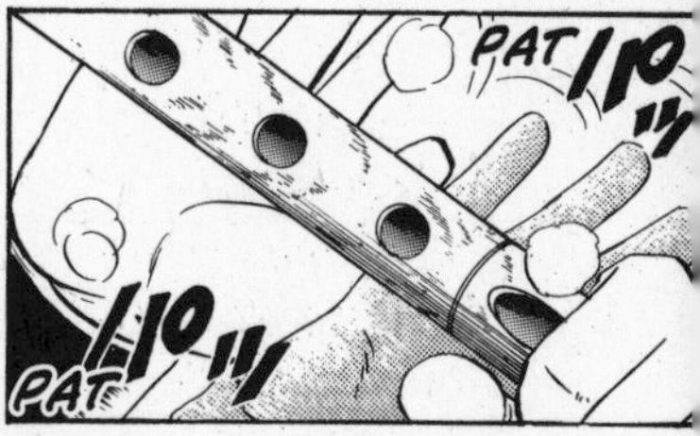
PAT
PAT
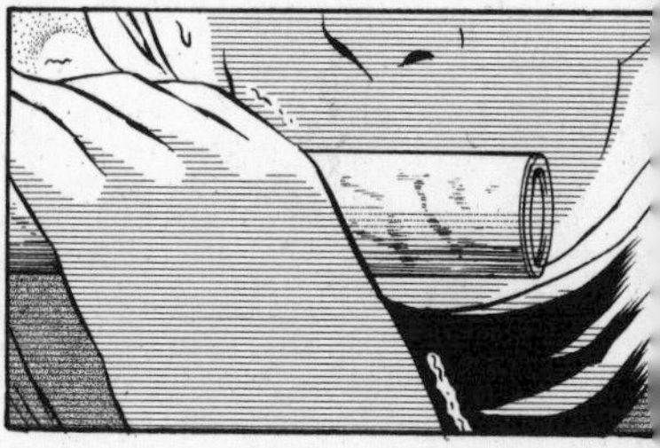
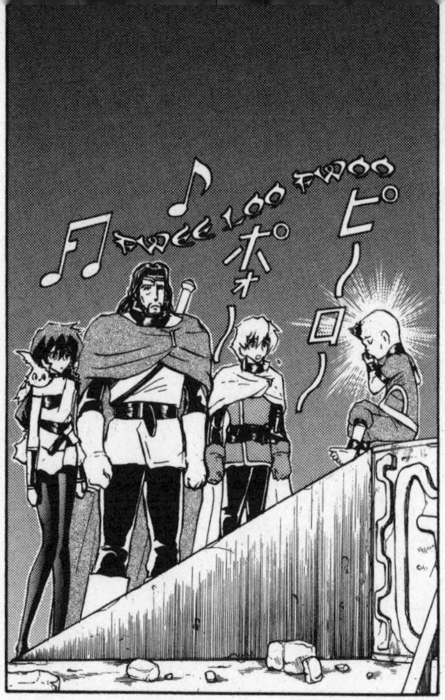
PWEE-LOO PWOO
ピーローー
ポォーー
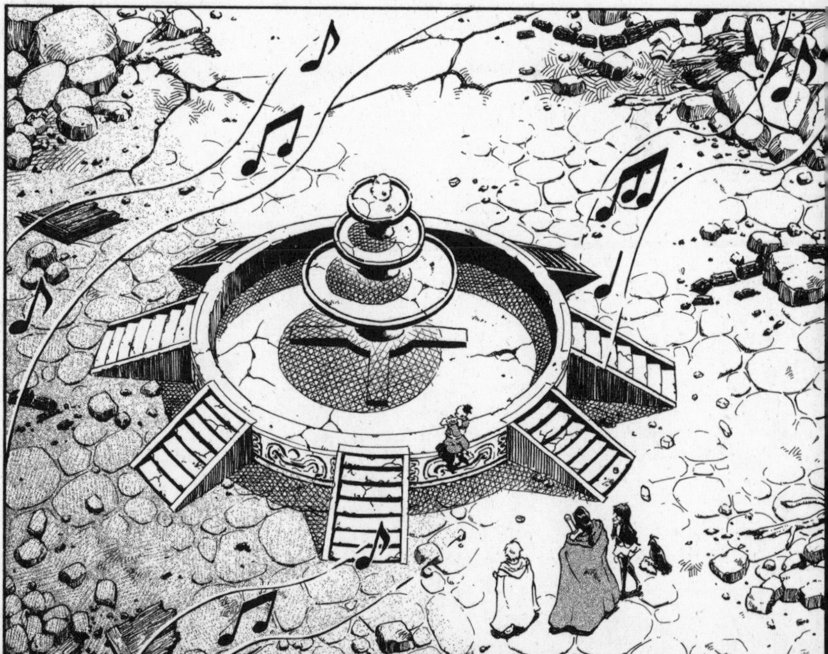

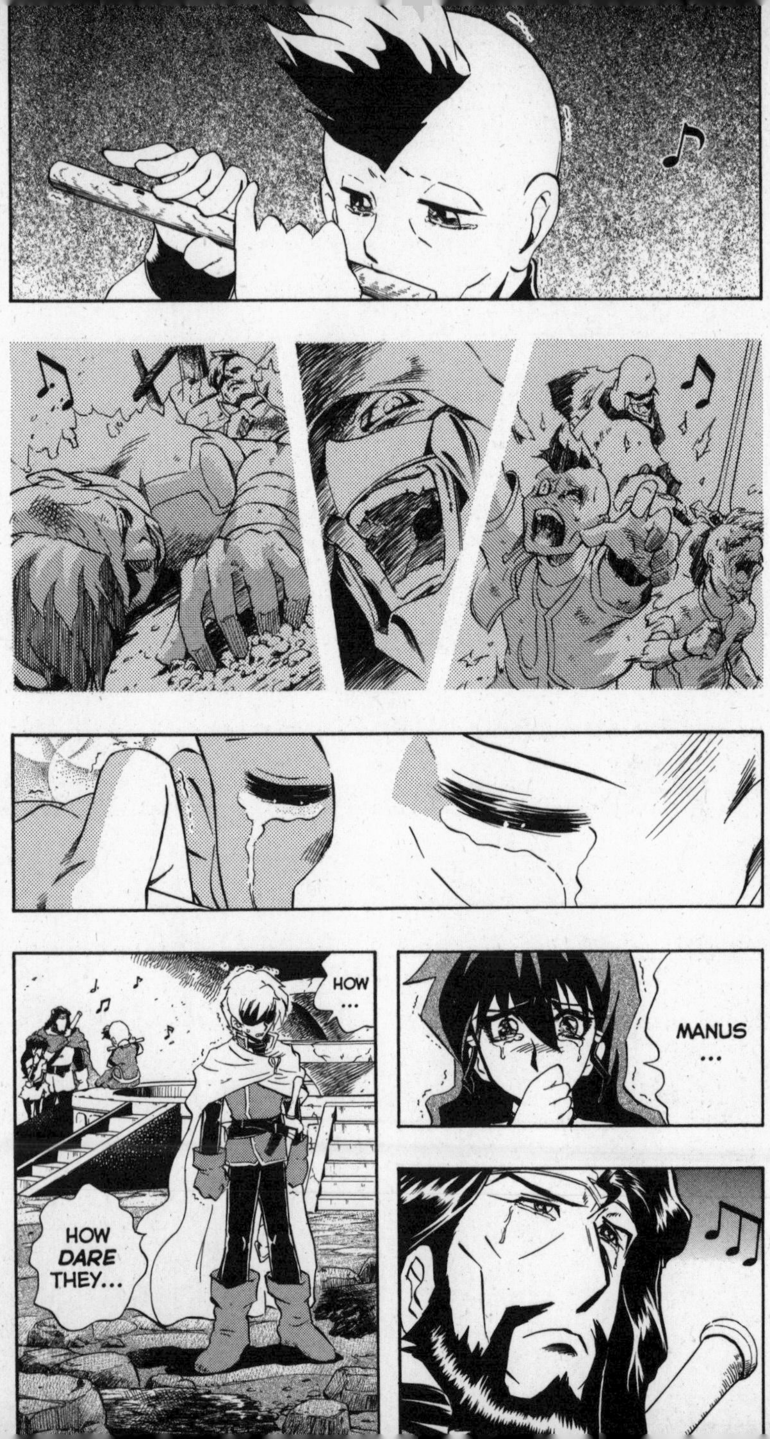
MANUS ...
HOW ...
HOW DARE THEY...

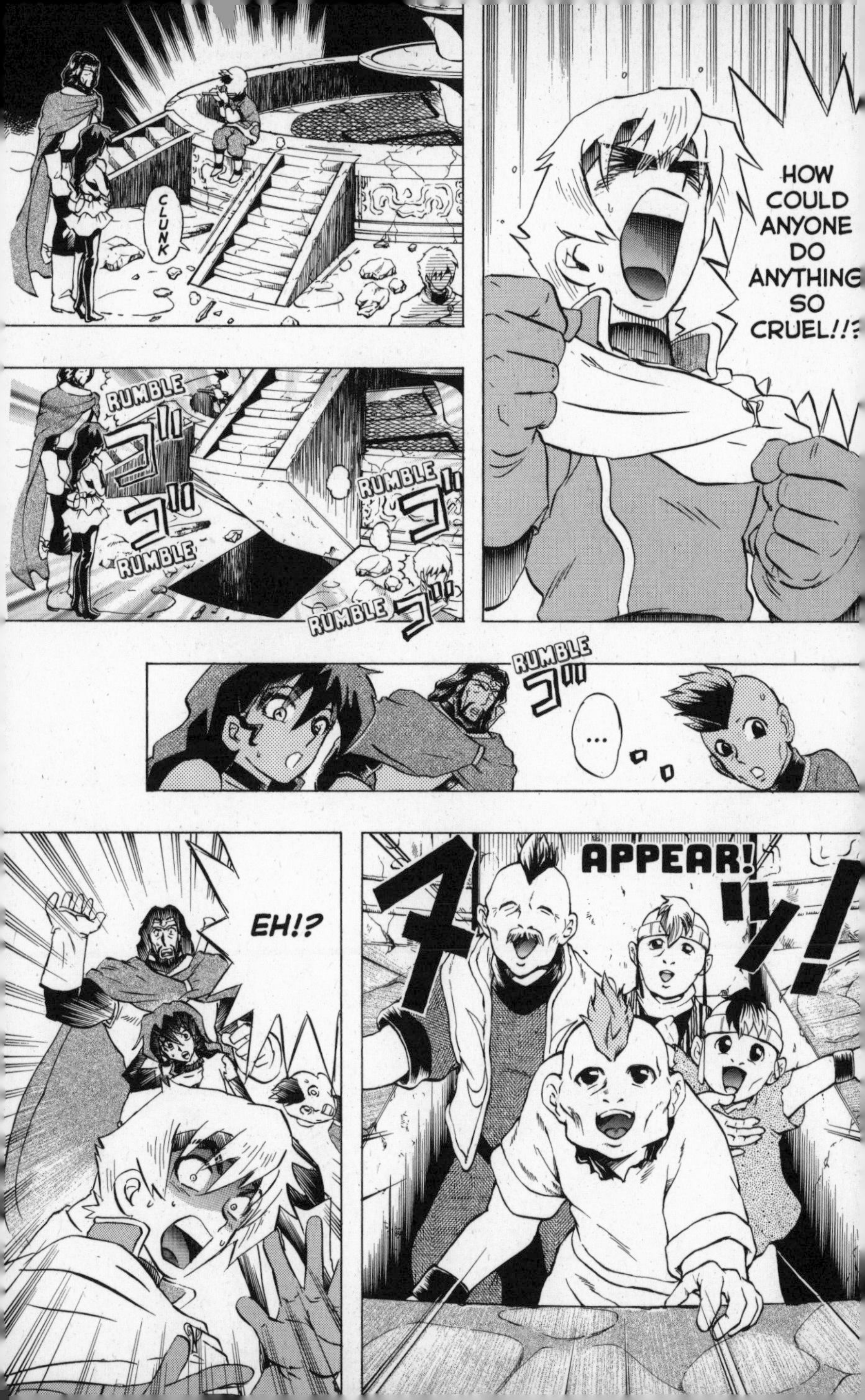
HOW COULD ANYONE DO ANYTHING SO CRUEL!!?
CLUNK
RUMBLE
RUMBLE
RUMBLE
RUMBLE
RUMBLE
...
APPEAR!
EH!?

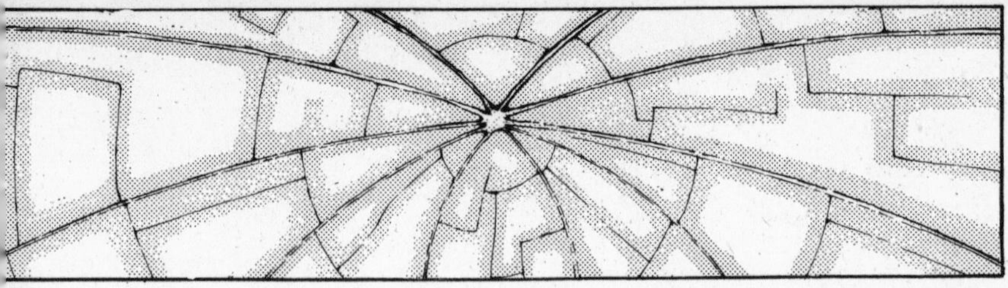
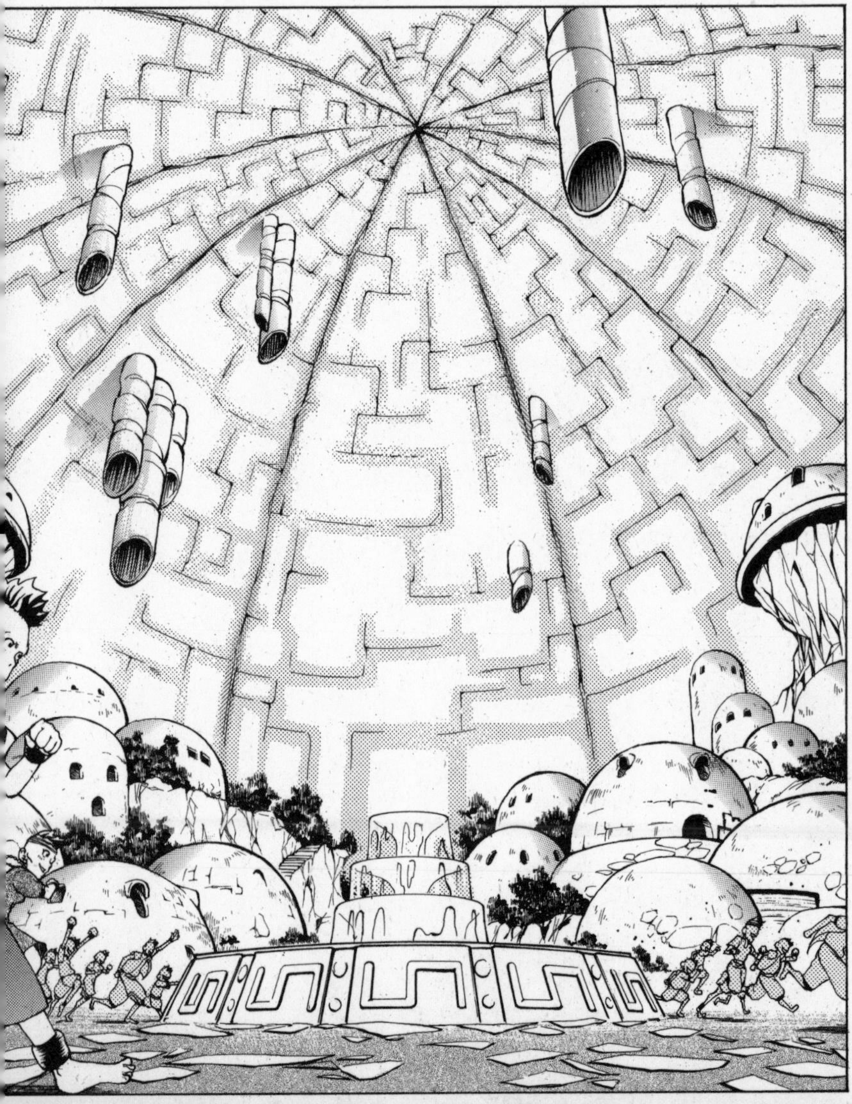

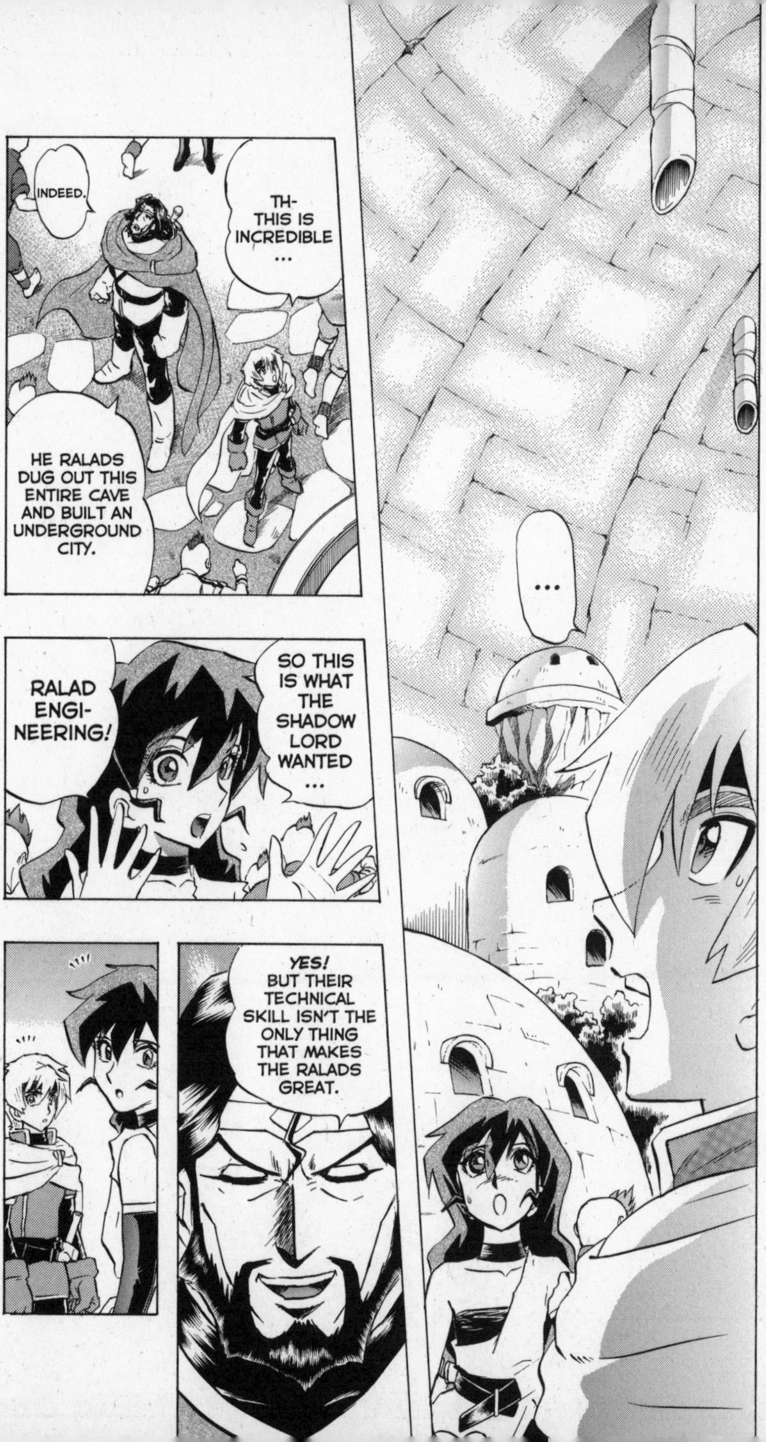
...
TH- THIS IS INCREDIBLE ...
INDEED.
HE RALADS DUG OUT THIS ENTIRE CAVE AND BUILT AN UNDERGROUND CITY.
SO THIS IS WHAT THE SHADOW LORD WANTED ...
RALAD ENGI-NEERING!
YES! BUT THEIR TECHNICAL SKILL ISN'T THE ONLY THING THAT MAKES THE RALADS GREAT.

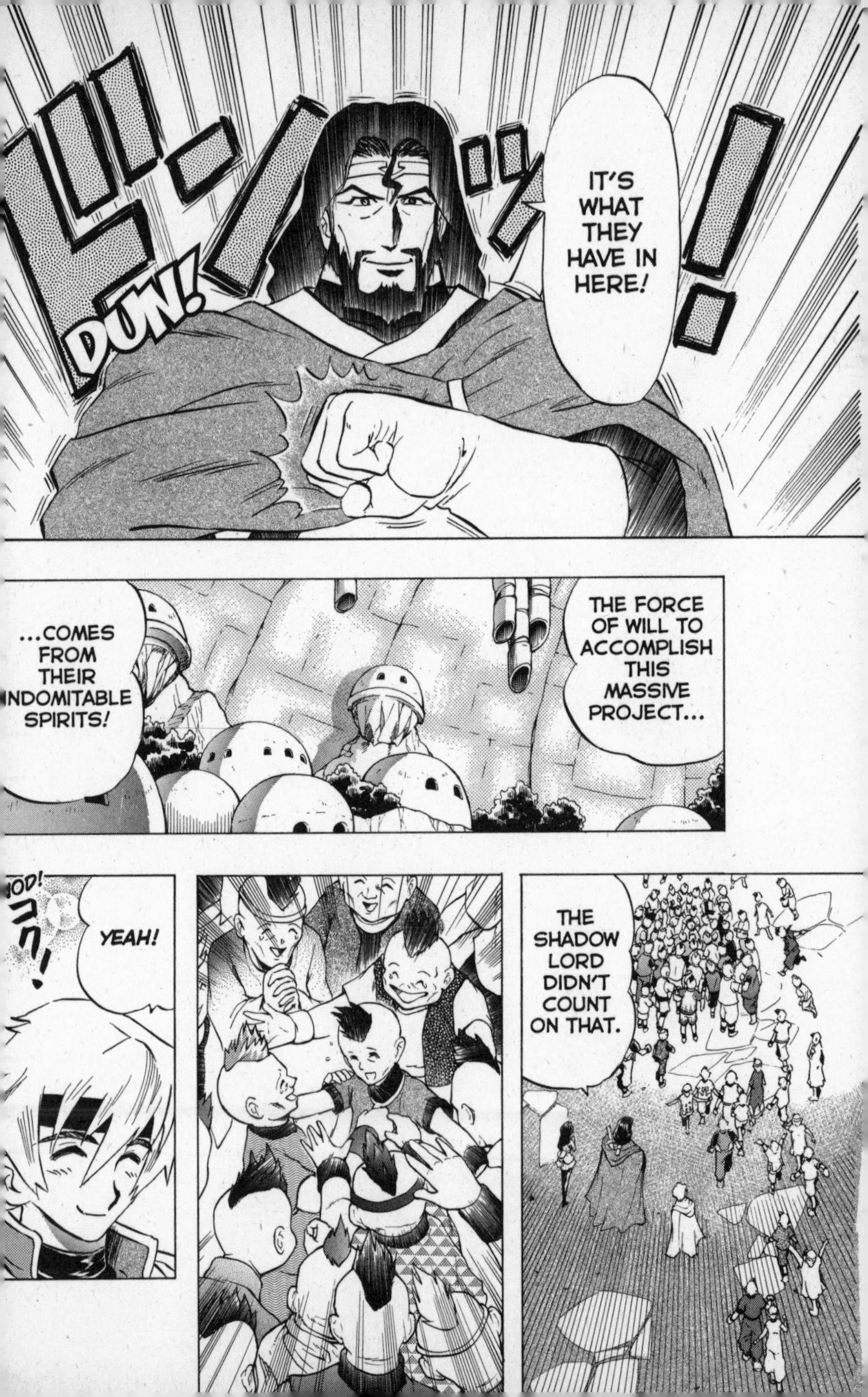
DUN!
IT'S WHAT THEY HAVE IN HERE!
THE FORCE OF WILL TO ACCOMPLISH THIS MASSIVE PROJECT...
...COMES FROM THEIR INDOMITABLE SPIRITS!
THE SHADOW LORD DIDN'T COUNT ON THAT.
YEAH!

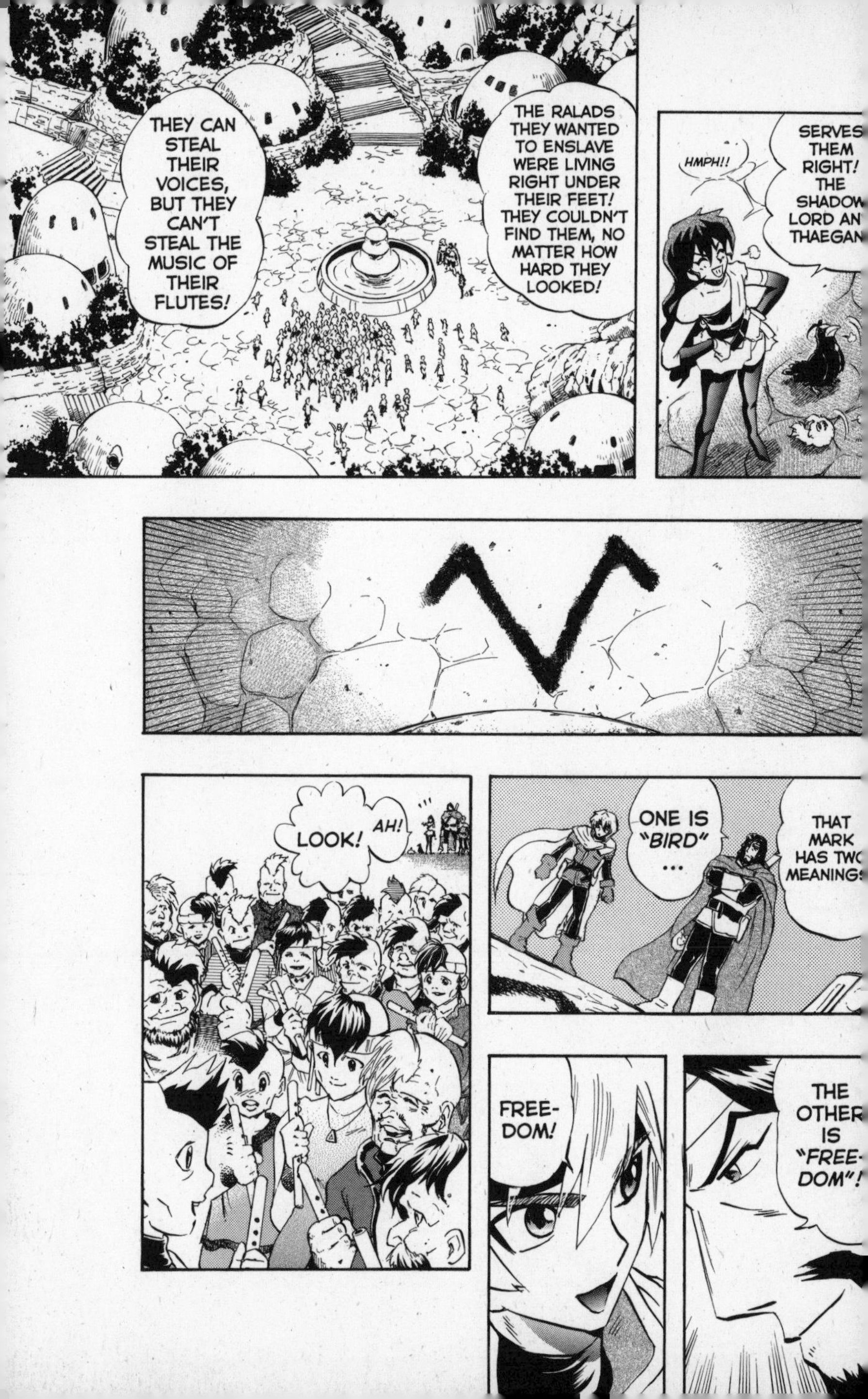
SERVES THEM RIGHT! THE SHADOW LORD AN THAEGAN
HMPH!!
THE RALADS THEY WANTED TO ENSLAVE WERE LIVING RIGHT UNDER THEIR FEET! THEY COULDN'T FIND THEM, NO MATTER HOW HARD THEY LOOKED!
THEY CAN STEAL THEIR VOICES, BUT THEY CAN'T STEAL THE MUSIC OF THEIR FLUTES!
THAT MARK HAS TWO MEANINGS
ONE IS "BIRD" ...
THE OTHER IS "FREE-DOM"!
FREE-DOM!
AH!
LOOK!

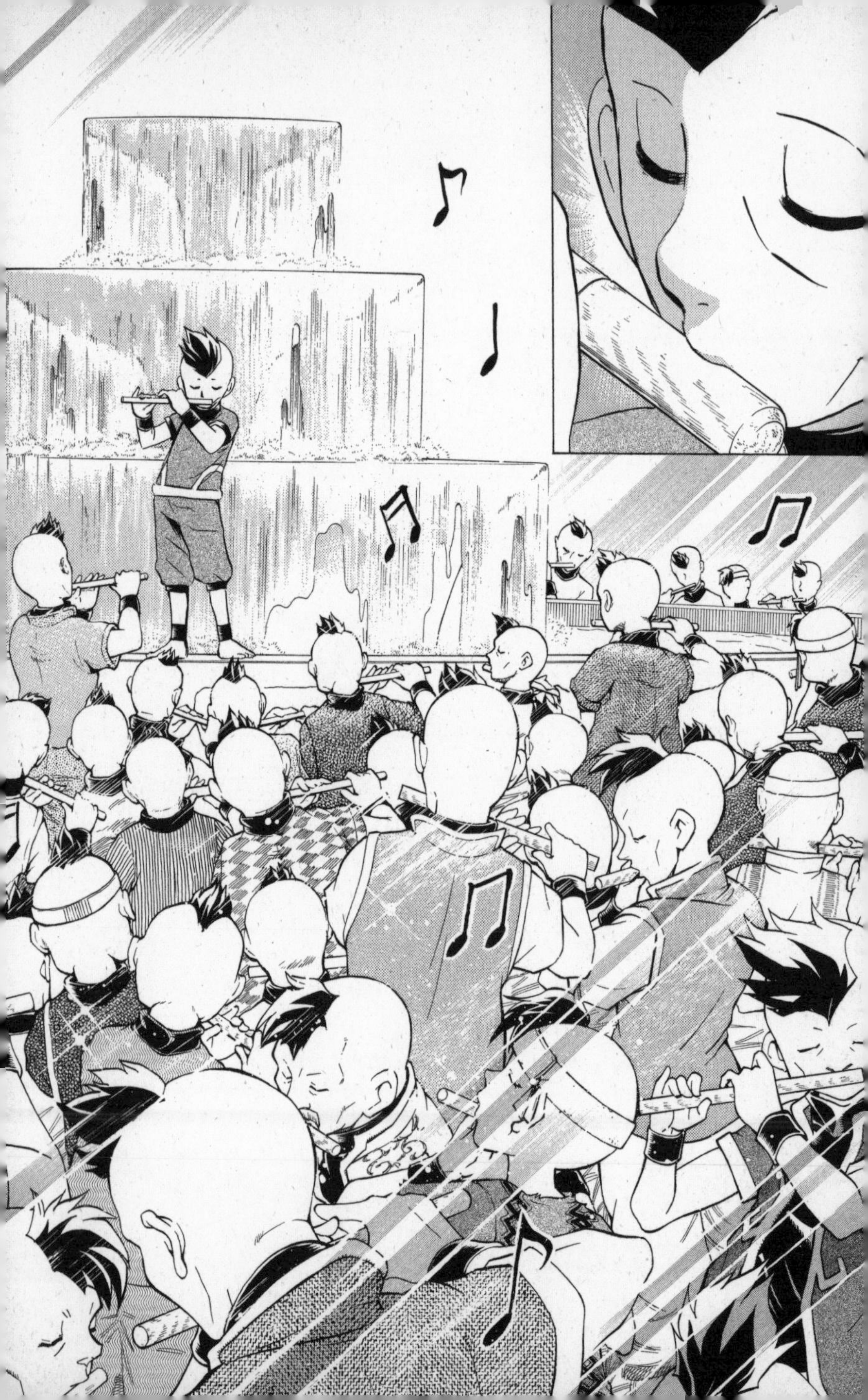

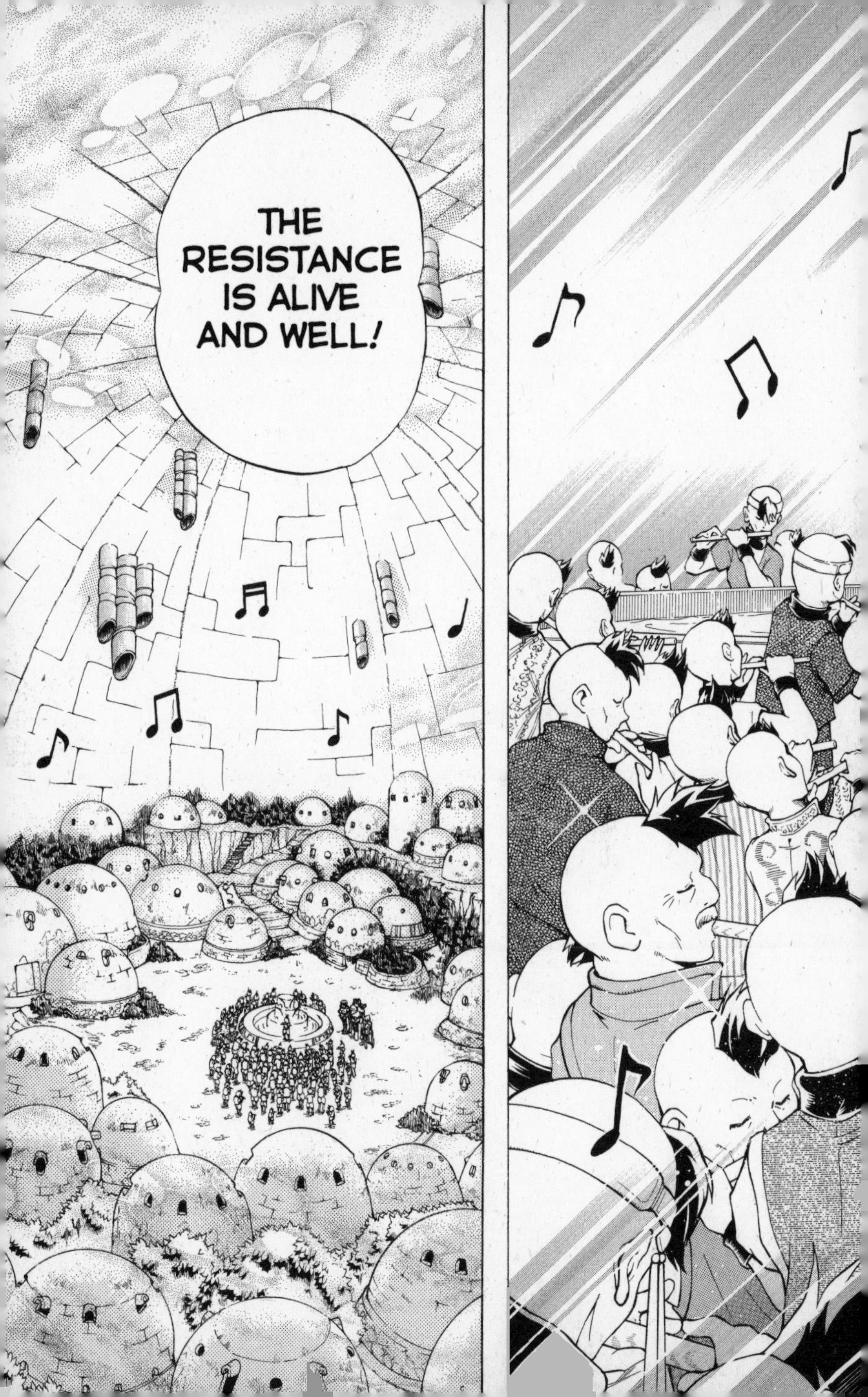
THE RESISTANCE IS ALIVE AND WELL!

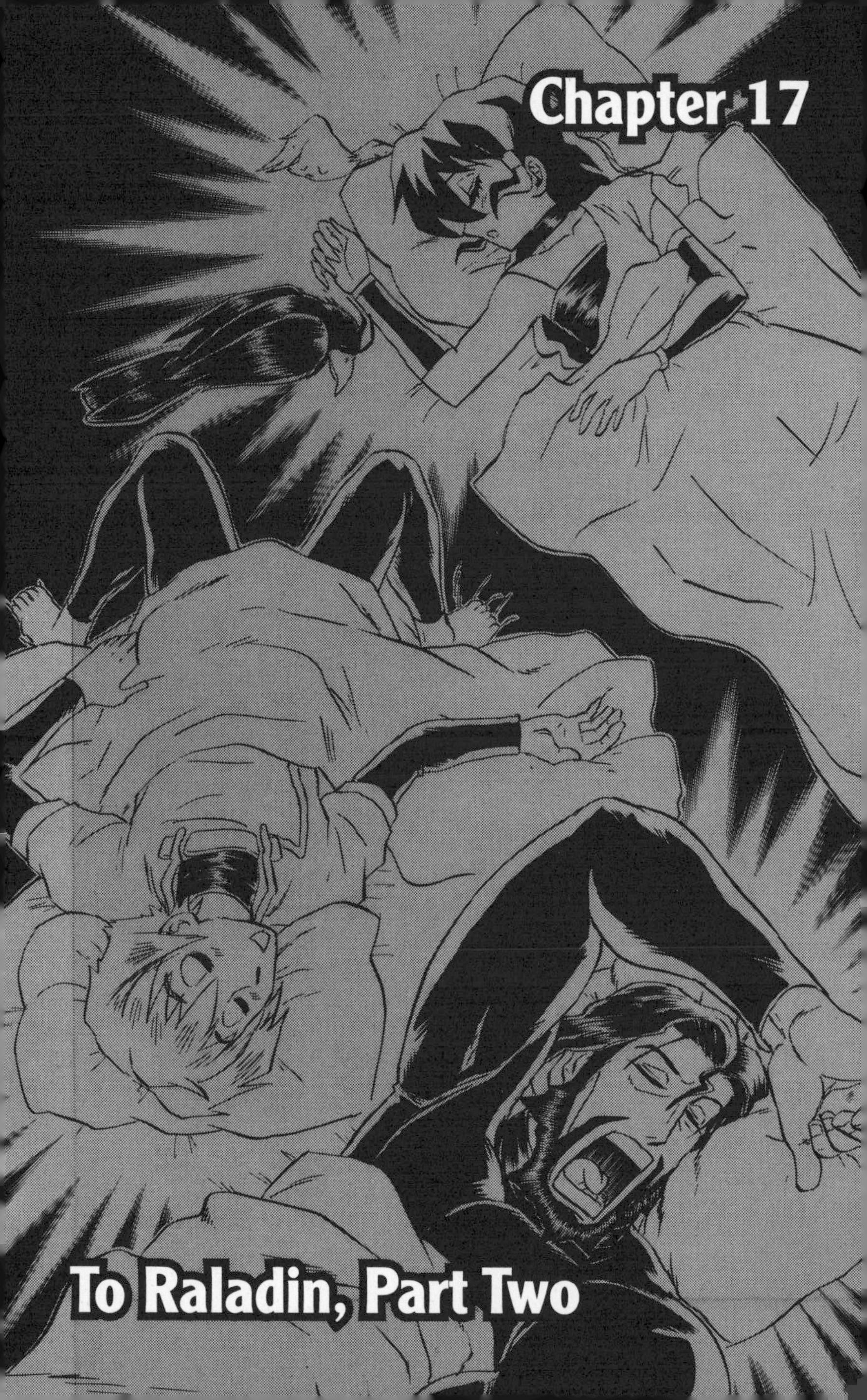
Chapter 17
To Raladin, Part Two

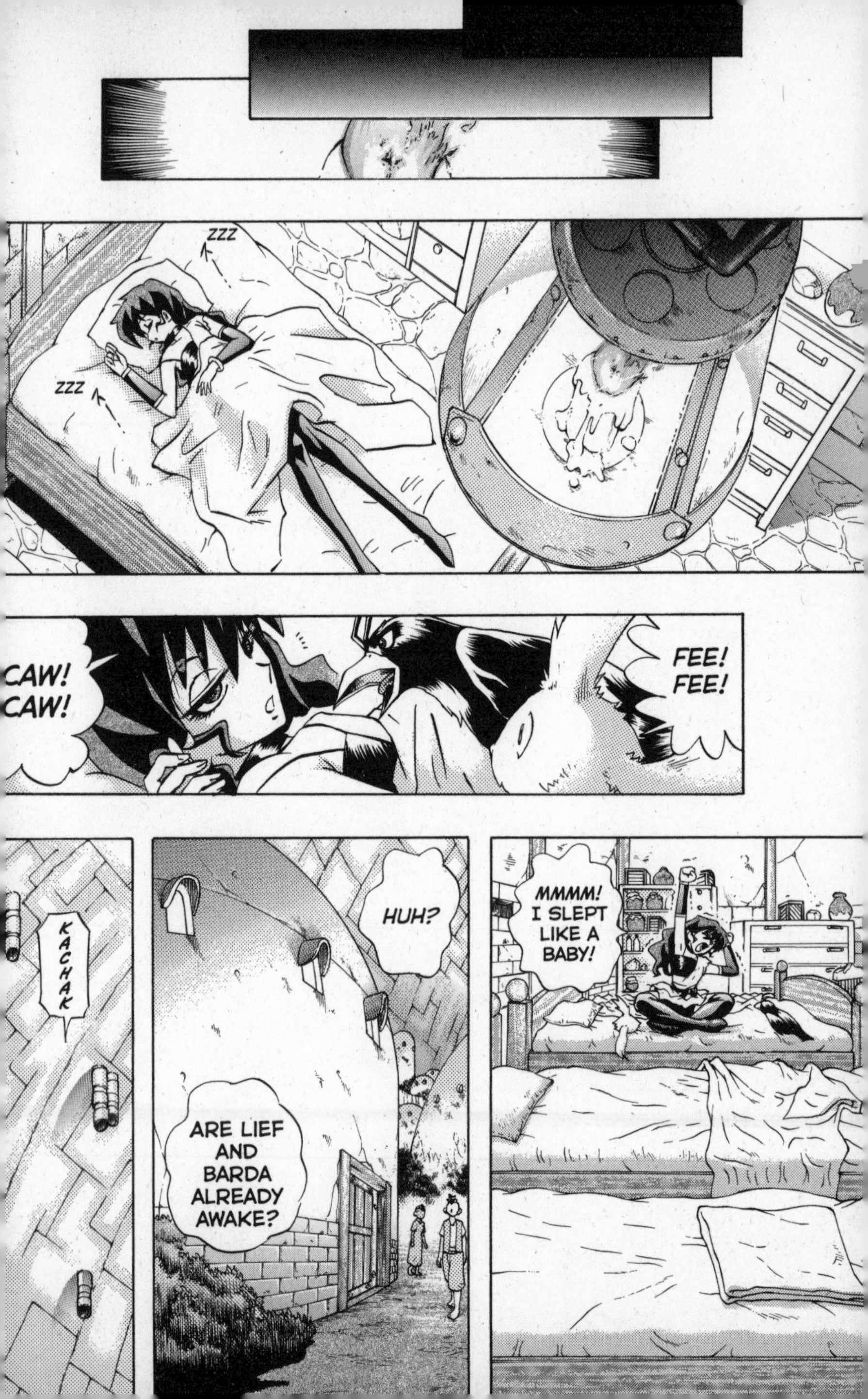
ZZZ
ZZZ
FEE! FEE!
CAW! CAW!
MMMM! I SLEPT LIKE A BABY!
HUH?
ARE LIEF AND BARDA ALREADY AWAKE?
KACHAK

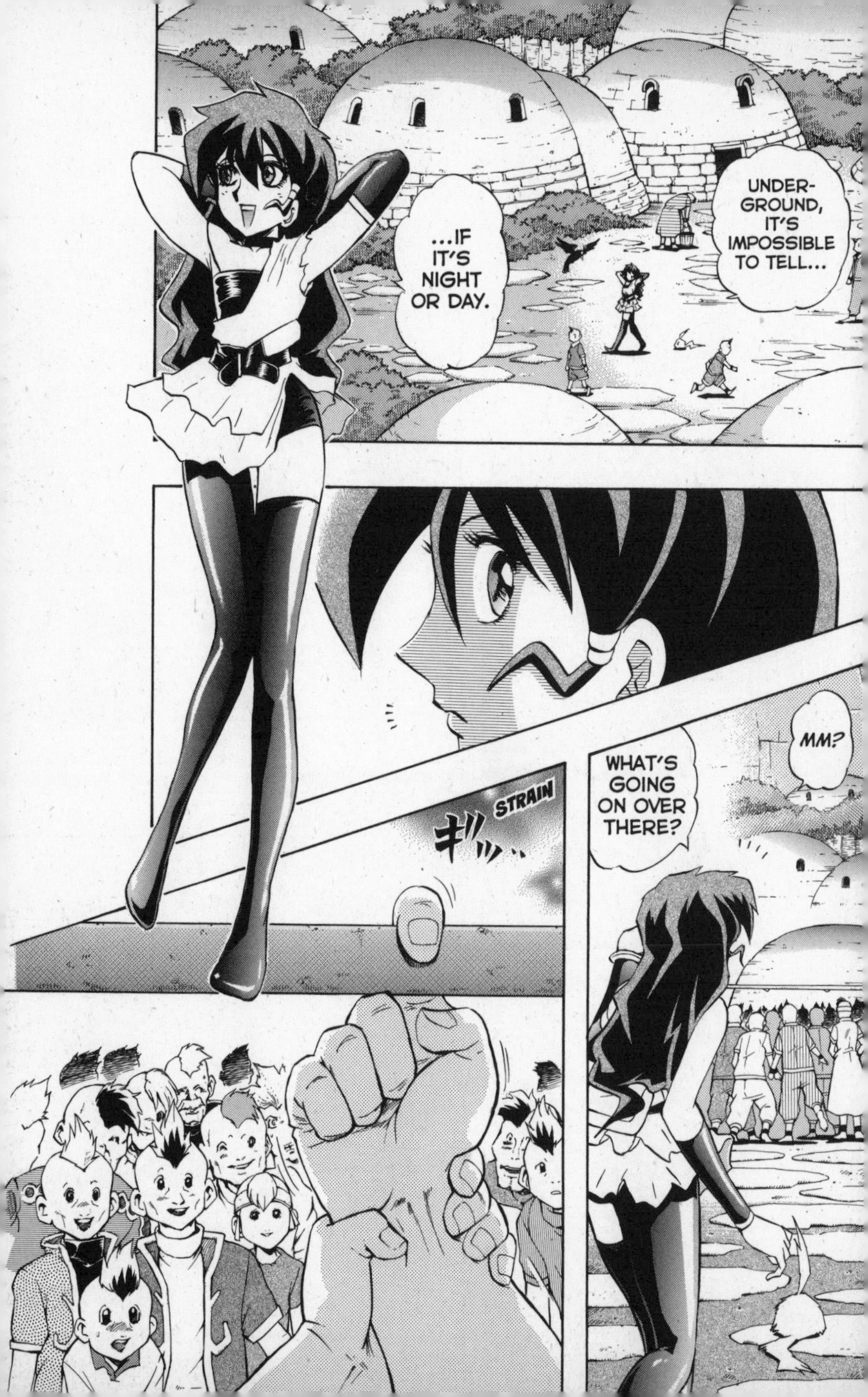
UNDER-GROUND, IT'S IMPOSSIBLE TO TELL...
...IF IT'S NIGHT OR DAY.
MM?
WHAT'S GOING ON OVER THERE?
STRAIN

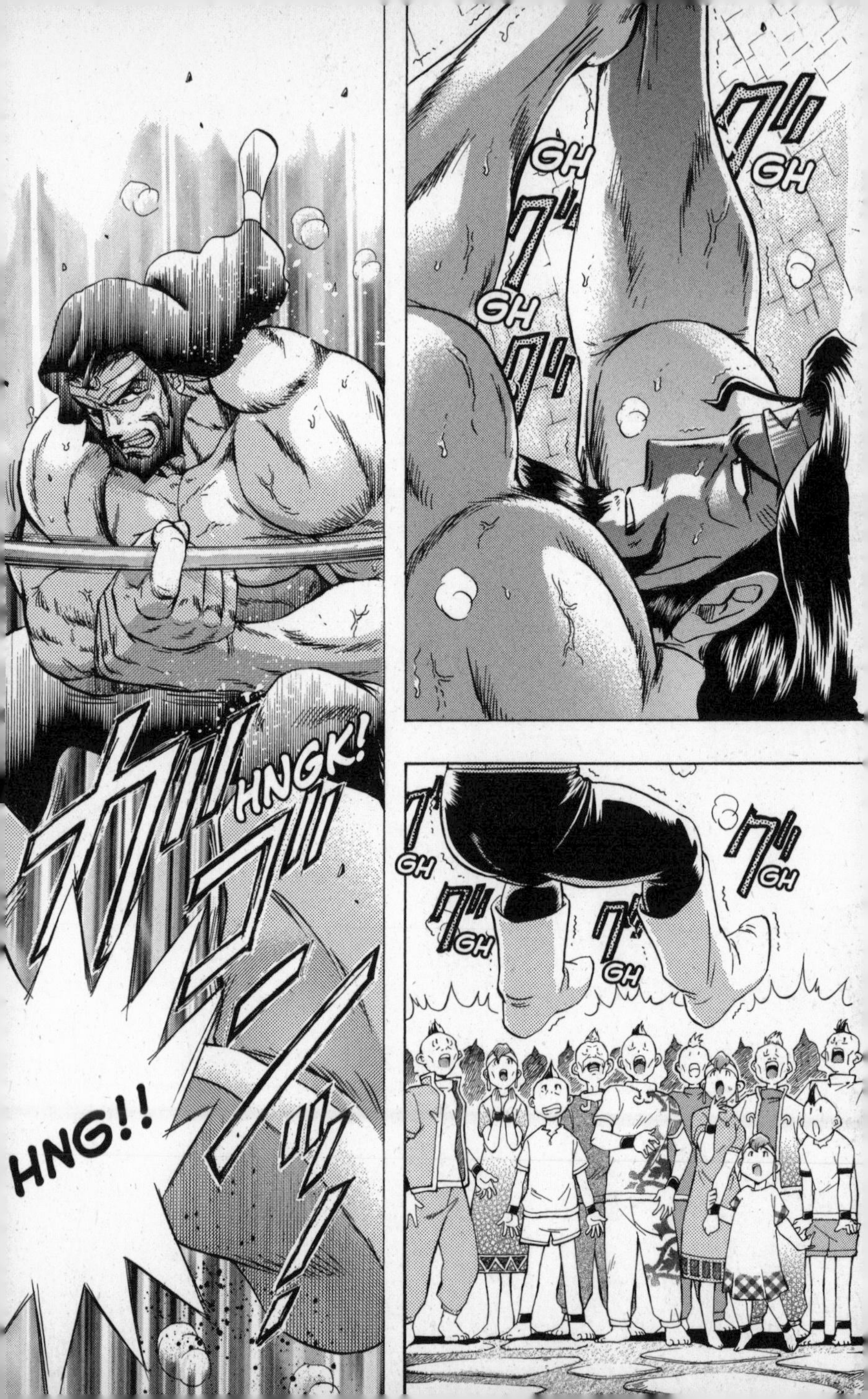
GH
GH
GH
GH
GH
GH
GH
HNGK!
HNG!!

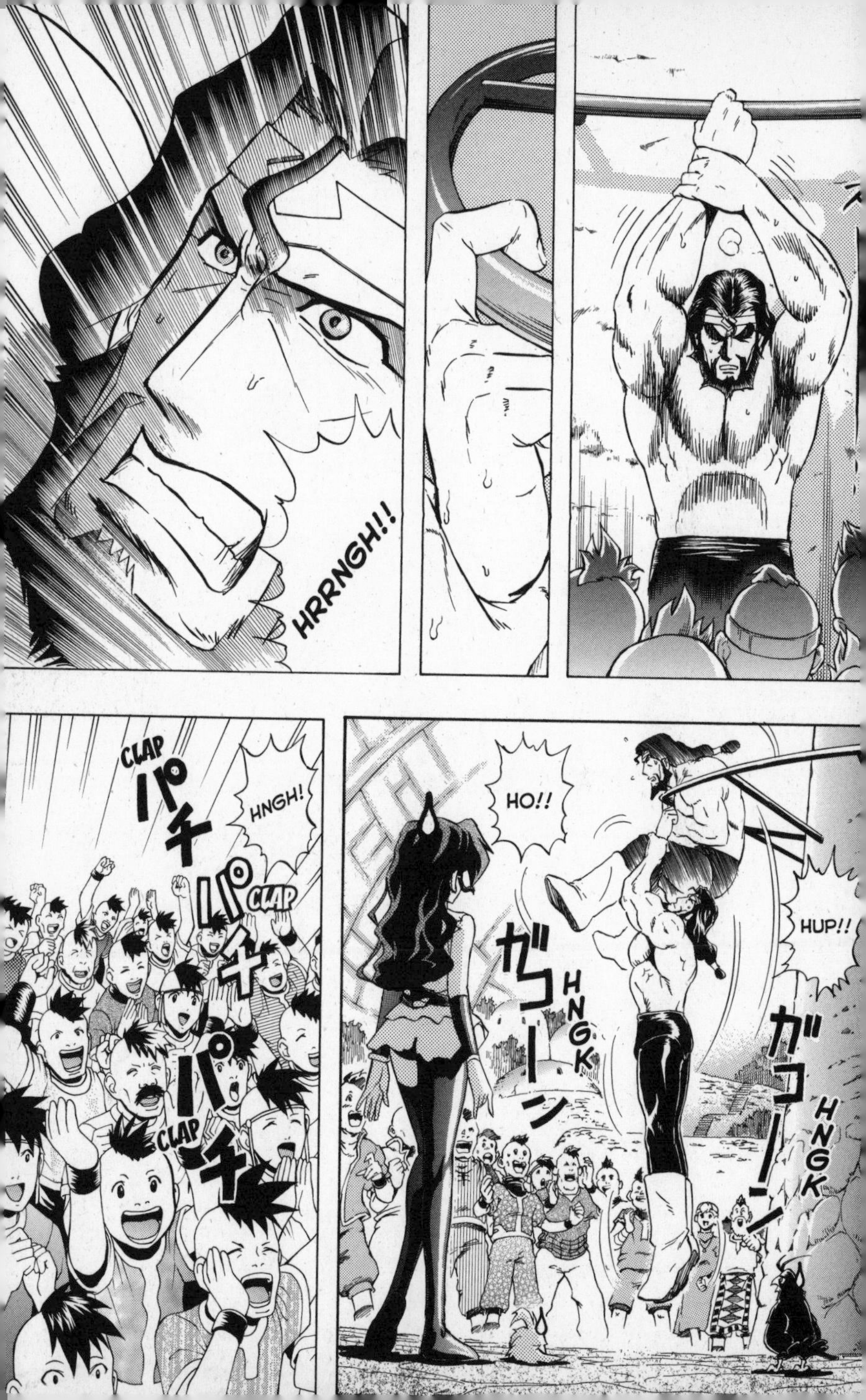
HRRNGH!!
HO!!
HUP!!
ガコーン
HNGK
ガコーン
HNGK
HNGH!
CLAP
パチ
CLAP
パチ
CLAP
パチ

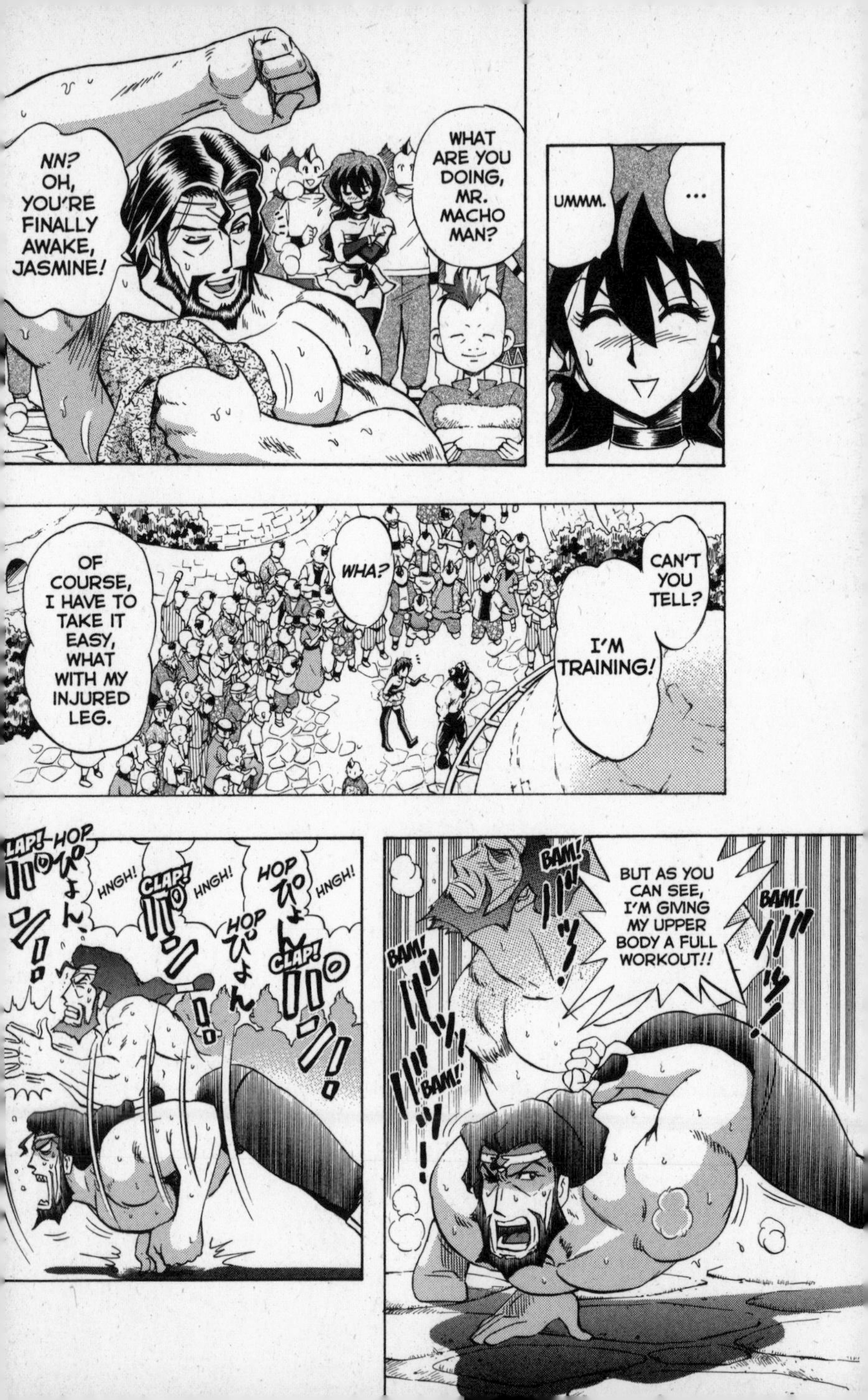

UMMM.
...
WHAT ARE YOU DOING, MR. MACHO MAN?
NN? OH, YOU'RE FINALLY AWAKE, JASMINE!
CAN'T YOU TELL?
I'M TRAINING!
WHA?
OF COURSE, I HAVE TO TAKE IT EASY, WHAT WITH MY INJURED LEG.
BAM!
BUT AS YOU CAN SEE, I'M GIVING MY UPPER BODY A FULL WORKOUT!!
BAM!
BAM!
BAM!
HNGH!
HOP ぴょん
CLAP!
HOP ぴょん
HNGH!
CLAP!
HNGH!
HOP ぴょん
CLAP!

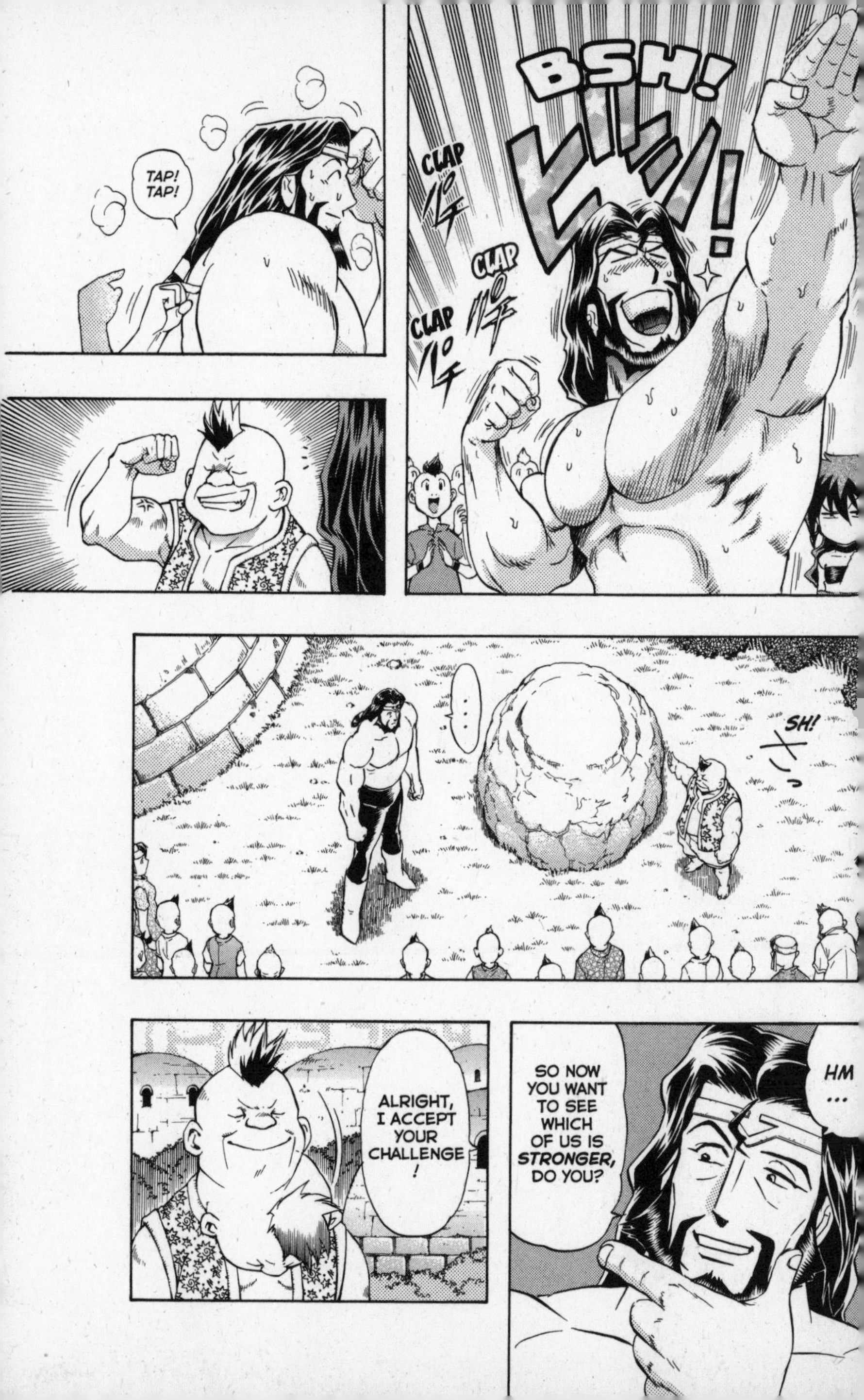
BSH!
CLAP
CLAP
CLAP
TAP! TAP!
...
SH!
HM ...
SO NOW YOU WANT TO SEE WHICH OF US IS STRONGER, DO YOU?
ALRIGHT, I ACCEPT YOUR CHALLENGE!

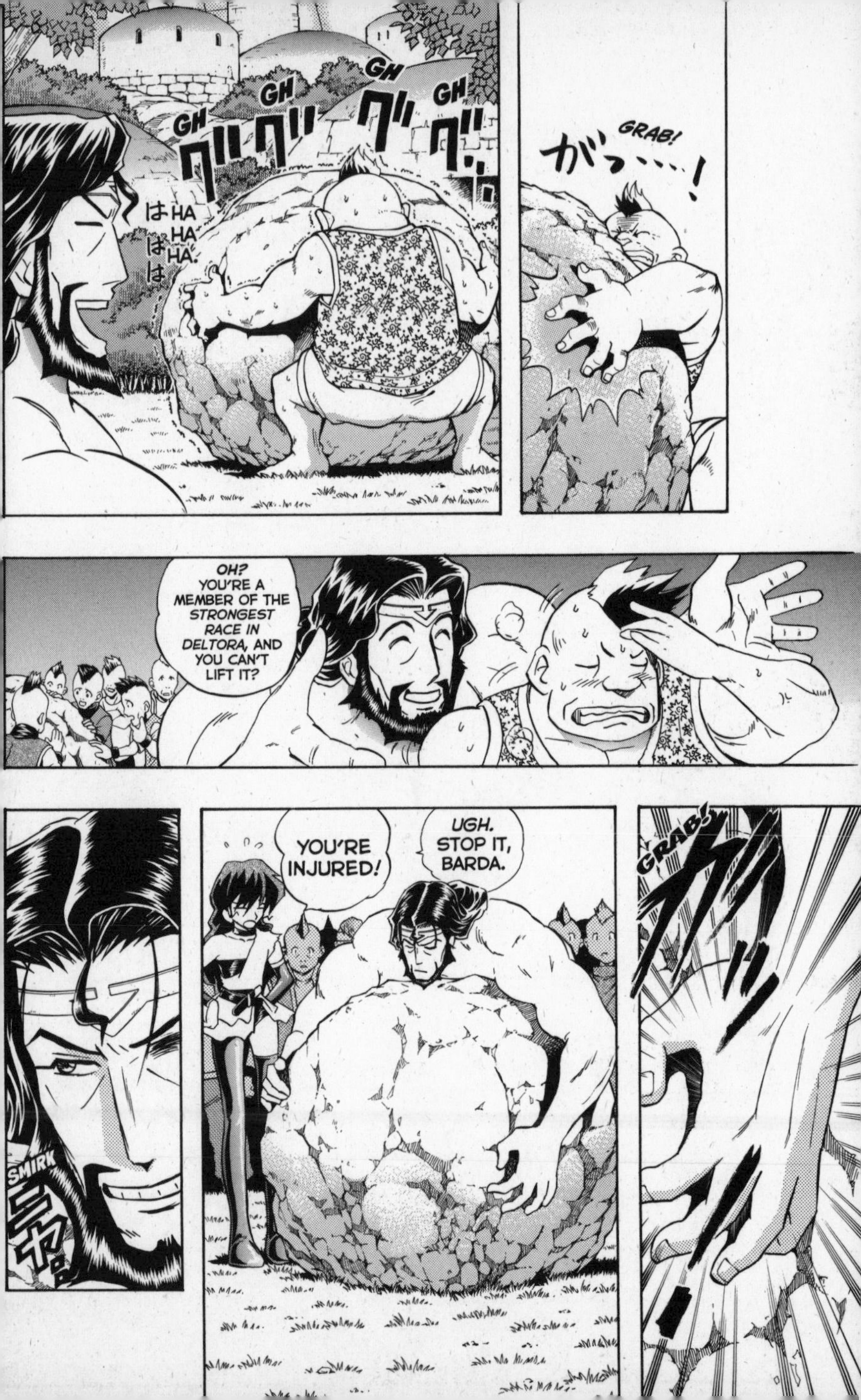

GRAB!
がっ……!
GH GH GH GH
HA HA HA
ははは
OH? YOU'RE A MEMBER OF THE STRONGEST RACE IN DELTORA, AND YOU CAN'T LIFT IT?
GRAB!
UGH. STOP IT, BARDA.
YOU'RE INJURED!
SMIRK

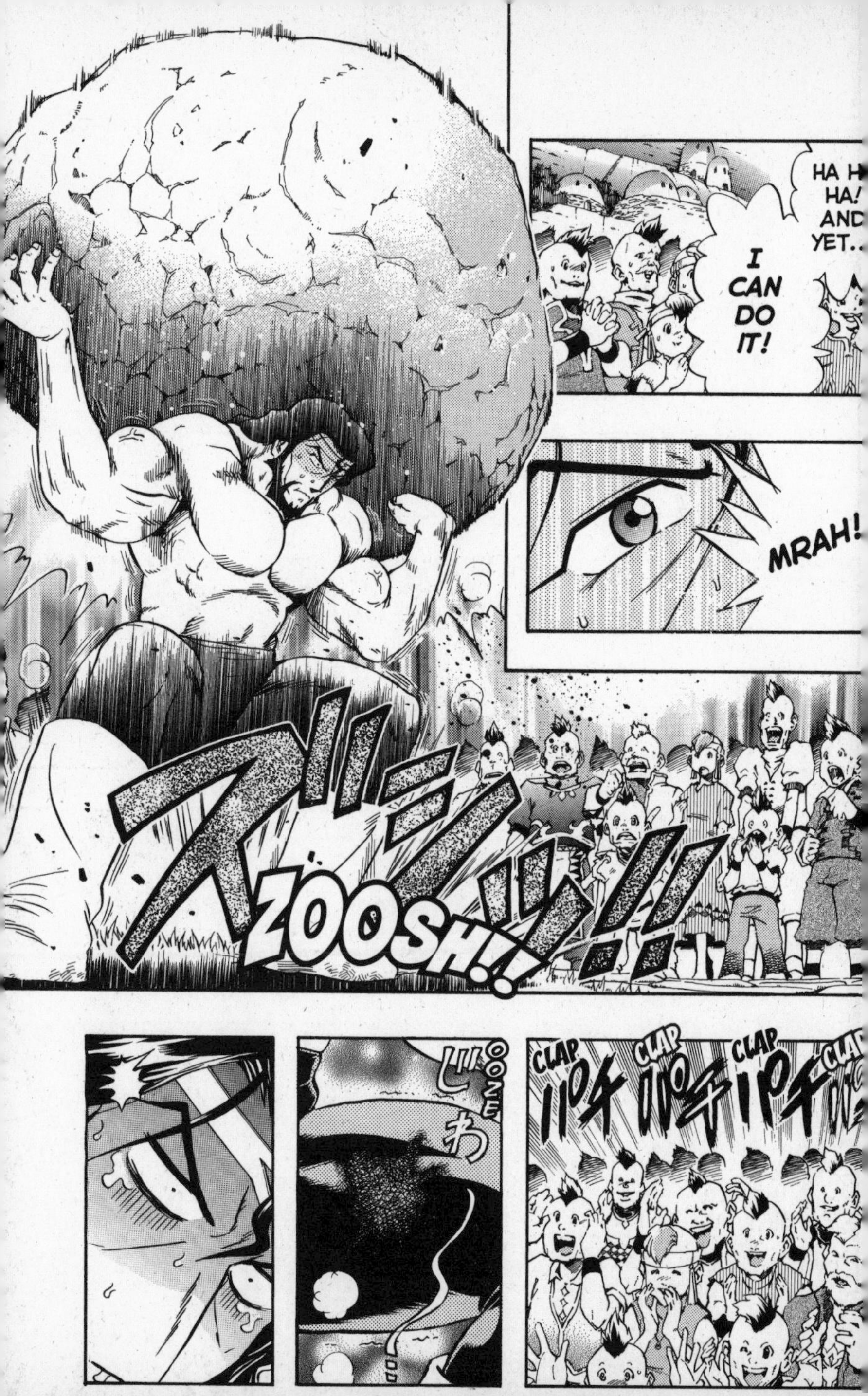

HA HA HA! AND YET...
I CAN DO IT!
MRAH!
ZOOSH!!
CLAP CLAP CLAP CLAP
OOZE

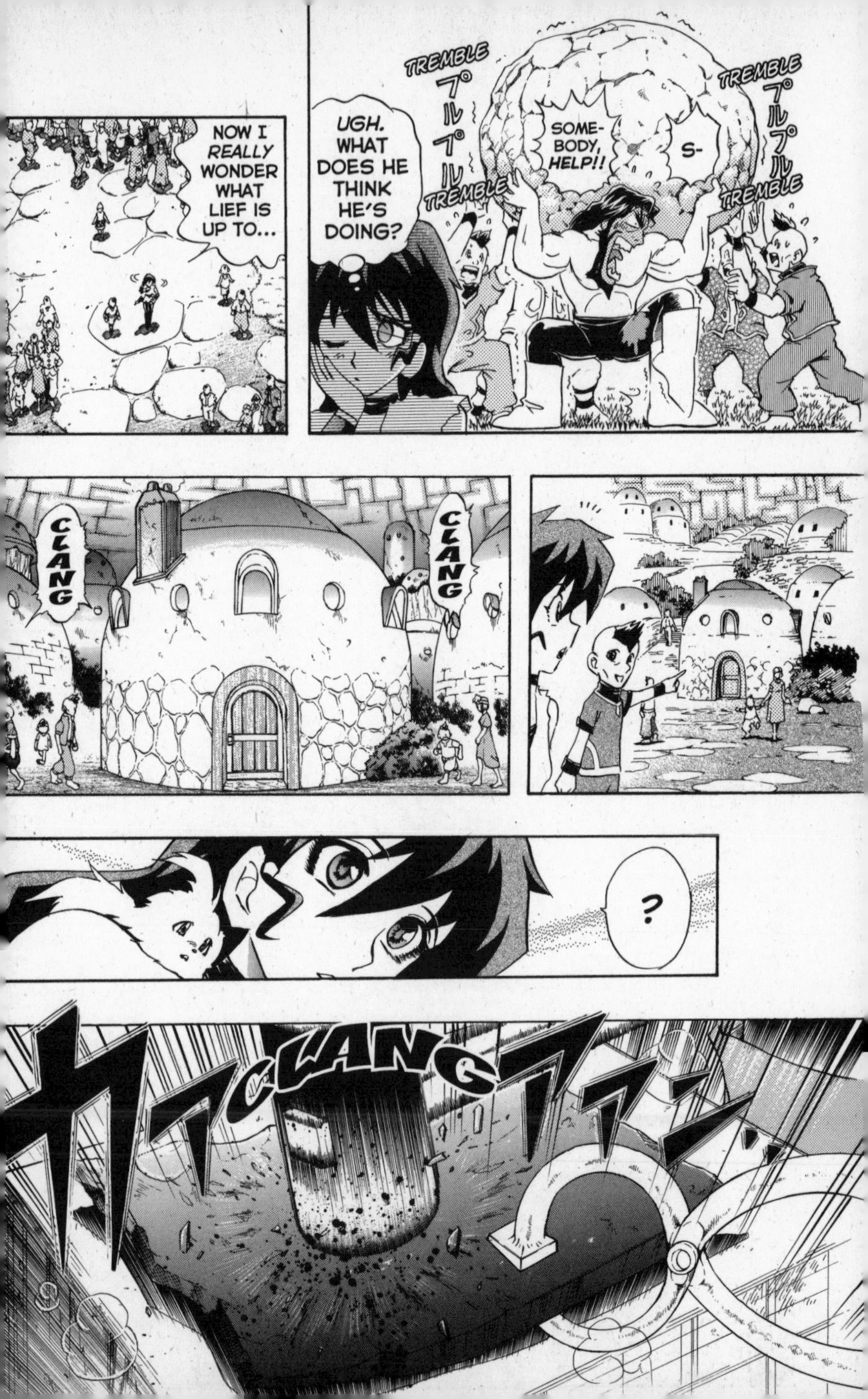
TREMBLE
プルプル
TREMBLE
S-
SOMEBODY, HELP!!
TREMBLE
プルプル
TREMBLE
UGH. WHAT DOES HE THINK HE'S DOING?
NOW I REALLY WONDER WHAT LIEF IS UP TO...
CLANG
CLANG
?
CLANG

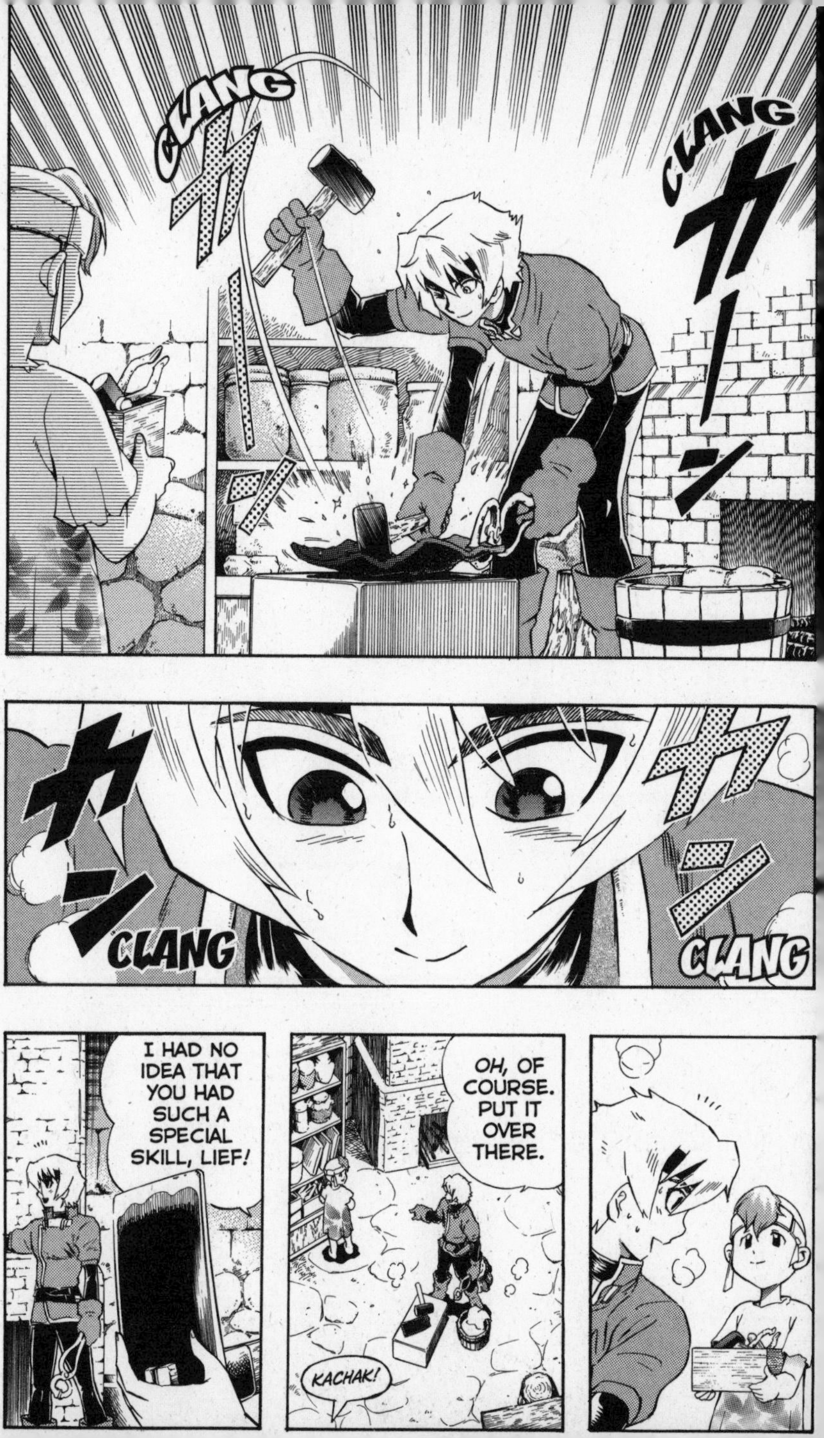
CLANG
CLANG
CLANG
CLANG
OH, OF COURSE. PUT IT OVER THERE.
KACHAK!
I HAD NO IDEA THAT YOU HAD SUCH A SPECIAL SKILL, LIEF!

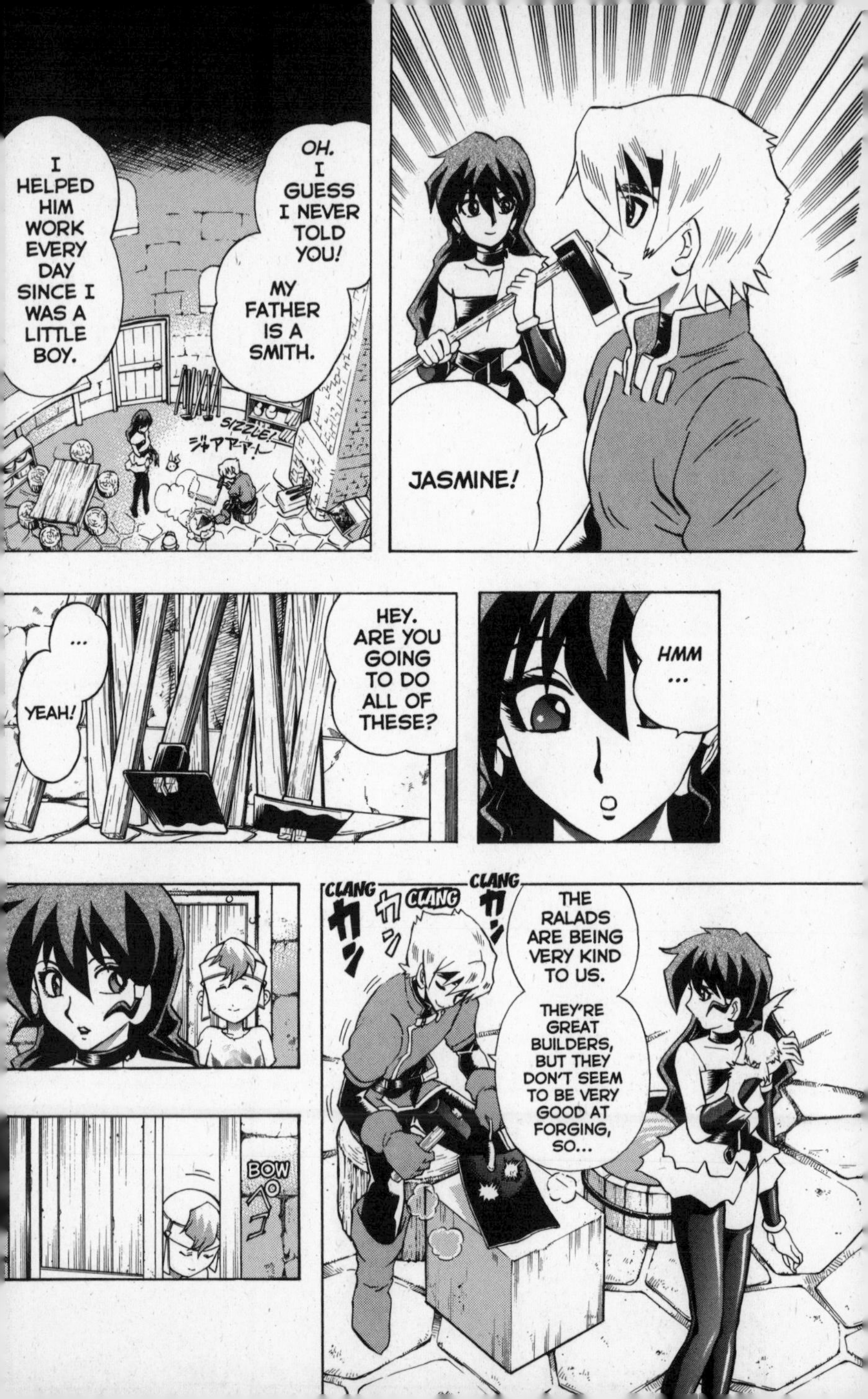
JASMINE!
OH. I GUESS I NEVER TOLD YOU!
MY FATHER IS A SMITH.
I HELPED HIM WORK EVERY DAY SINCE I WAS A LITTLE BOY.
SIZZLE!
HMM ...
HEY. ARE YOU GOING TO DO ALL OF THESE?
...
YEAH!
CLANG
CLANG
CLANG
THE RALADS ARE BEING VERY KIND TO US.
THEY'RE GREAT BUILDERS, BUT THEY DON'T SEEM TO BE VERY GOOD AT FORGING, SO...
BOW

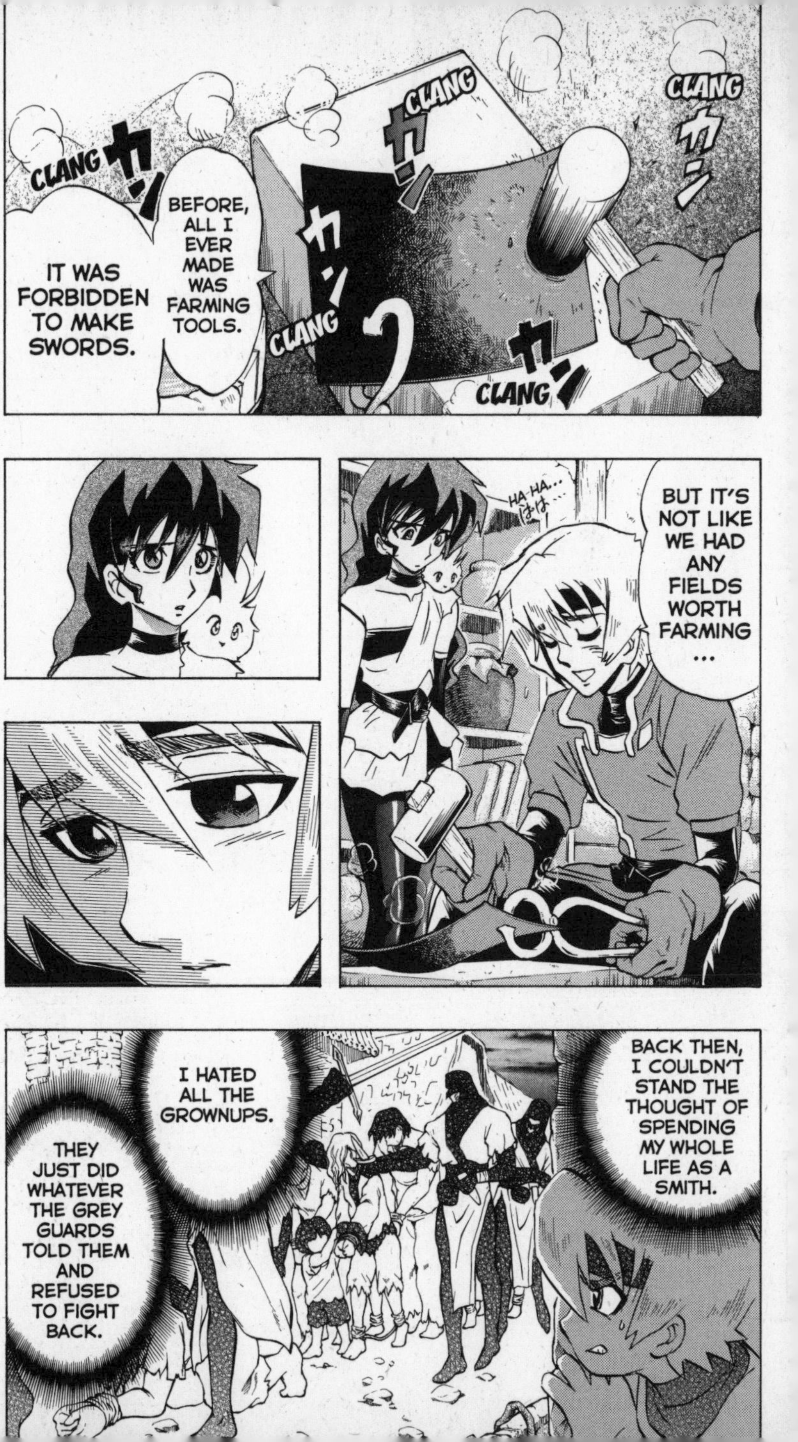
CLANG
カン
CLANG
カン
BEFORE, ALL I EVER MADE WAS FARMING TOOLS.
CLANG
カン
IT WAS FORBIDDEN TO MAKE SWORDS.
CLANG
カン
CLANG
カン
BUT IT'S NOT LIKE WE HAD ANY FIELDS WORTH FARMING ...
HA-HA... はは…
BACK THEN, I COULDN'T STAND THE THOUGHT OF SPENDING MY WHOLE LIFE AS A SMITH.
I HATED ALL THE GROWNUPS.
THEY JUST DID WHATEVER THE GREY GUARDS TOLD THEM AND REFUSED TO FIGHT BACK.

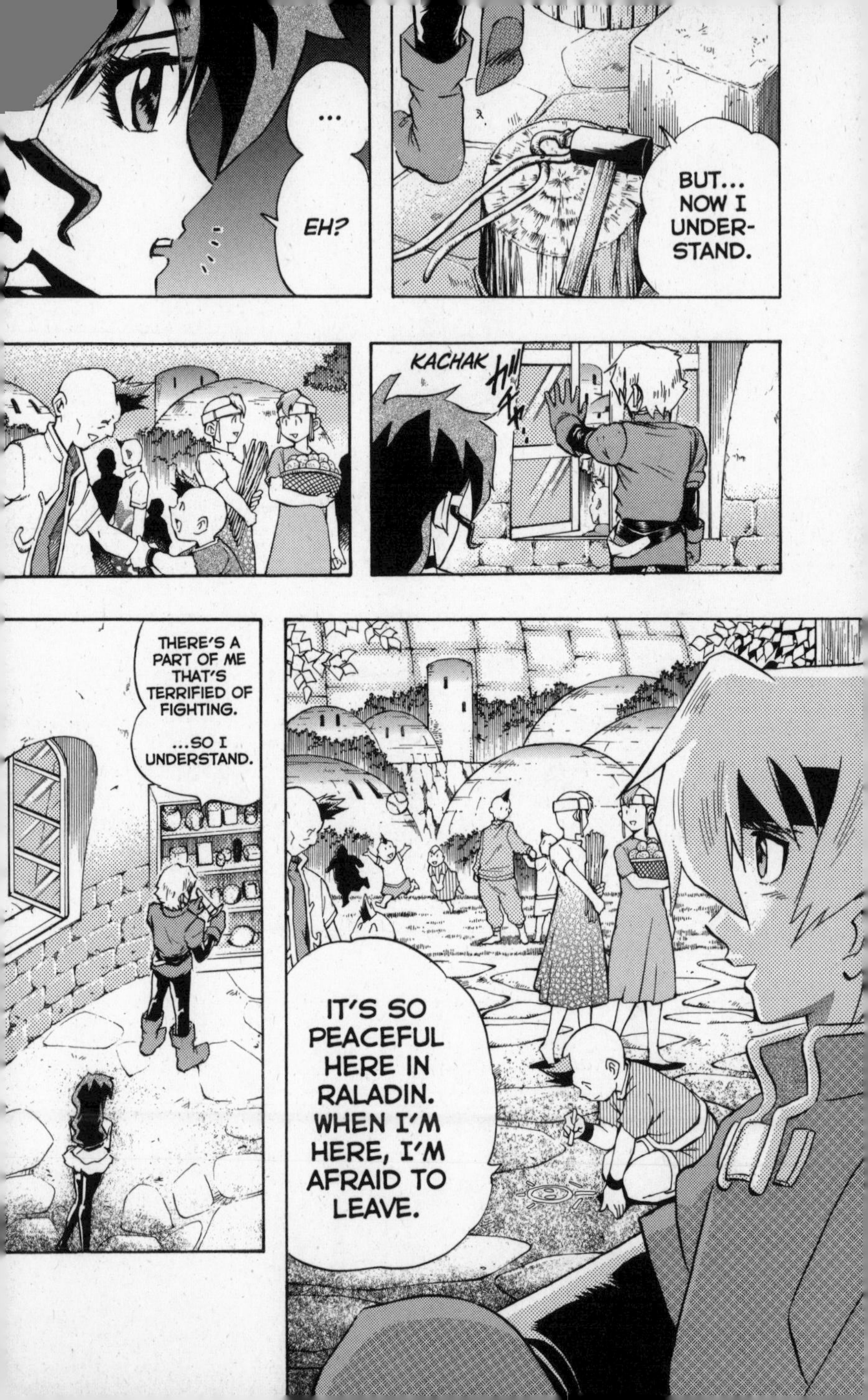
BUT... NOW I UNDER-STAND.
...
EH?
KACHAK
IT'S SO PEACEFUL HERE IN RALADIN. WHEN I'M HERE, I'M AFRAID TO LEAVE.
THERE'S A PART OF ME THAT'S TERRIFIED OF FIGHTING.
...SO I UNDERSTAND.

GLARE

LIEF
...

L...

SPIN
IV.

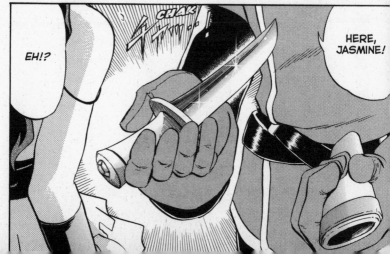

EH!?

CHAK!

HERE, JASMINE!

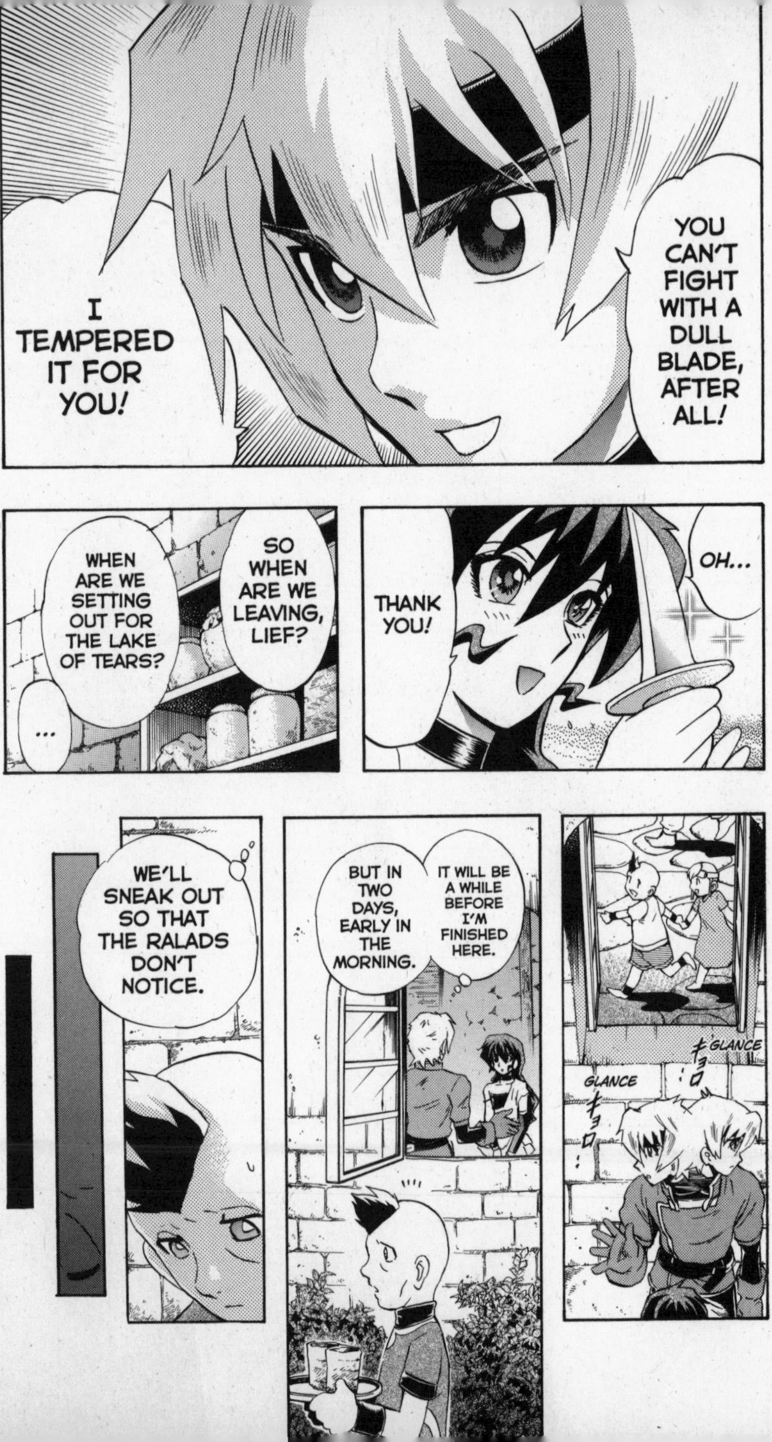
YOU CAN'T FIGHT WITH A DULL BLADE, AFTER ALL!
I TEMPERED IT FOR YOU!
OH...
THANK YOU!
SO WHEN ARE WE LEAVING, LIEF?
WHEN ARE WE SETTING OUT FOR THE LAKE OF TEARS?
...
キョロ GLANCE
キョロ GLANCE
IT WILL BE A WHILE BEFORE I'M FINISHED HERE.
BUT IN TWO DAYS, EARLY IN THE MORNING.
WE'LL SNEAK OUT SO THAT THE RALADS DON'T NOTICE.

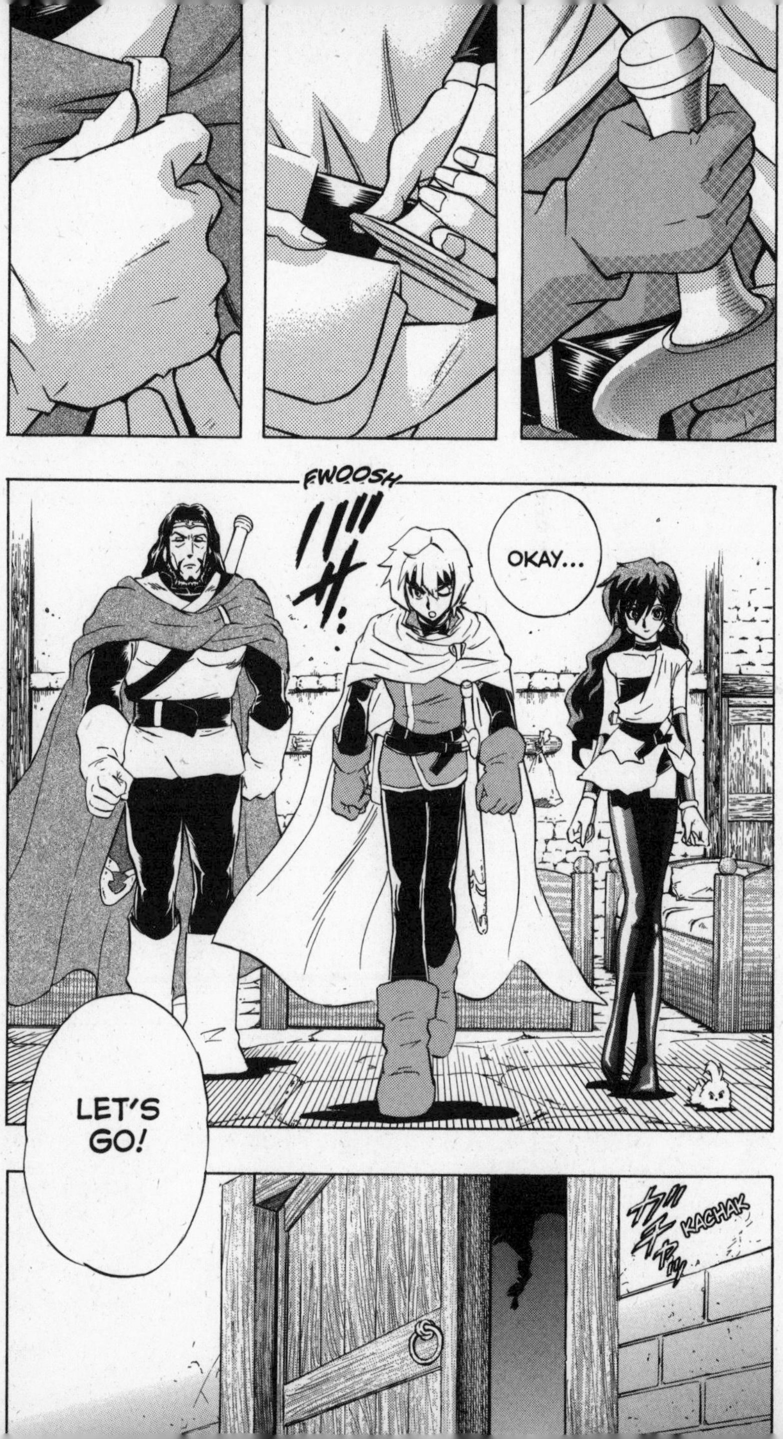
OKAY...
FWOOSH
LET'S GO!
KACHAK

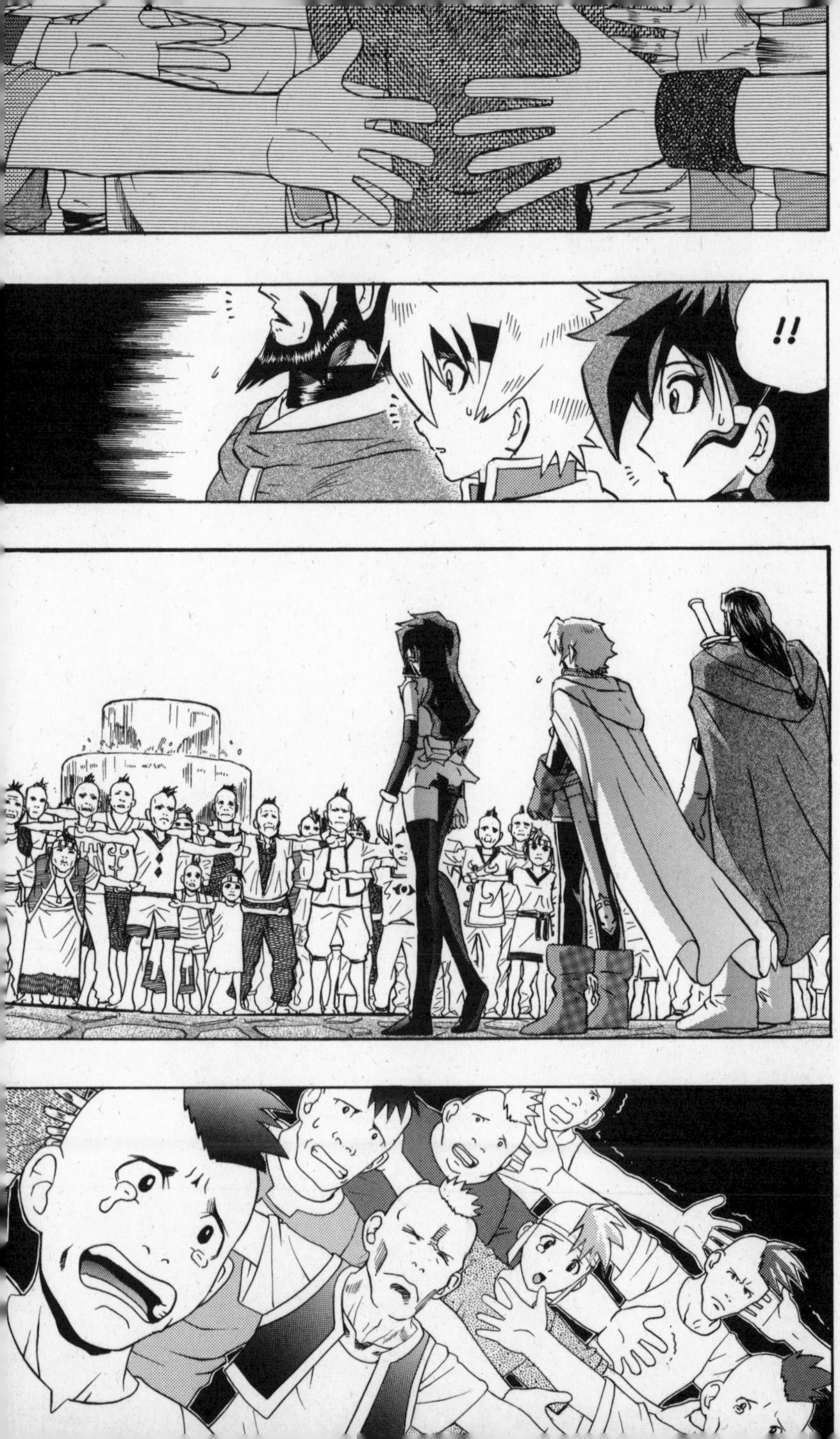
!!

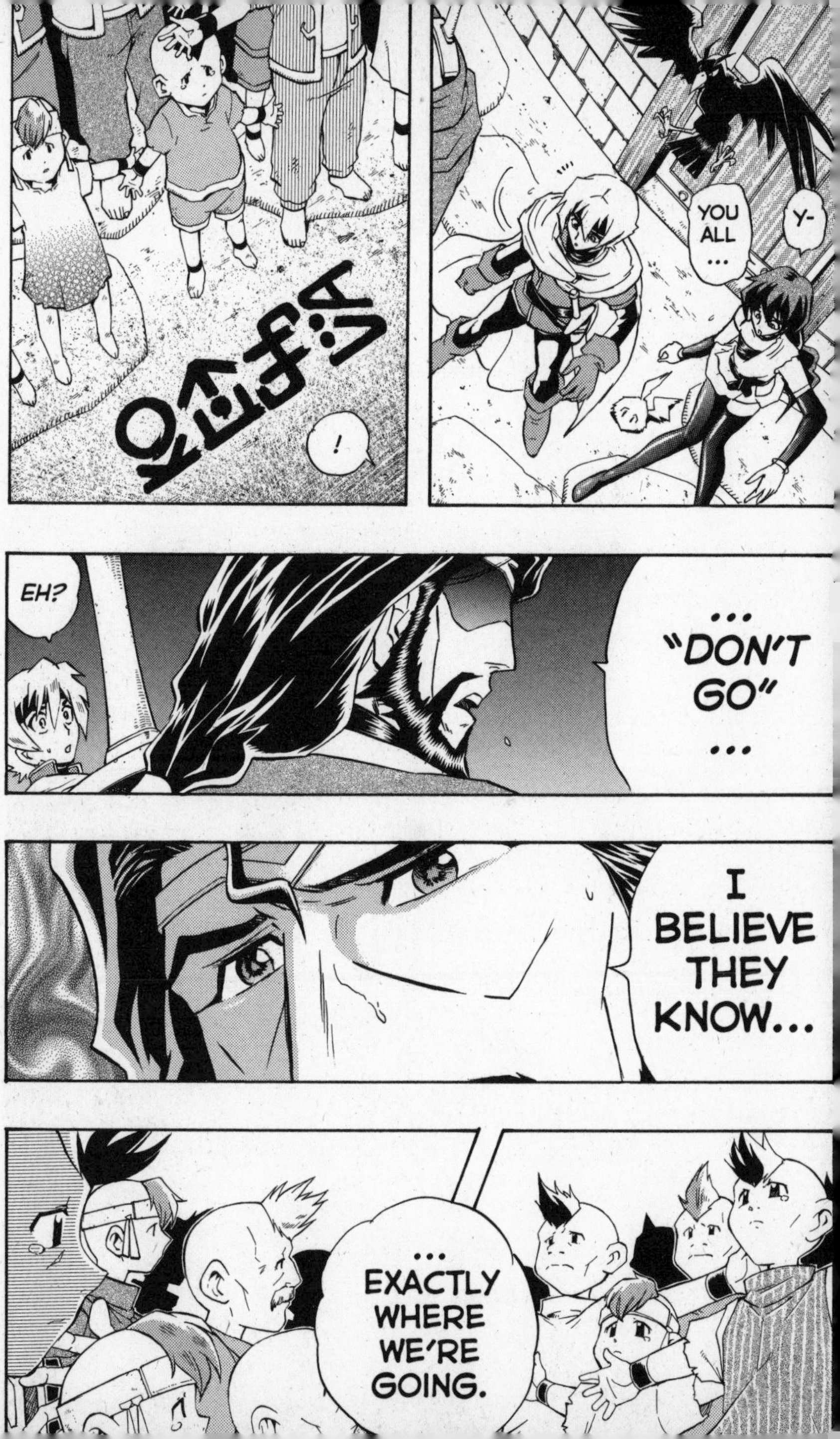
Y-
YOU ALL ...
!
EH?
... "DON'T GO" ...
I BELIEVE THEY KNOW...
... EXACTLY WHERE WE'RE GOING.

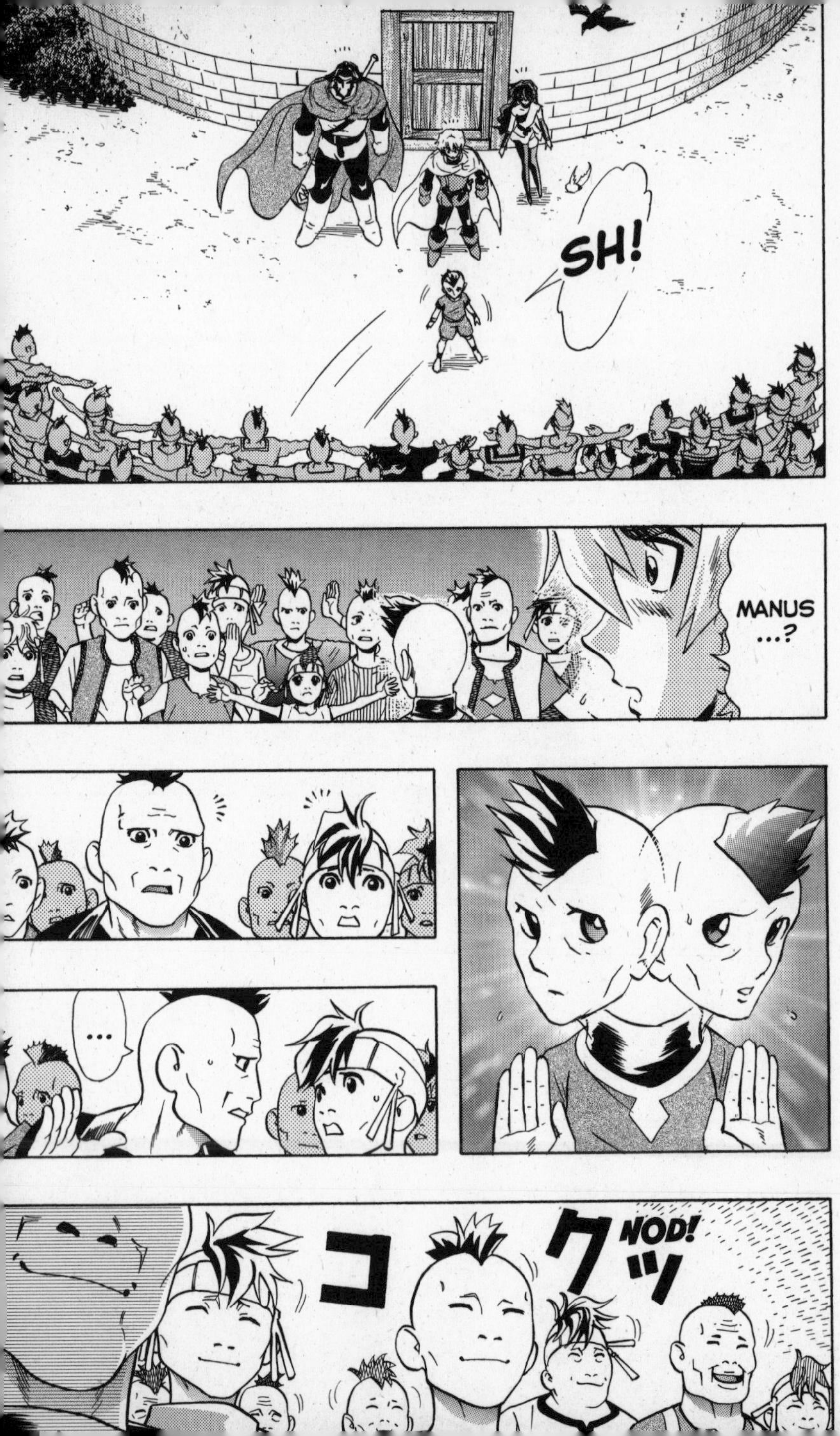
SH!
MANUS ...?
...
コクッ
NOD!

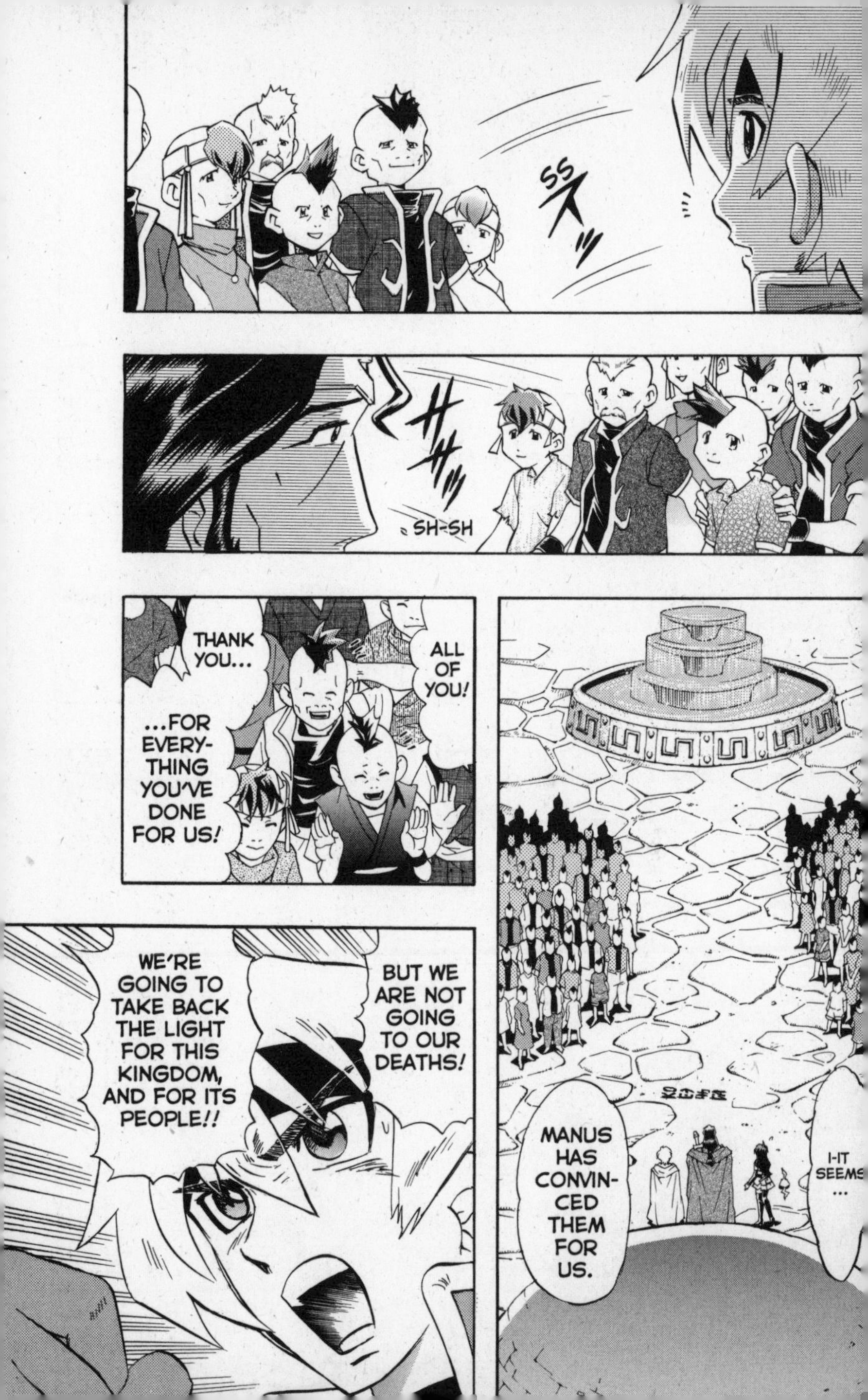
SS
SH-SH
I-IT SEEMS...
MANUS HAS CONVINCED THEM FOR US.
THANK YOU...
ALL OF YOU!
...FOR EVERYTHING YOU'VE DONE FOR US!
BUT WE ARE NOT GOING TO OUR DEATHS!
WE'RE GOING TO TAKE BACK THE LIGHT FOR THIS KINGDOM, AND FOR ITS PEOPLE!!

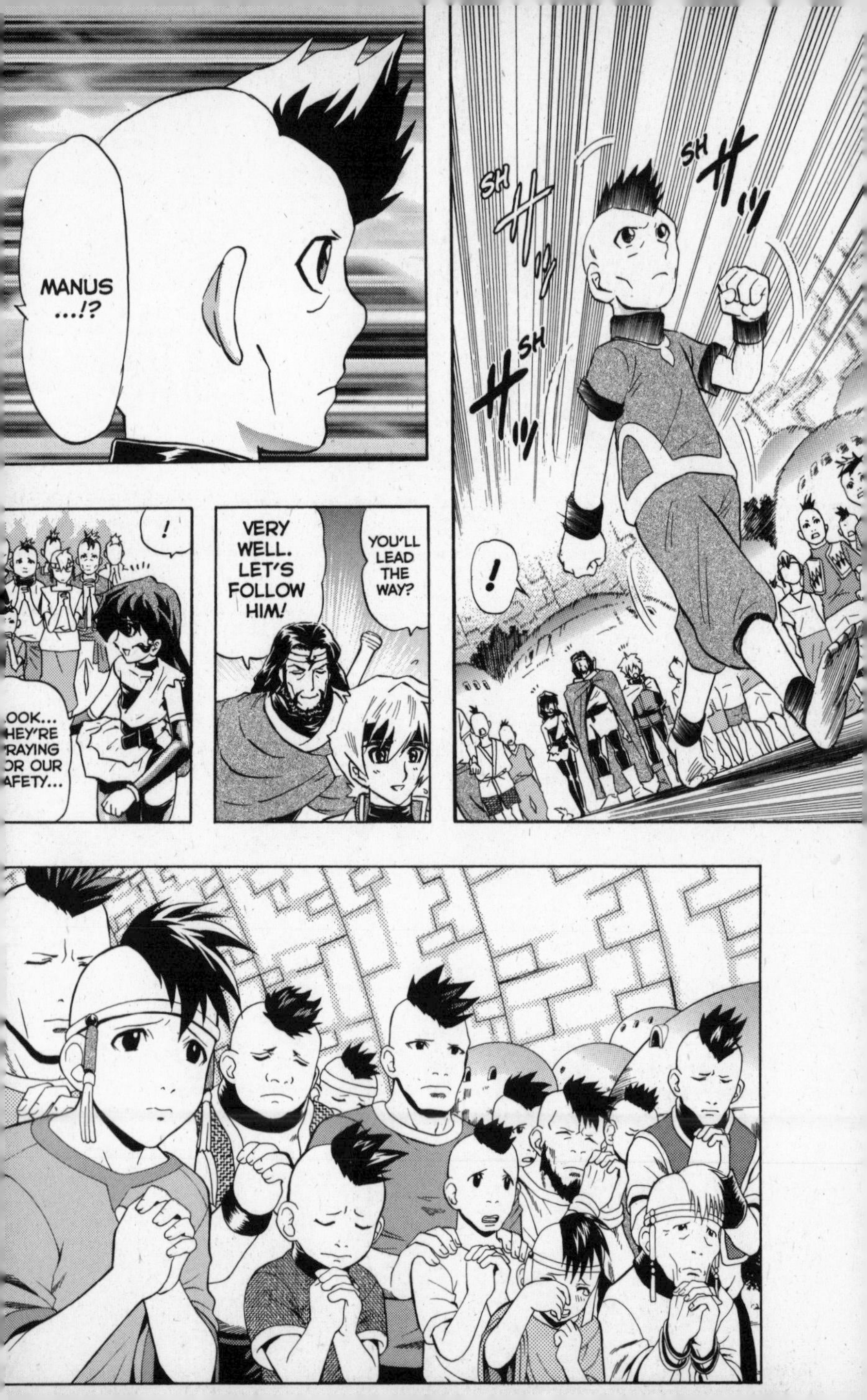
SH
SH
SH
!
MANUS ...!?
YOU'LL LEAD THE WAY?
VERY WELL. LET'S FOLLOW HIM!
!
OOK... HEY'RE RAYING OR OUR AFETY...

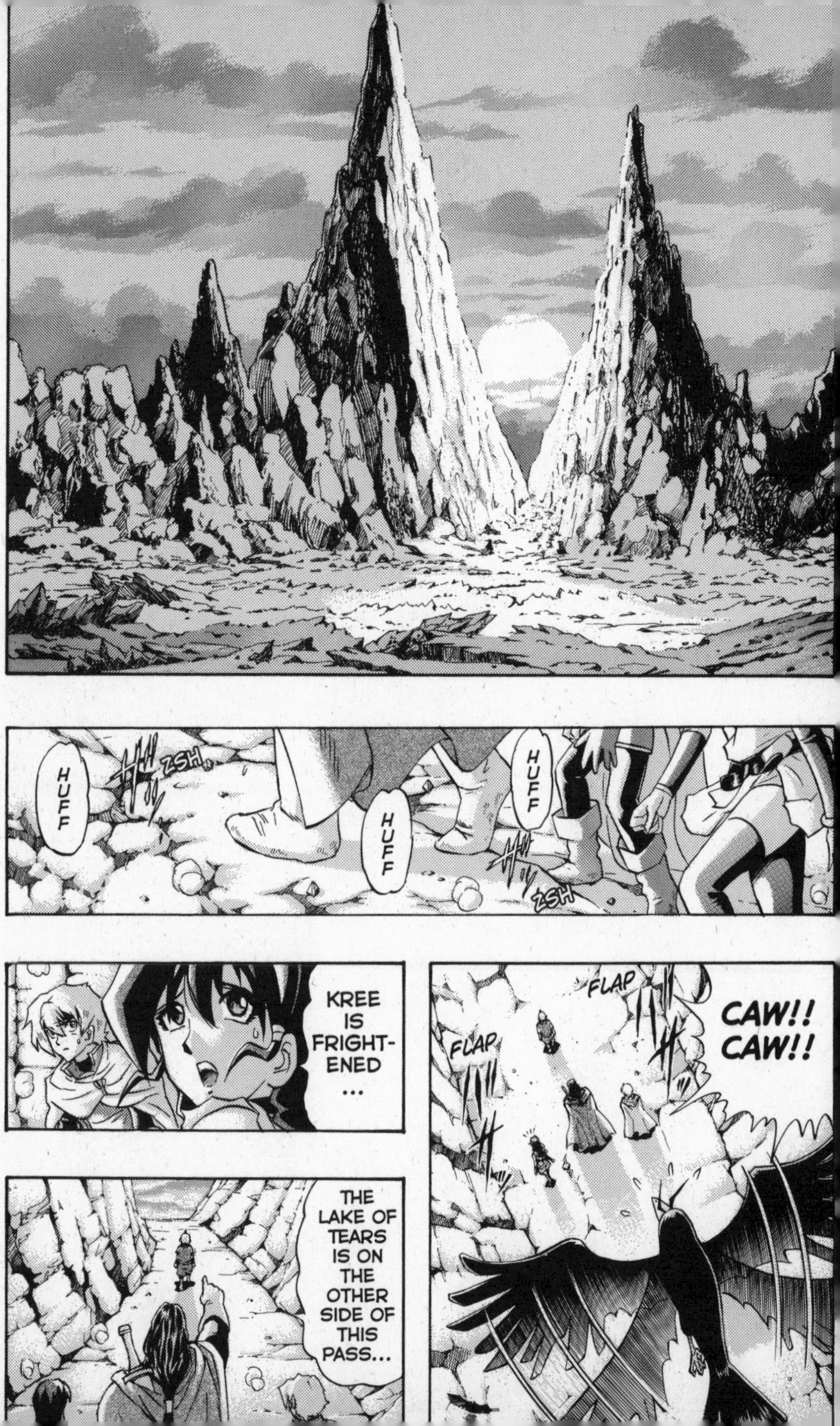
HUFF
ZSH
HUFF
ZSH
HUFF
CAW!! CAW!!
FLAP
FLAP
KREE IS FRIGHTENED...
THE LAKE OF TEARS IS ON THE OTHER SIDE OF THIS PASS...

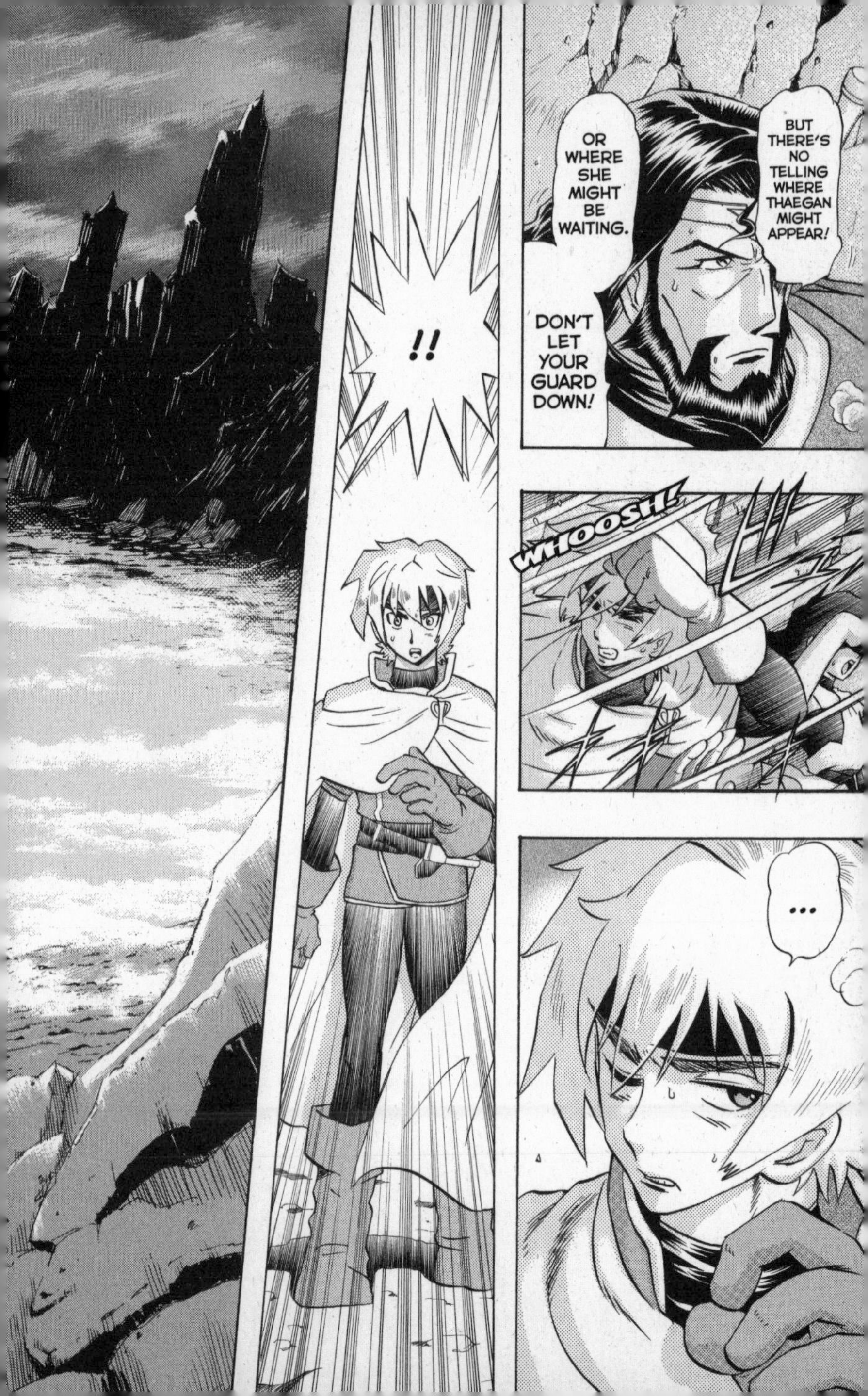
BUT THERE'S NO TELLING WHERE THAEGAN MIGHT APPEAR!
OR WHERE SHE MIGHT BE WAITING.
DON'T LET YOUR GUARD DOWN!
WHOOSH!
...
!!

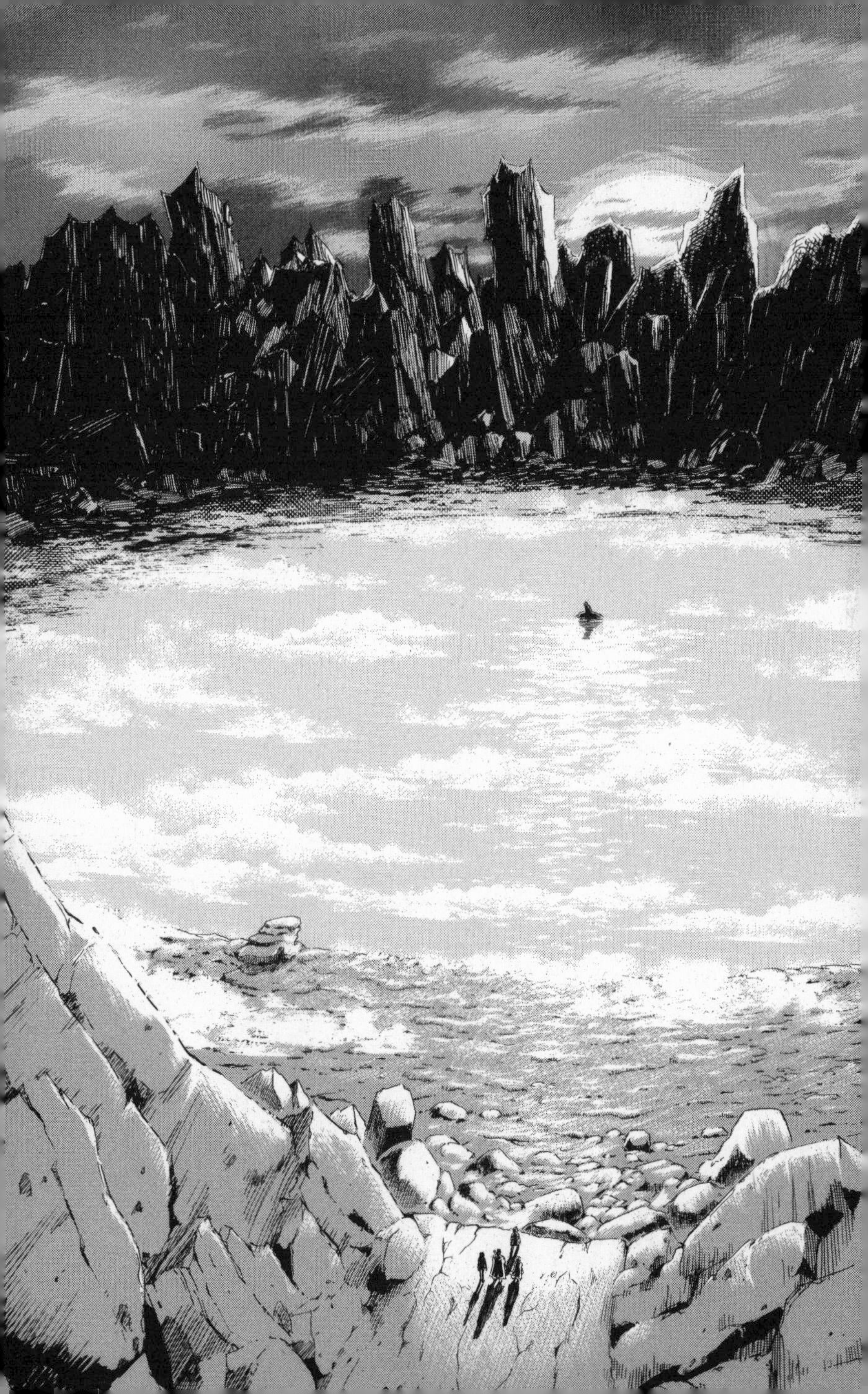

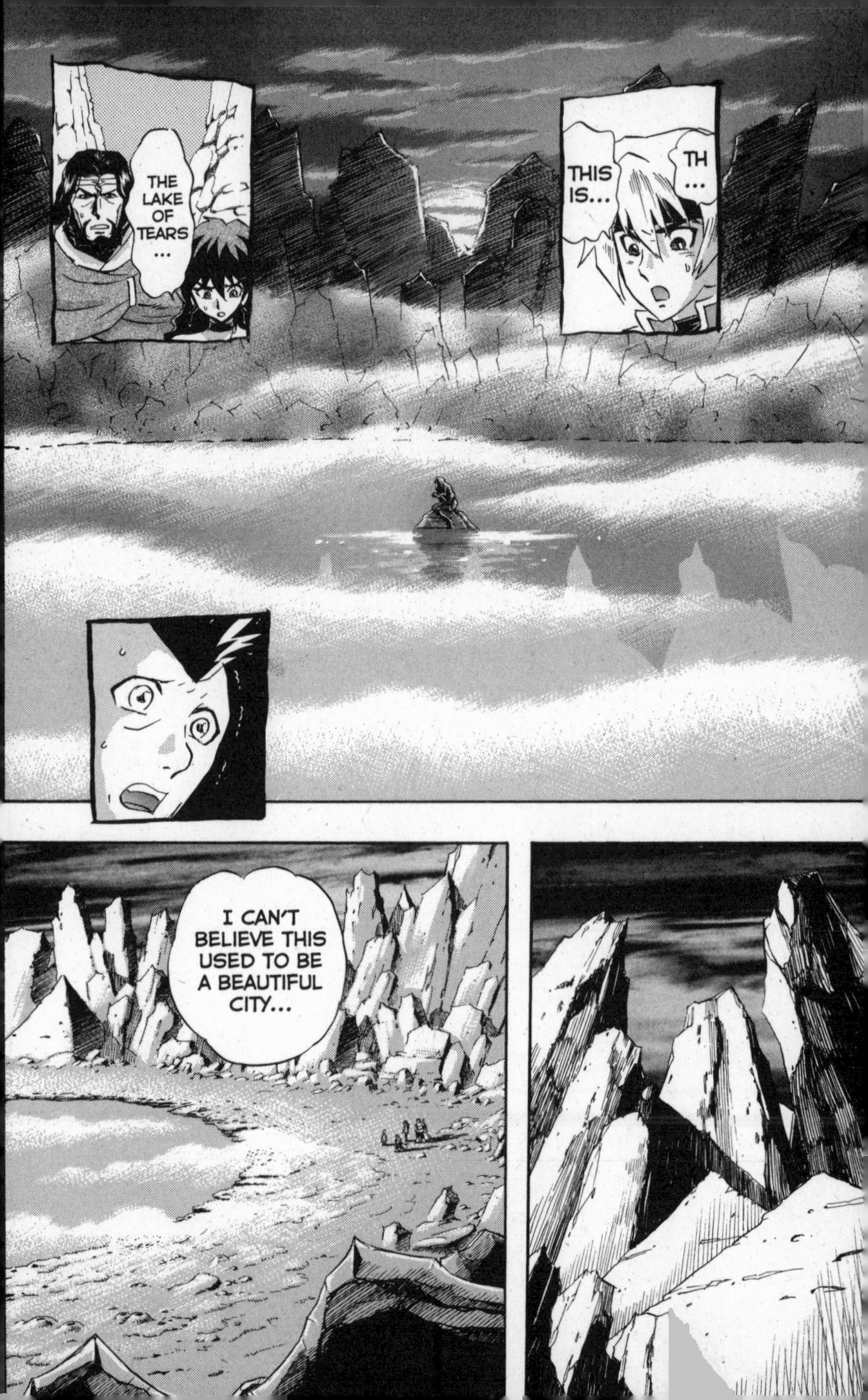
TH ...
THIS IS...
THE LAKE OF TEARS ...
I CAN'T BELIEVE THIS USED TO BE A BEAUTIFUL CITY...

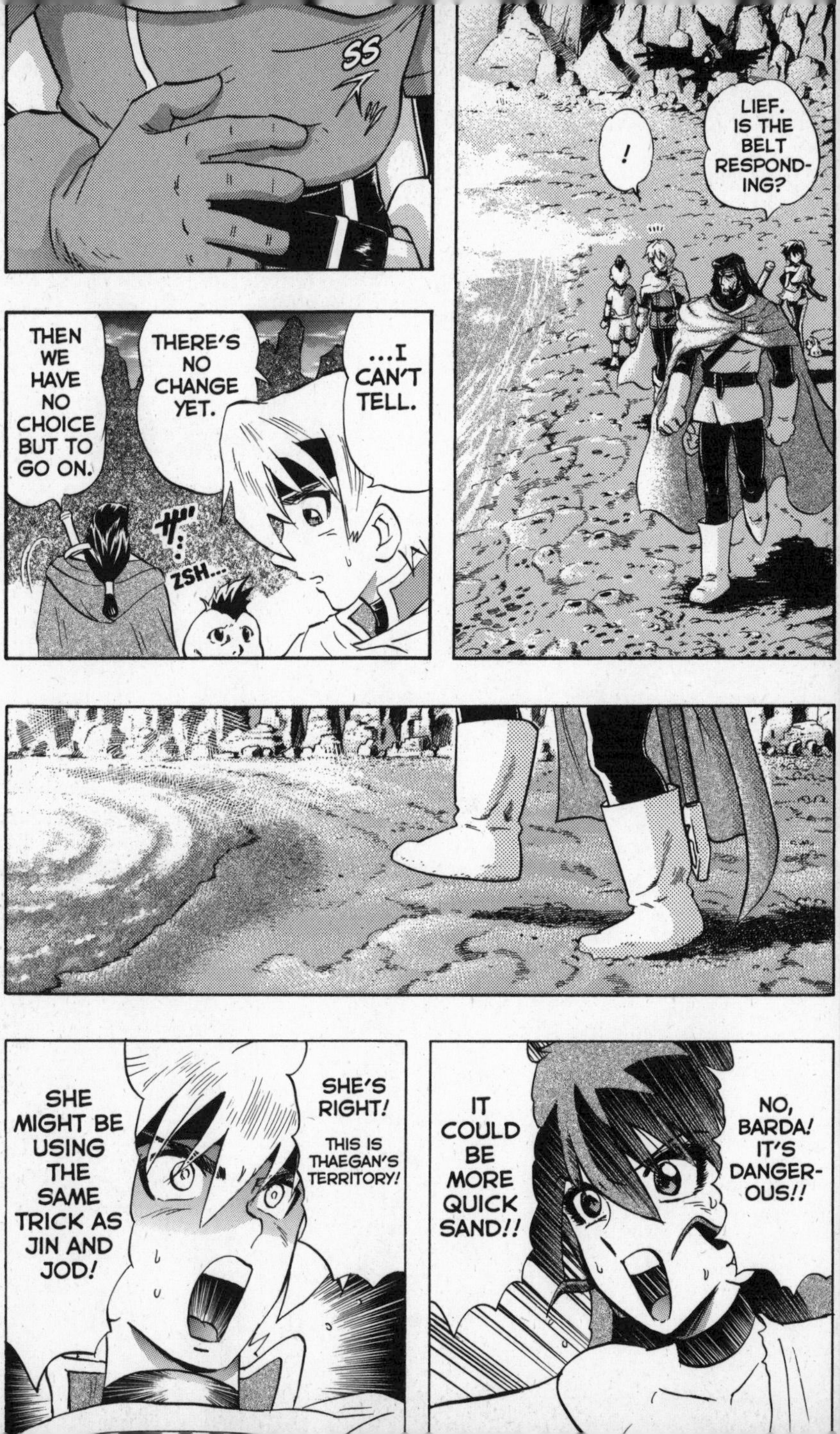
LIEF. IS THE BELT RESPOND-ING?
!
SS
...I CAN'T TELL.
THERE'S NO CHANGE YET.
THEN WE HAVE NO CHOICE BUT TO GO ON.
ZSH...
NO, BARDA! IT'S DANGER-OUS!!
IT COULD BE MORE QUICK SAND!!
SHE'S RIGHT!
THIS IS THAEGAN'S TERRITORY!
SHE MIGHT BE USING THE SAME TRICK AS JIN AND JOD!

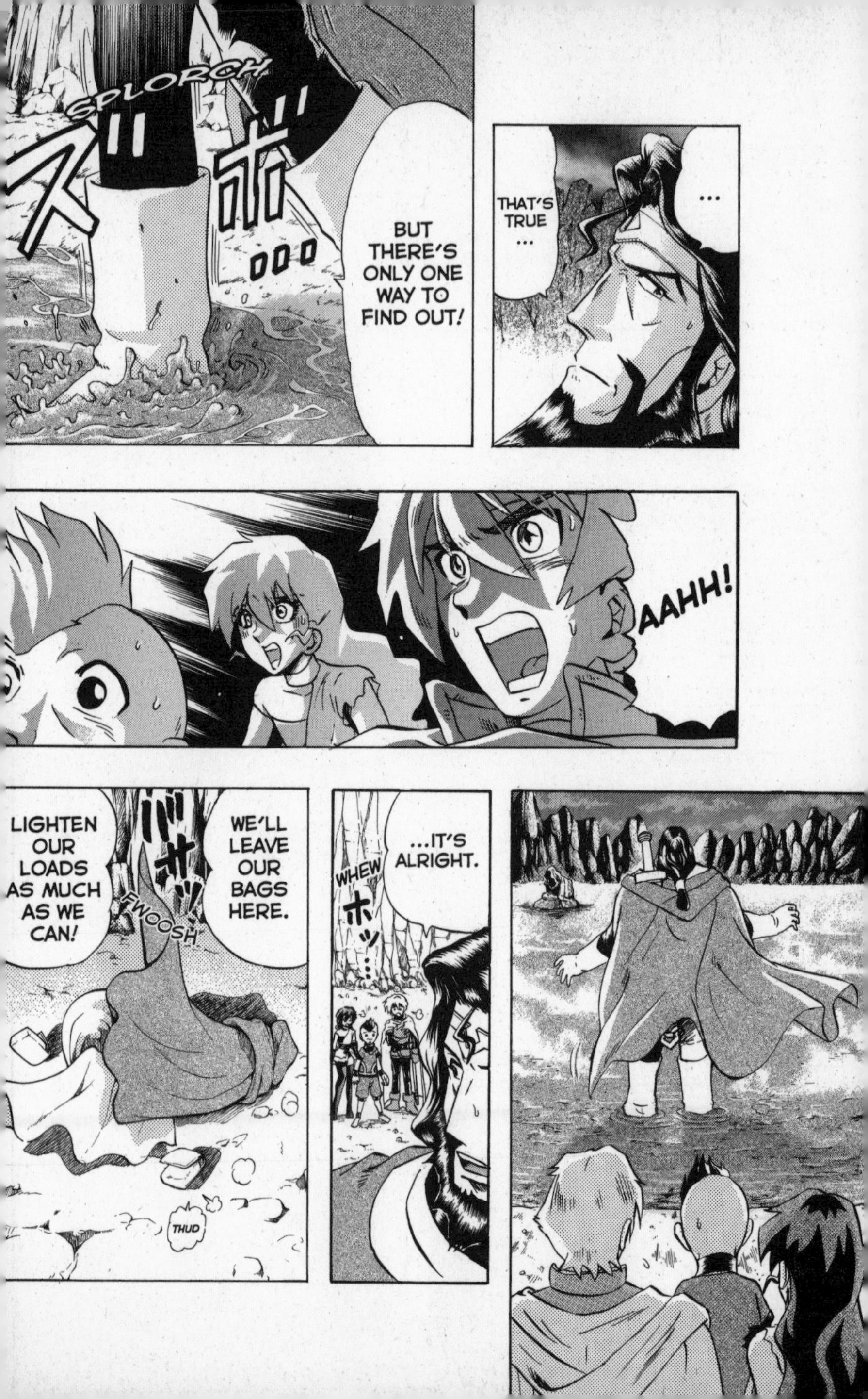
...
THAT'S TRUE ...
SPLORCH
ズボ
BUT THERE'S ONLY ONE WAY TO FIND OUT!
AAHH!
...IT'S ALRIGHT.
WHEW
ホッ…
WE'LL LEAVE OUR BAGS HERE.
LIGHTEN OUR LOADS AS MUCH AS WE CAN!
バサッ
FWOOSH
THUD

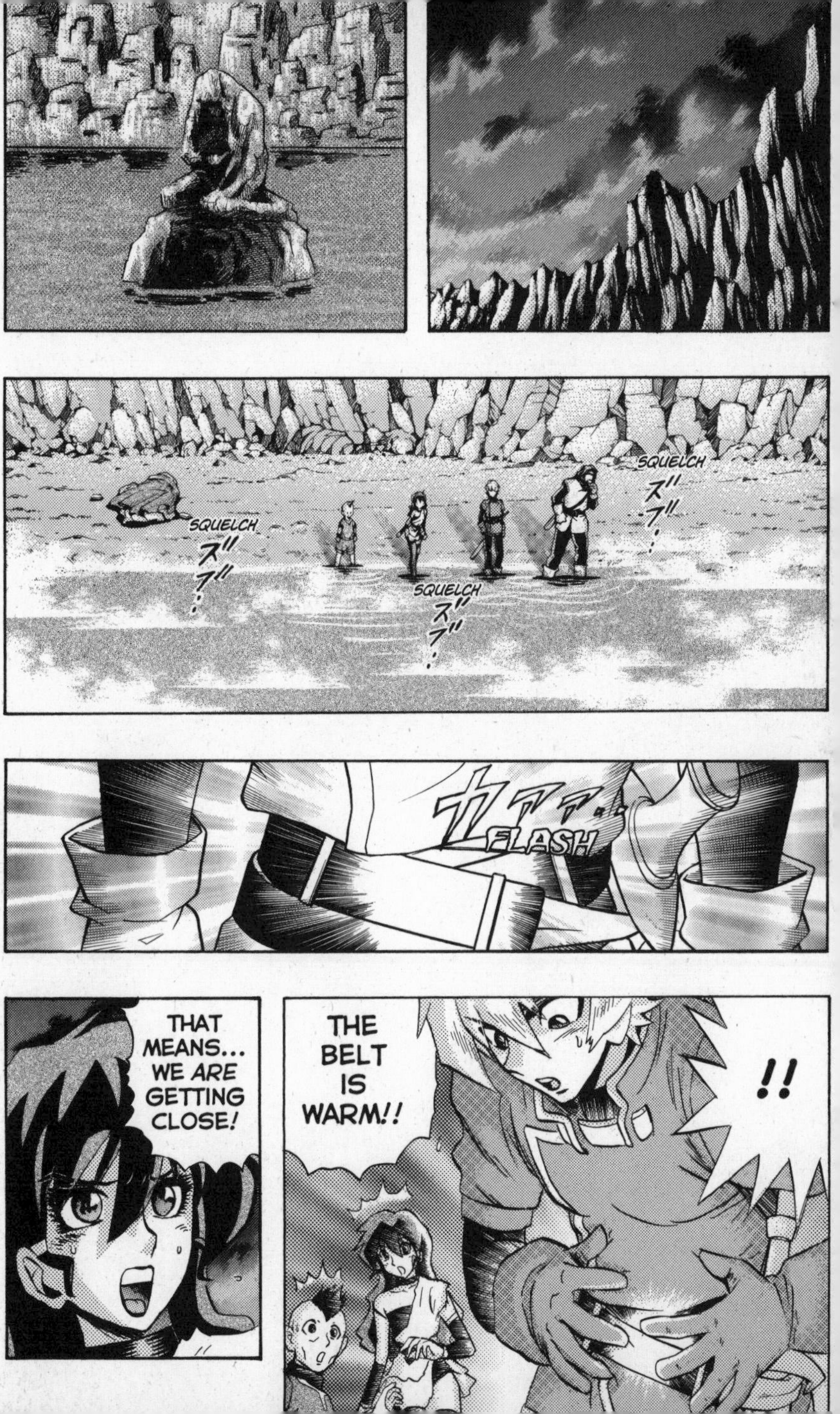

SQUELCH
ズブ…
SQUELCH
ズブ…
SQUELCH
ズブ…
カァァ..
FLASH
!!
THE BELT IS WARM!!
THAT MEANS... WE ARE GETTING CLOSE!

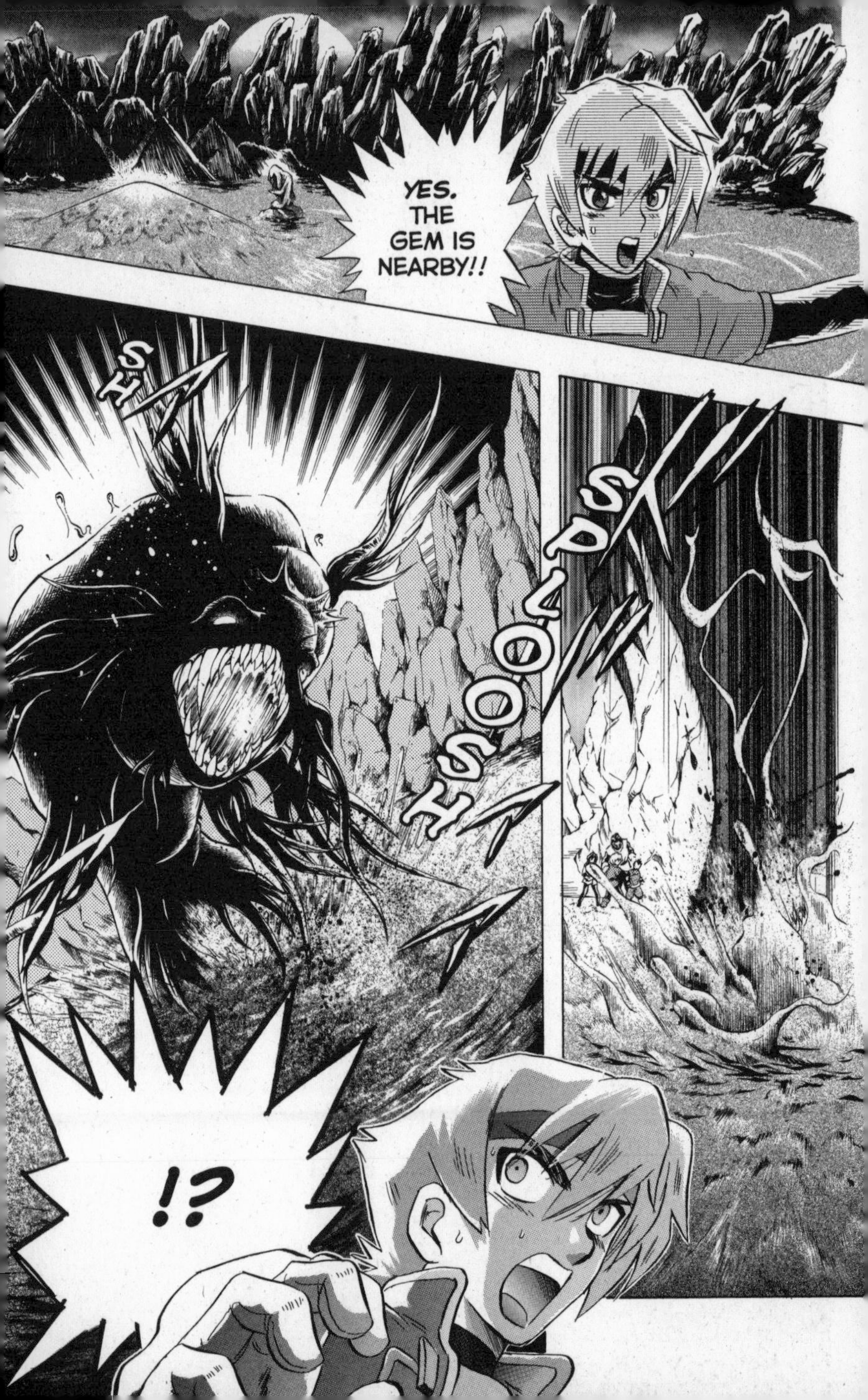
YES. THE GEM IS NEARBY!!
SPLOOSH
SH
!?

Chapter 18: The Monster in the Lake

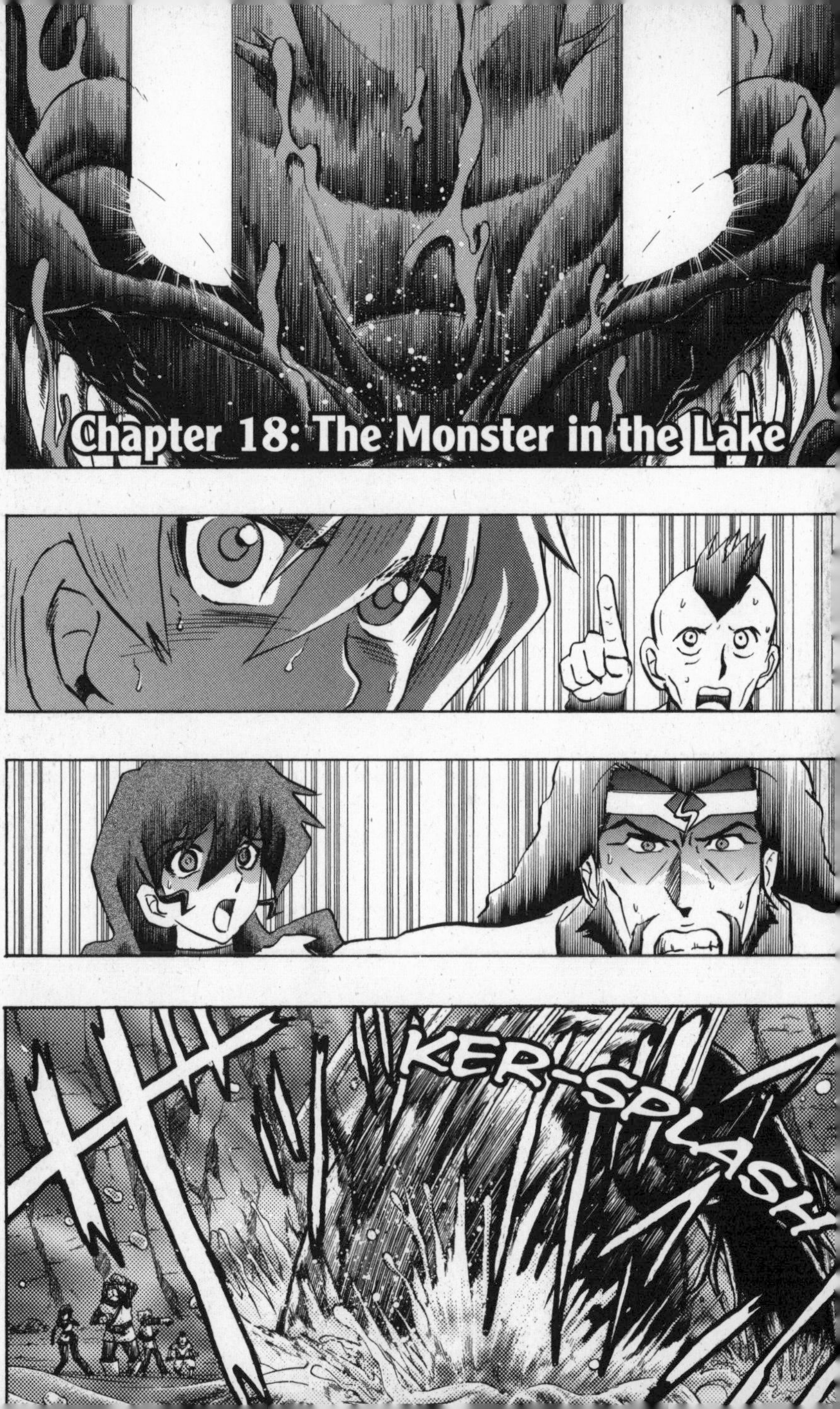
KER-SPLASH

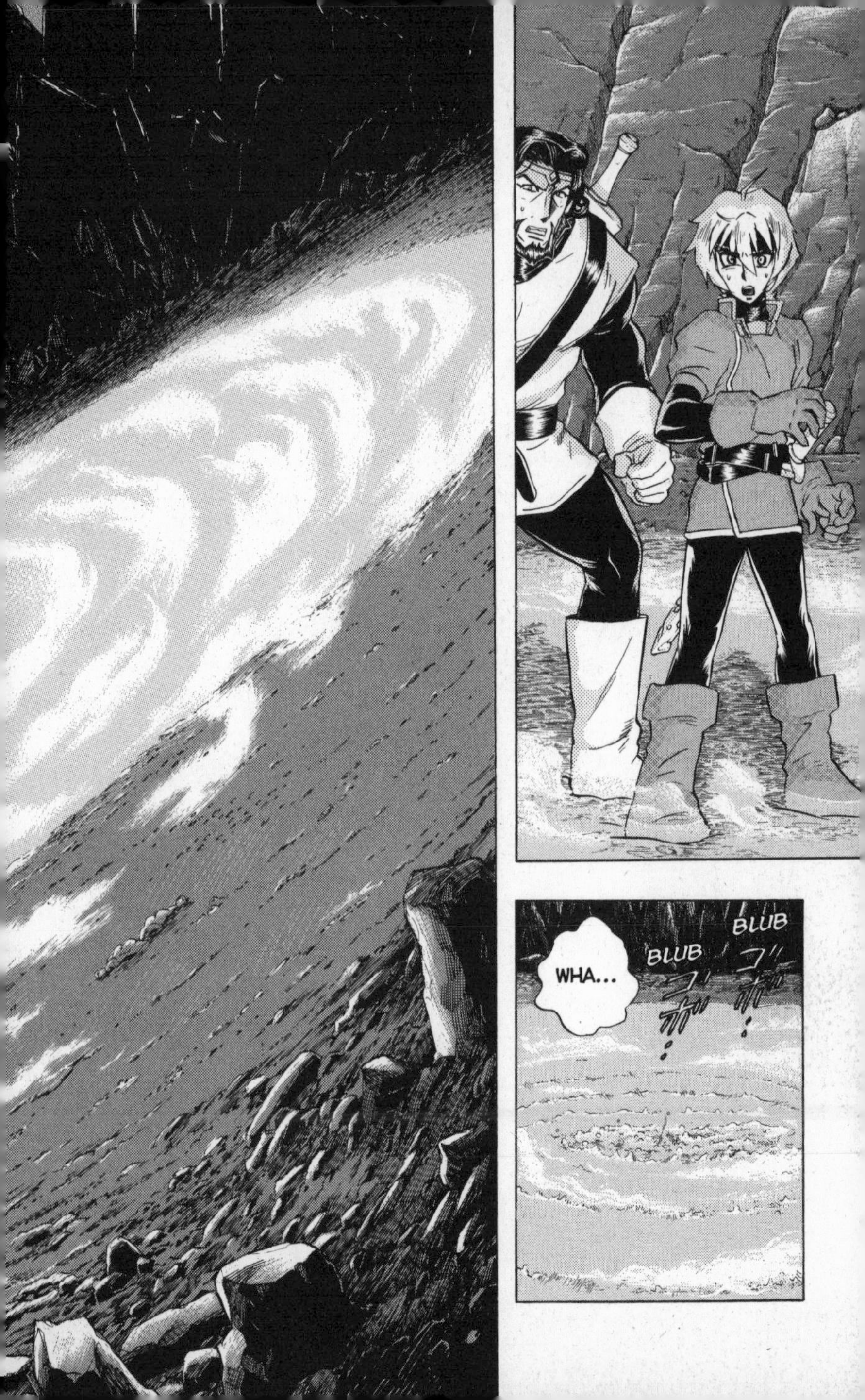
WHA...
BLUB
BLUB

Chapter 18: The Monster in the Lake

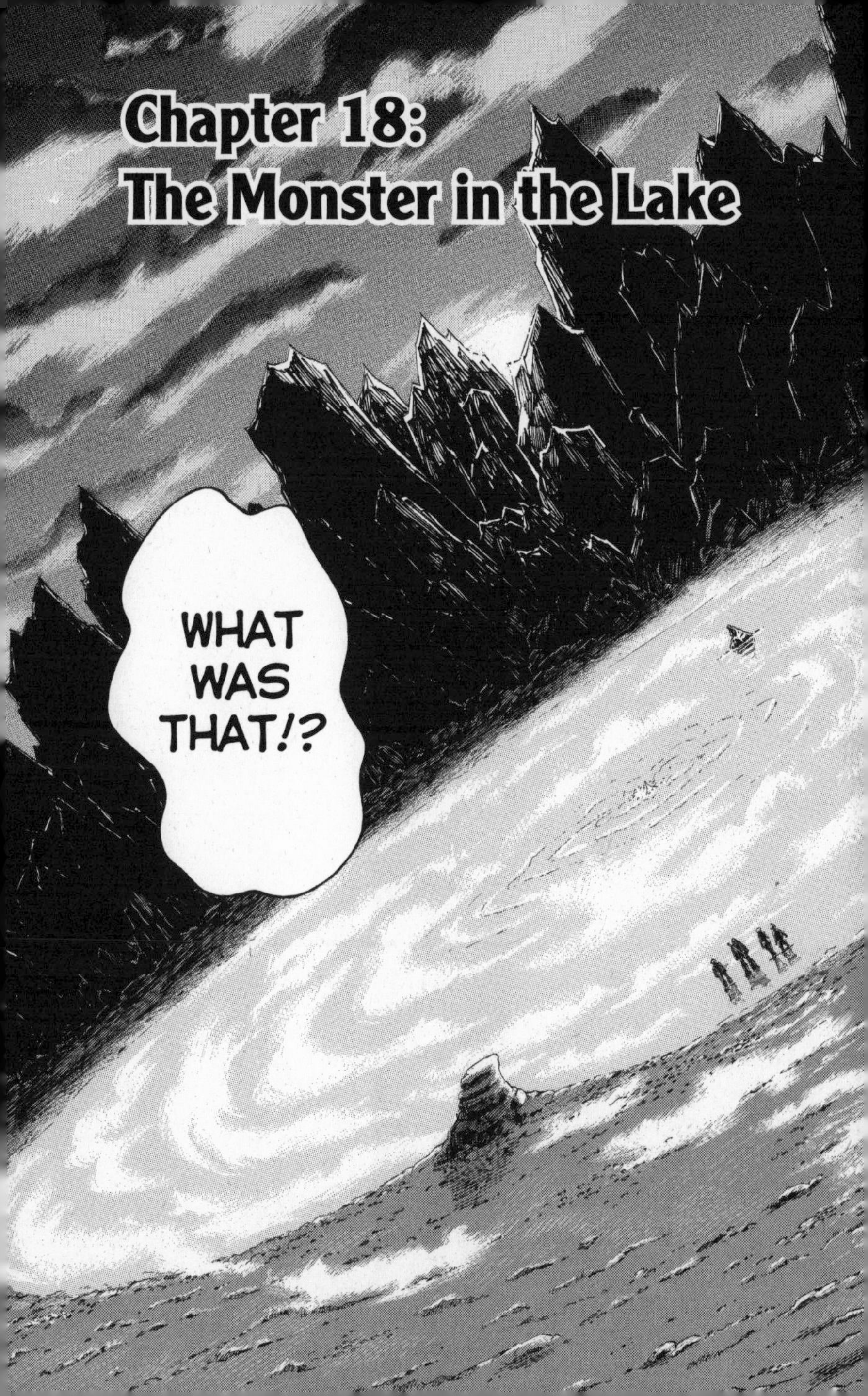
WHAT WAS THAT!?

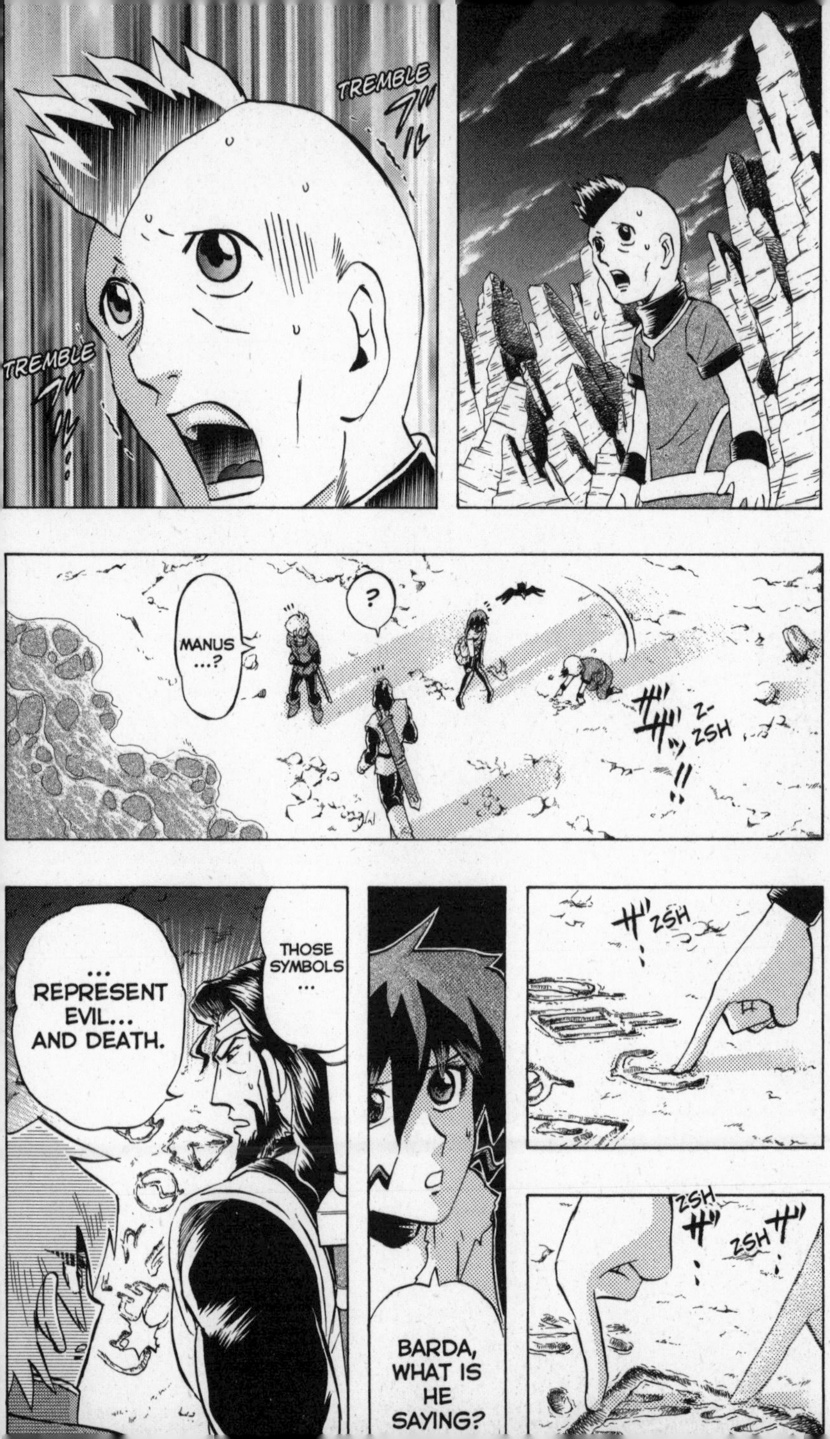
TREMBLE
TREMBLE
?
MANUS ...?
Z-ZSH!!
ZSH
ZSH
ZSH
BARDA, WHAT IS HE SAYING?
THOSE SYMBOLS ...
... REPRESENT EVIL... AND DEATH.

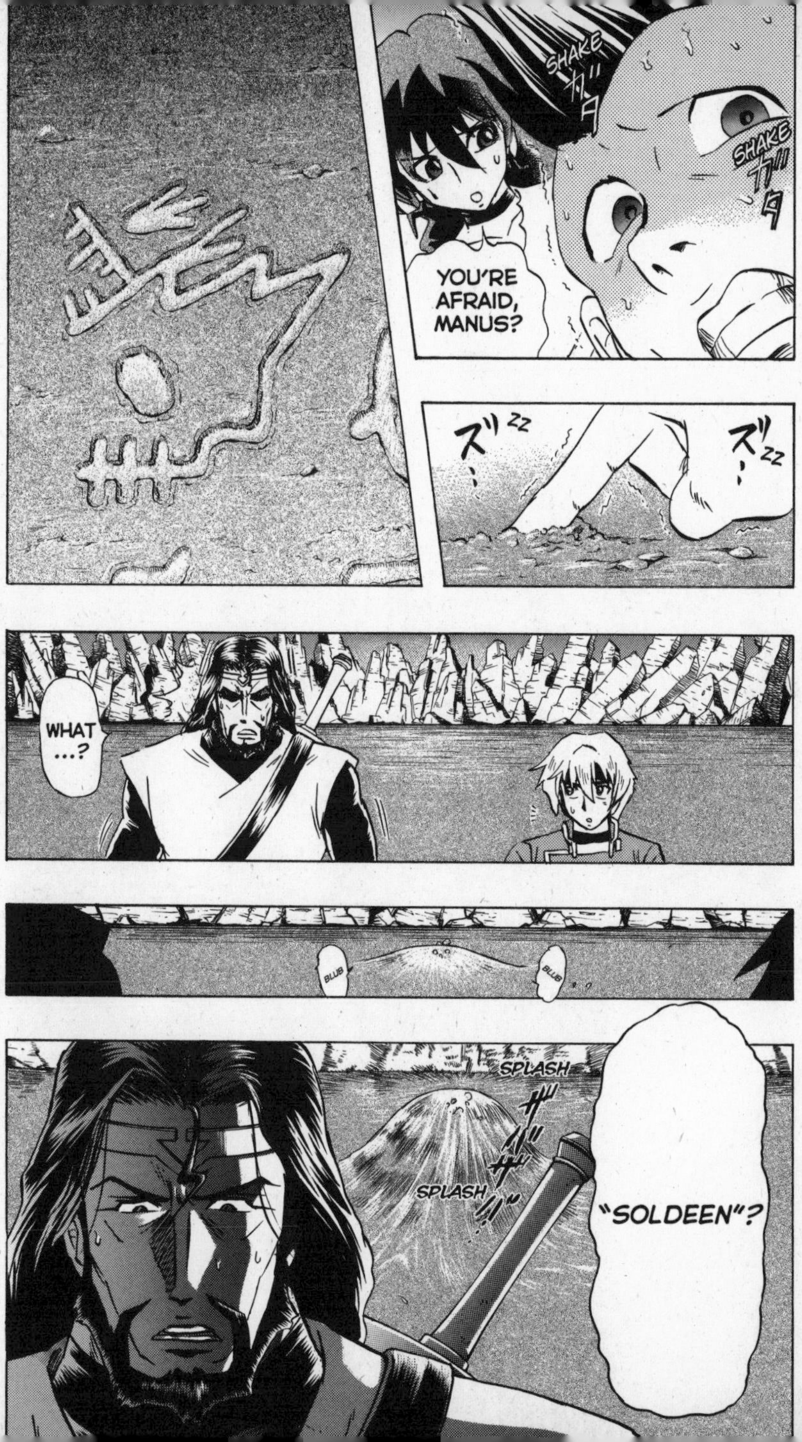
SHAKE
ガタ
SHAKE
ガタ
YOU'RE AFRAID, MANUS?
ズ ZZ
ズ ZZ
WHAT ...?
BLUB
BLUB
SPLASH
SPLASH
"SOLDEEN"?

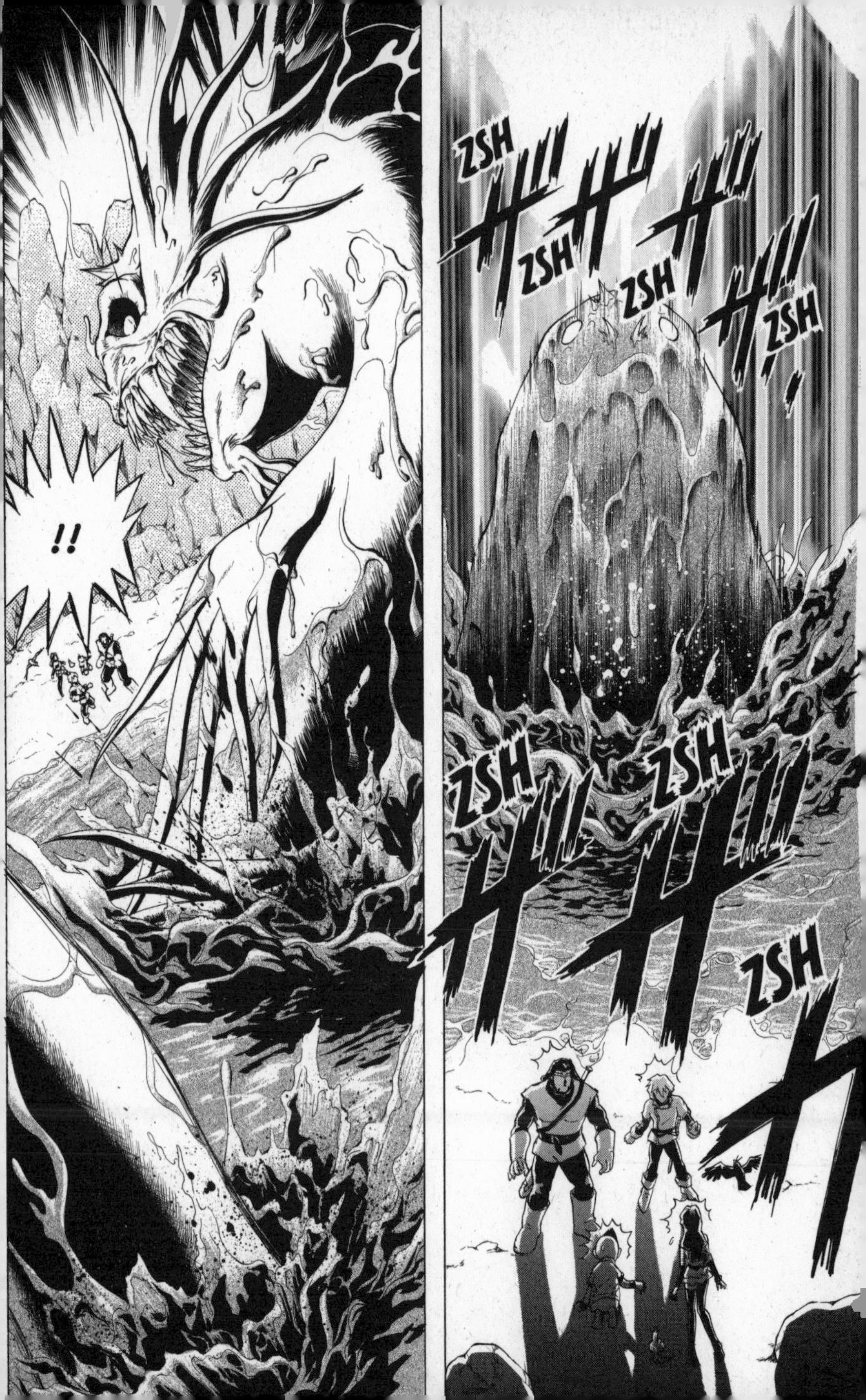
ZSH
ZSH
ZSH
ZSH
ZSH
ZSH
ZSH
!!

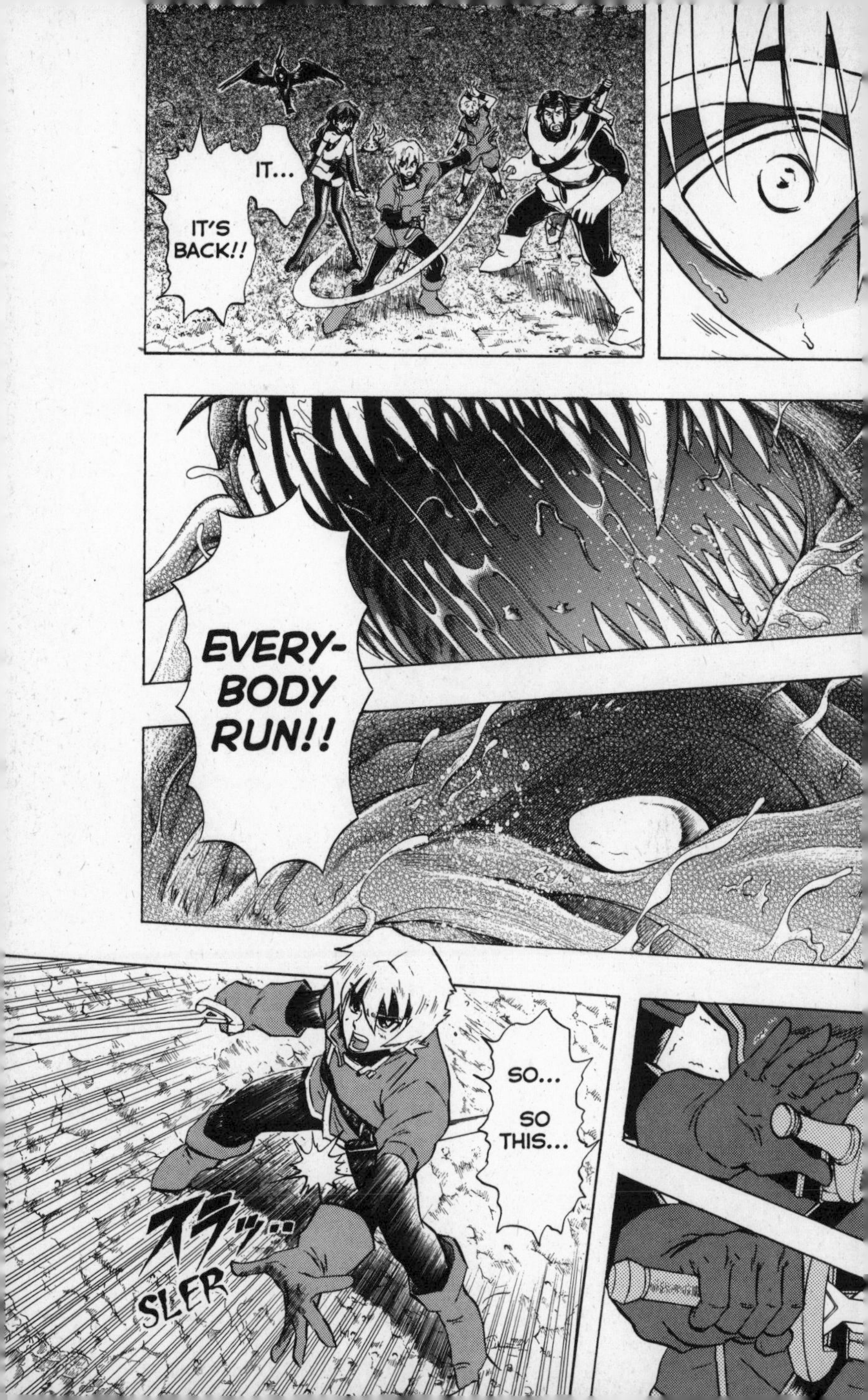
IT...
IT'S BACK!!
EVERY-BODY RUN!!
SO...
SO THIS...
スラッ..
SLER

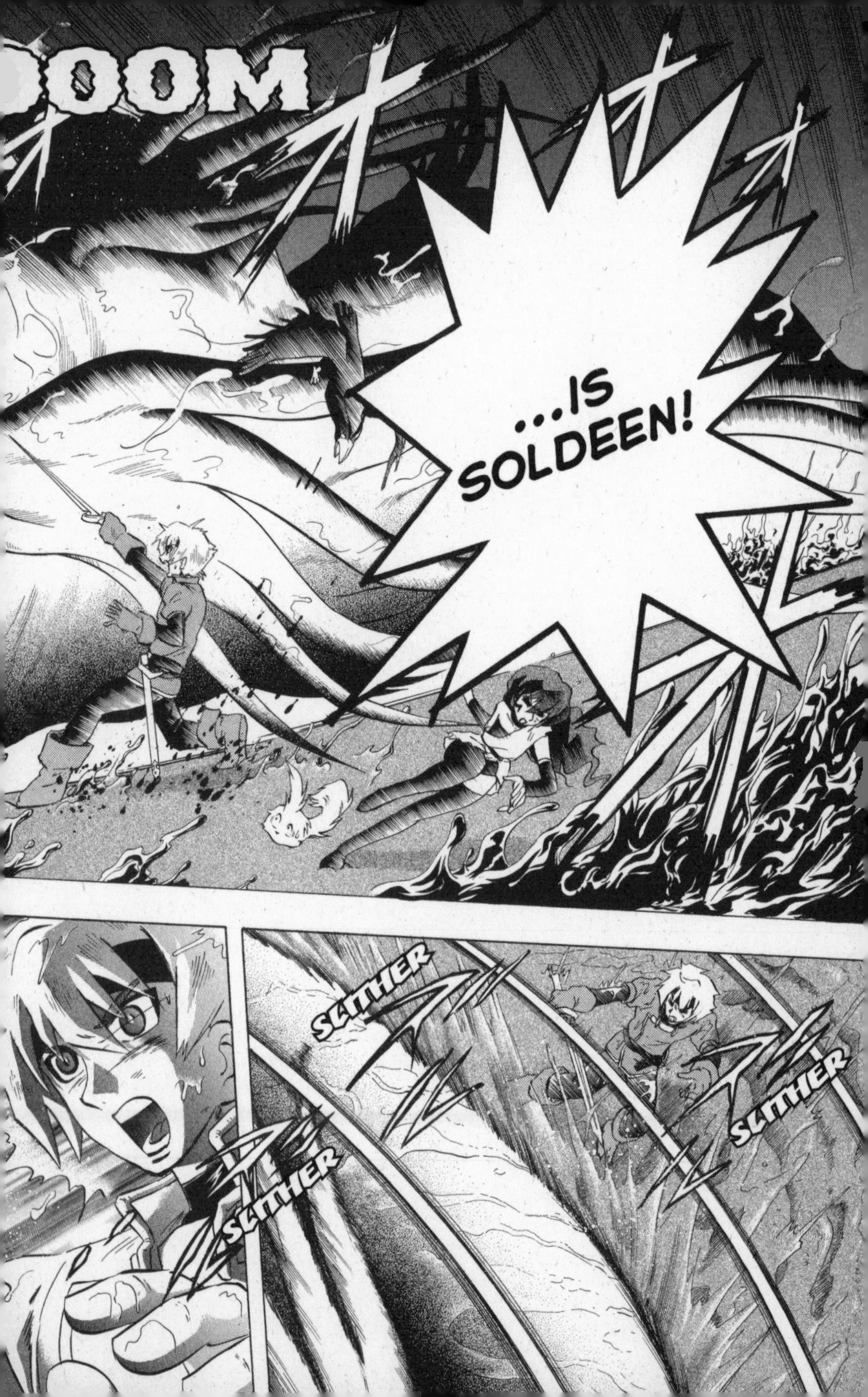
OOM
...IS SOLDEEN!
SLITHER
SLITHER
SLITHER

ZWOO

AH!!

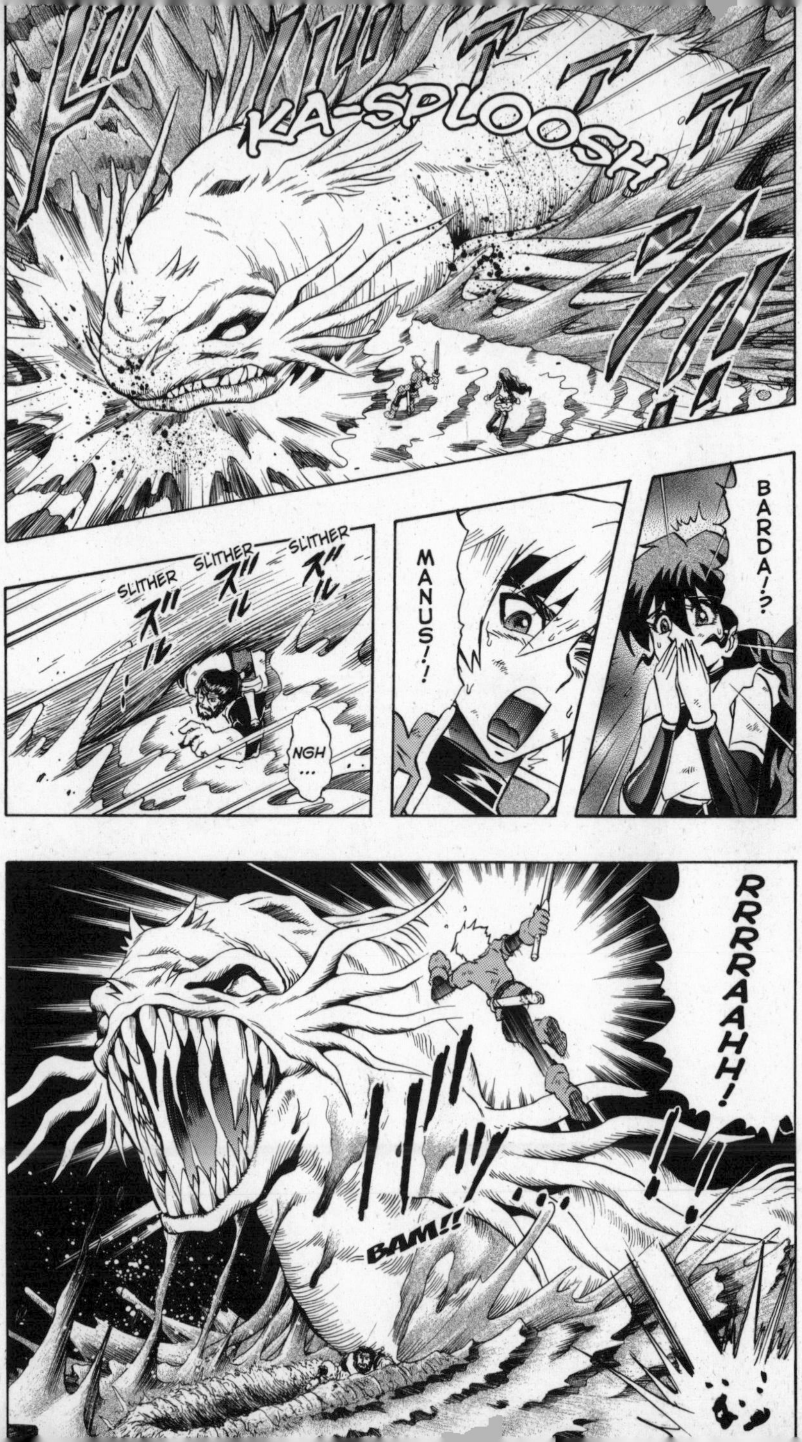
KA-SPLOOSH
BARDA!?
MANUS!!
SLITHER
ズル
SLITHER
ズル
SLITHER
ズル
NGH...
RRRRAAHH!
BAM!!

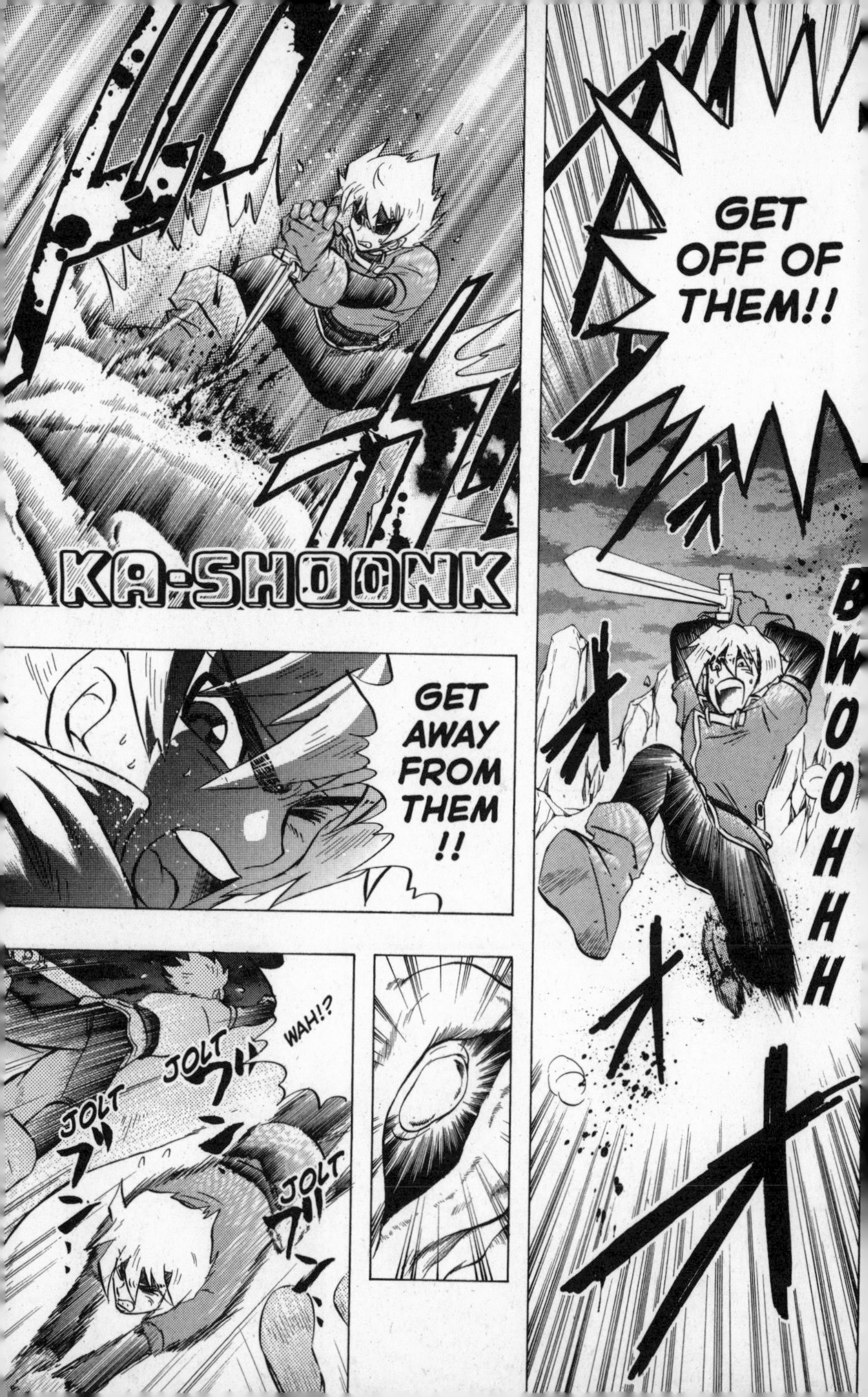
GET OFF OF THEM!!
BWOOOHHHH
KA-SHOONK
GET AWAY FROM THEM !!
WAH!?
JOLT
JOLT
JOLT

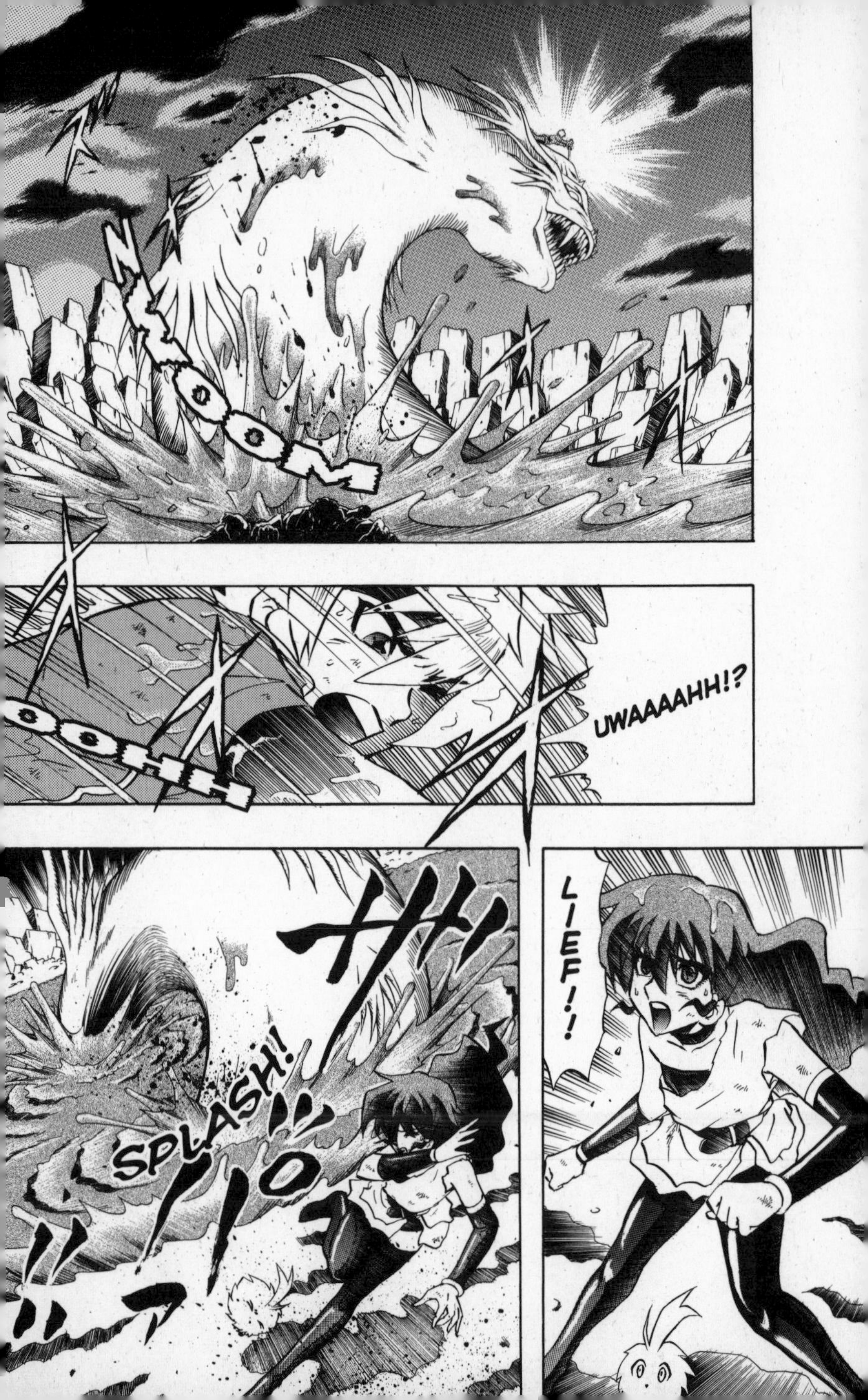
NHOOOM
UWAAAAHH!?
LIEF!!
SPLASH!!

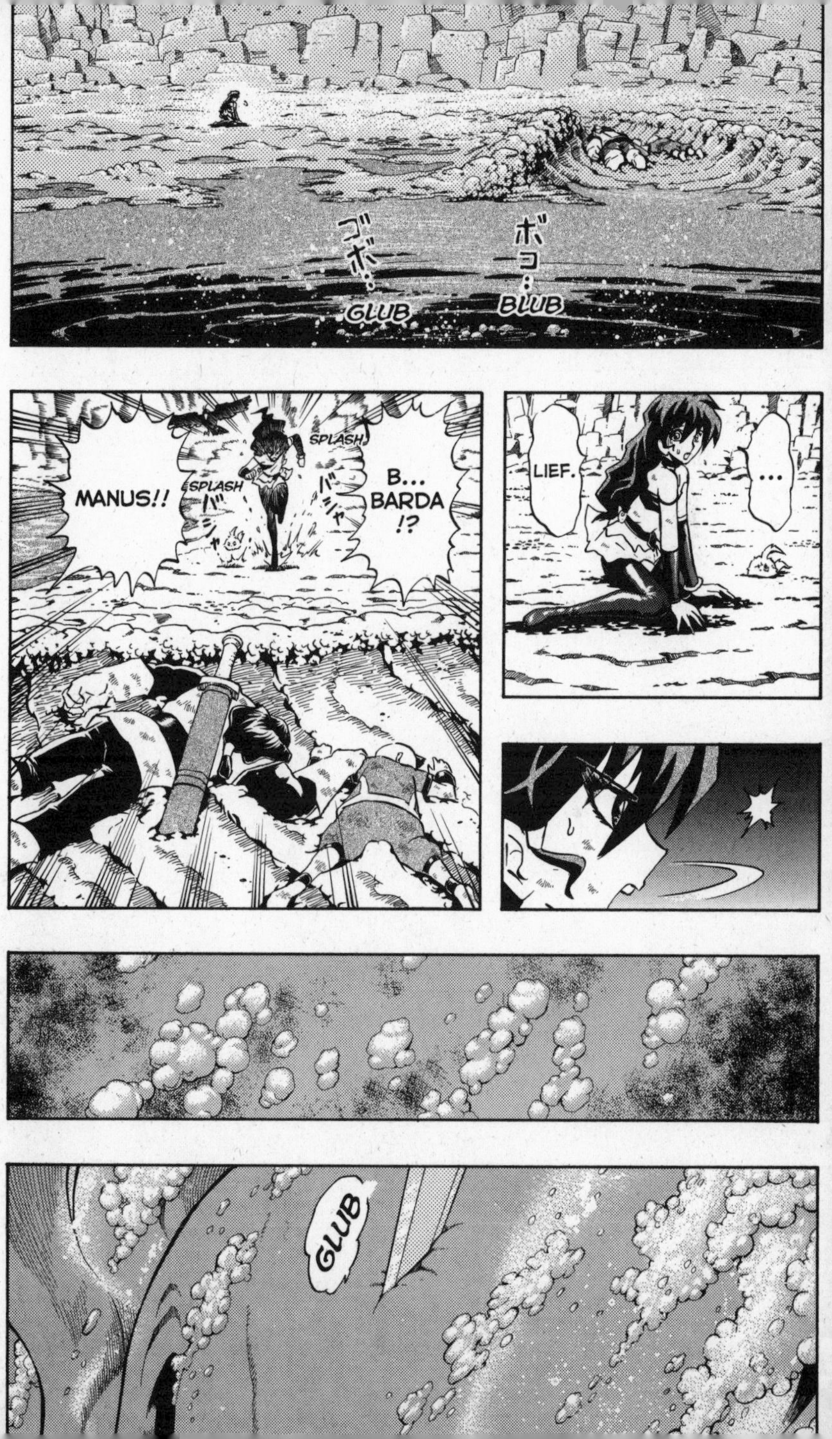
ボコ…
BLUB
ゴボ…
GLUB
…
LIEF.
B… BARDA !?
SPLASH
バシャ
SPLASH
バシャ
MANUS!!
GLUB

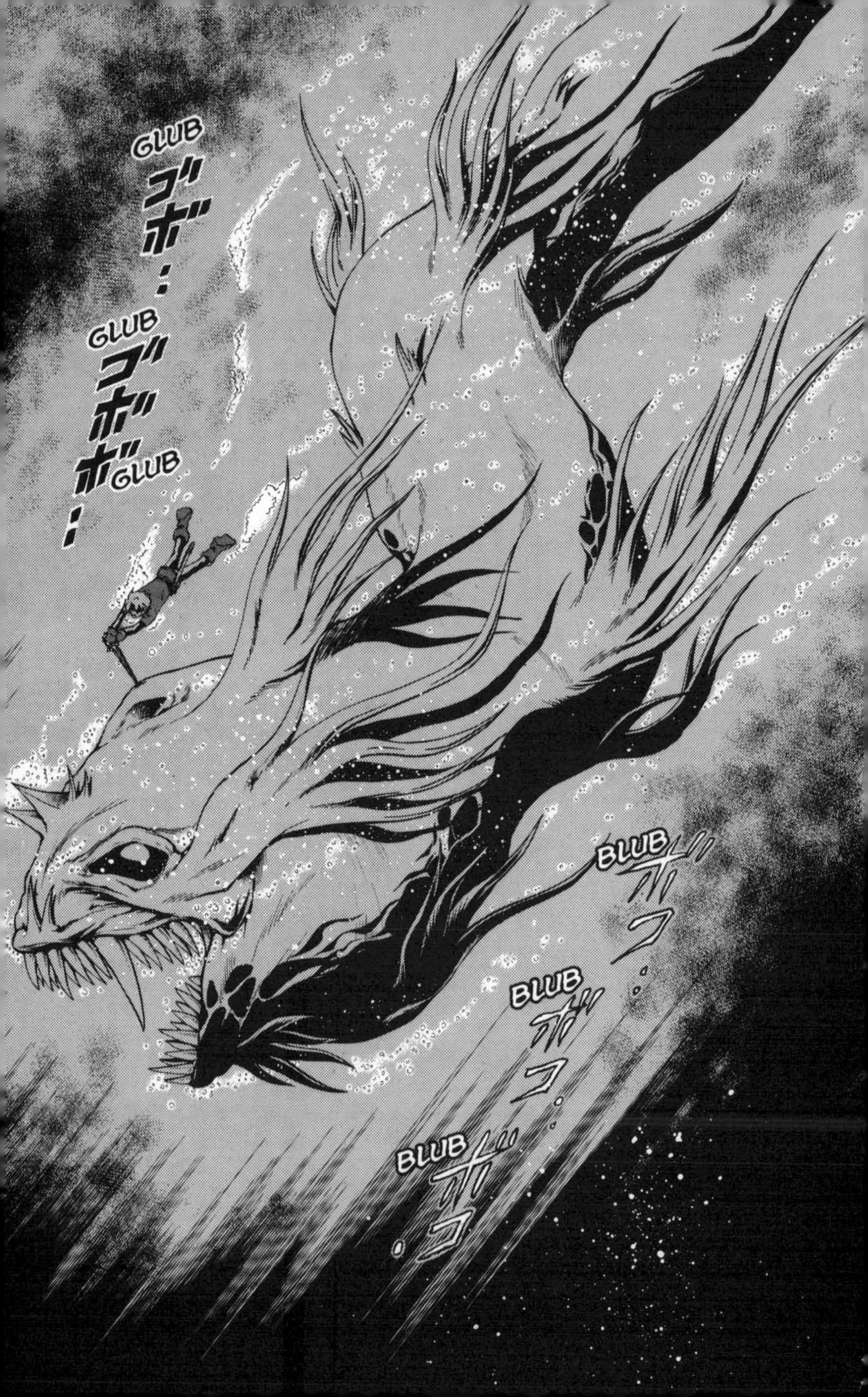
GLUB
ゴボ…
GLUB
ゴボボ…
GLUB
BLUB
ボコ…
BLUB
ボコ…
BLUB
ボコ

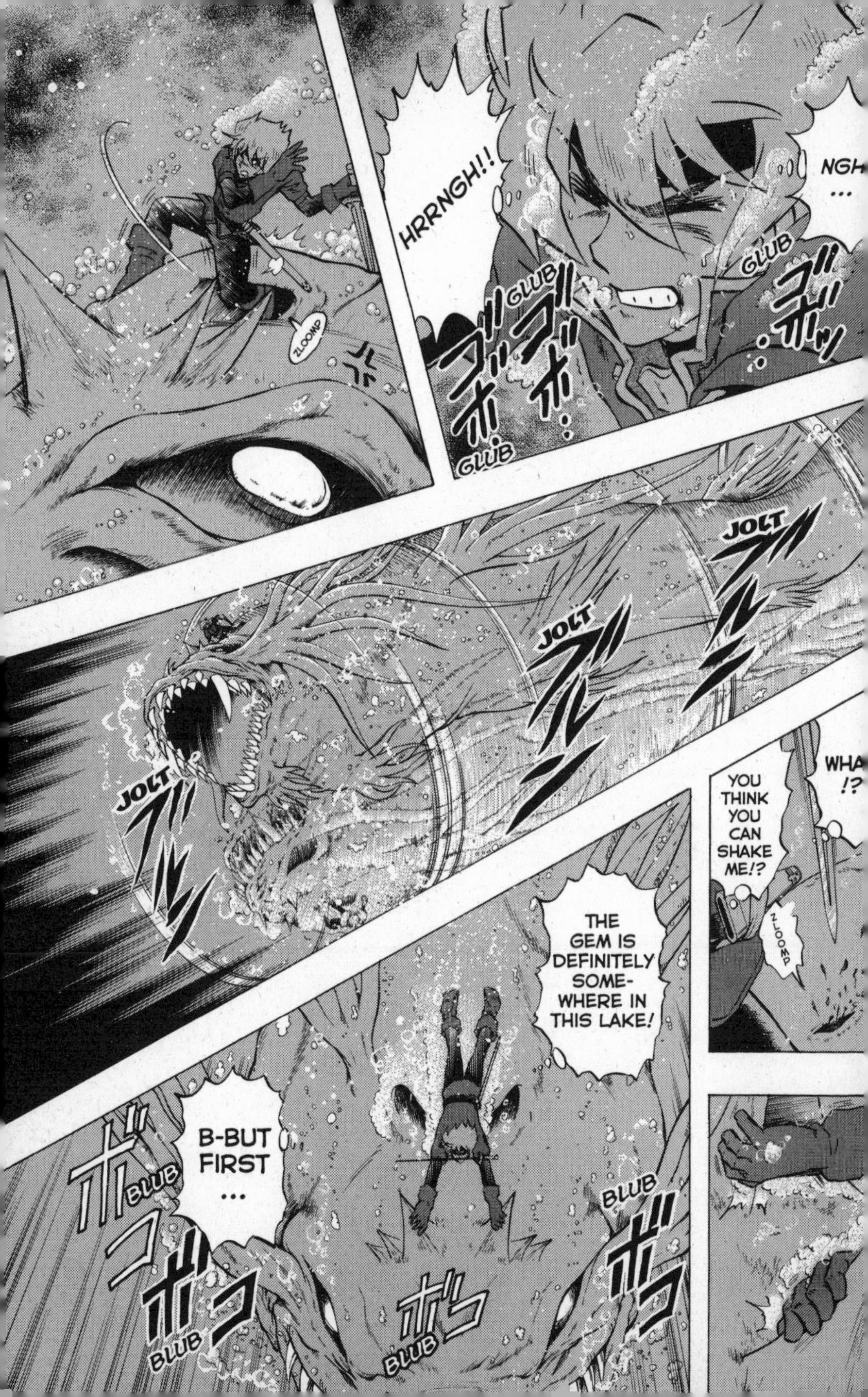

NGH...
HRRNGH!!
GLUB
GLUB
GLUB
ZLOOMP
JOLT
JOLT
JOLT
WHA!?
YOU THINK YOU CAN SHAKE ME!?
ZLOOMP
THE GEM IS DEFINITELY SOME-WHERE IN THIS LAKE!
BLUB
BLUB
B-BUT FIRST...
BLUB
BLUB

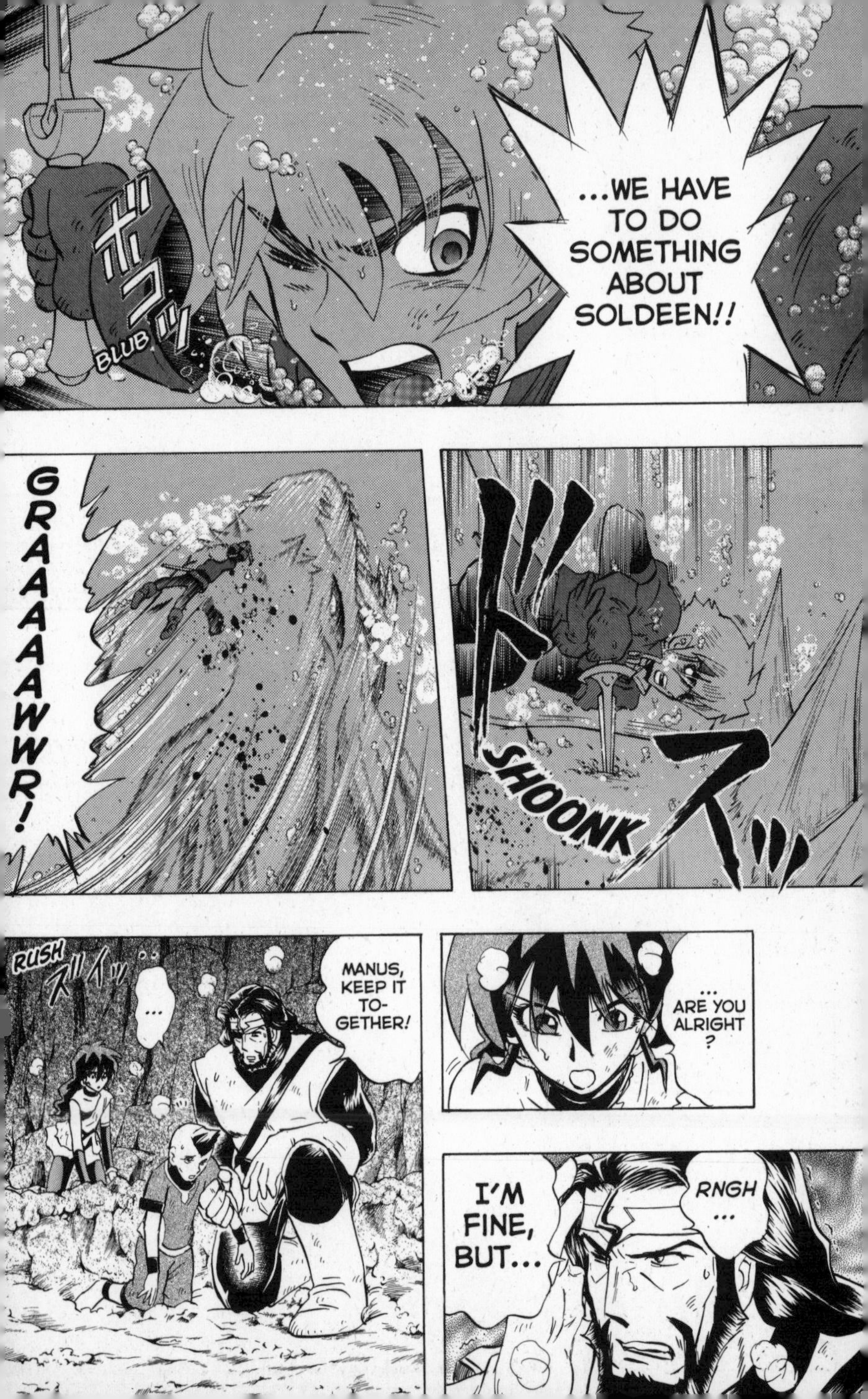
...WE HAVE TO DO SOMETHING ABOUT SOLDEEN!!
BLUB
SHOONK
GRAAAAAAAWWR!
...ARE YOU ALRIGHT?
RNGH...
I'M FINE, BUT...
MANUS, KEEP IT TO-GETHER!
...
RUSH

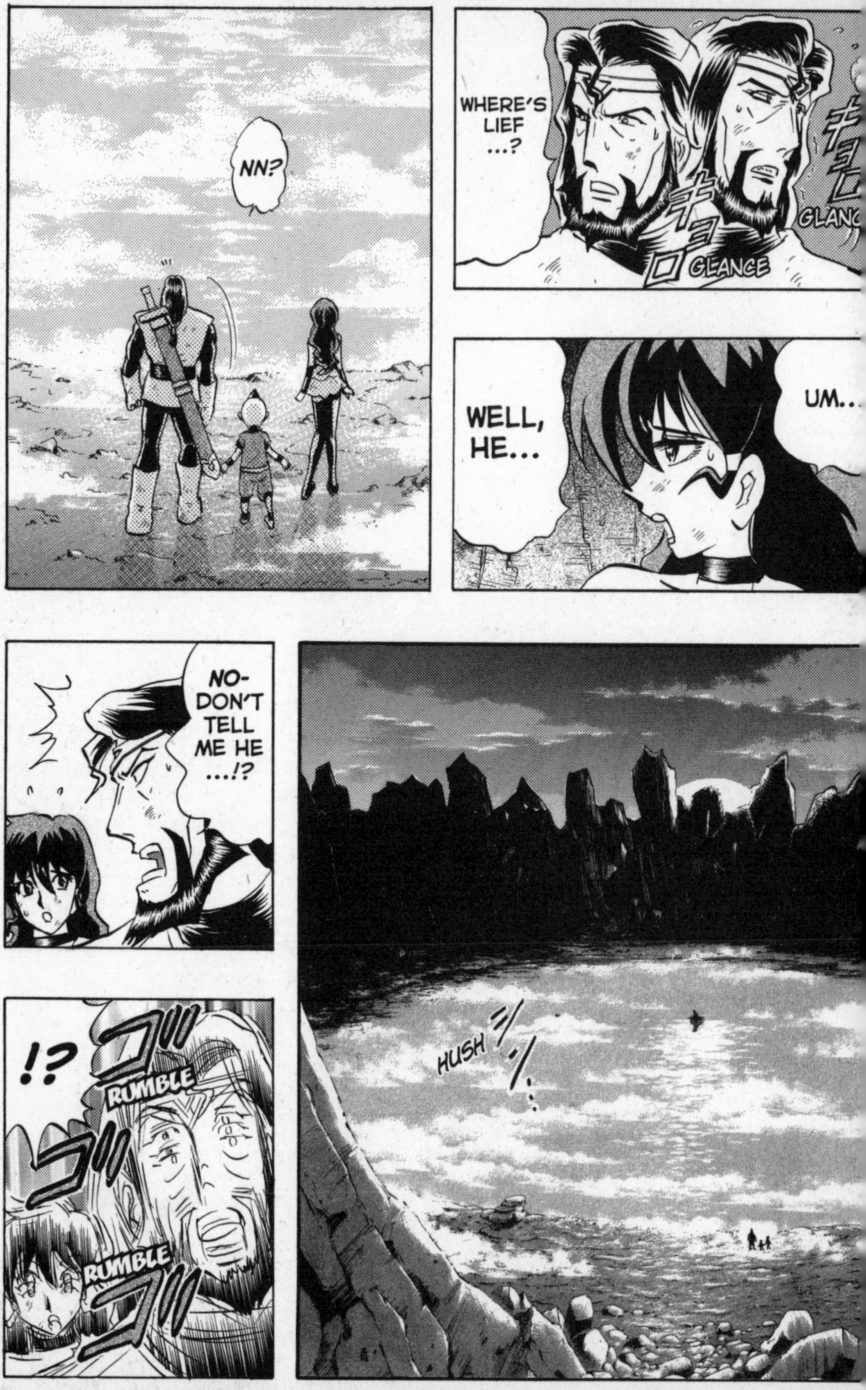
WHERE'S LIEF ...?
キョロ
GLANC
キョロ
GLANCE
UM...
WELL, HE...
NN?
HUSH
NO- DON'T TELL ME HE ...!?
!?
RUMBLE
RUMBLE

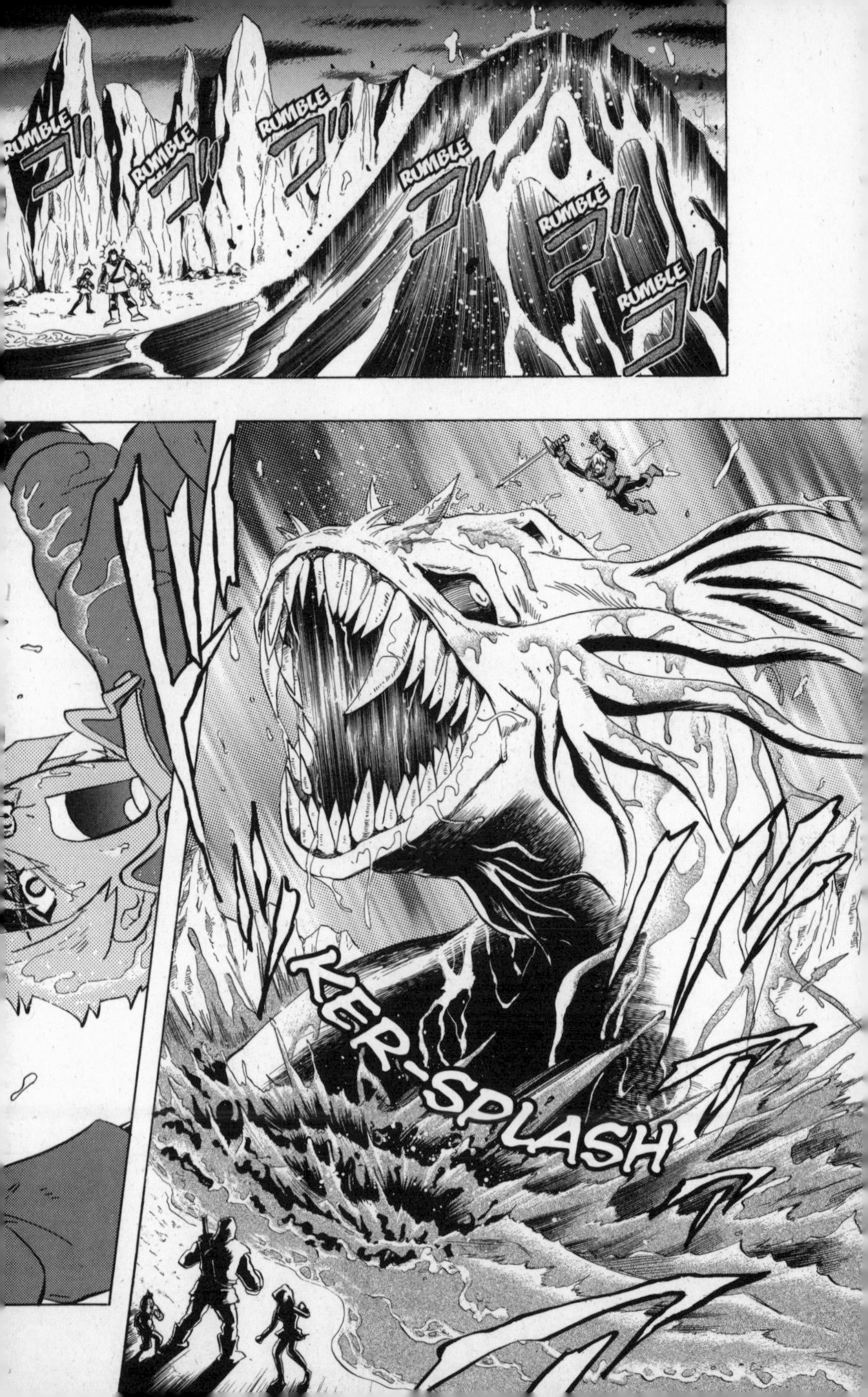
RUMBLE
RUMBLE
RUMBLE
RUMBLE
RUMBLE
RUMBLE
KER-SPLASH

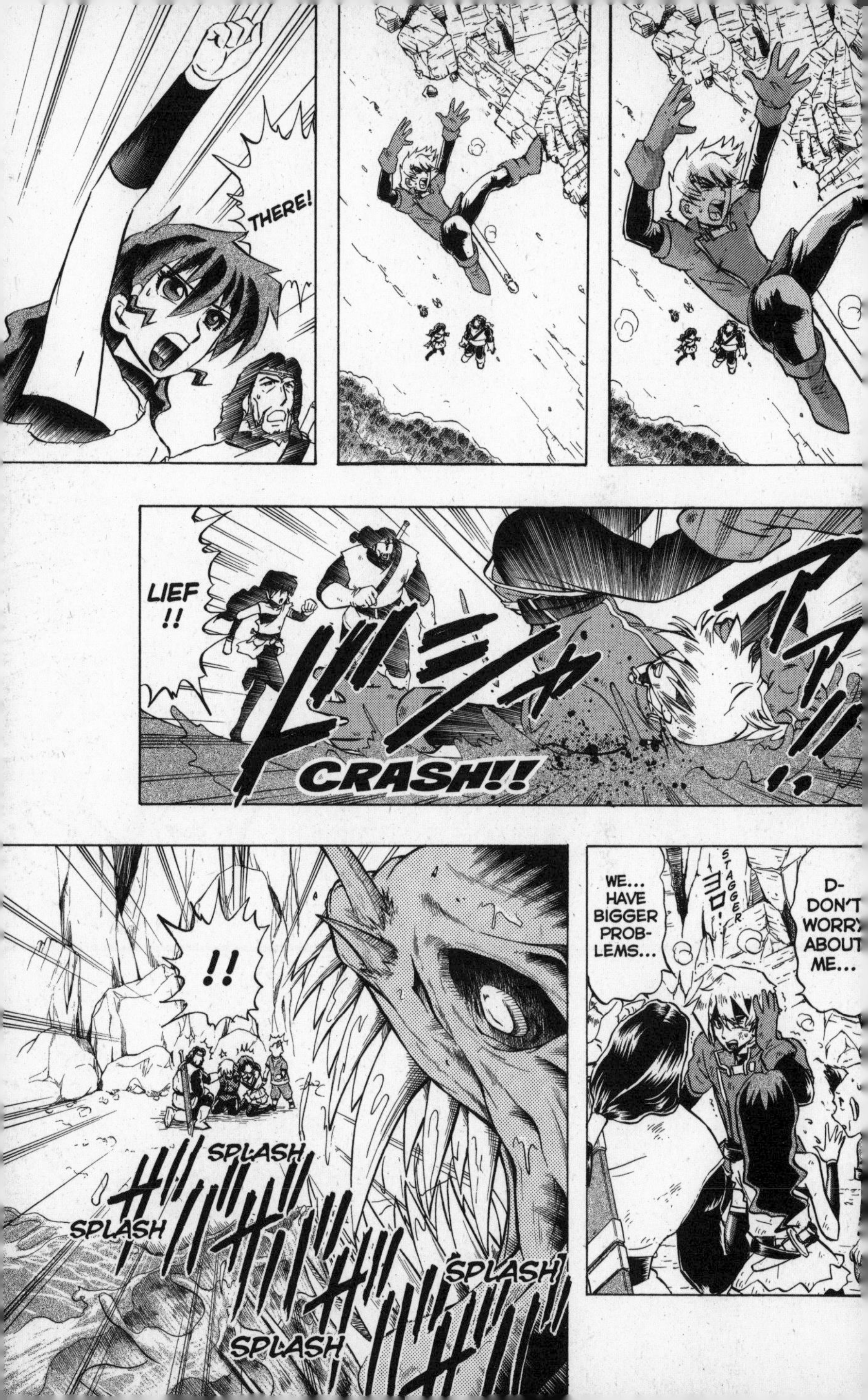
THERE!
LIEF !!
CRASH!!
D-DON'T WORRY ABOUT ME...
STAGGER
WE... HAVE BIGGER PROBLEMS...
!!
SPLASH
SPLASH
SPLASH
SPLASH

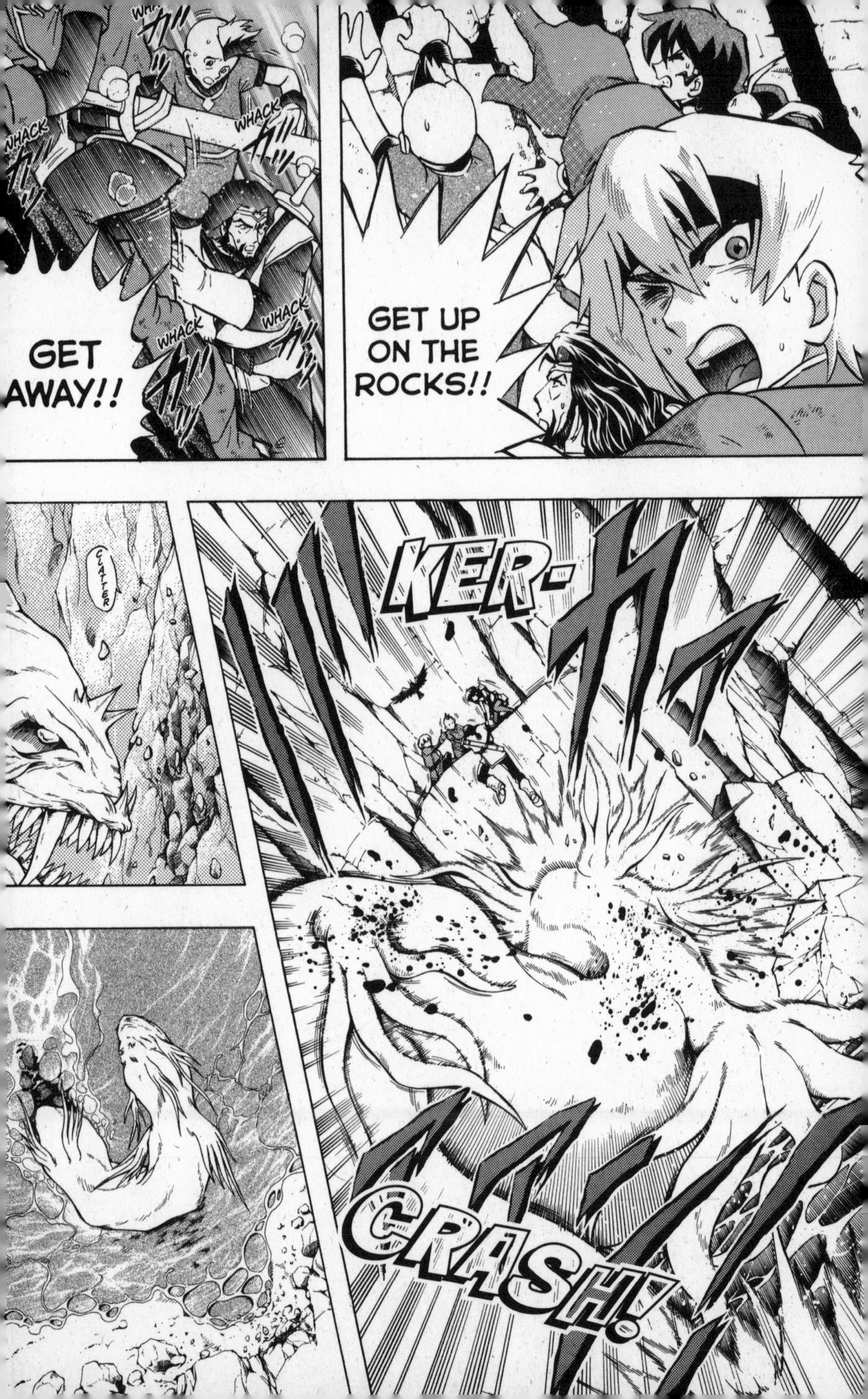
GET UP ON THE ROCKS!!
WHACK
WHACK
WHACK
WHACK
GET AWAY!!
KER-
CRASH!
CLATTER

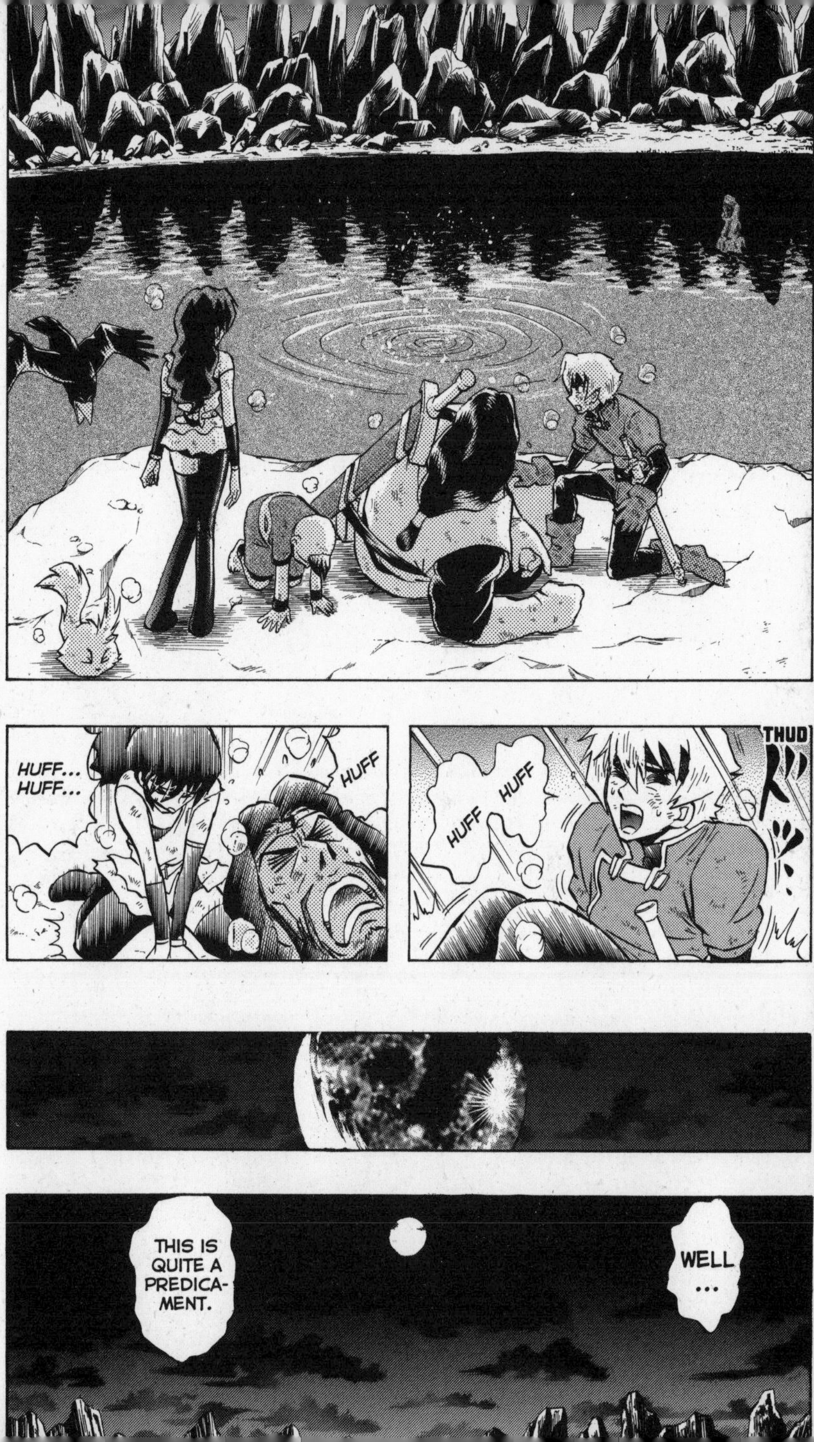
THUD
HUFF HUFF
HUFF
HUFF... HUFF...
WELL ...
THIS IS QUITE A PREDICA-MENT.

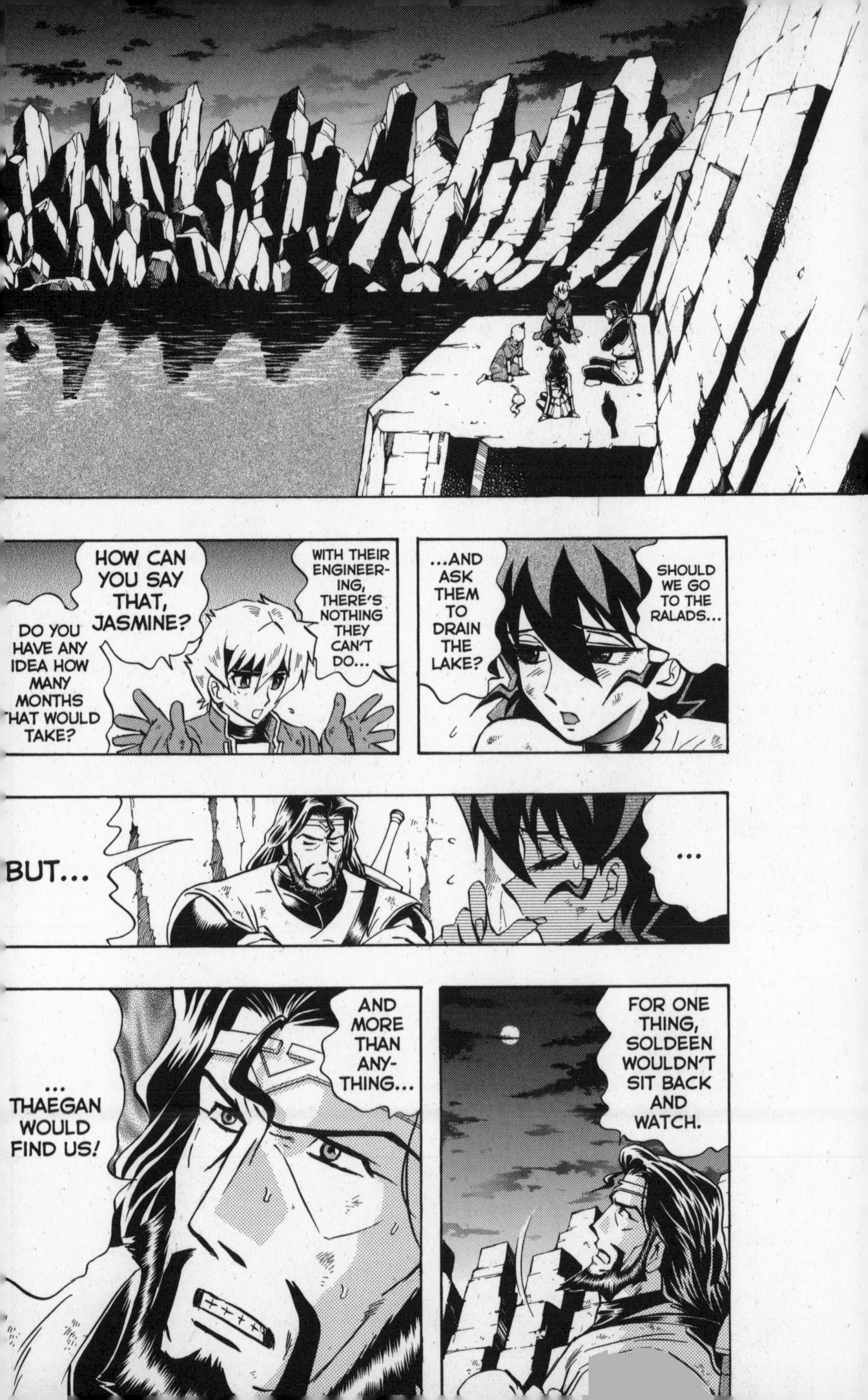

SHOULD WE GO TO THE RALADS...
...AND ASK THEM TO DRAIN THE LAKE?
WITH THEIR ENGINEER-ING, THERE'S NOTHING THEY CAN'T DO...
HOW CAN YOU SAY THAT, JASMINE?
DO YOU HAVE ANY IDEA HOW MANY MONTHS THAT WOULD TAKE?
...
BUT...
FOR ONE THING, SOLDEEN WOULDN'T SIT BACK AND WATCH.
AND MORE THAN ANY-THING...
... THAEGAN WOULD FIND US!

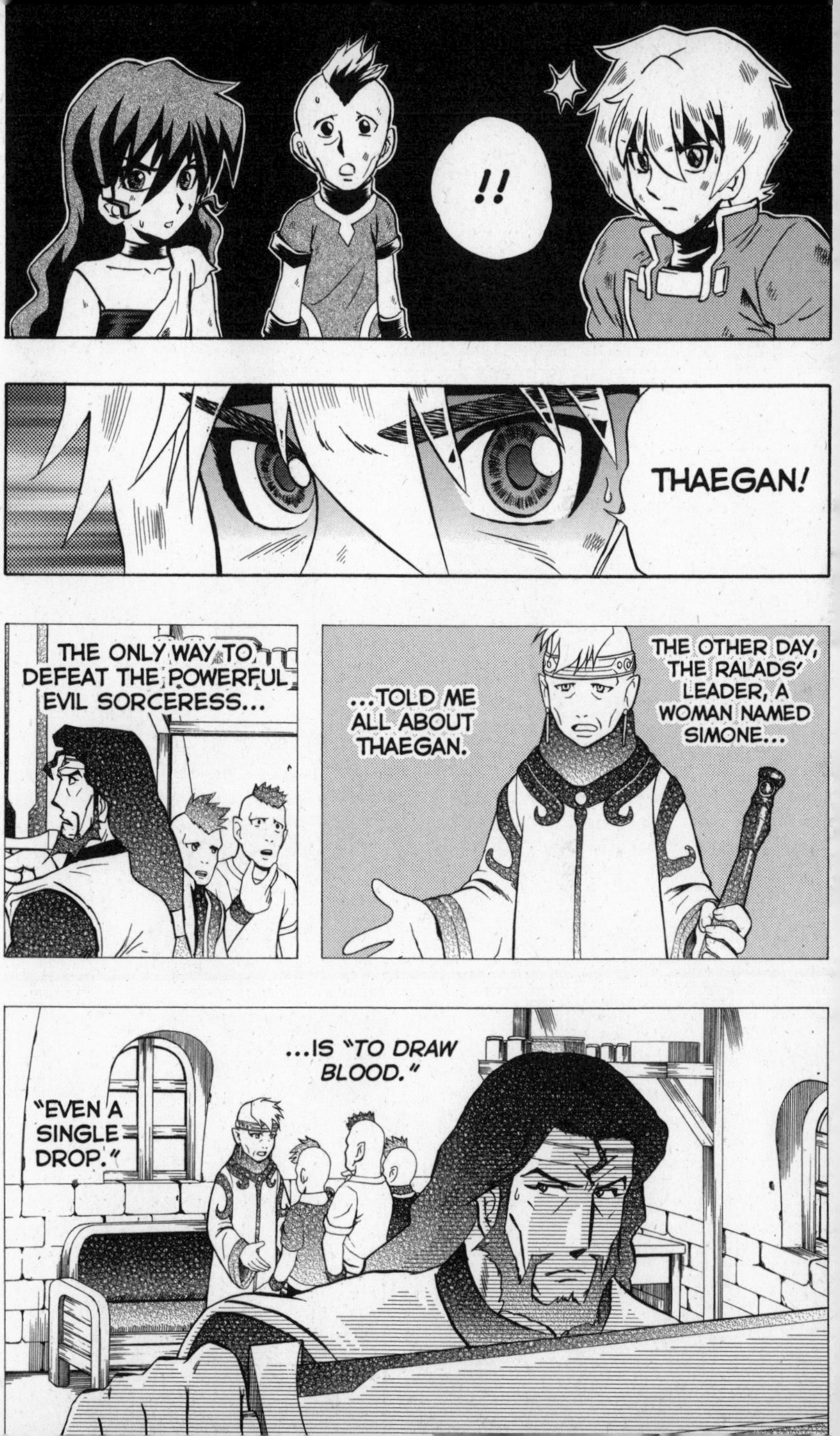
!!
THAEGAN!
THE OTHER DAY, THE RALADS' LEADER, A WOMAN NAMED SIMONE...
...TOLD ME ALL ABOUT THAEGAN.
THE ONLY WAY TO DEFEAT THE POWERFUL EVIL SORCERESS...
...IS "TO DRAW BLOOD."
"EVEN A SINGLE DROP."

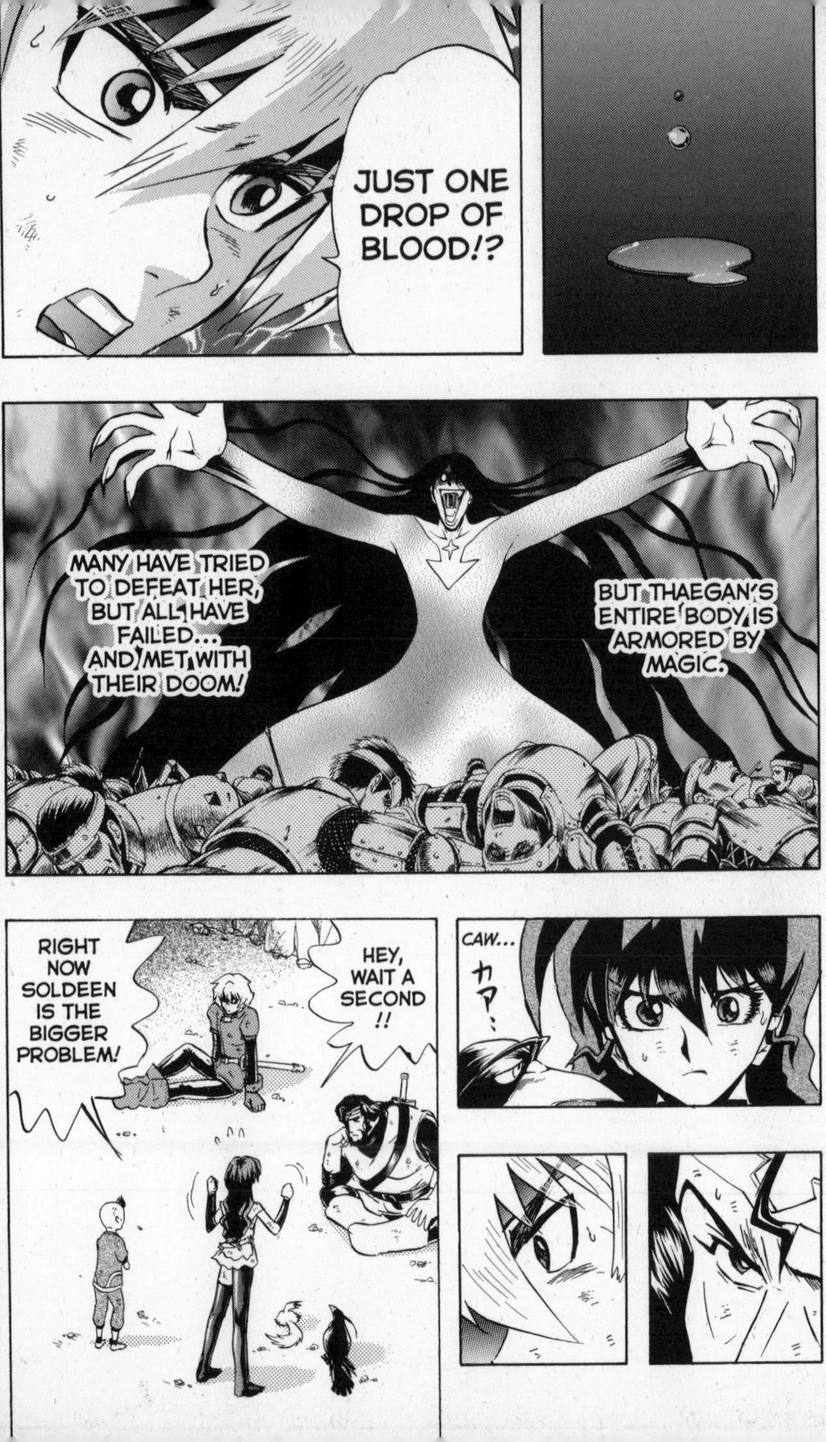
JUST ONE DROP OF BLOOD!?
BUT THAEGAN'S ENTIRE BODY IS ARMORED BY MAGIC.
MANY HAVE TRIED TO DEFEAT HER, BUT ALL HAVE FAILED... AND MET WITH THEIR DOOM!
CAW...
カア
HEY, WAIT A SECOND !!
RIGHT NOW SOLDEEN IS THE BIGGER PROBLEM!

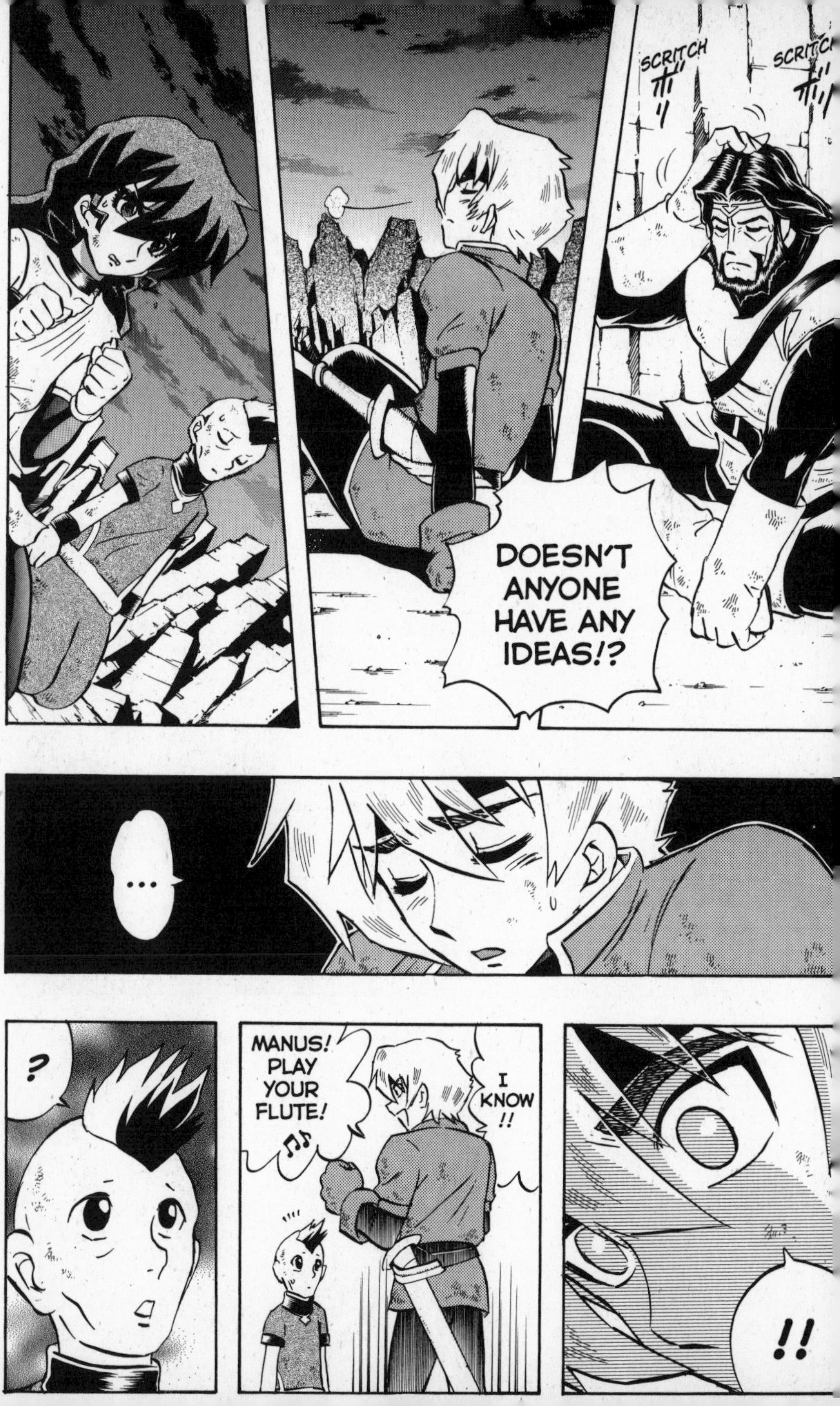
SCRITCH
SCRITCH
DOESN'T ANYONE HAVE ANY IDEAS!?
...
!!
MANUS! PLAY YOUR FLUTE!
I KNOW!!
?

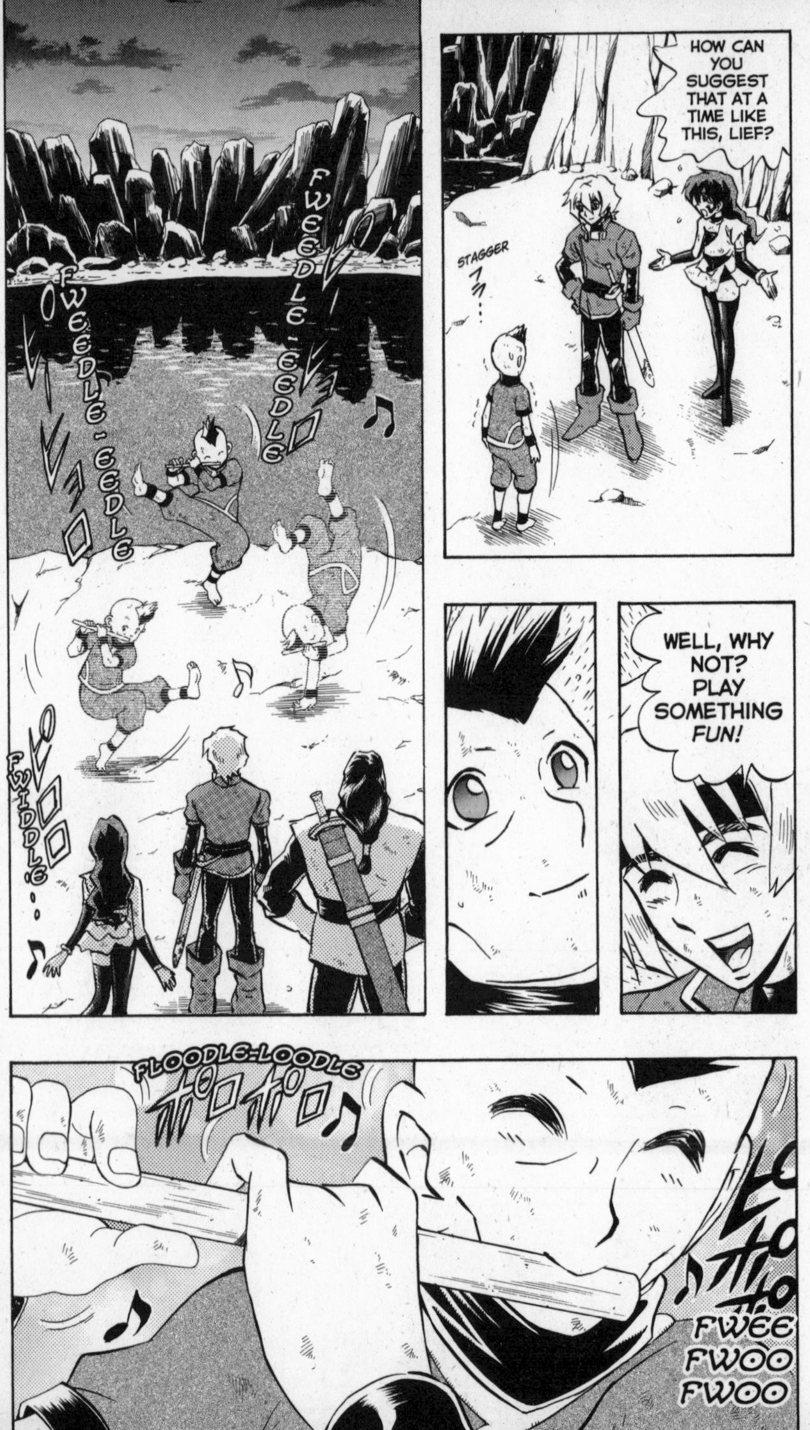

HOW CAN YOU SUGGEST THAT AT A TIME LIKE THIS, LIEF?
STAGGER
WELL, WHY NOT? PLAY SOMETHING FUN!
FWEEDLE-EEDLE
FWEEDLE-EEDLE
FWIDDLE...
FLOODLE-LOODLE
FWEE FWOO FWOO

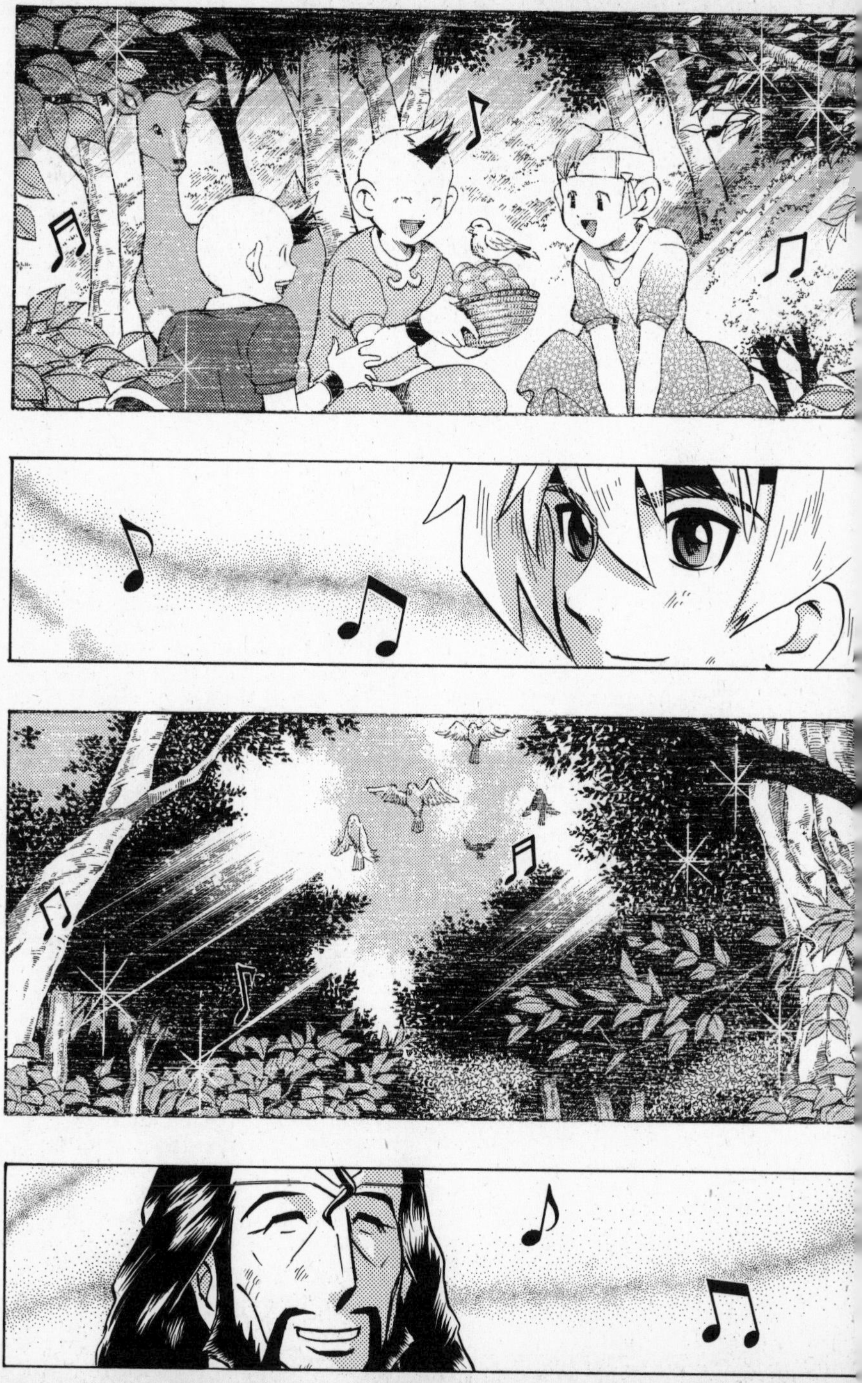

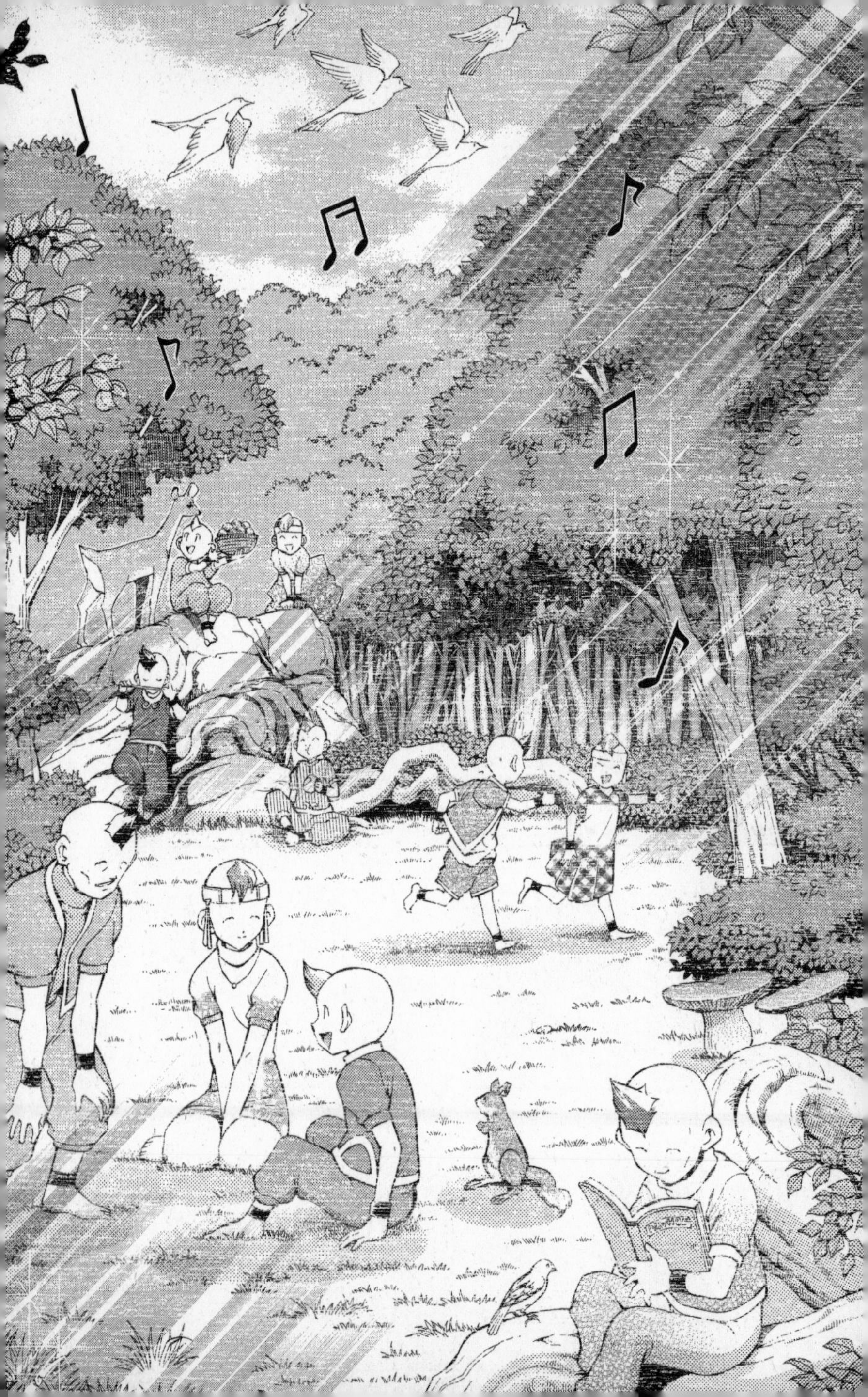

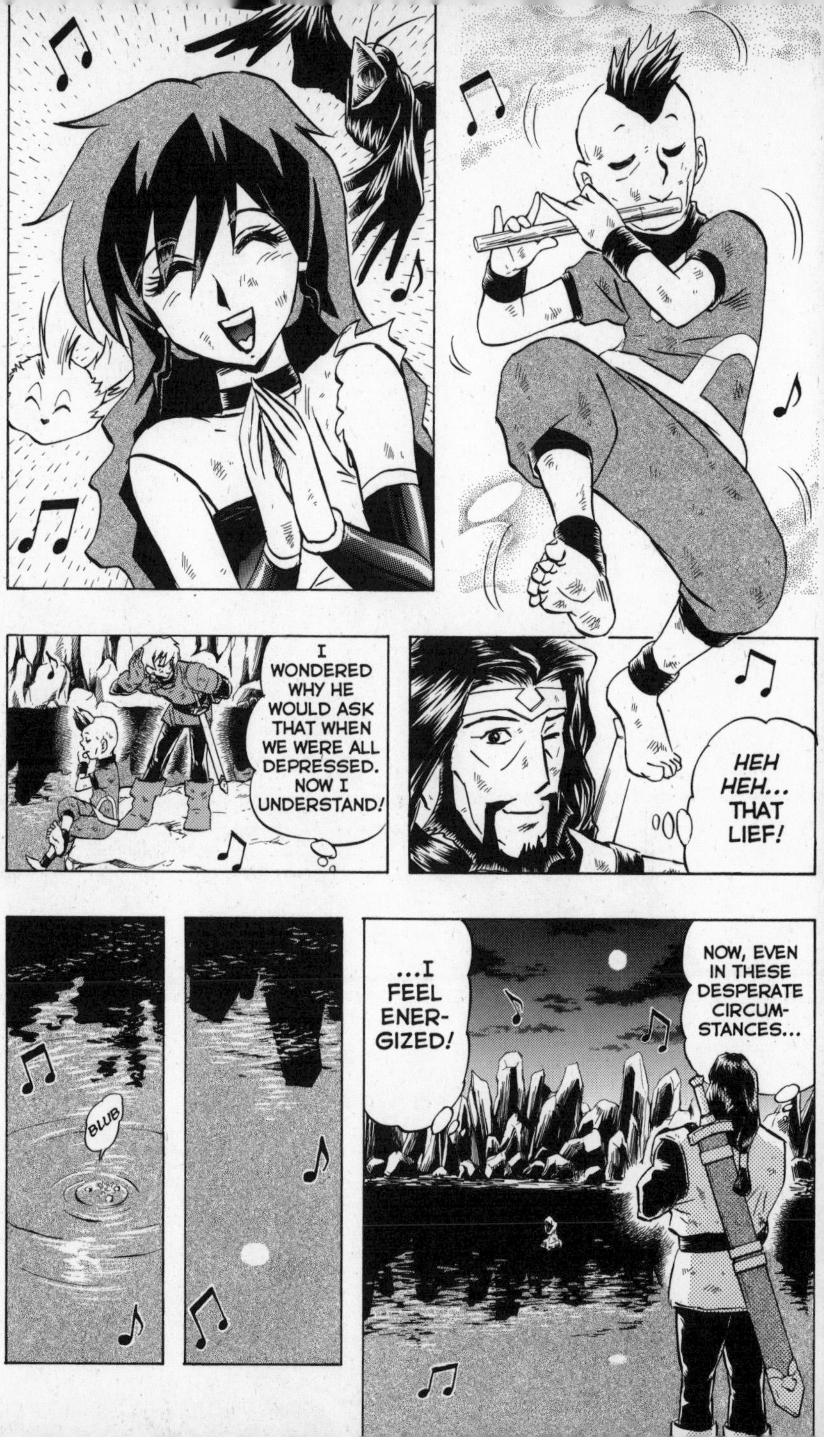
HEH HEH... THAT LIEF!
I WONDERED WHY HE WOULD ASK THAT WHEN WE WERE ALL DEPRESSED. NOW I UNDERSTAND!
NOW, EVEN IN THESE DESPERATE CIRCUM-STANCES...
...I FEEL ENER-GIZED!
BLUB

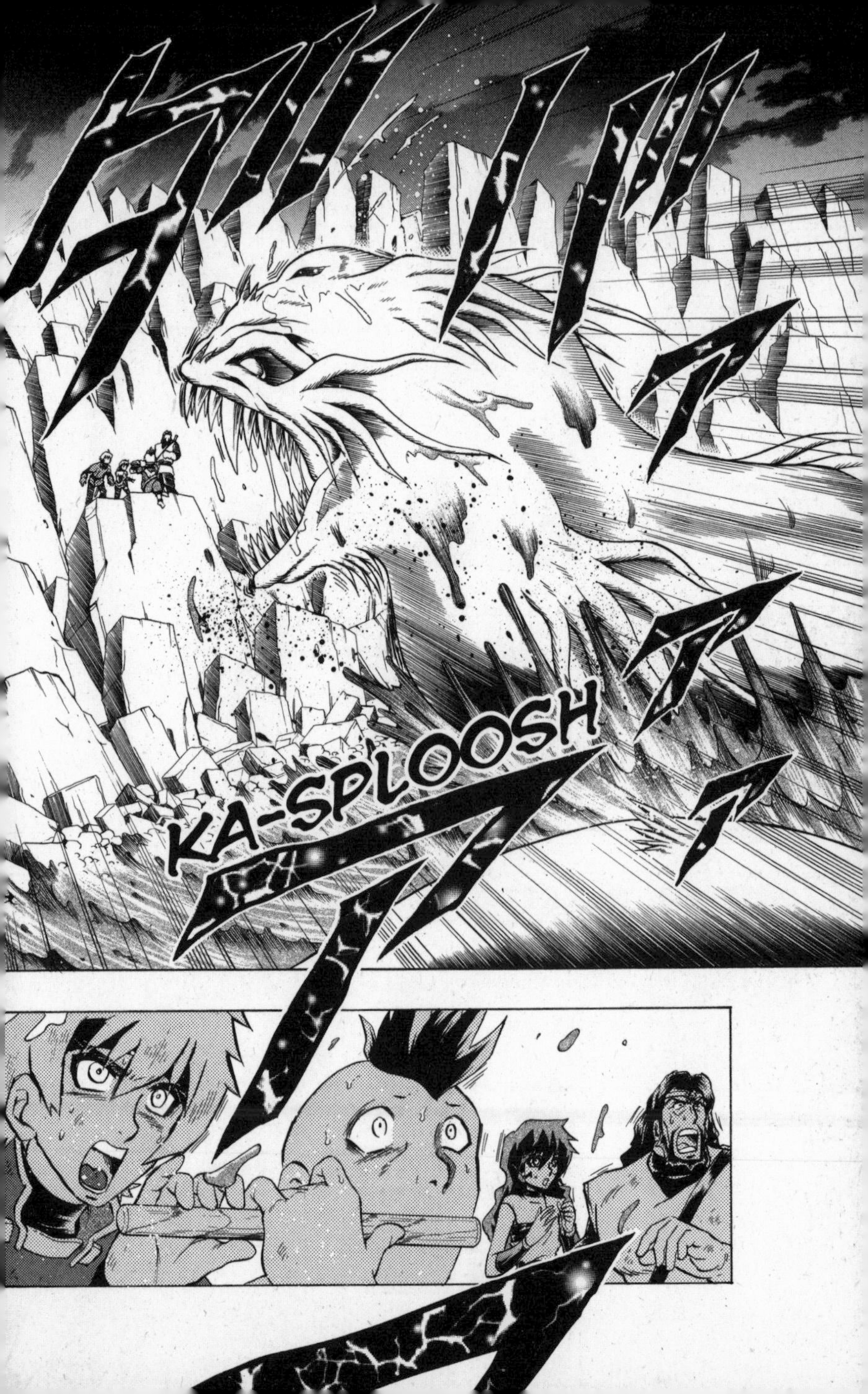
KA-SPLOOSH

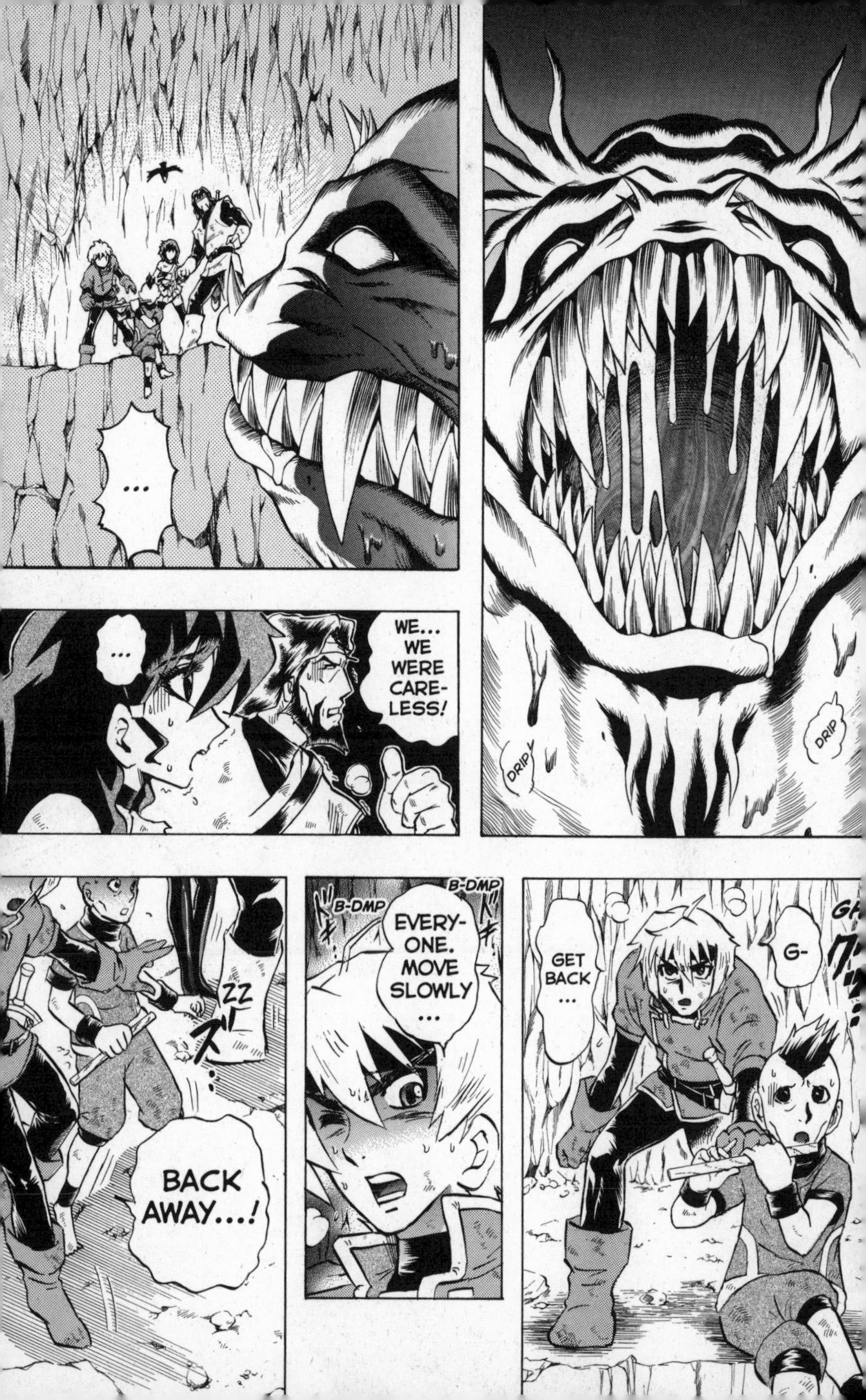
DRIP
DRIP
...
...
WE... WE WERE CARE-LESS!
GH
G-
GET BACK ...
B-DMP
B-DMP
EVERY-ONE. MOVE SLOWLY ...
ZZ
BACK AWAY...!

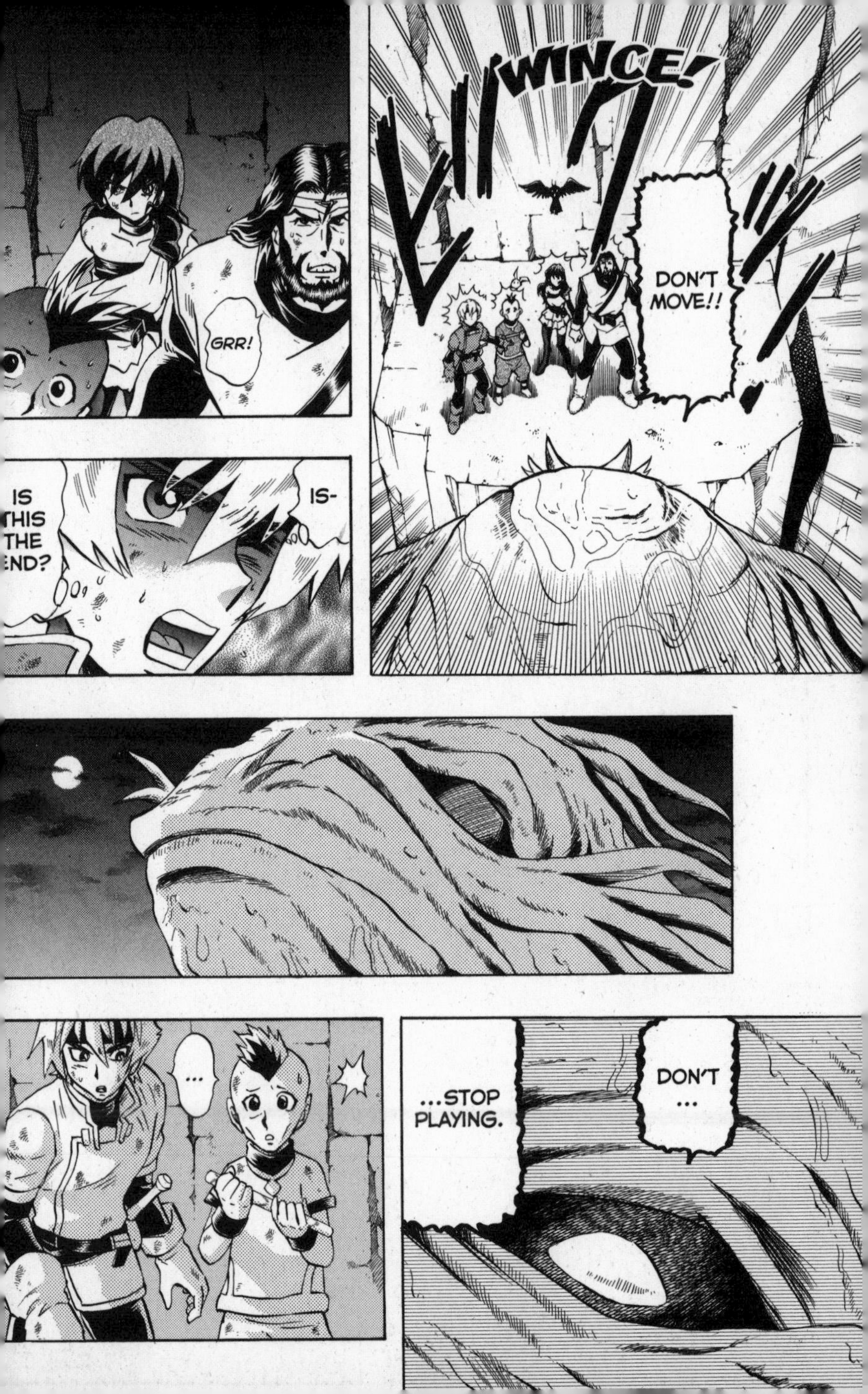
WINCE!
DON'T MOVE!!
GRR!
IS-
IS THIS THE END?
DON'T ...
...STOP PLAYING.
...

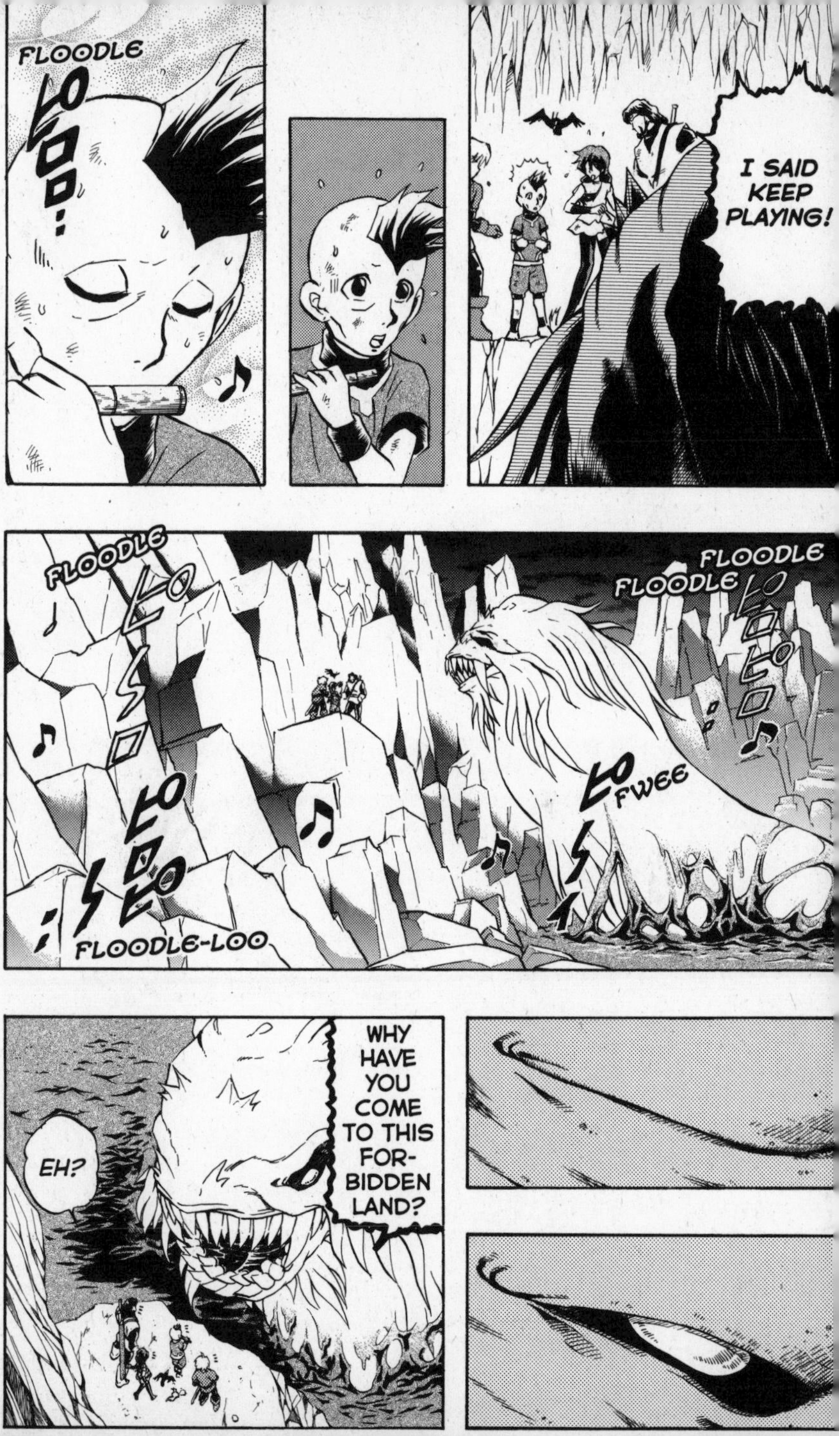
I SAID KEEP PLAYING!
FLOODLE
FLOODLE
FLOODLE
FWEE
FLOODLE
FLOODLE-LOO
WHY HAVE YOU COME TO THIS FOR-BIDDEN LAND?
EH?

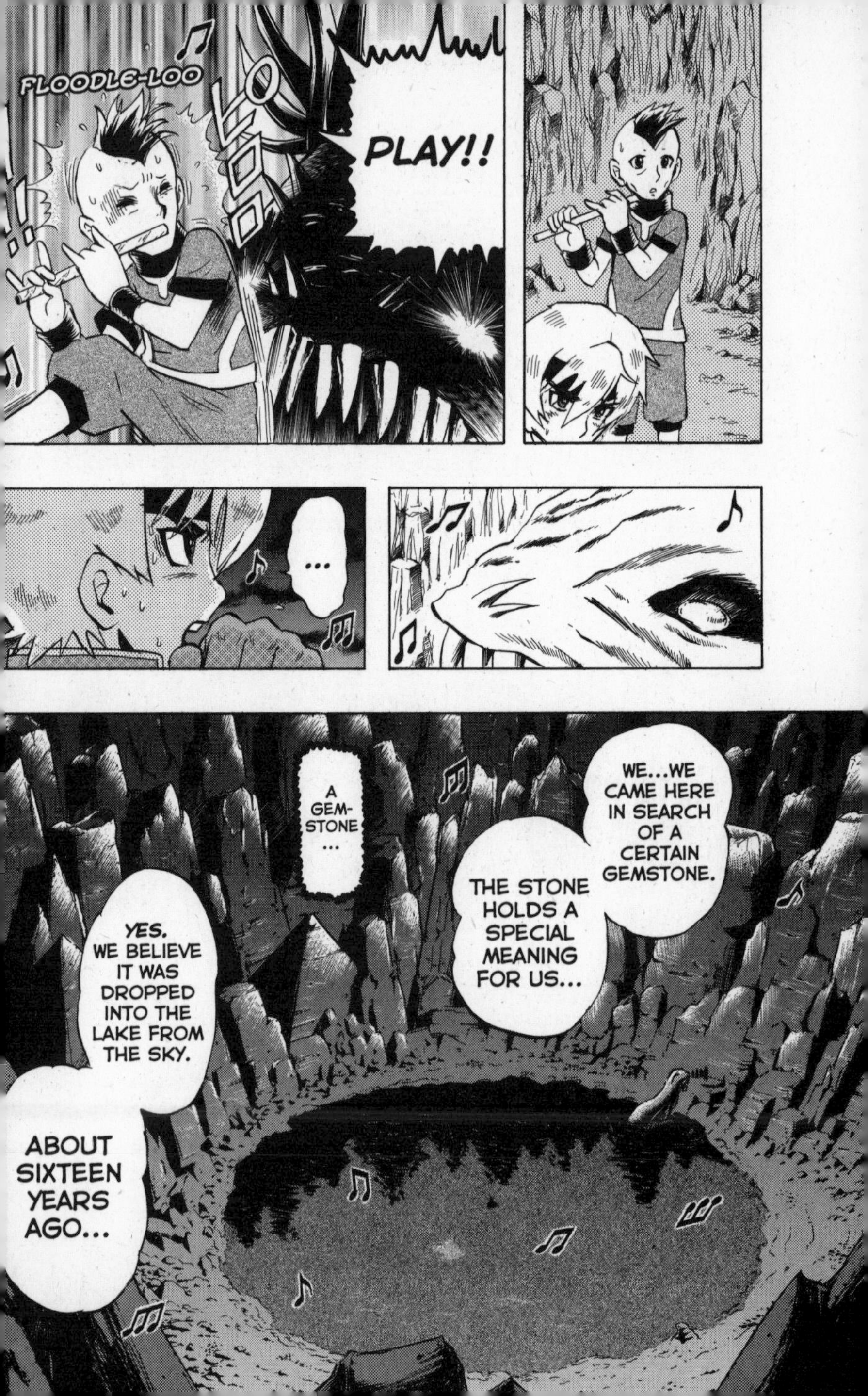
PLAY!!
LOLOLO
FLOODLE-LOO
...
WE...WE CAME HERE IN SEARCH OF A CERTAIN GEMSTONE.
THE STONE HOLDS A SPECIAL MEANING FOR US...
A GEM-STONE ...
YES. WE BELIEVE IT WAS DROPPED INTO THE LAKE FROM THE SKY.
ABOUT SIXTEEN YEARS AGO...

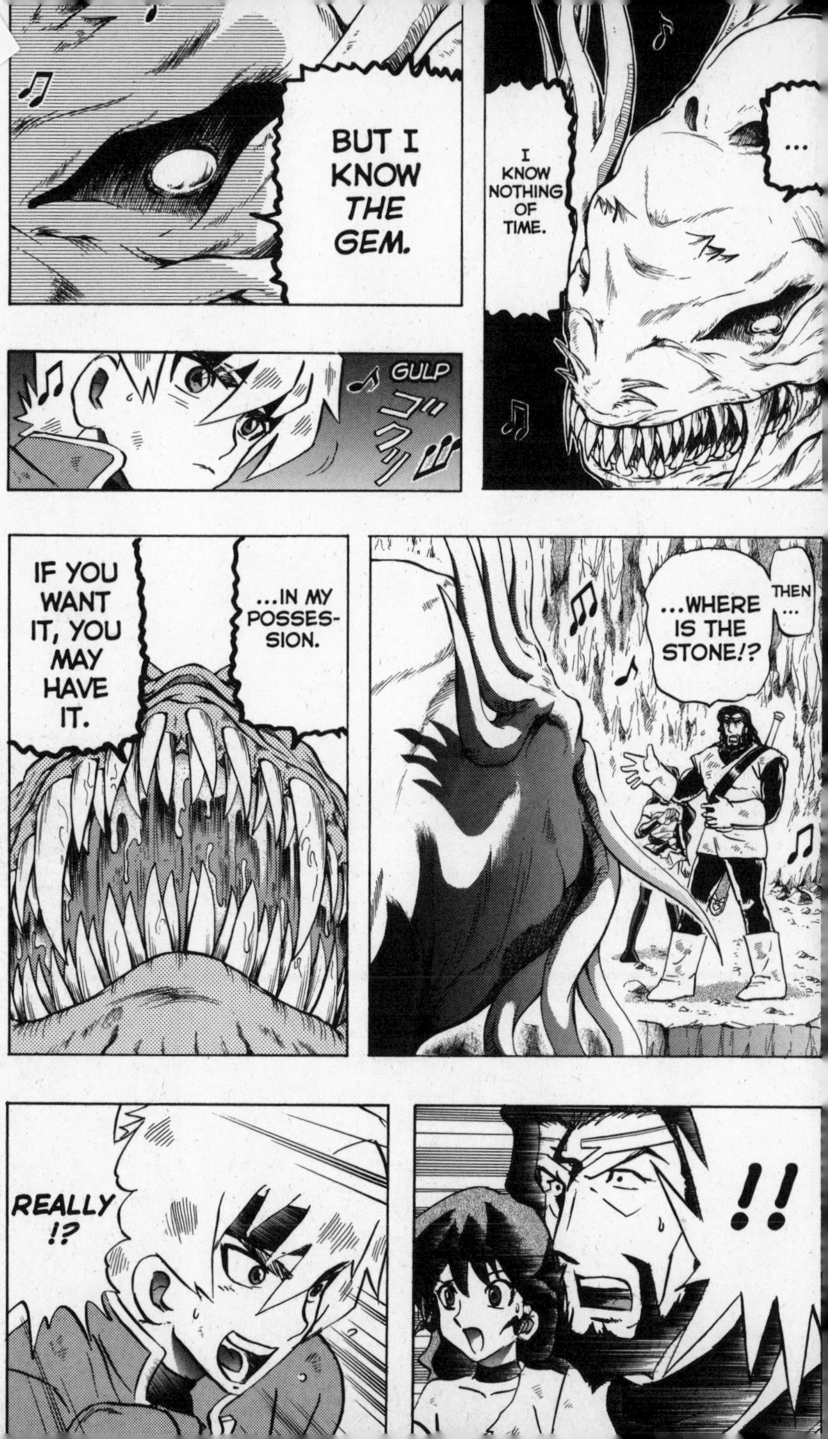
...
I KNOW NOTHING OF TIME.
BUT I KNOW THE GEM.
GULP
ゴクッ
THEN...
...WHERE IS THE STONE!?
...IN MY POSSESSION.
IF YOU WANT IT, YOU MAY HAVE IT.
!!
REALLY!?

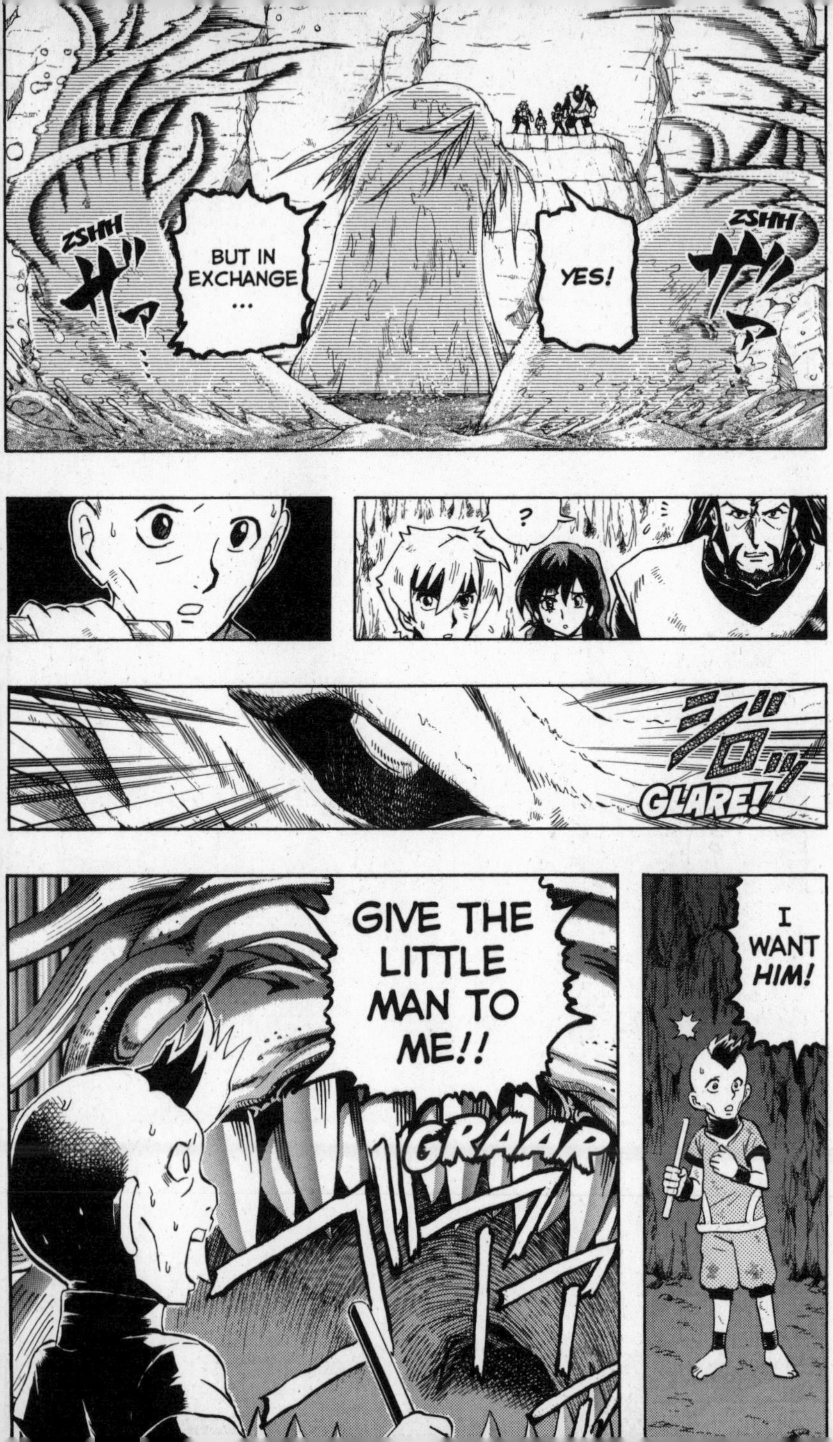
ZSHH
YES!
BUT IN EXCHANGE ...
ZSHH
?
ジロッ
GLARE!
I WANT HIM!
GIVE THE LITTLE MAN TO ME!!
GRAAR

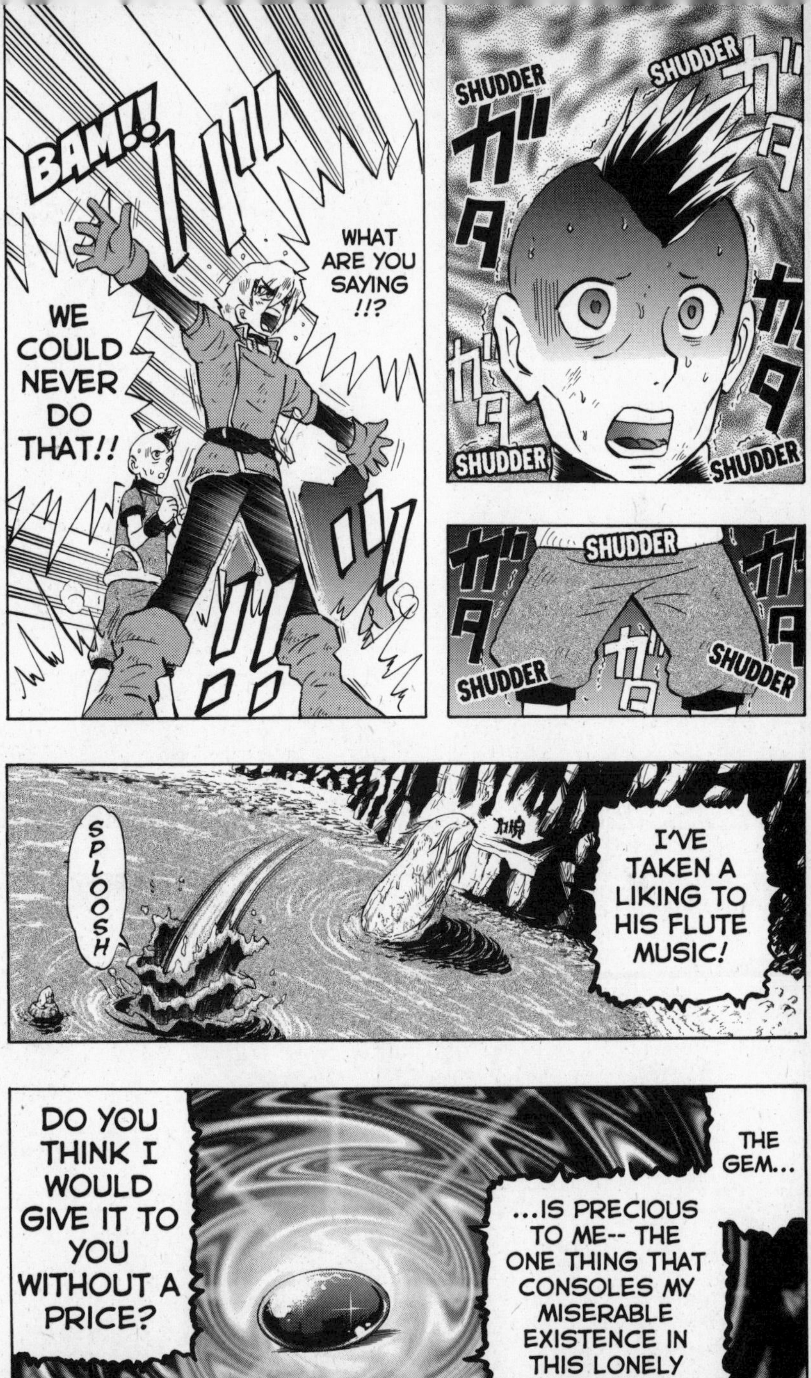

SHUDDER
SHUDDER
ガタ
ガタ
ガタ
ガタ
SHUDDER
SHUDDER
SHUDDER
ガタ
ガタ
ガタ
SHUDDER
SHUDDER
BAM!!
WHAT ARE YOU SAYING !!?
WE COULD NEVER DO THAT!!
I'VE TAKEN A LIKING TO HIS FLUTE MUSIC!
SPLOOSH
THE GEM...
...IS PRECIOUS TO ME-- THE ONE THING THAT CONSOLES MY MISERABLE EXISTENCE IN THIS LONELY PLACE.
DO YOU THINK I WOULD GIVE IT TO YOU WITHOUT A PRICE?

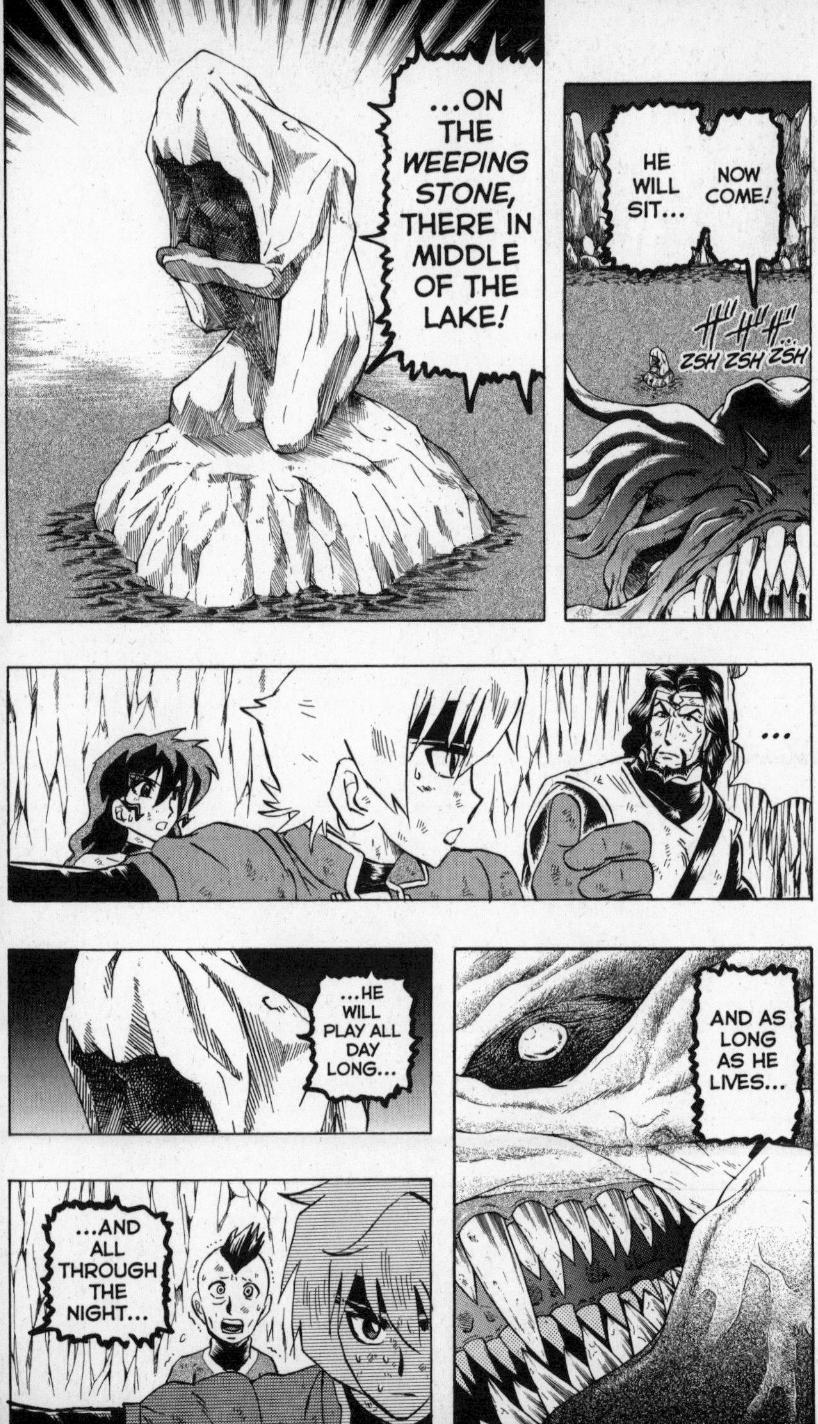
NOW COME!
HE WILL SIT...
ZSH ZSH ZSH
...ON THE *WEEPING STONE*, THERE IN MIDDLE OF THE LAKE!
...
AND AS LONG AS HE LIVES...
...HE WILL PLAY ALL DAY LONG...
...AND ALL THROUGH THE NIGHT...

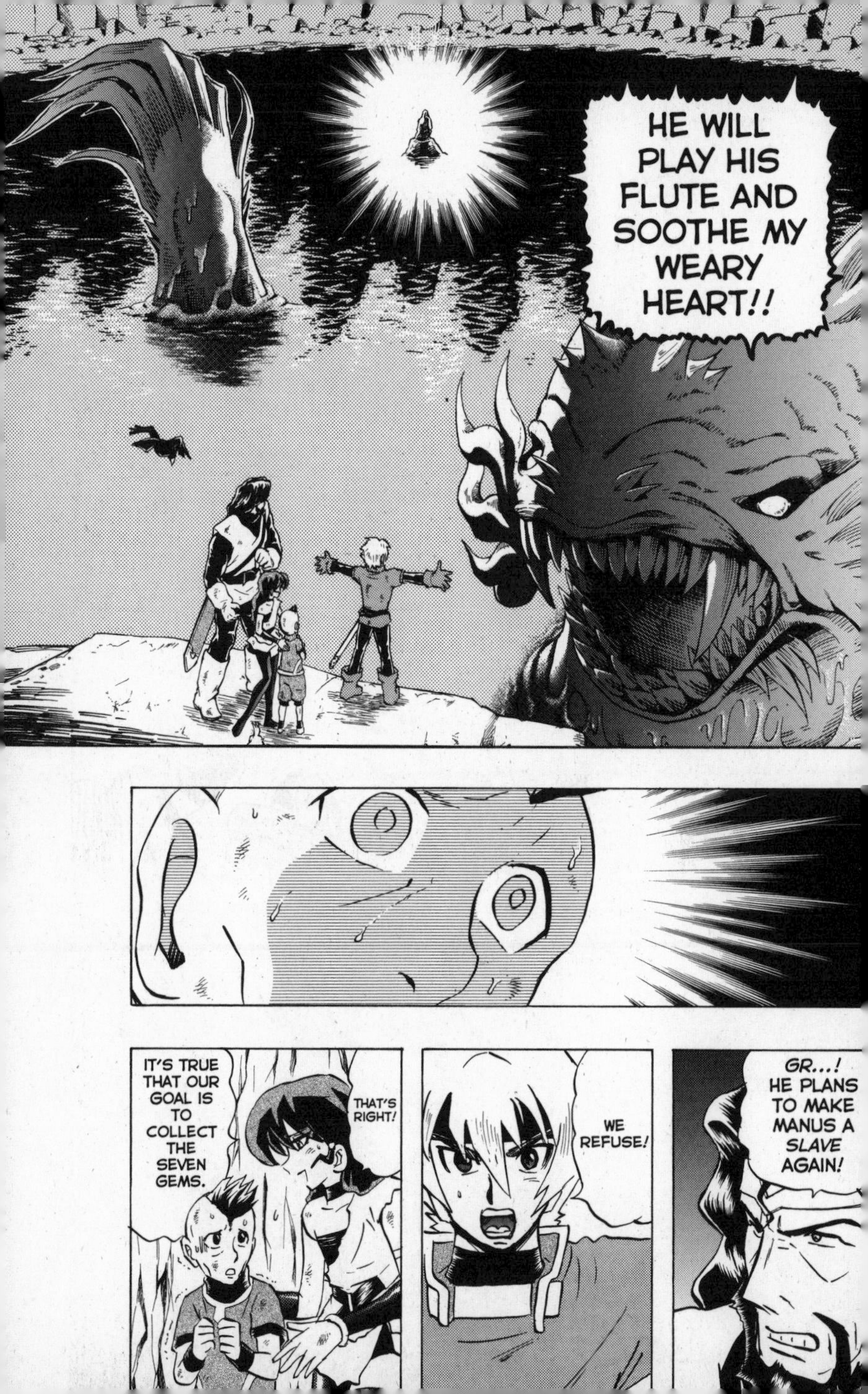
HE WILL PLAY HIS FLUTE AND SOOTHE MY WEARY HEART!!
GR...! HE PLANS TO MAKE MANUS A SLAVE AGAIN!
WE REFUSE!
THAT'S RIGHT!
IT'S TRUE THAT OUR GOAL IS TO COLLECT THE SEVEN GEMS.

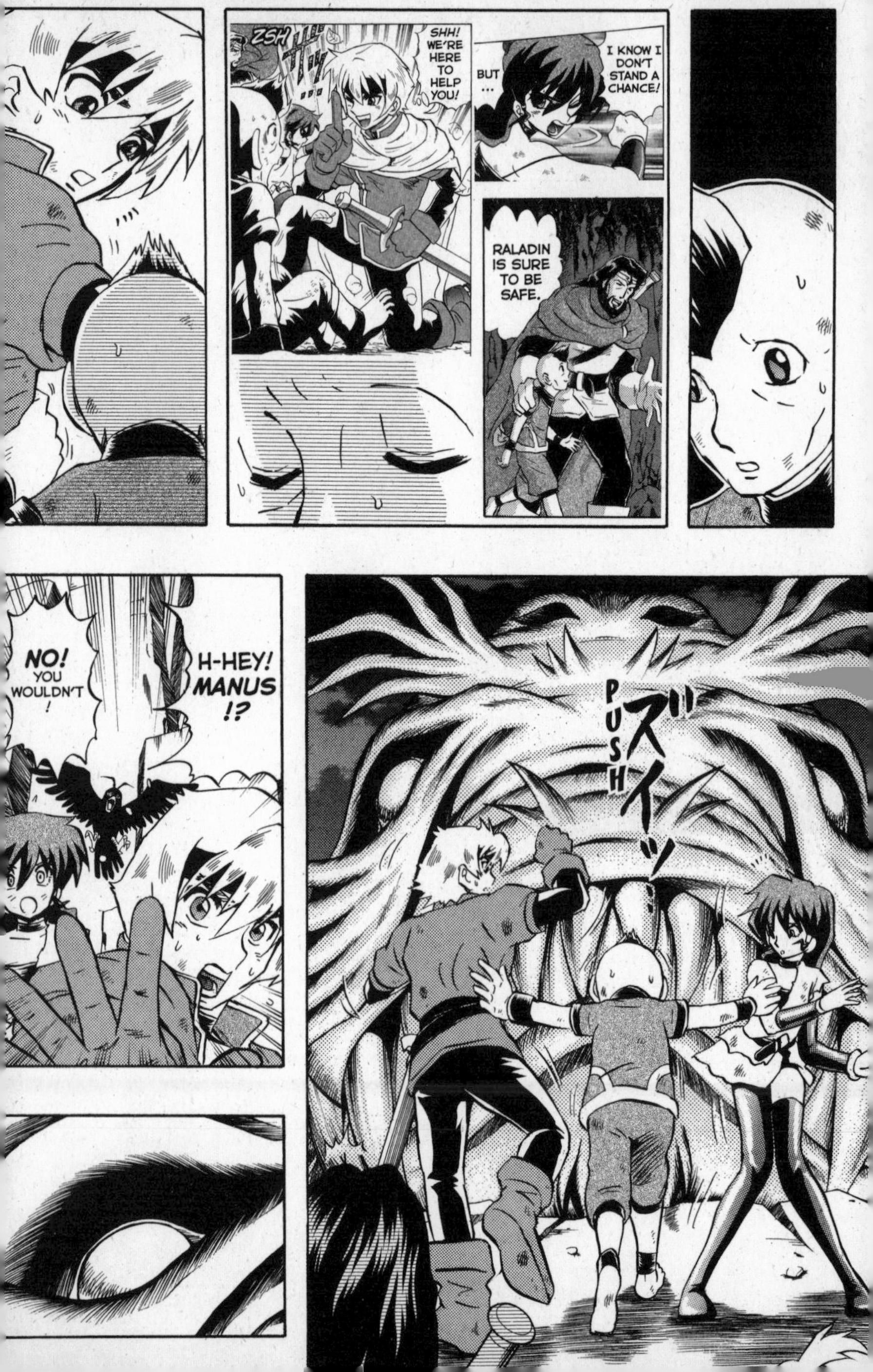
I KNOW I DON'T STAND A CHANCE!
BUT ...
RALADIN IS SURE TO BE SAFE.
SHH! WE'RE HERE TO HELP YOU!
ZSH
PUSH
H-HEY! MANUS !?
NO! YOU WOULDN'T !

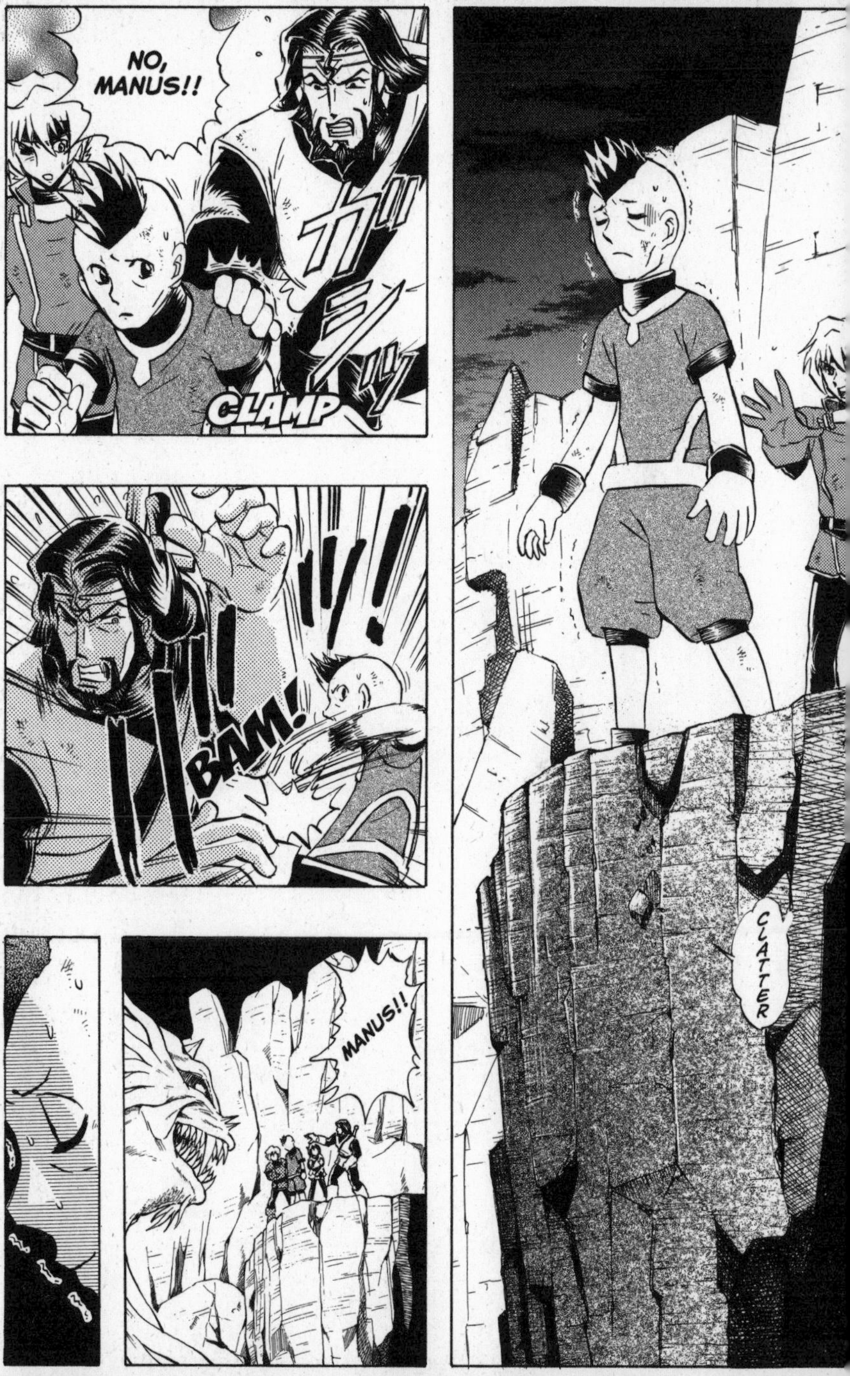
CLATTER
NO, MANUS!!
CLAMP
BAM!
MANUS!!

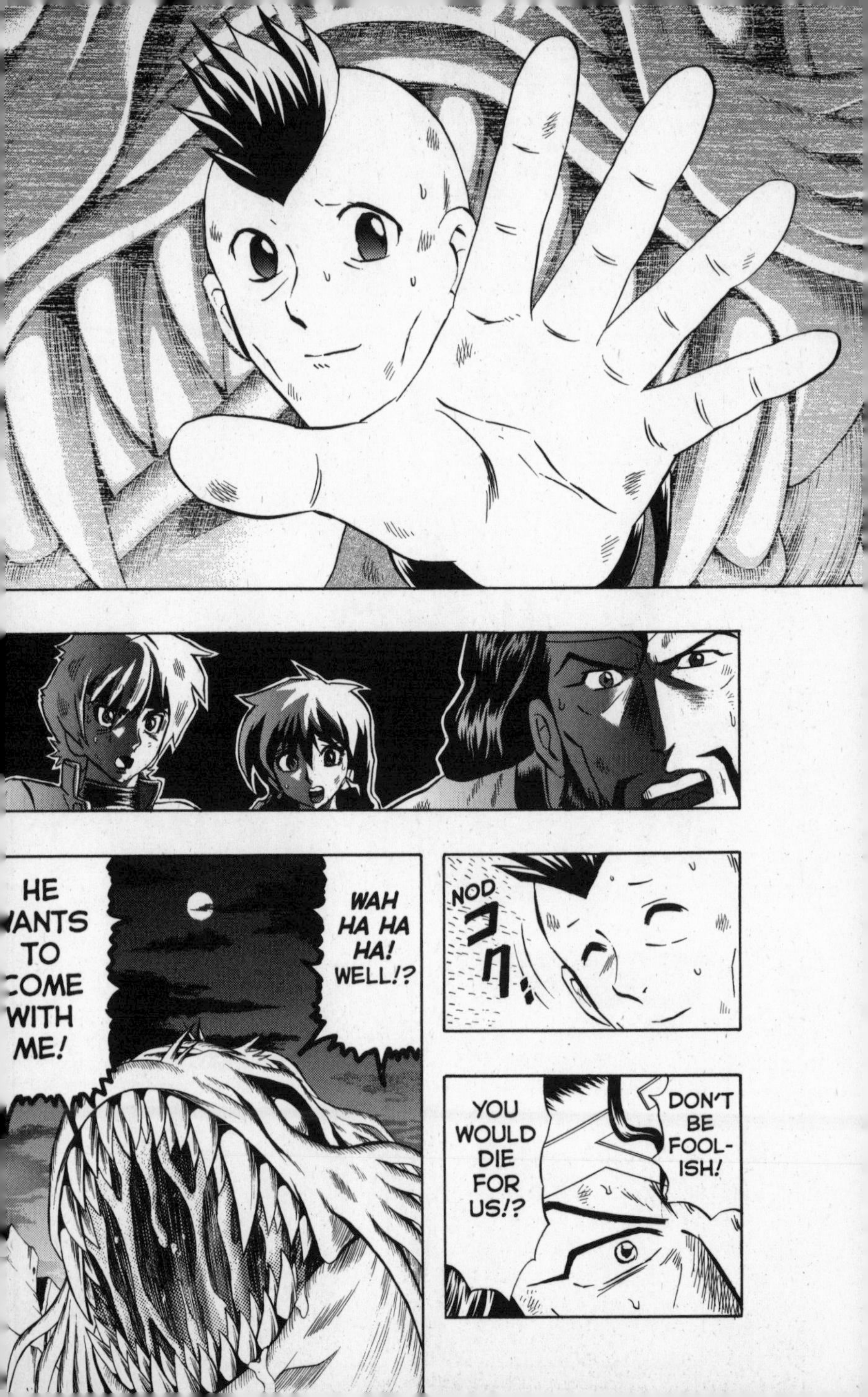
NOD
DON'T BE FOOL-ISH!
YOU WOULD DIE FOR US!?
WAH HA HA HA! WELL!?
HE WANTS TO COME WITH ME!

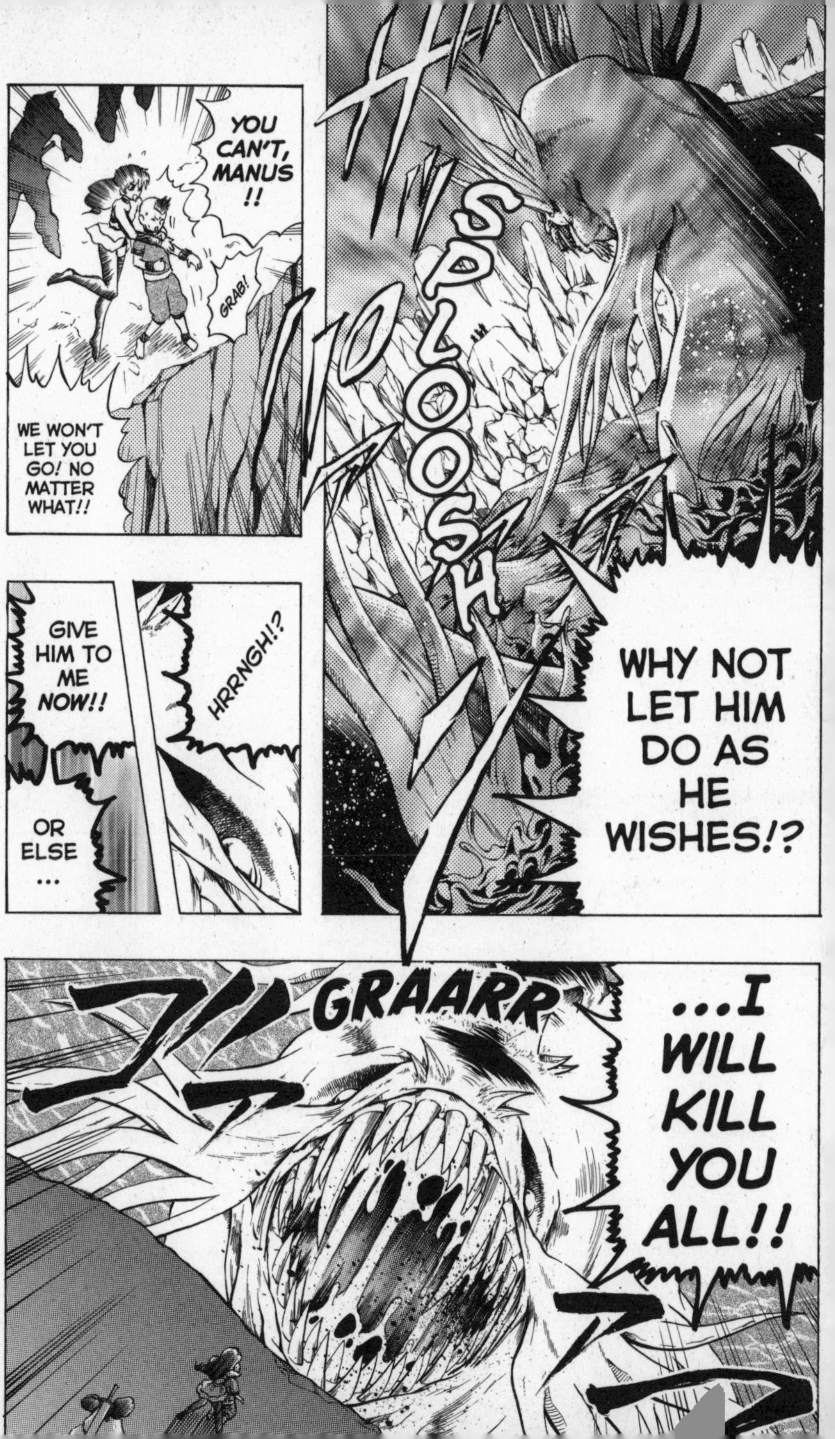
SPLOOSH
WHY NOT LET HIM DO AS HE WISHES!?
YOU CAN'T, MANUS!!
GRAB!
WE WON'T LET YOU GO! NO MATTER WHAT!!
HRRNGH!?
GIVE HIM TO ME NOW!!
OR ELSE ...
GRAARR
...I WILL KILL YOU ALL!!

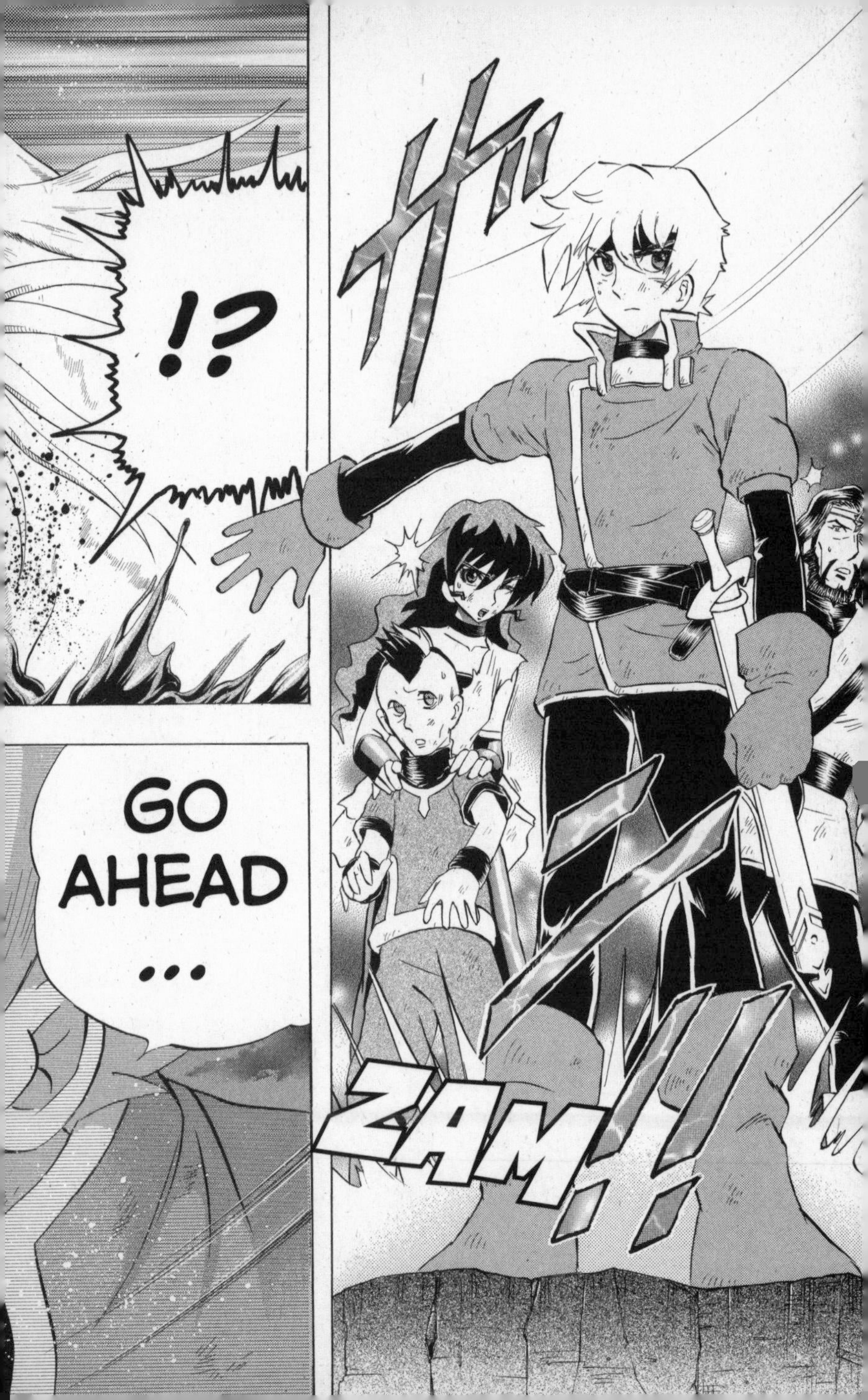
ZAM!!
!?
GO AHEAD ...

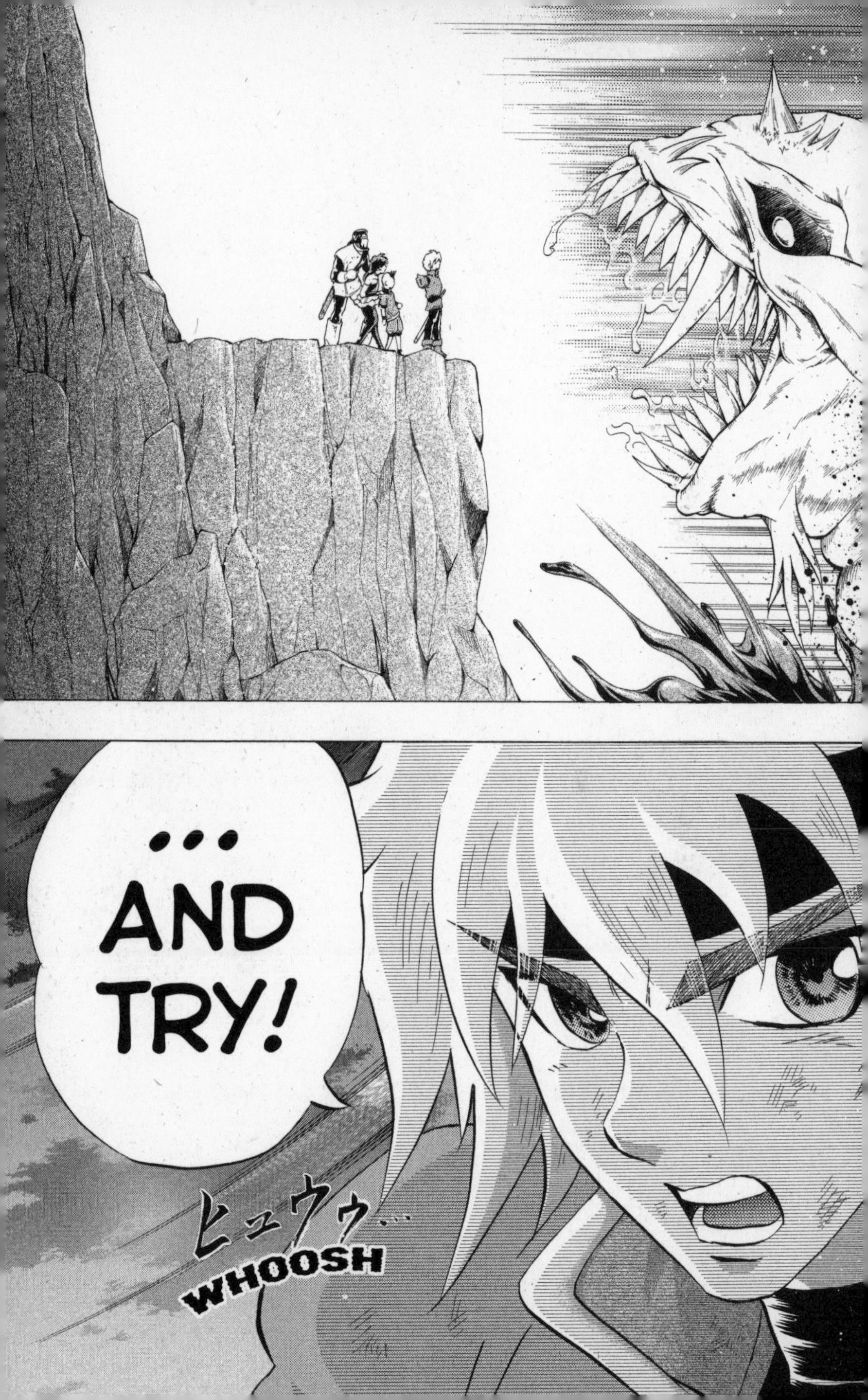

...AND TRY!
ヒュウゥ…
WHOOSH

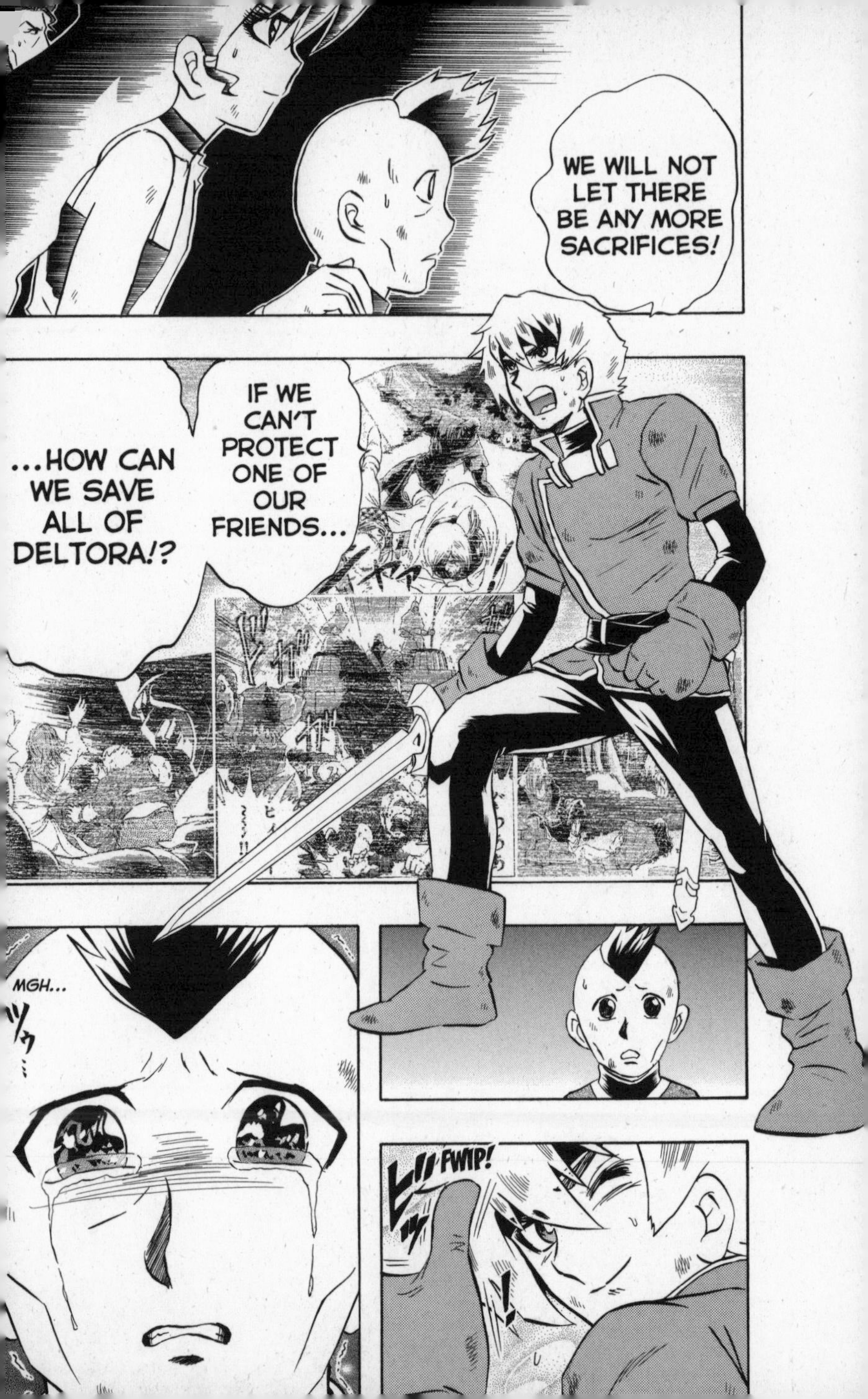
WE WILL NOT LET THERE BE ANY MORE SACRIFICES!
IF WE CAN'T PROTECT ONE OF OUR FRIENDS...
...HOW CAN WE SAVE ALL OF DELTORA!?
MGH...
FWIP!

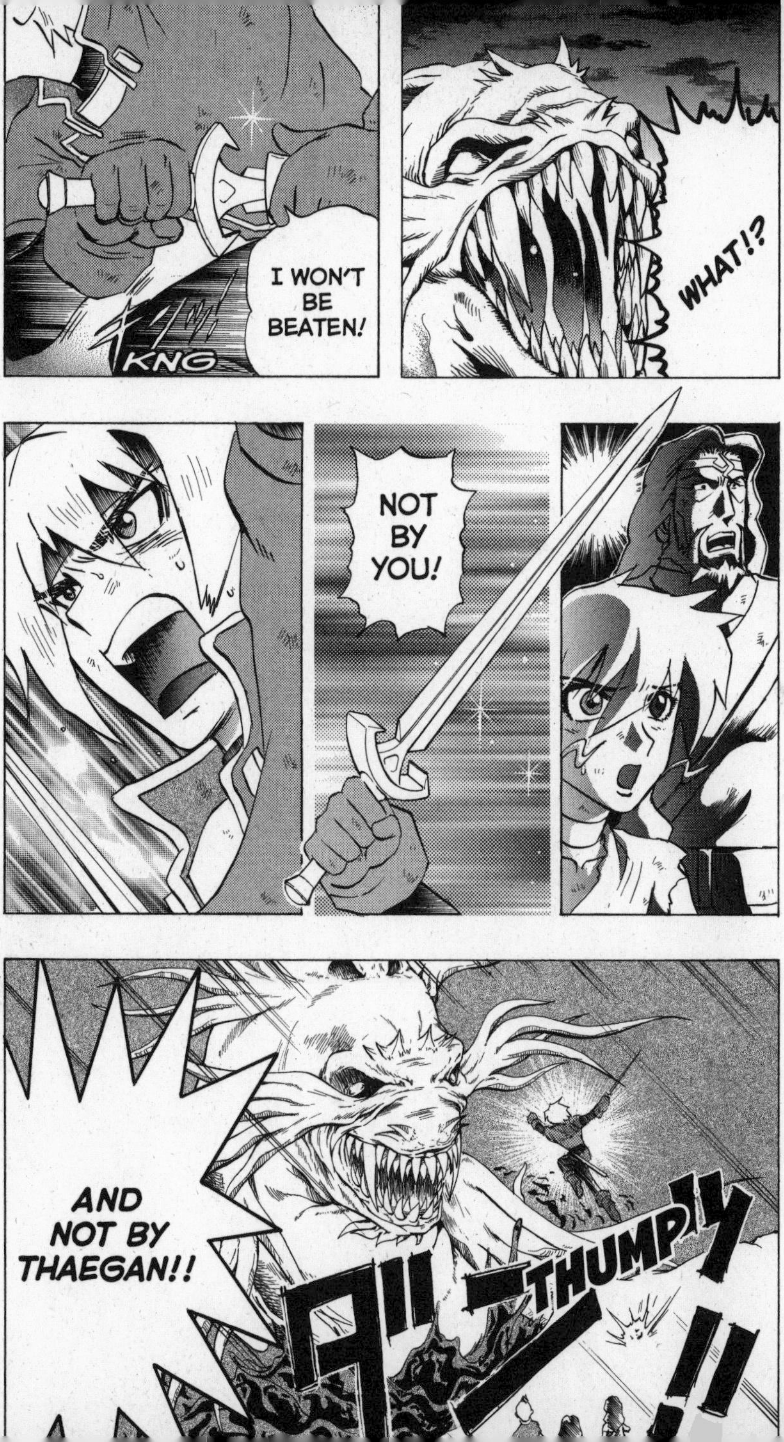
WHAT!?
I WON'T BE BEATEN!
KNG
NOT BY YOU!
AND NOT BY THAEGAN!!
THUMP

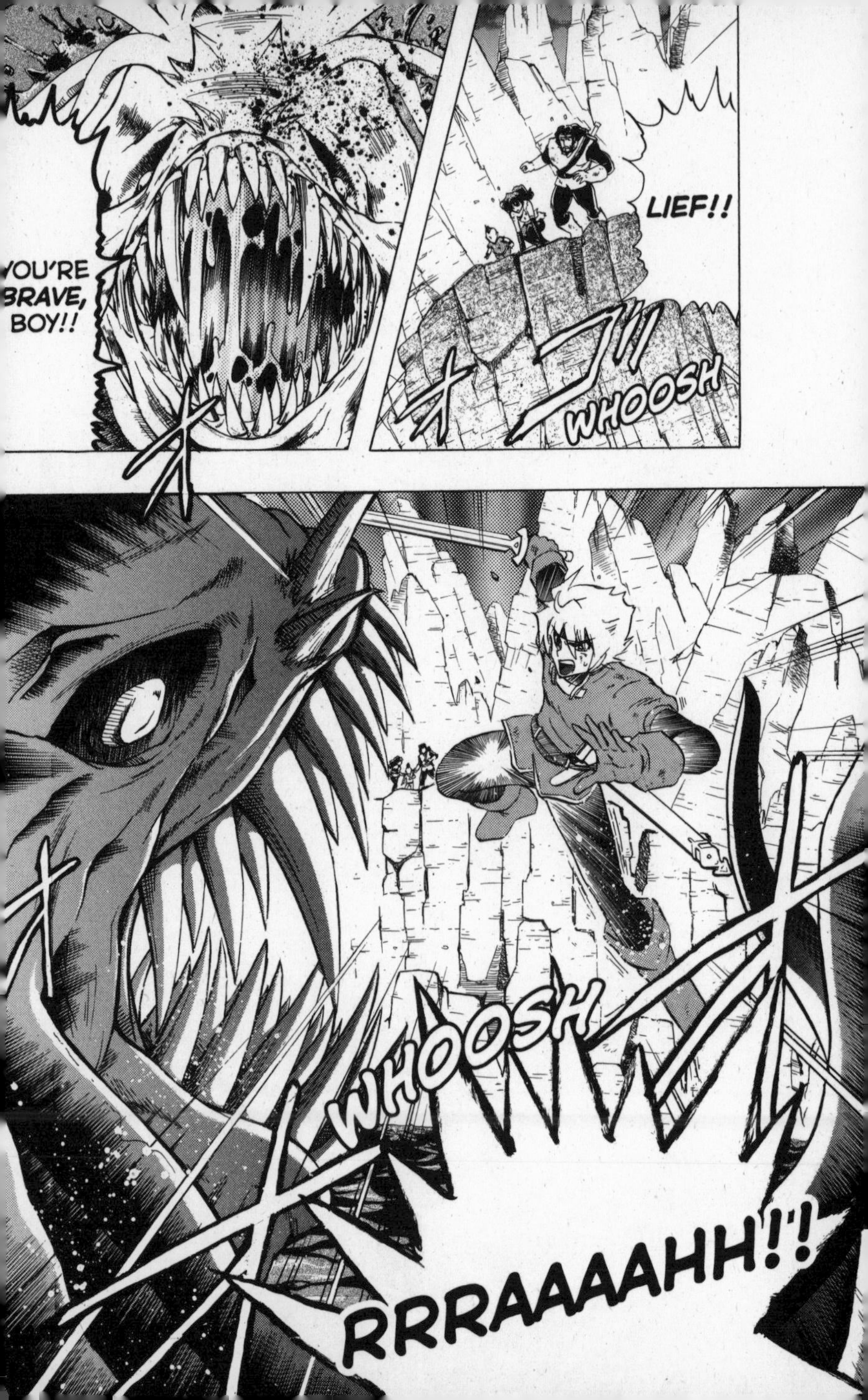
LIEF!!
WHOOSH
YOU'RE BRAVE, BOY!!
WHOOSH
RRRAAAAAHH!!

Chapter 19: The Sorceress Thaegan

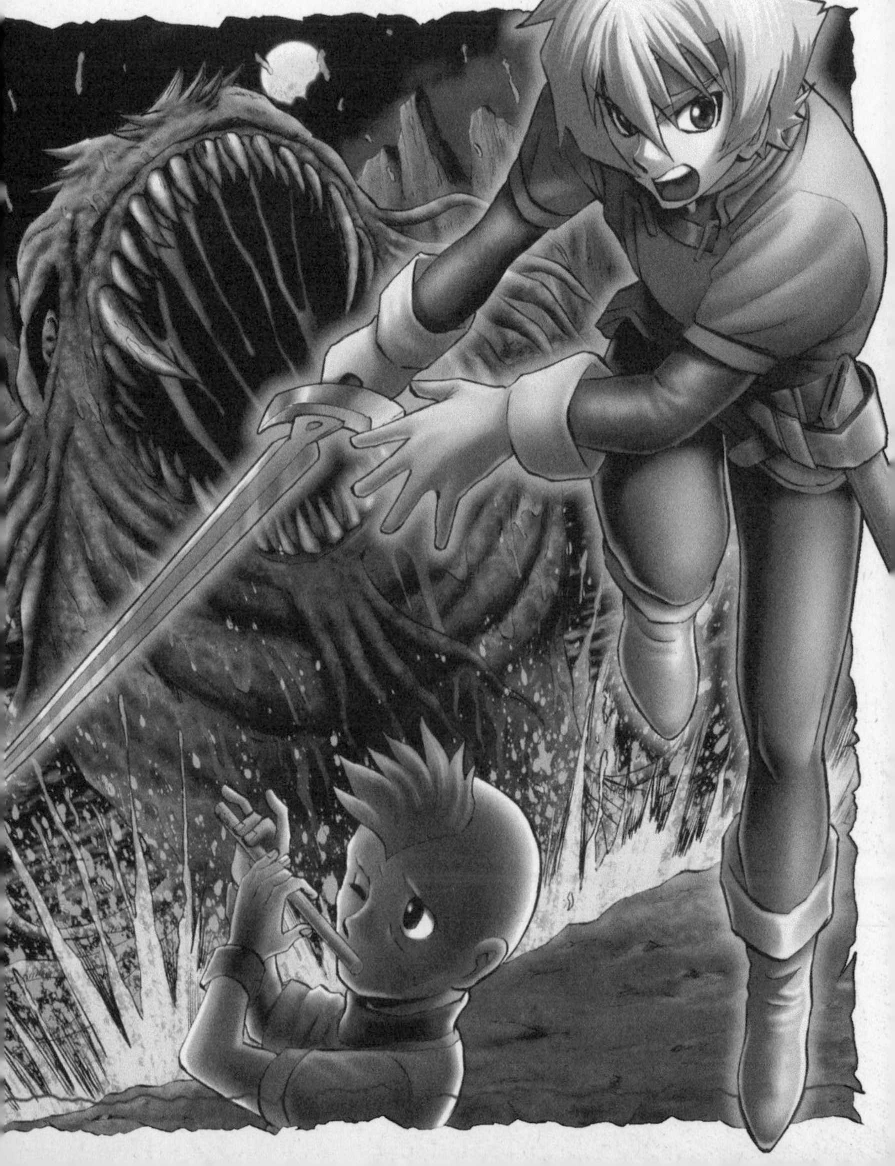

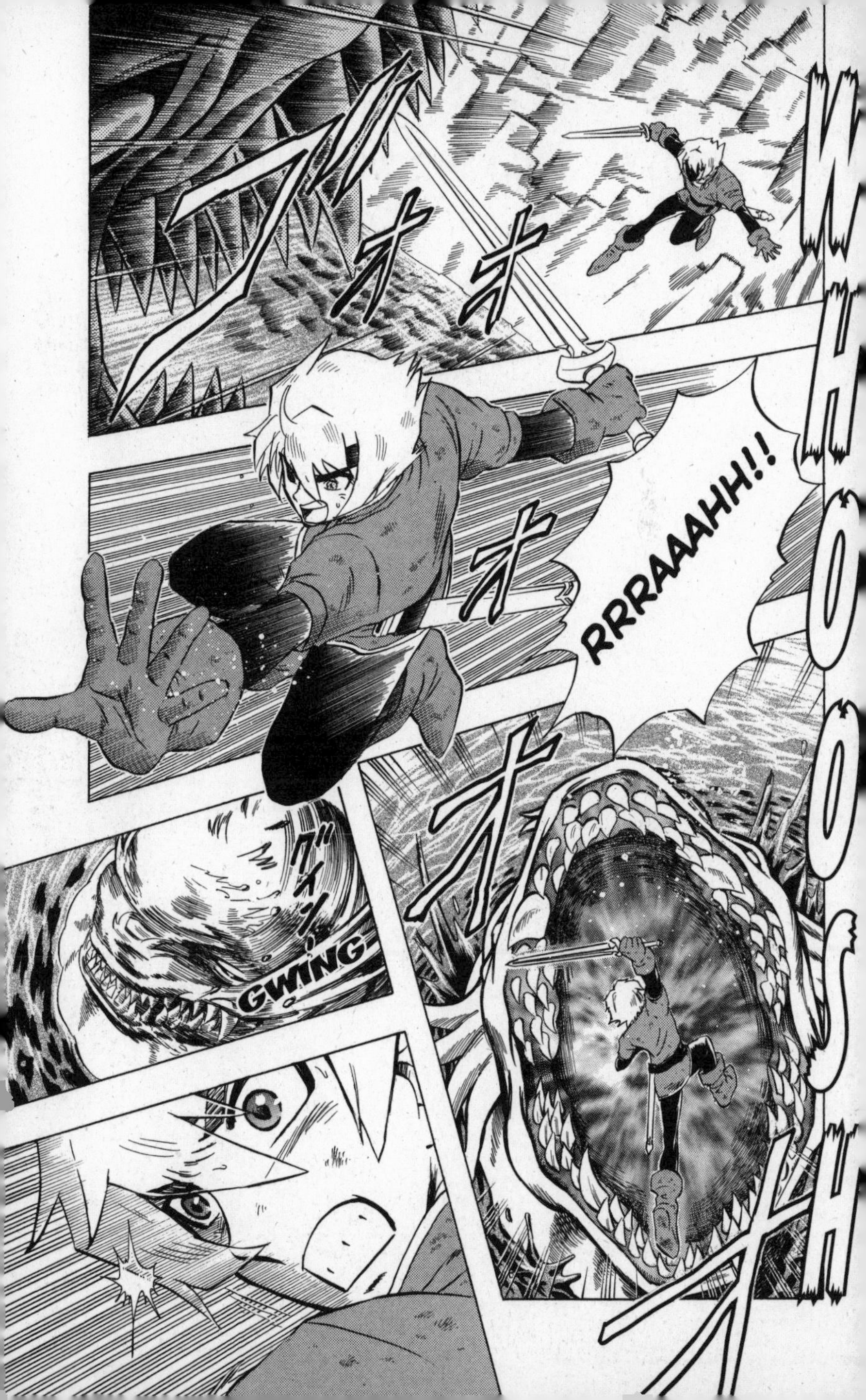

WHOOSH
RRRAAAHH!!
ブオオオオ
グイン
GWING

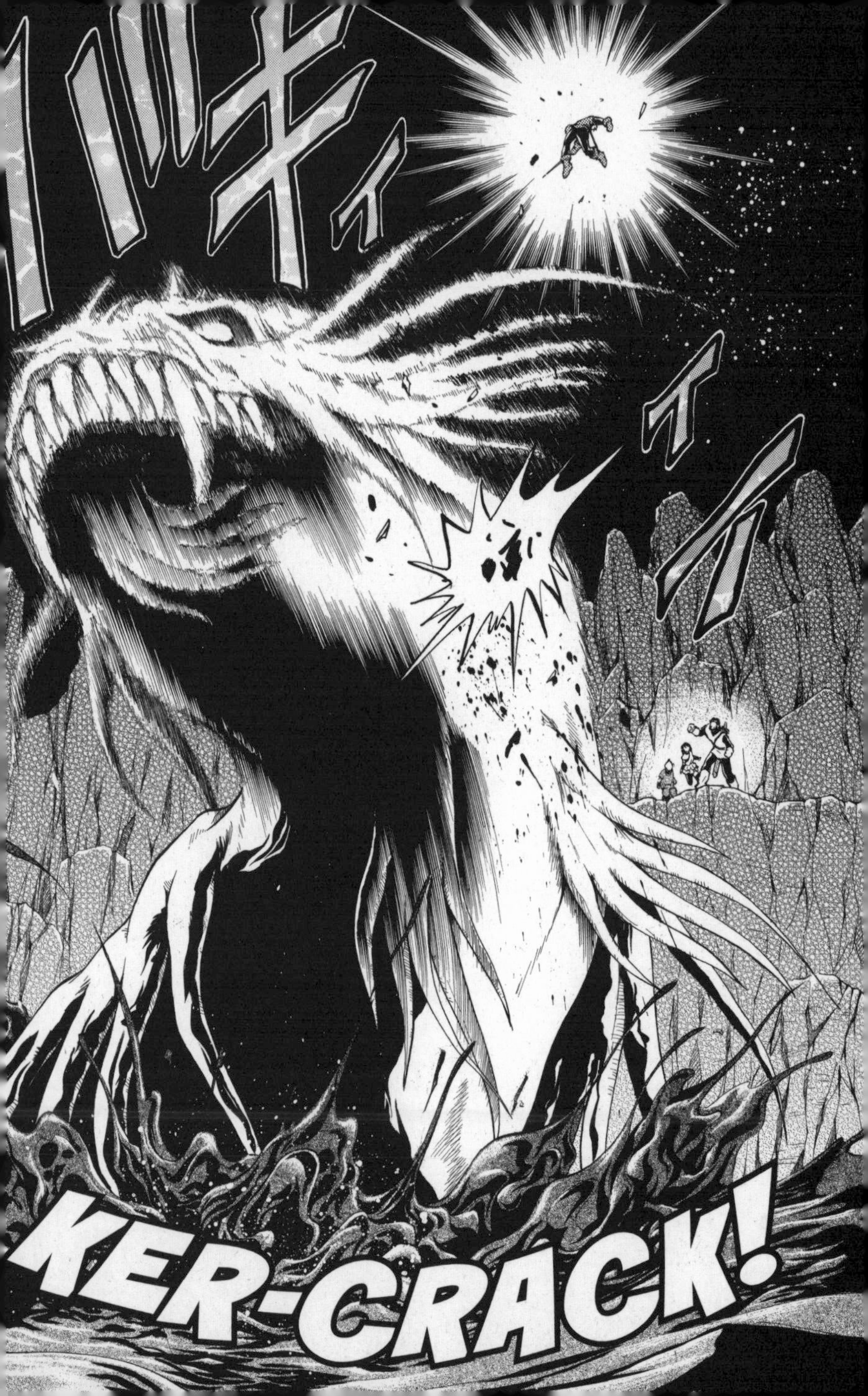
KER-CRACK!

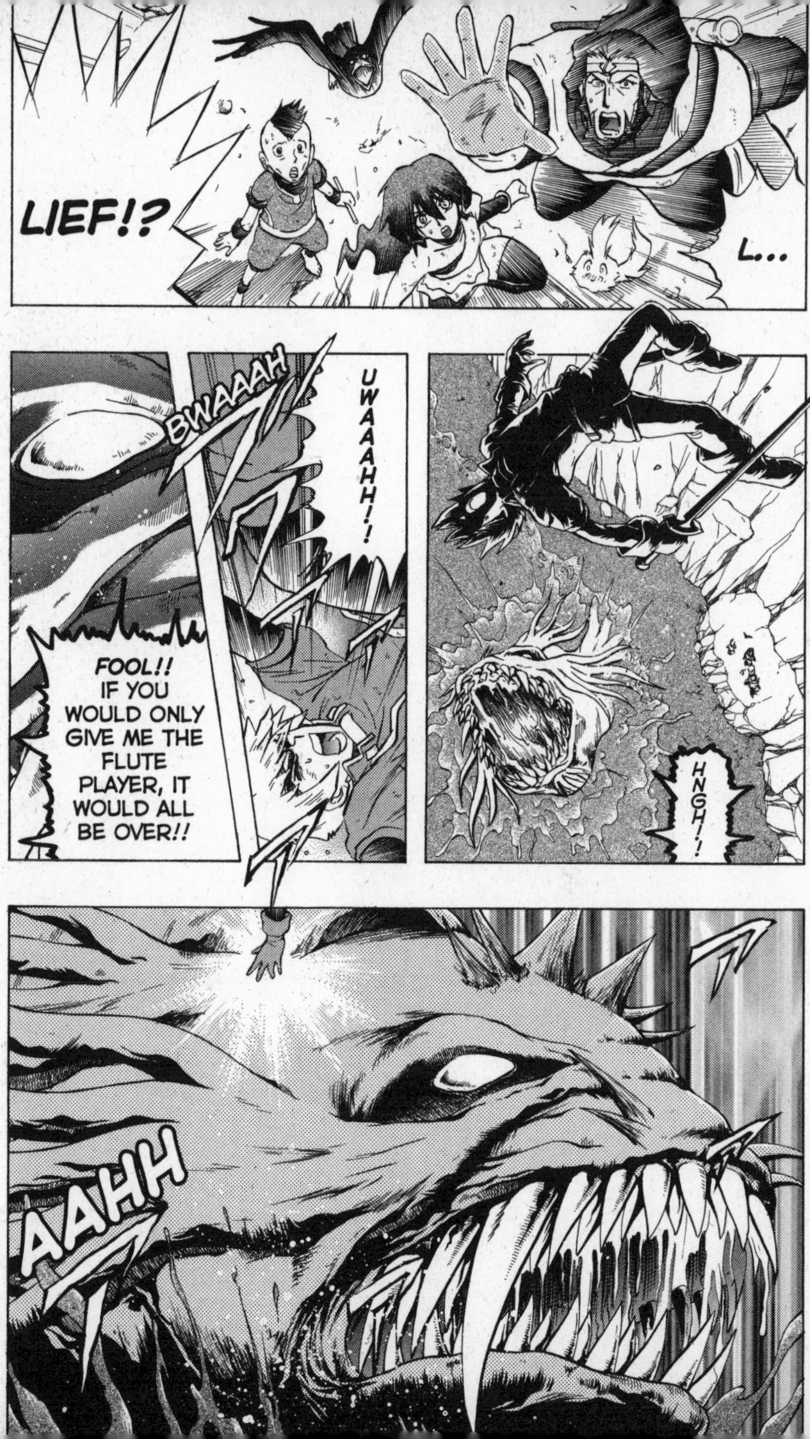
L...
LIEF!?
HNGH!!
UWAAAAHH!!
BWAAAH
FOOL!! IF YOU WOULD ONLY GIVE ME THE FLUTE PLAYER, IT WOULD ALL BE OVER!!
AAHH

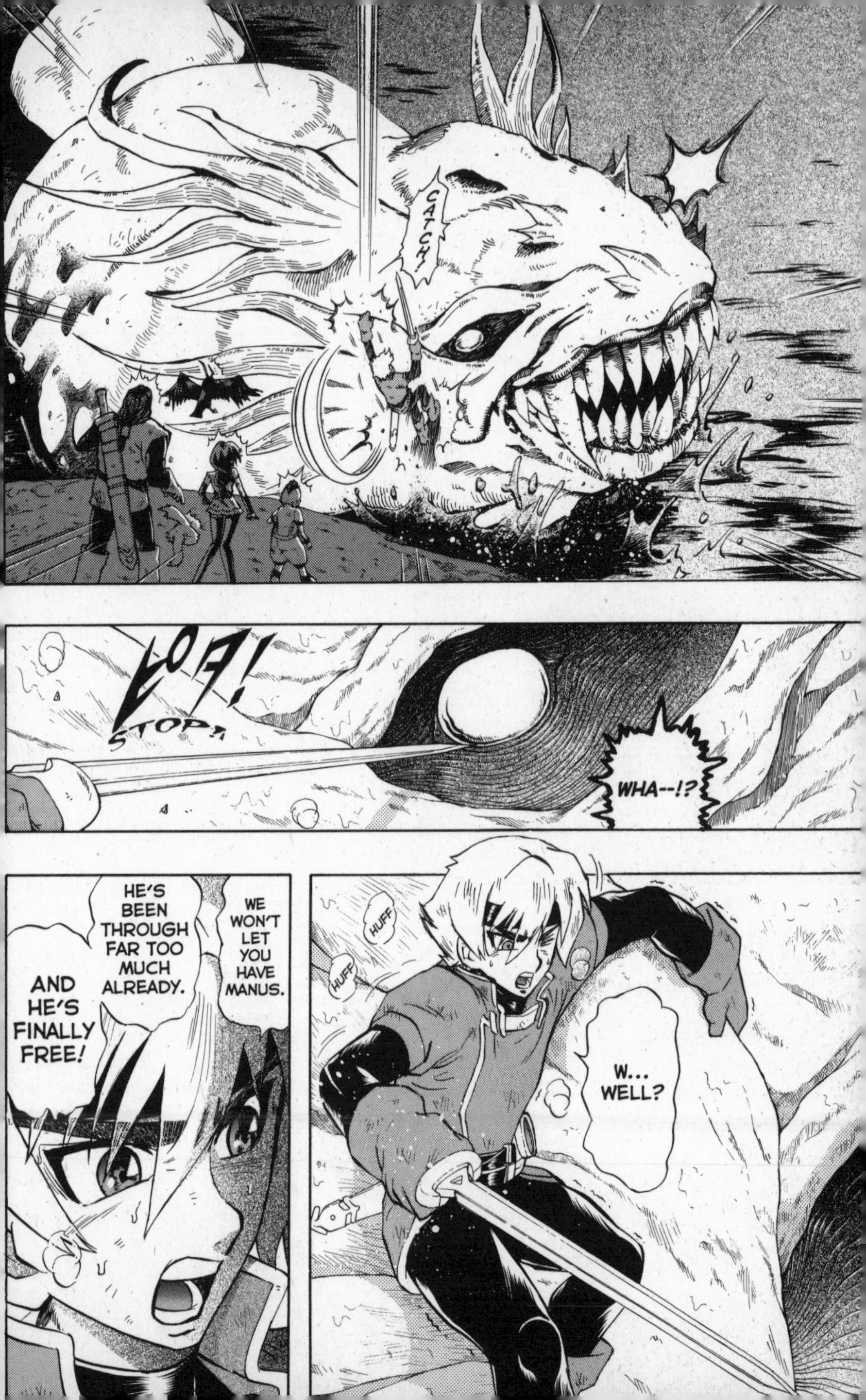
CATCH!
WHA--!?
STOP?!
HUFF
HUFF
HUFF
W... WELL?
WE WON'T LET YOU HAVE MANUS.
HE'S BEEN THROUGH FAR TOO MUCH ALREADY.
AND HE'S FINALLY FREE!

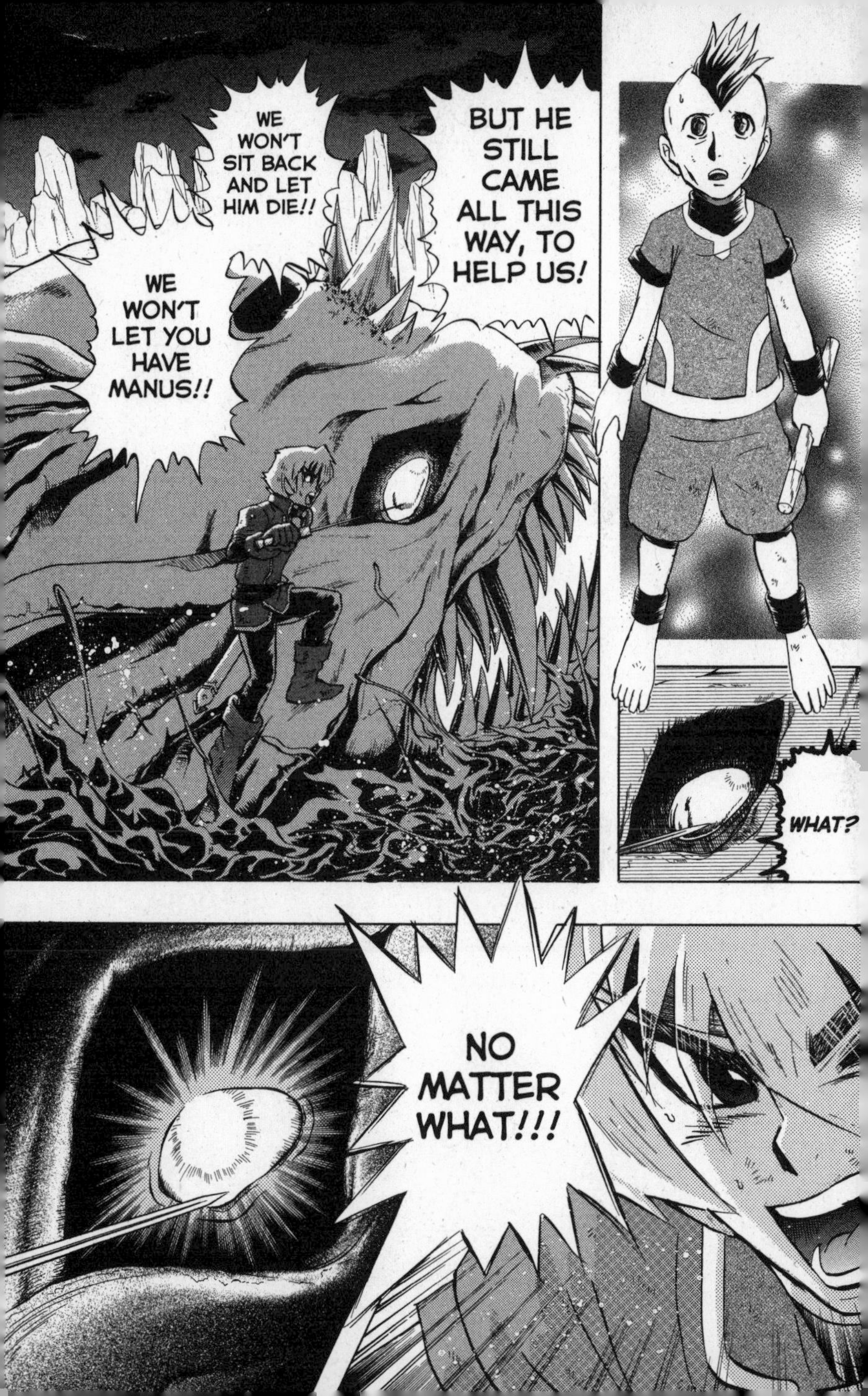
WHAT?
BUT HE STILL CAME ALL THIS WAY, TO HELP US!
WE WON'T SIT BACK AND LET HIM DIE!!
WE WON'T LET YOU HAVE MANUS!!
NO MATTER WHAT!!!

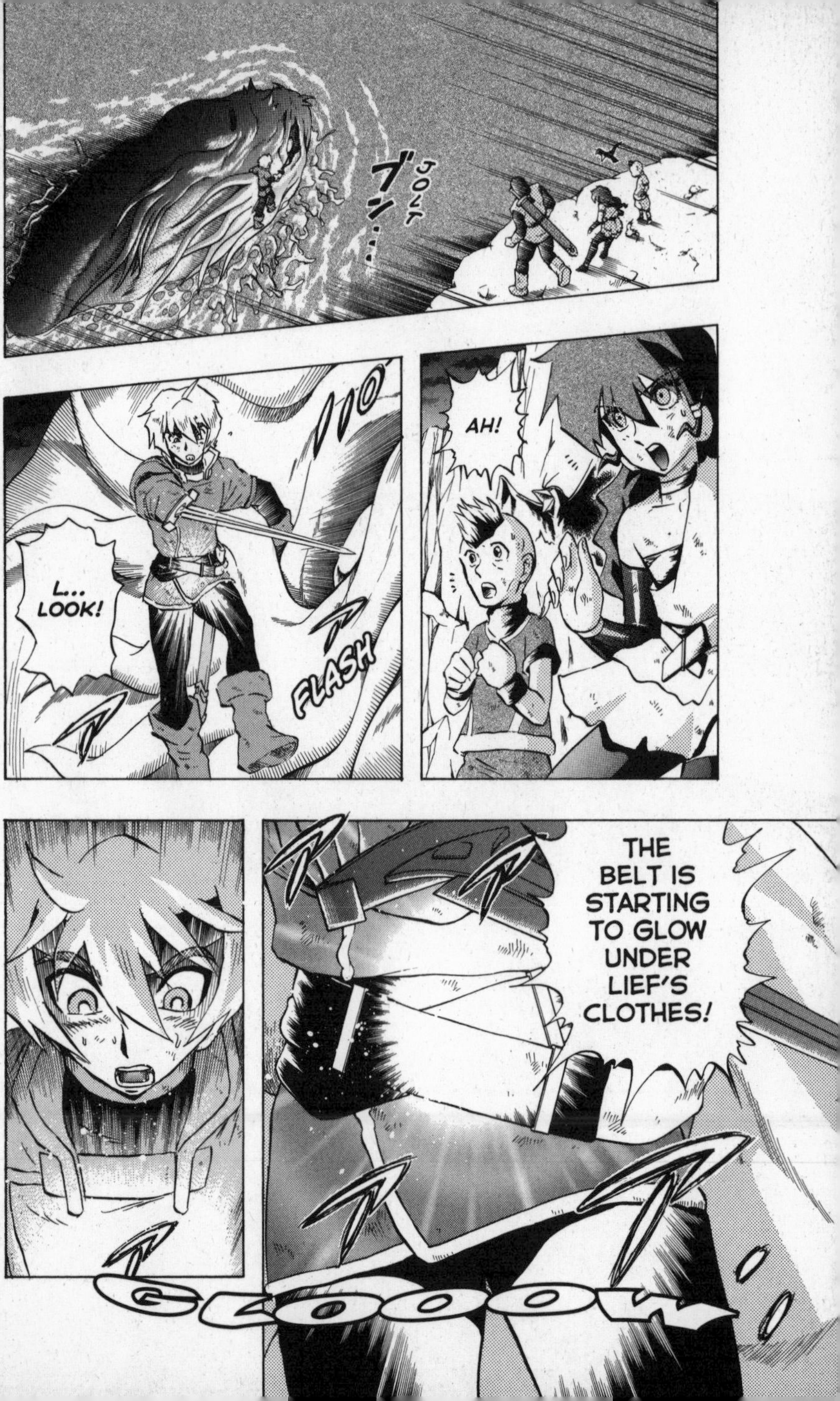
ブン…
JOLT
AH!
L... LOOK!
FLASH
THE BELT IS STARTING TO GLOW UNDER LIEF'S CLOTHES!
GLOOOW

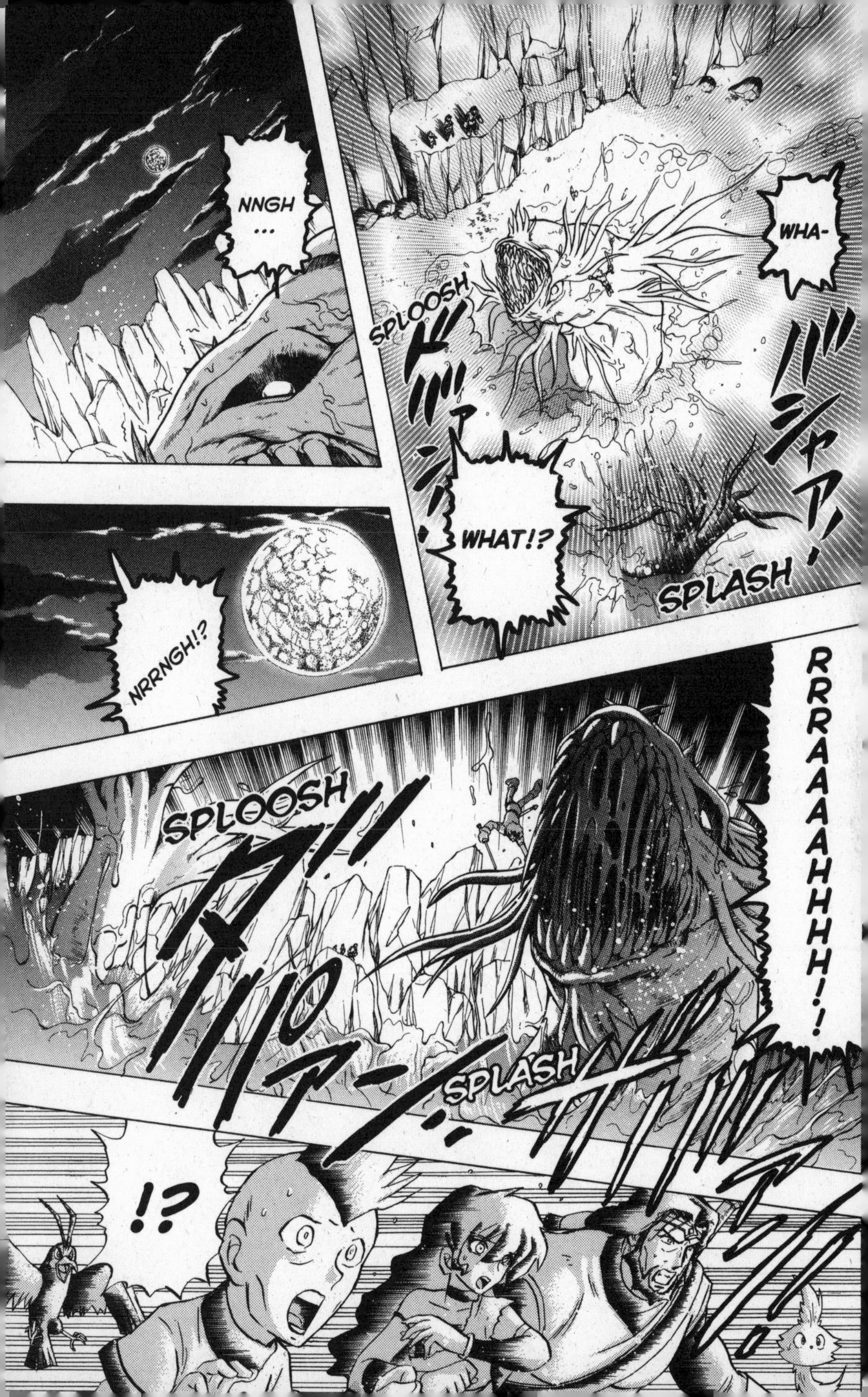
WHA-
SPLOOSH
WHAT!?
SPLASH
NNGH ...
NRRNGH!?
RRRAAAAHHHHH!!
SPLOOSH
SPLASH
!?

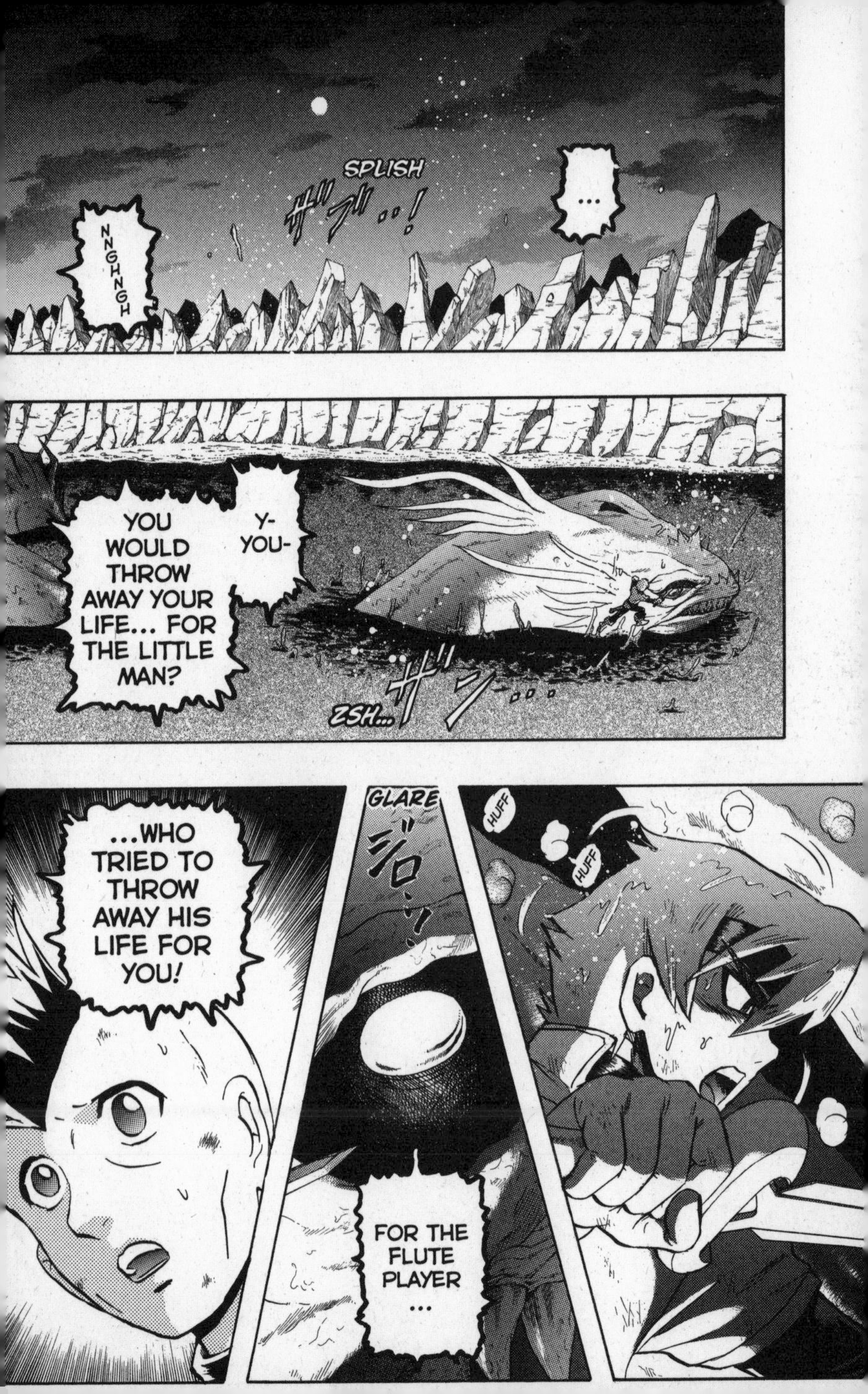
...
SPLISH
NNGHNGH
Y-YOU-
YOU WOULD THROW AWAY YOUR LIFE... FOR THE LITTLE MAN?
ZSH...
HUFF
HUFF
GLARE
FOR THE FLUTE PLAYER ...
...WHO TRIED TO THROW AWAY HIS LIFE FOR YOU!

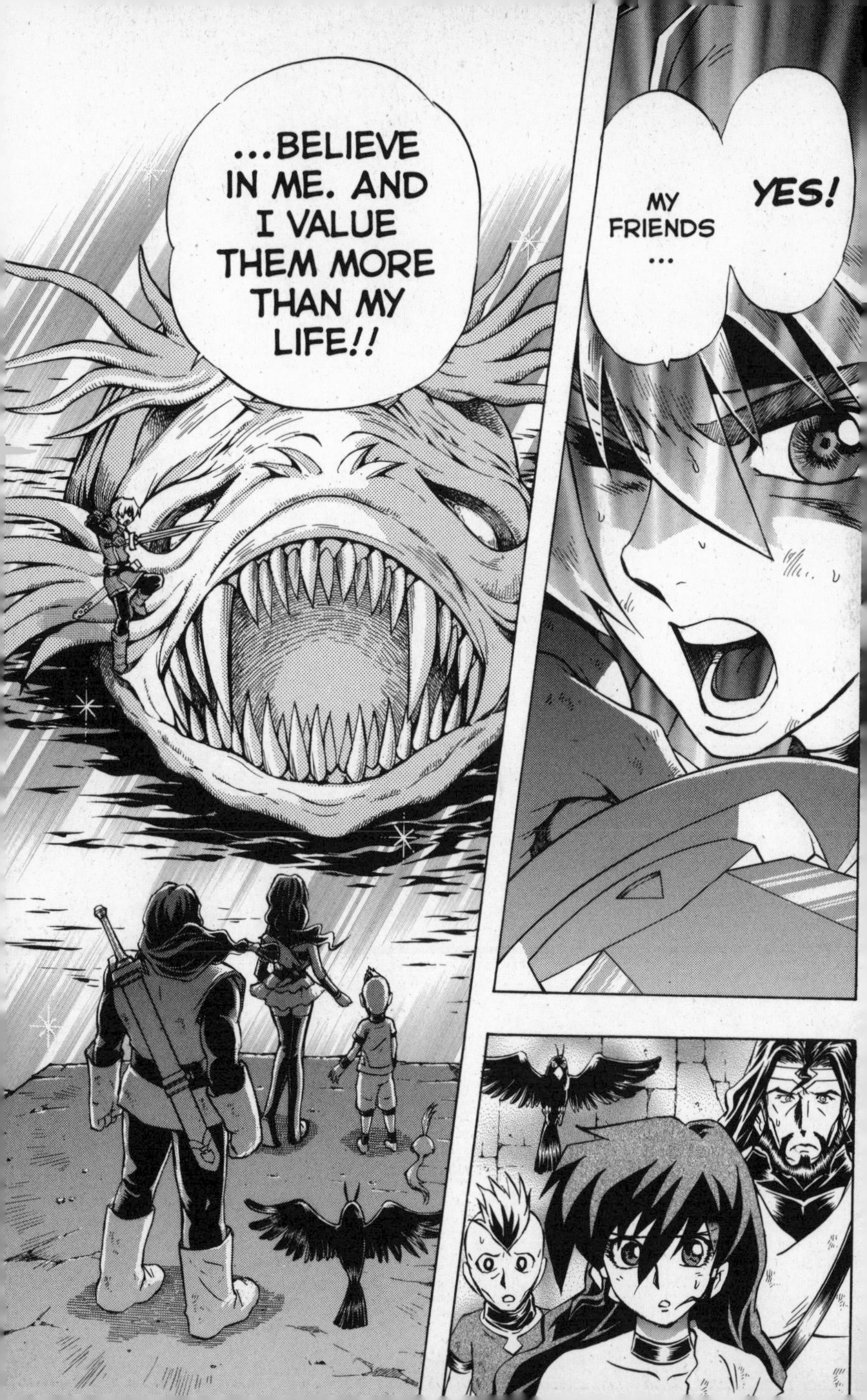
YES!
MY FRIENDS ...
...BELIEVE IN ME. AND I VALUE THEM MORE THAN MY LIFE!!

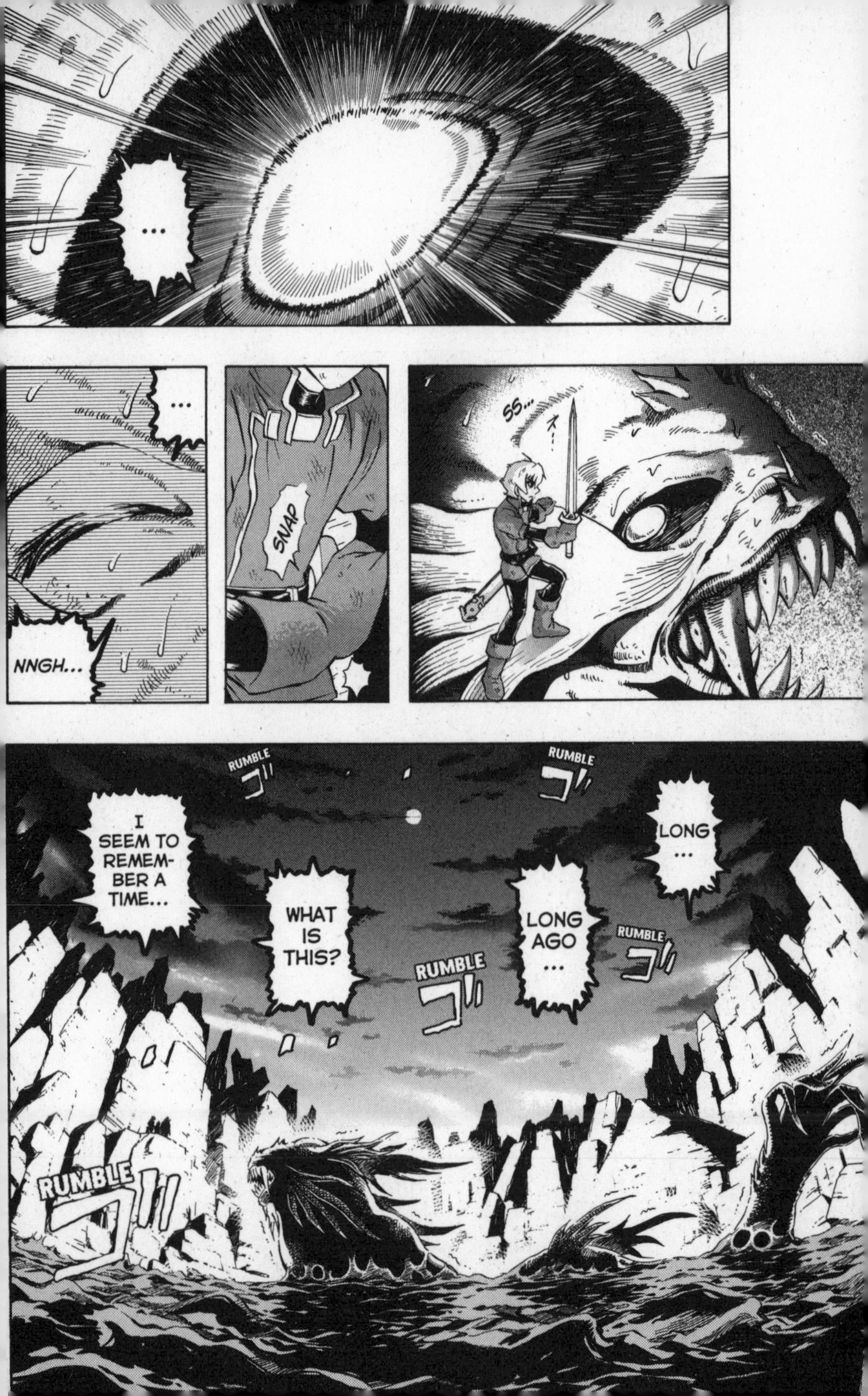
...
SS...
SNAP
...
NNGH...
RUMBLE
LONG ...
RUMBLE
LONG AGO ...
RUMBLE
WHAT IS THIS?
RUMBLE
I SEEM TO REMEMBER A TIME...
RUMBLE

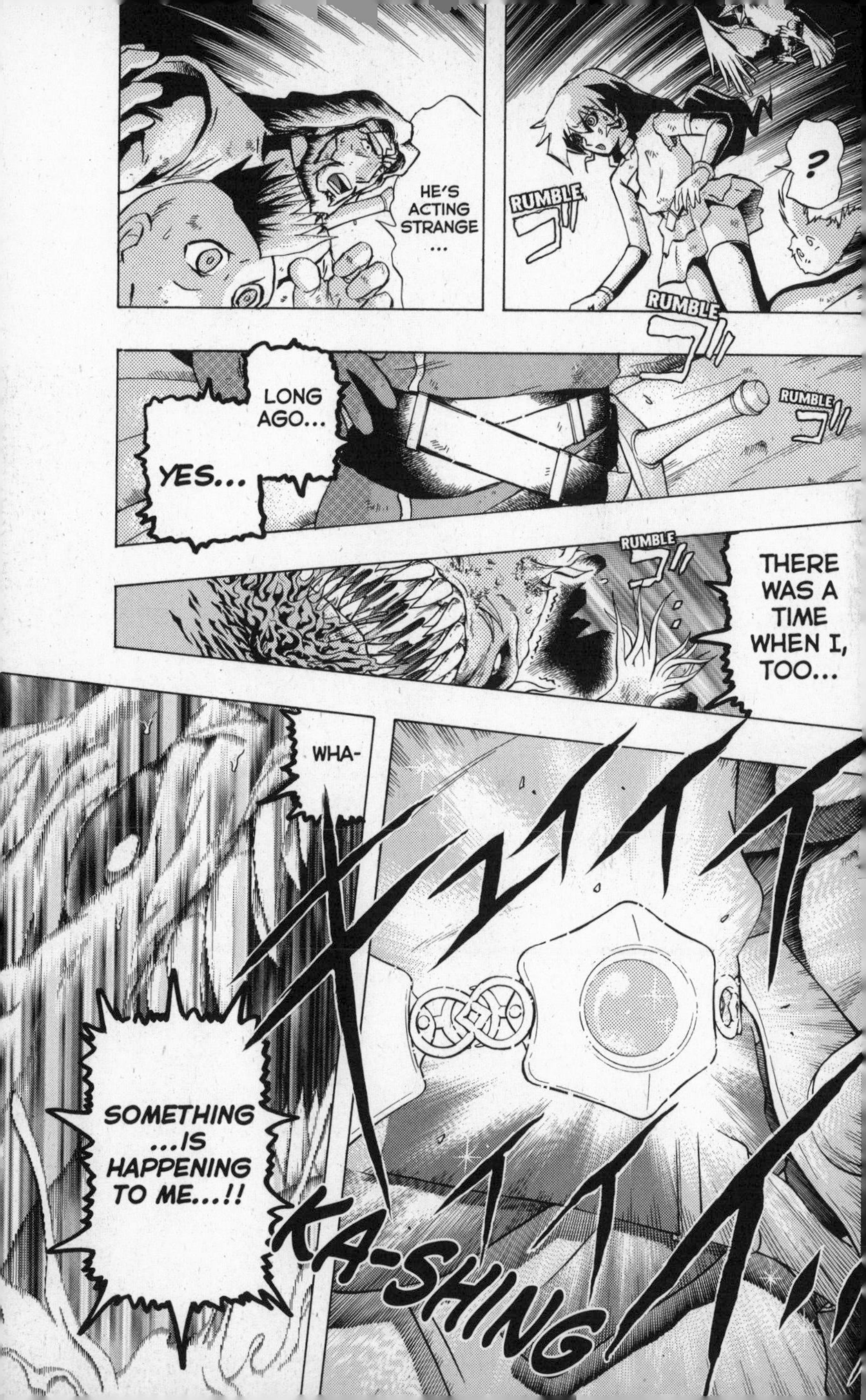
?
RUMBLE
RUMBLE
HE'S ACTING STRANGE ...
RUMBLE
LONG AGO...
YES...
RUMBLE
THERE WAS A TIME WHEN I, TOO...
KA-SHING
WHA-
SOMETHING ...IS HAPPENING TO ME...!!

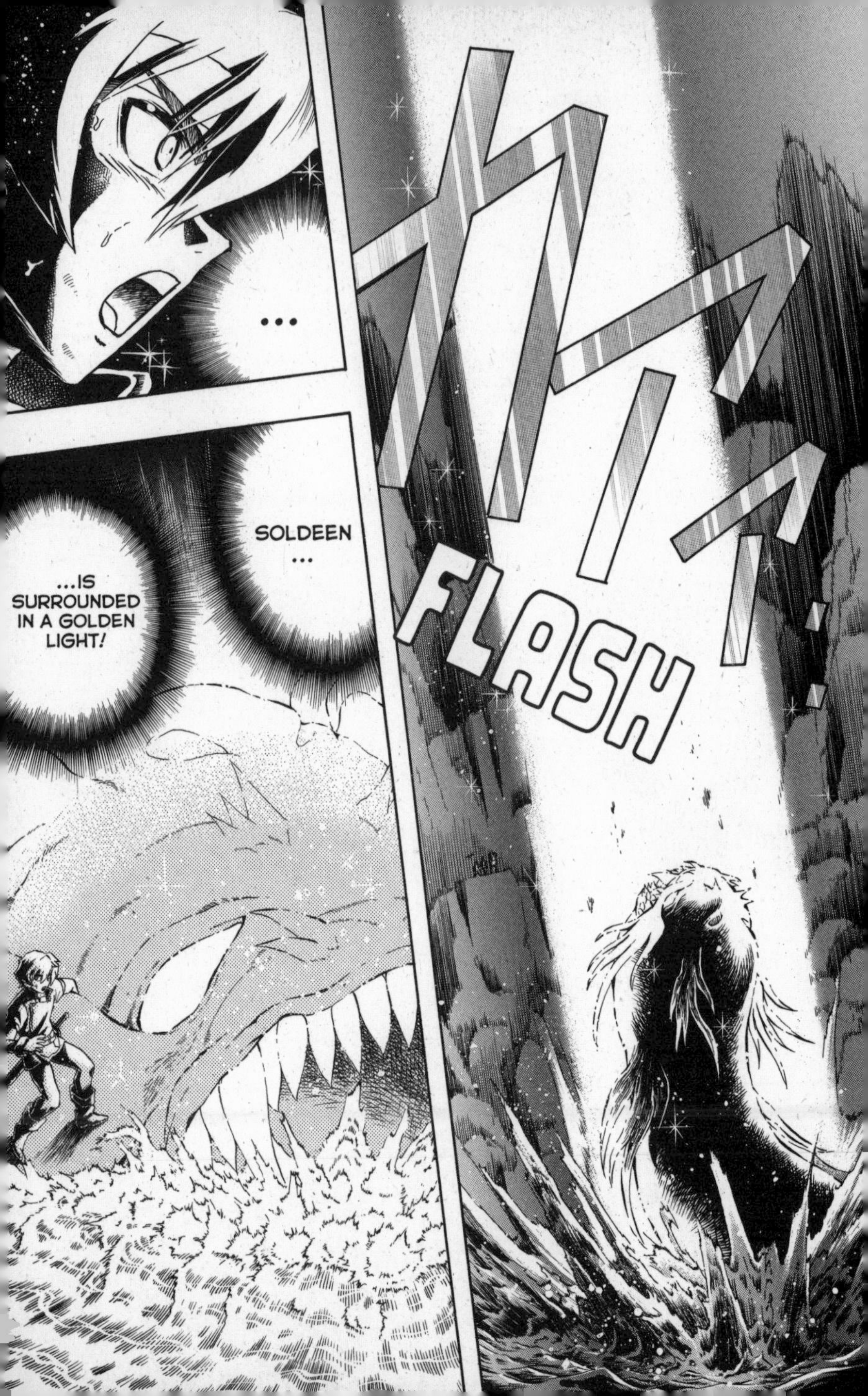
FLASH
...
SOLDEEN ...
...IS SURROUNDED IN A GOLDEN LIGHT!

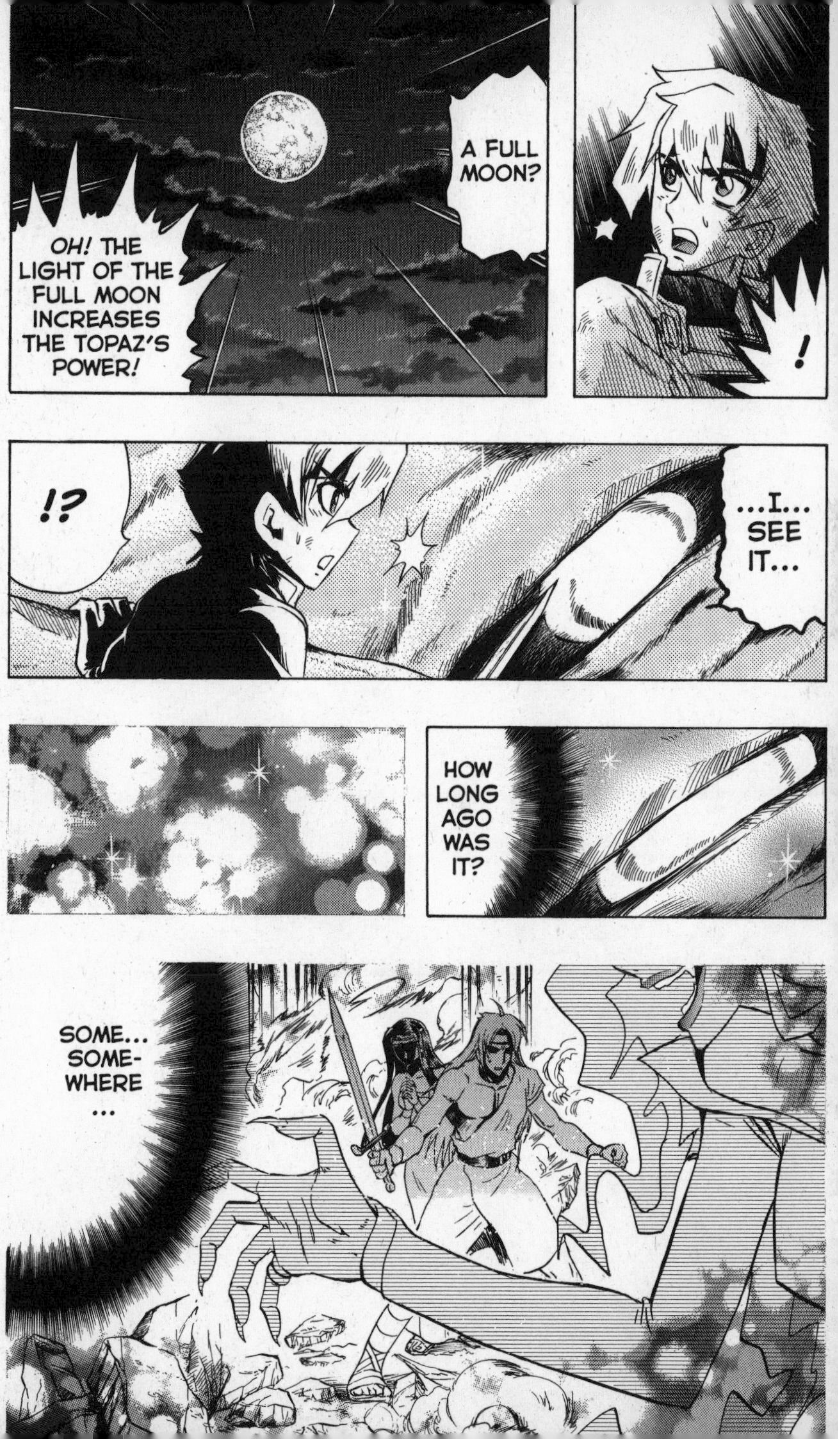
!
A FULL MOON?
OH! THE LIGHT OF THE FULL MOON INCREASES THE TOPAZ'S POWER!
...I... SEE IT...
!?
HOW LONG AGO WAS IT?
SOME... SOME-WHERE ...

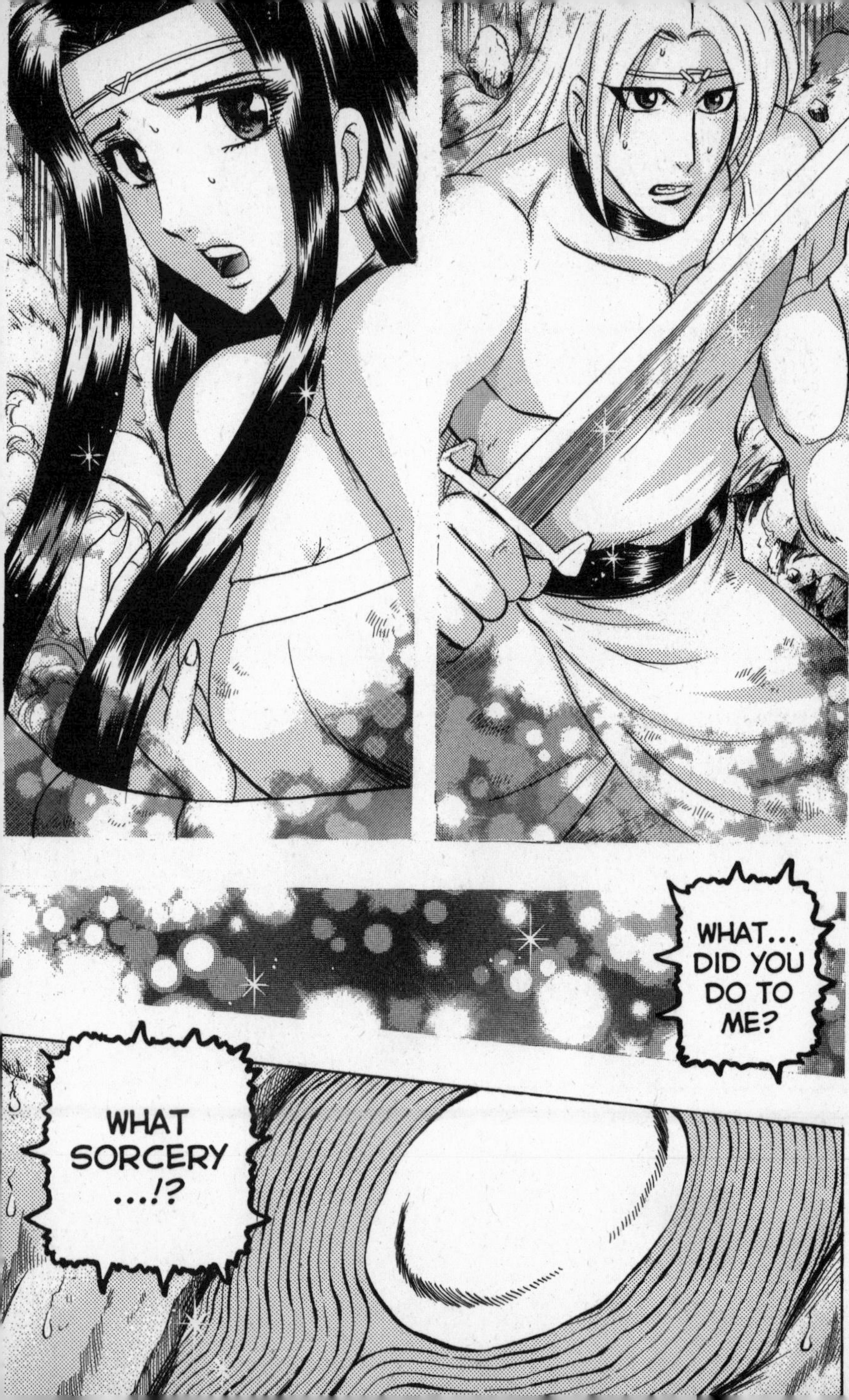
WHAT... DID YOU DO TO ME?
WHAT SORCERY ...!?

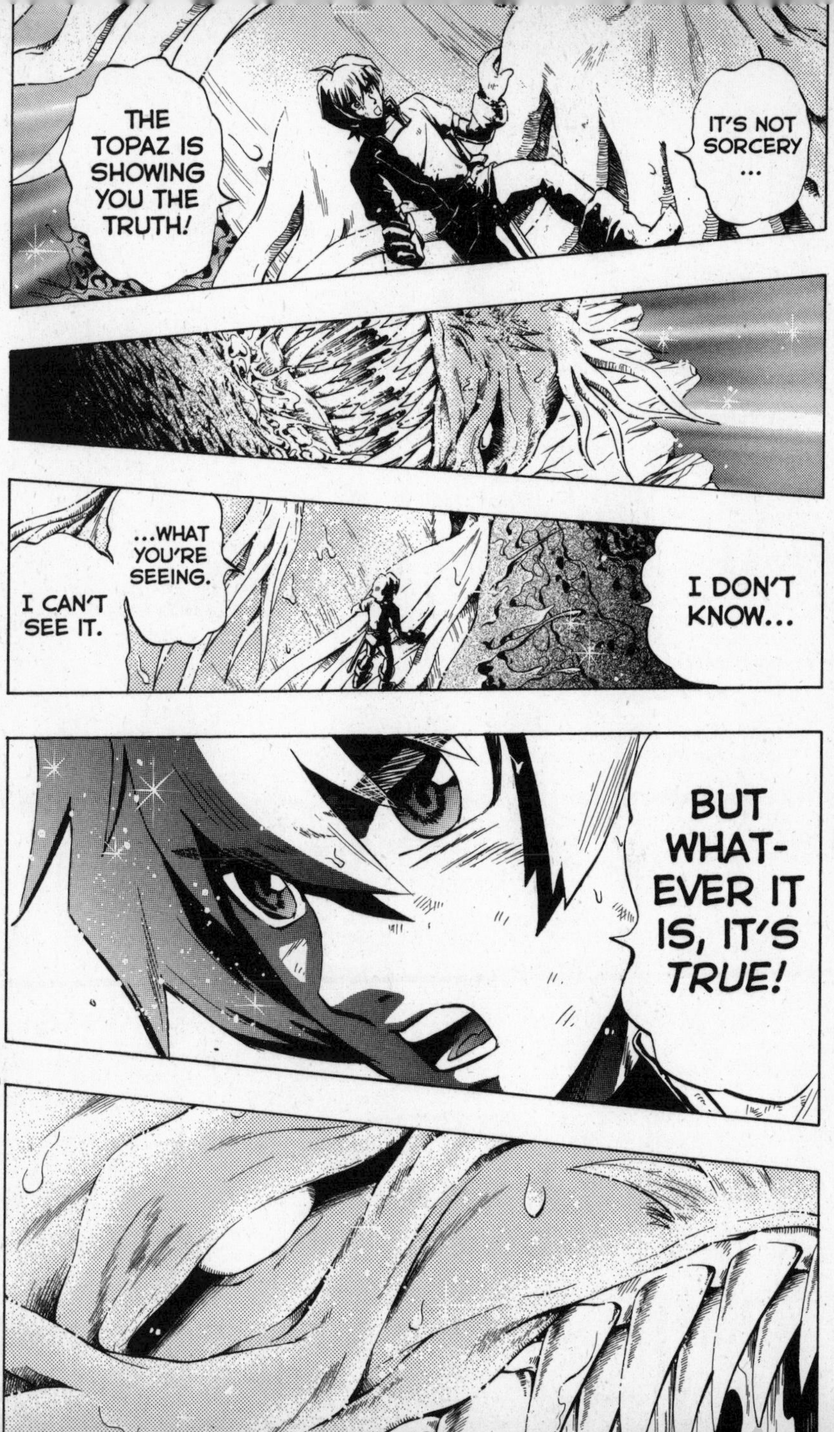
IT'S NOT SORCERY ...
THE TOPAZ IS SHOWING YOU THE TRUTH!
I DON'T KNOW...
...WHAT YOU'RE SEEING.
I CAN'T SEE IT.
BUT WHAT-EVER IT IS, IT'S *TRUE!*

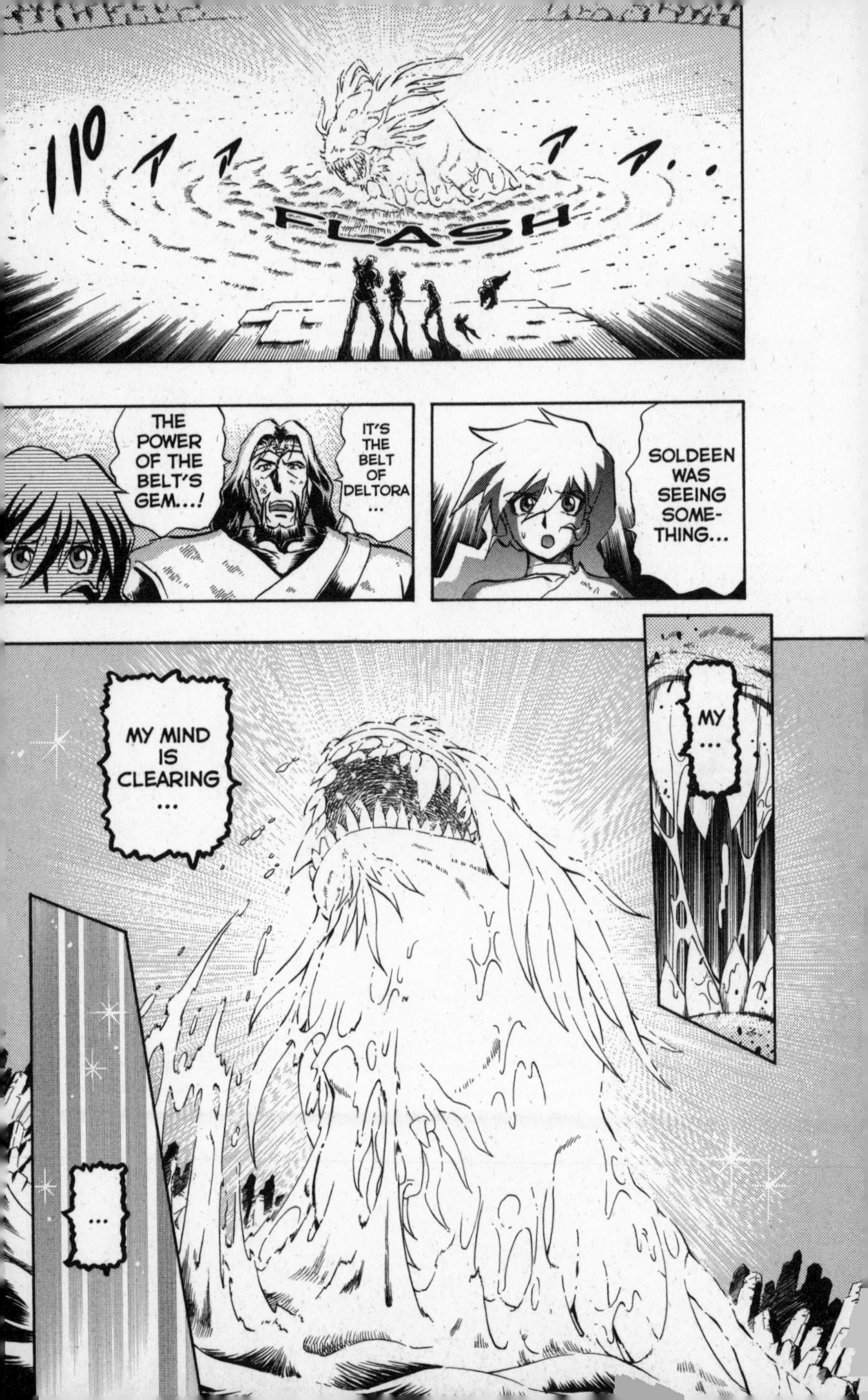

パアア アア...
FLASH
SOLDEEN WAS SEEING SOME-THING...
IT'S THE BELT OF DELTORA ...
THE POWER OF THE BELT'S GEM...!
MY ...
MY MIND IS CLEARING ...
...

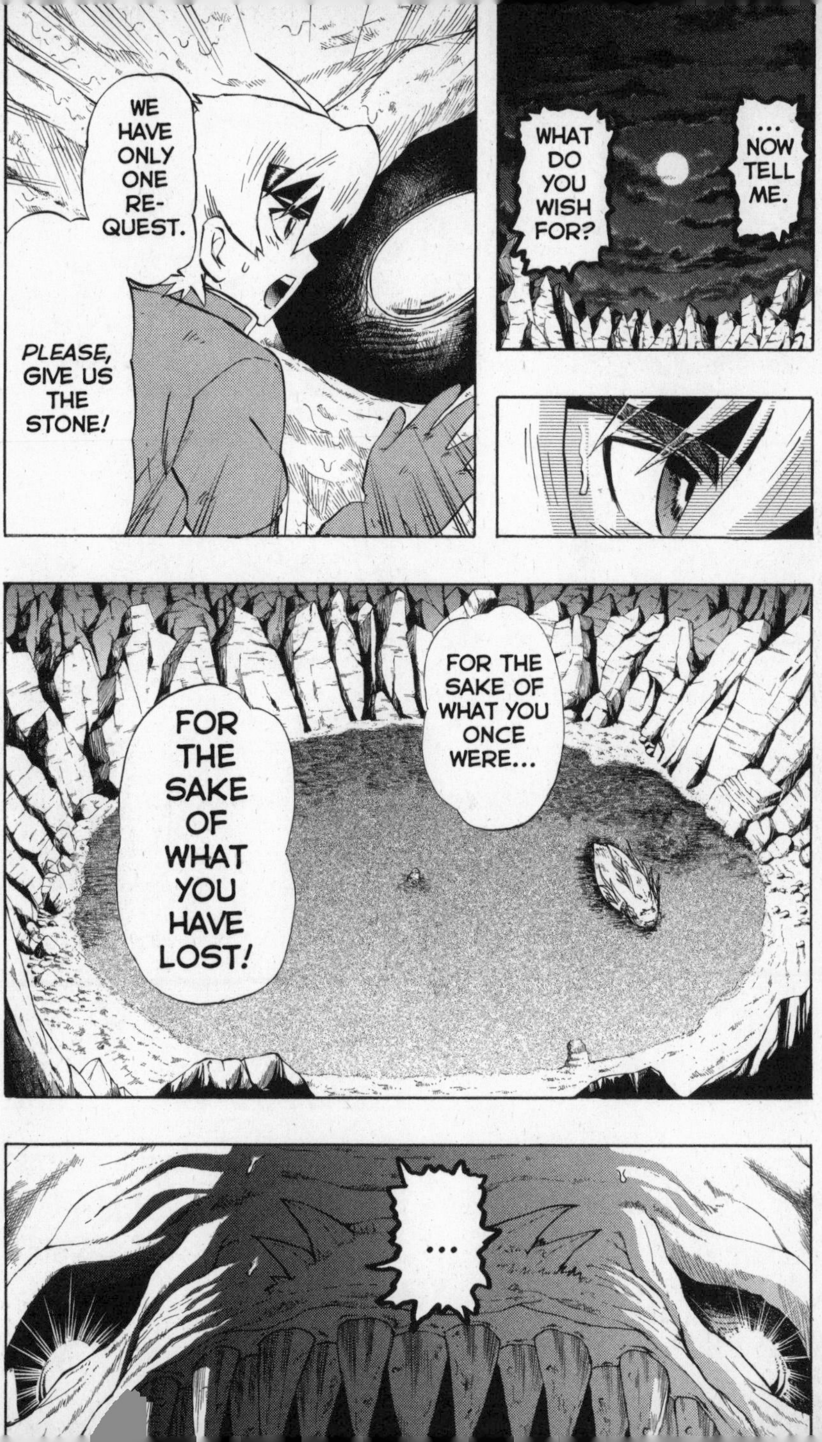
...NOW TELL ME.
WHAT DO YOU WISH FOR?
WE HAVE ONLY ONE REQUEST.
PLEASE, GIVE US THE STONE!
FOR THE SAKE OF WHAT YOU ONCE WERE...
FOR THE SAKE OF WHAT YOU HAVE LOST!
...

VERY
WELL.

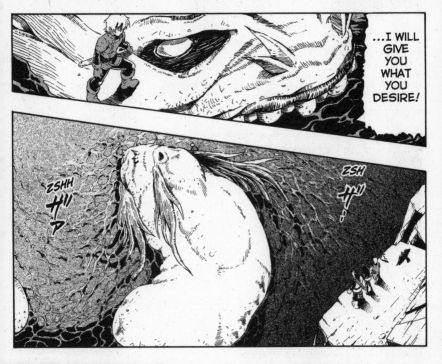

...I WILL
GIVE
YOU
WHAT
YOU
DESIRE!

ZSHH

ZSH

COME!

ZSH

ZSH

ZSH

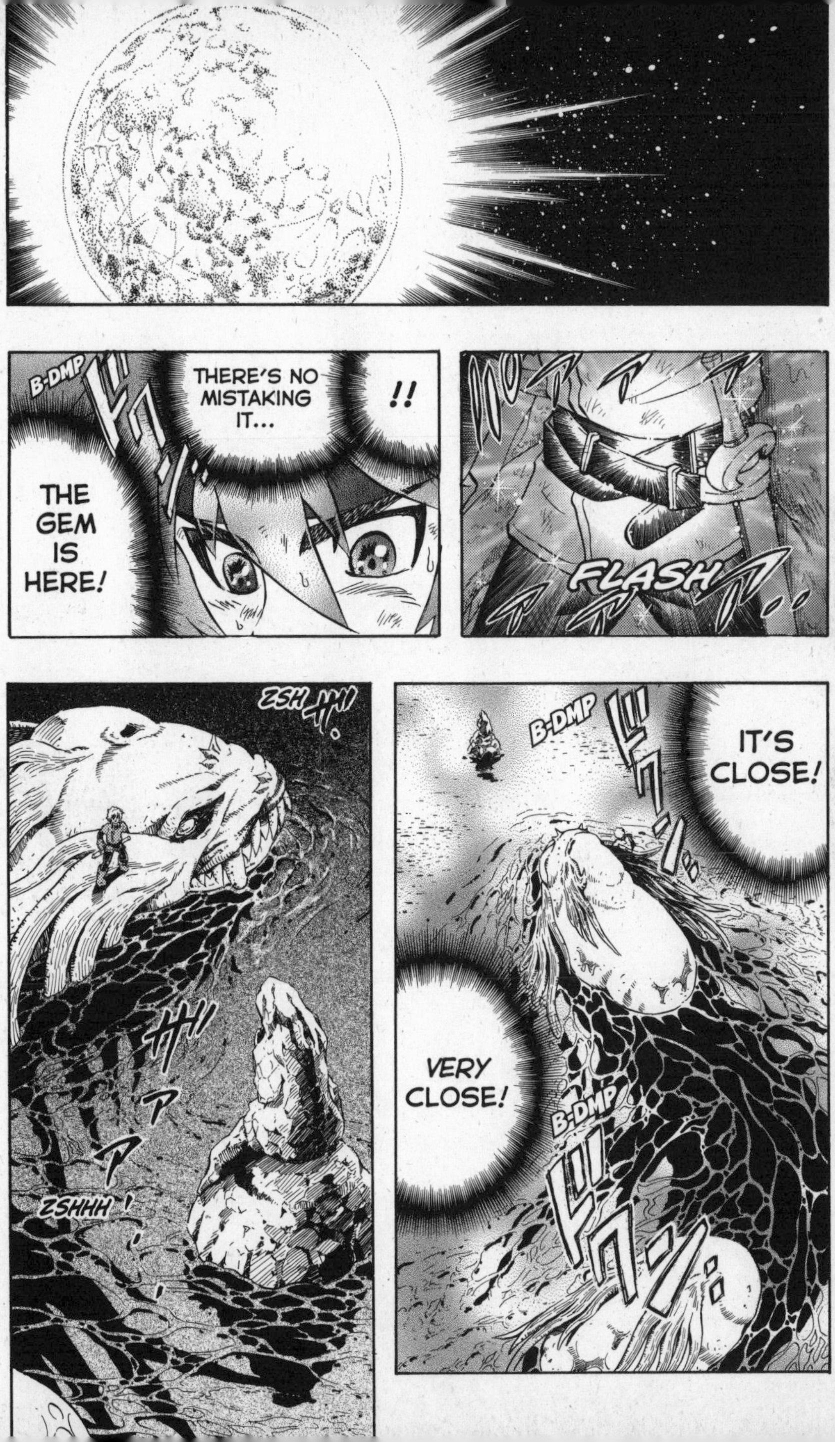
FLASH
!!
THERE'S NO MISTAKING IT...
B-DMP
THE GEM IS HERE!
B-DMP
IT'S CLOSE!
VERY CLOSE!
B-DMP
ZSH
ZSHHH!

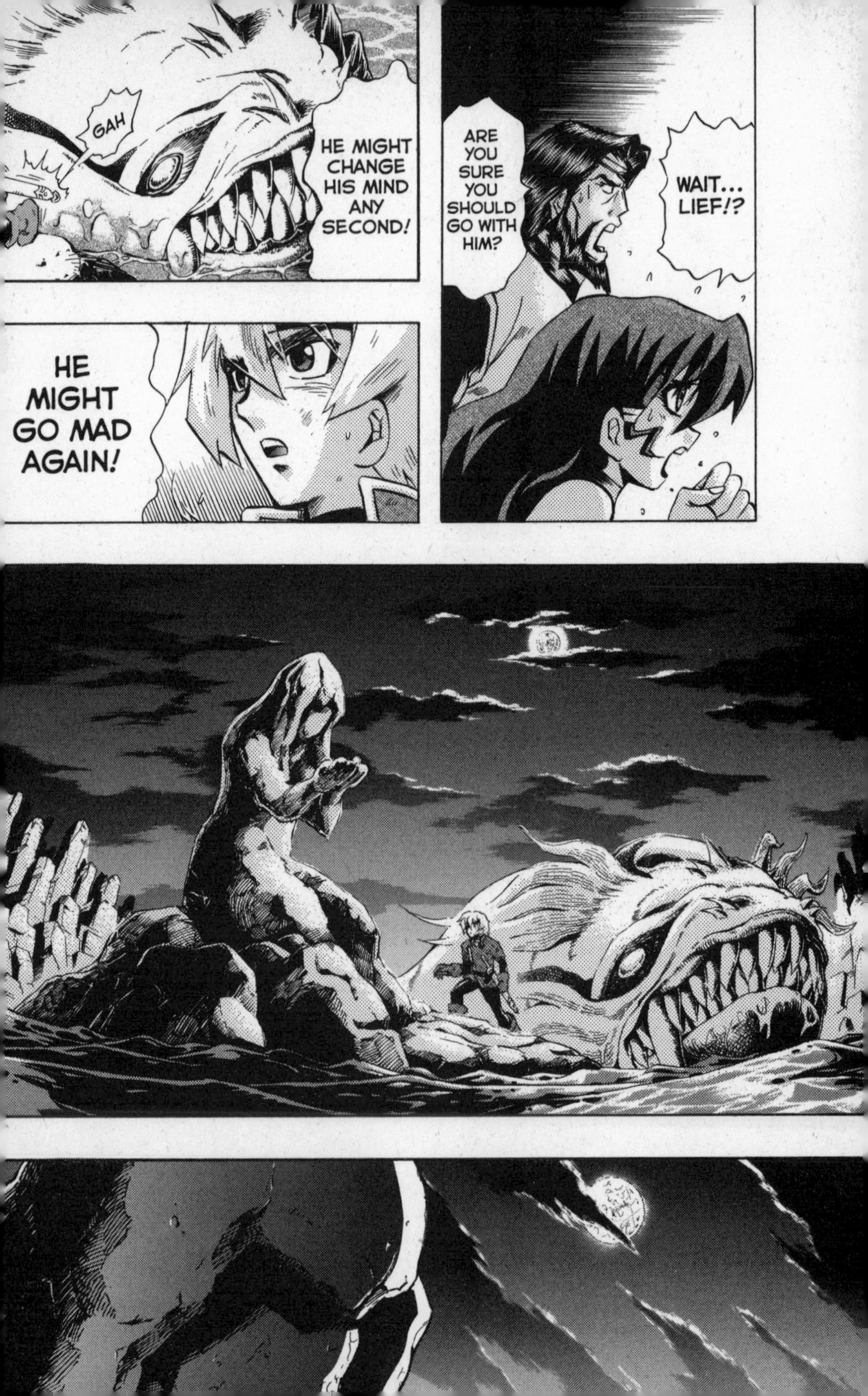
WAIT... LIEF!?
ARE YOU SURE YOU SHOULD GO WITH HIM?
HE MIGHT CHANGE HIS MIND ANY SECOND!
GAH
HE MIGHT GO MAD AGAIN!

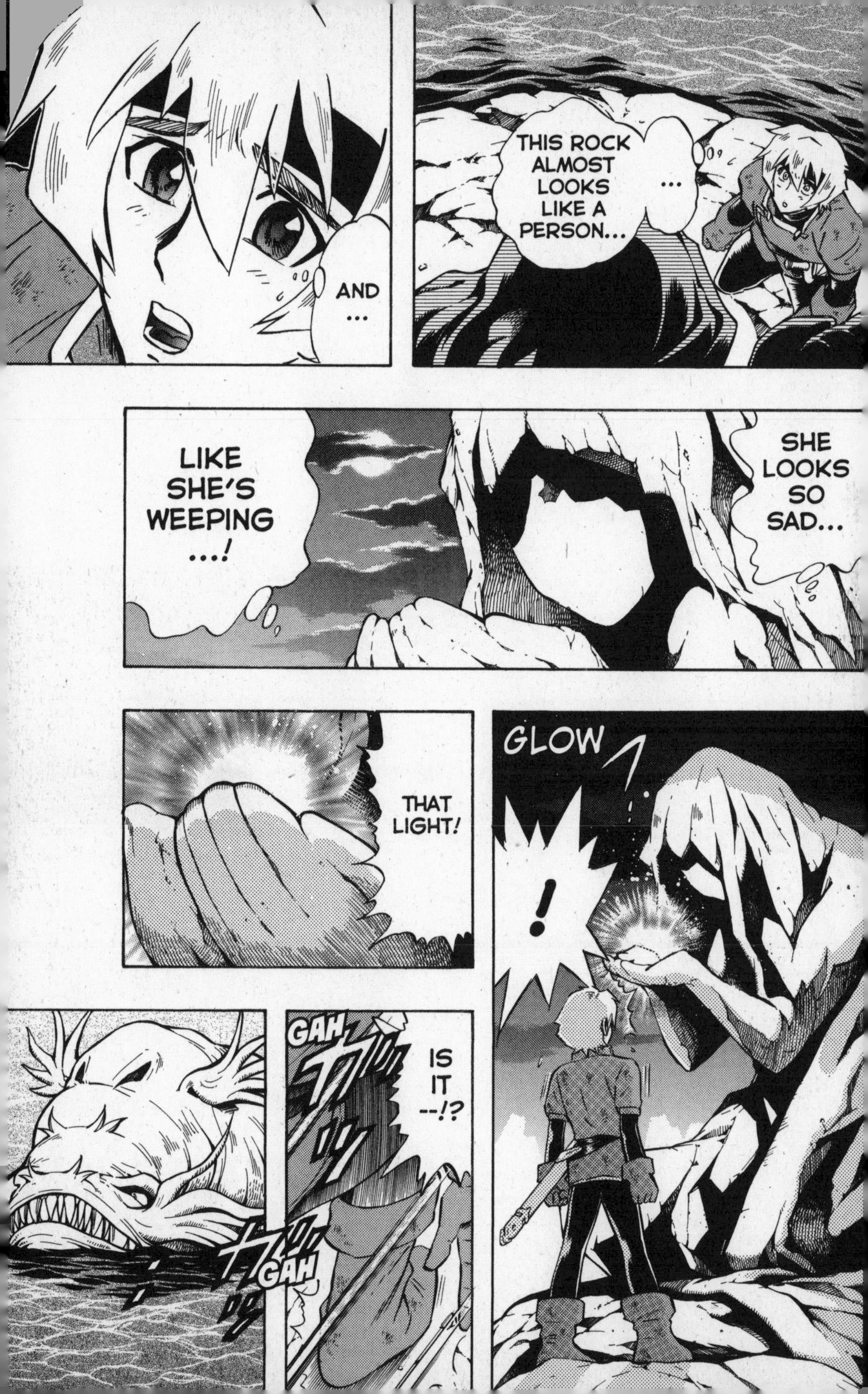
THIS ROCK ALMOST LOOKS LIKE A PERSON...
...
AND ...
SHE LOOKS SO SAD...
LIKE SHE'S WEEPING ...!
GLOW
!
THAT LIGHT!
GAH
IS IT --!?
GAH

IT IS!!

IT--

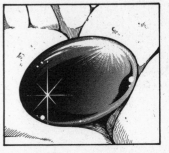

REALLY!?

R- WHAT !?

WE DID IT, EVERY- ONE!

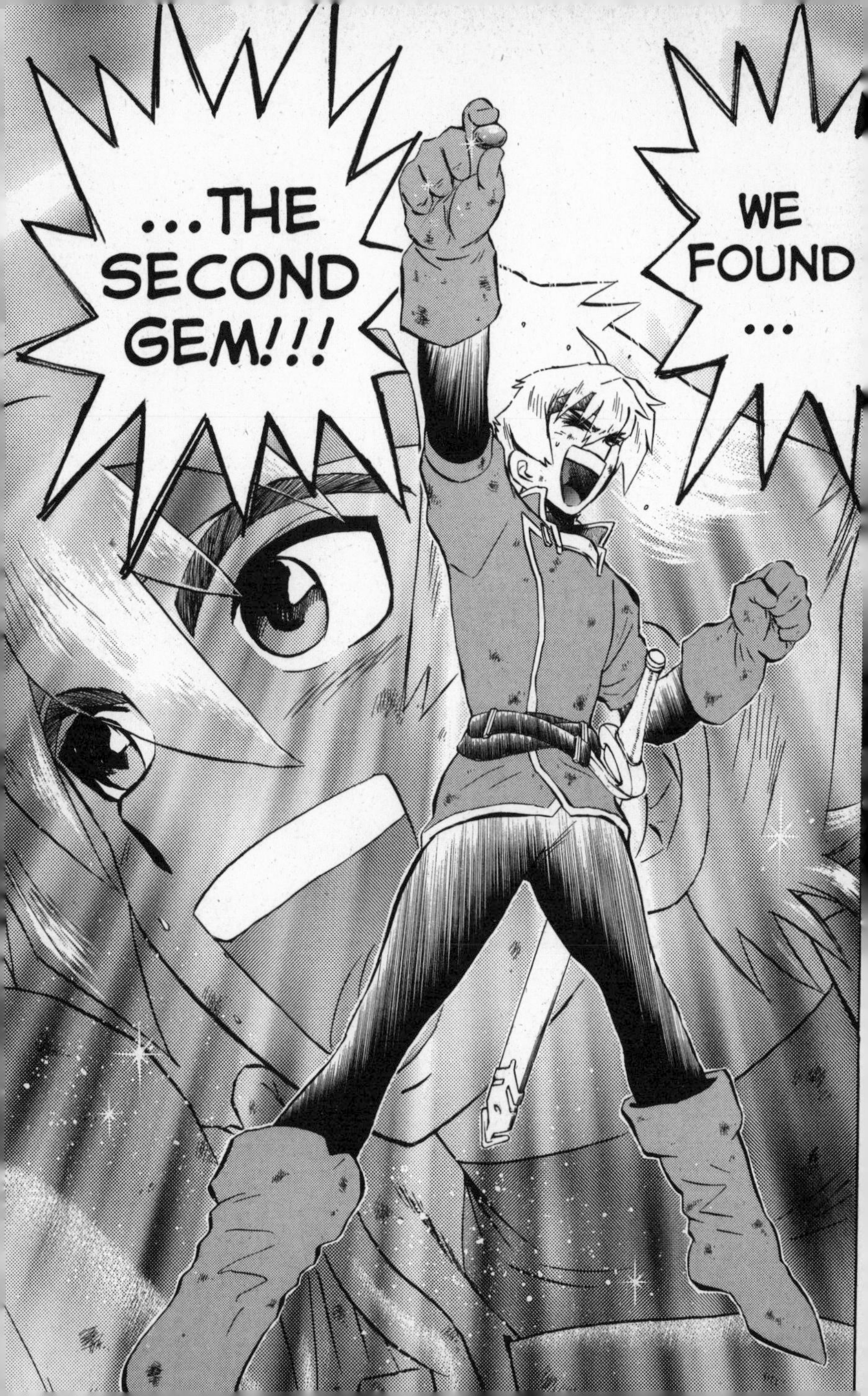
WE FOUND ...
...THE SECOND GEM!!!

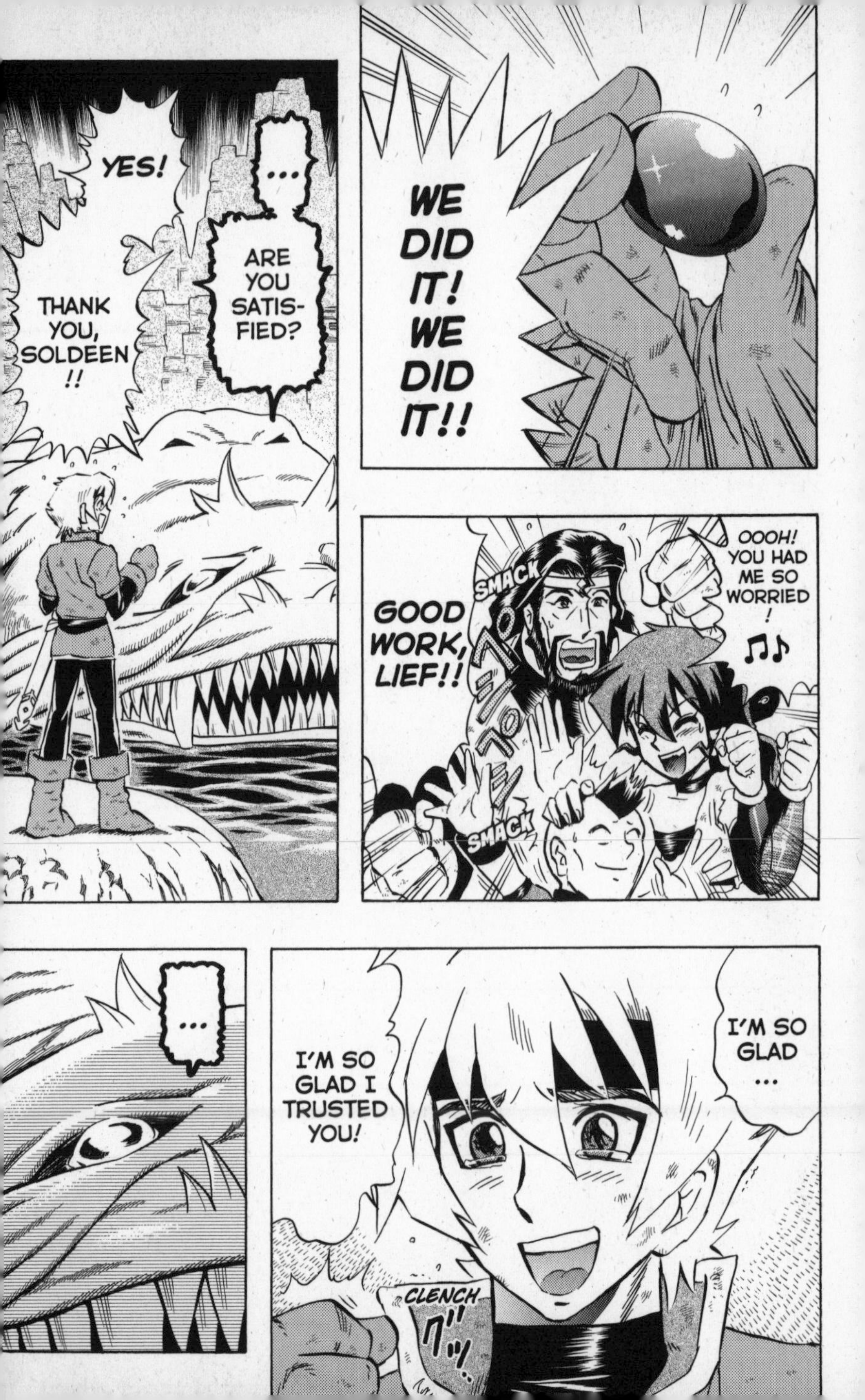
WE DID IT! WE DID IT!!
OOOH! YOU HAD ME SO WORRIED!
GOOD WORK, LIEF!!
SMACK
SMACK
...
ARE YOU SATISFIED?
YES!
THANK YOU, SOLDEEN!!
I'M SO GLAD...
I'M SO GLAD I TRUSTED YOU!
CLENCH
...

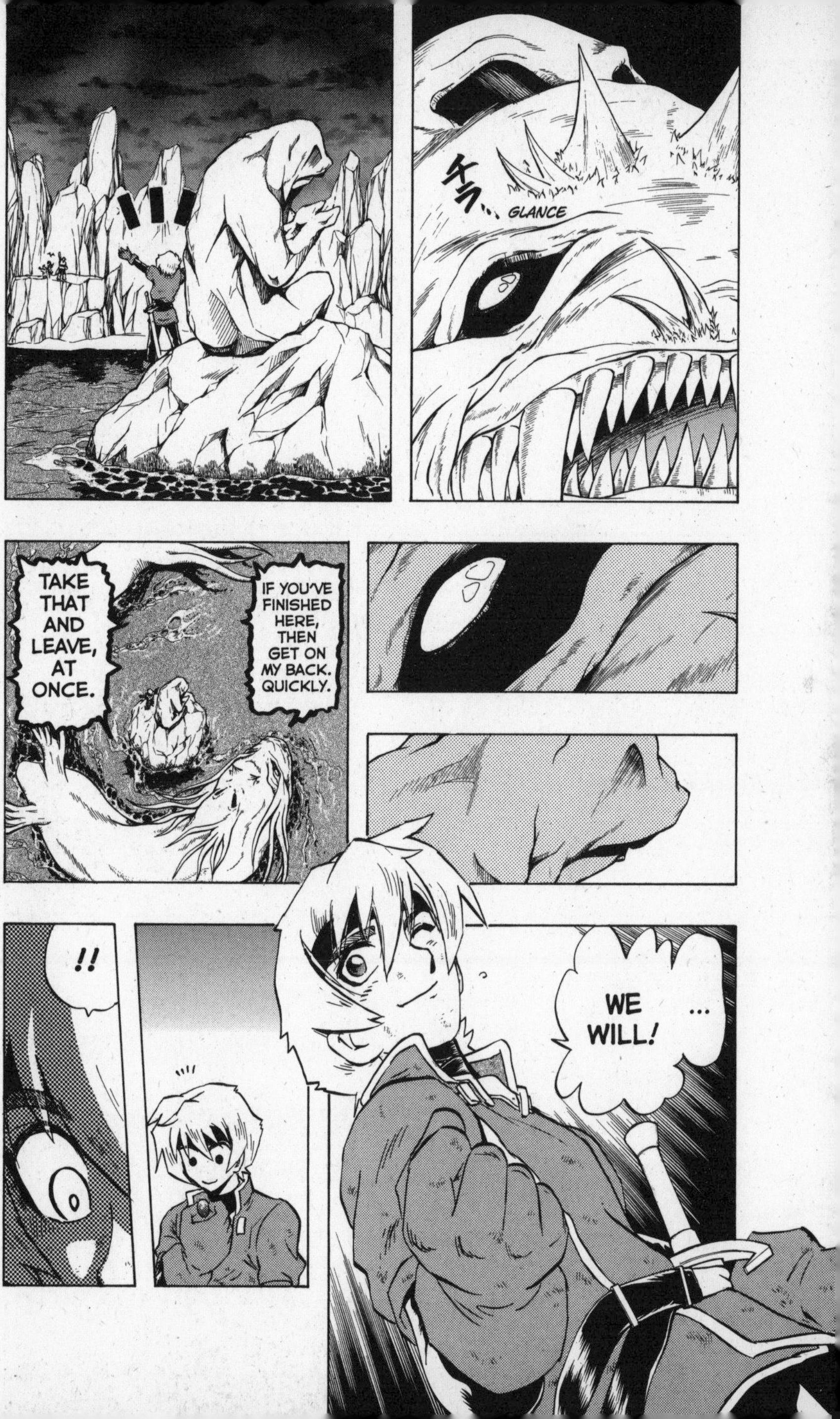

チラ... GLANCE
IF YOU'VE FINISHED HERE, THEN GET ON MY BACK. QUICKLY.
TAKE THAT AND LEAVE, AT ONCE.
WE WILL! ...
!!

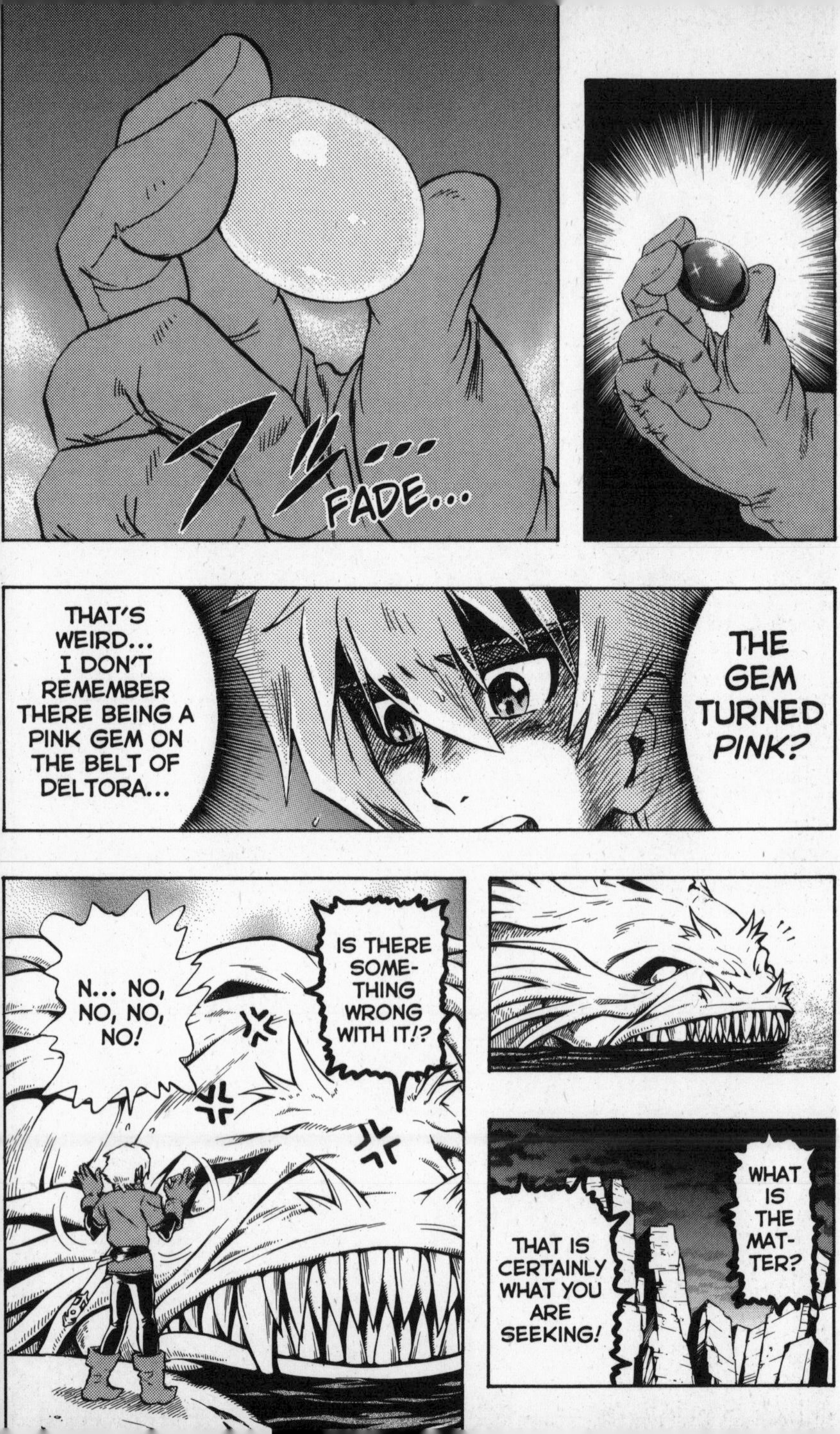
FADE...
THE GEM TURNED PINK?
THAT'S WEIRD... I DON'T REMEMBER THERE BEING A PINK GEM ON THE BELT OF DELTORA...
WHAT IS THE MAT-TER?
THAT IS CERTAINLY WHAT YOU ARE SEEKING!
IS THERE SOME-THING WRONG WITH IT!?
N... NO, NO, NO, NO!

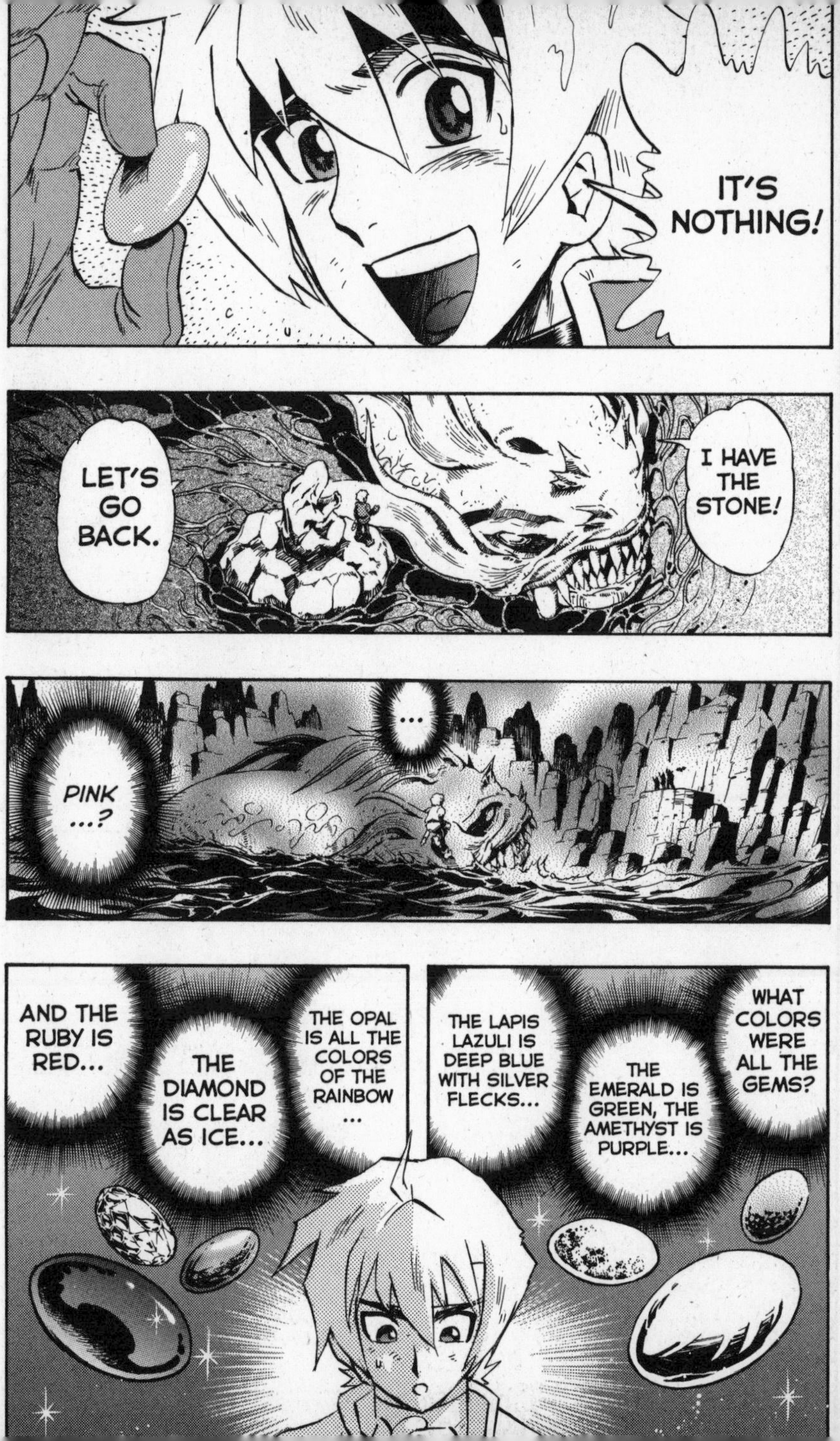
IT'S NOTHING!
I HAVE THE STONE!
LET'S GO BACK.
...
PINK ...?
WHAT COLORS WERE ALL THE GEMS?
THE EMERALD IS GREEN, THE AMETHYST IS PURPLE...
THE LAPIS LAZULI IS DEEP BLUE WITH SILVER FLECKS...
THE OPAL IS ALL THE COLORS OF THE RAINBOW ...
THE DIAMOND IS CLEAR AS ICE...
AND THE RUBY IS RED...

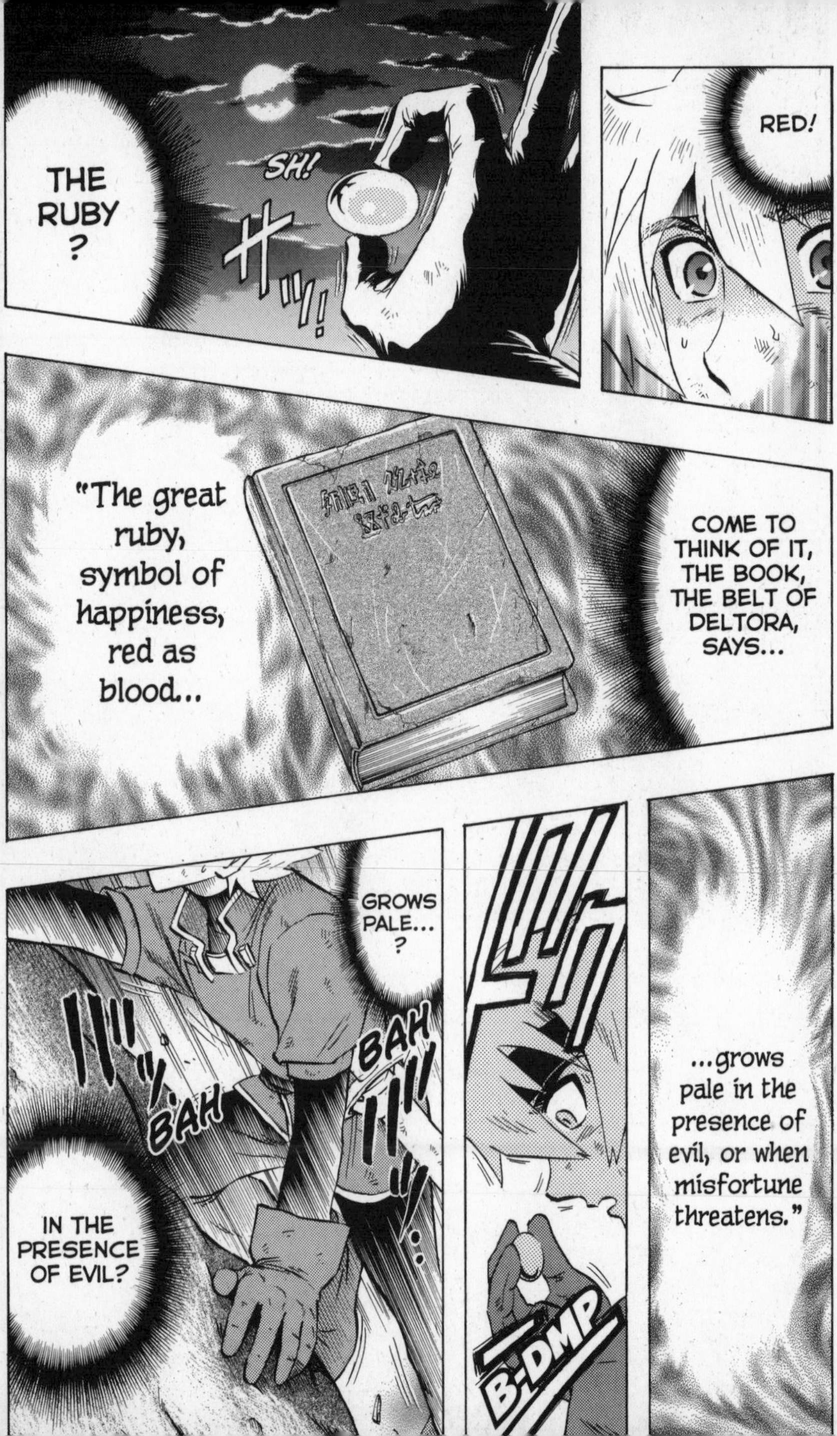
RED!
SH!
THE RUBY ?
COME TO THINK OF IT, THE BOOK, THE BELT OF DELTORA, SAYS...
"The great ruby, symbol of happiness, red as blood...
...grows pale in the presence of evil, or when misfortune threatens."
B-DMP
GROWS PALE... ?
BAH
BAH
IN THE PRESENCE OF EVIL?

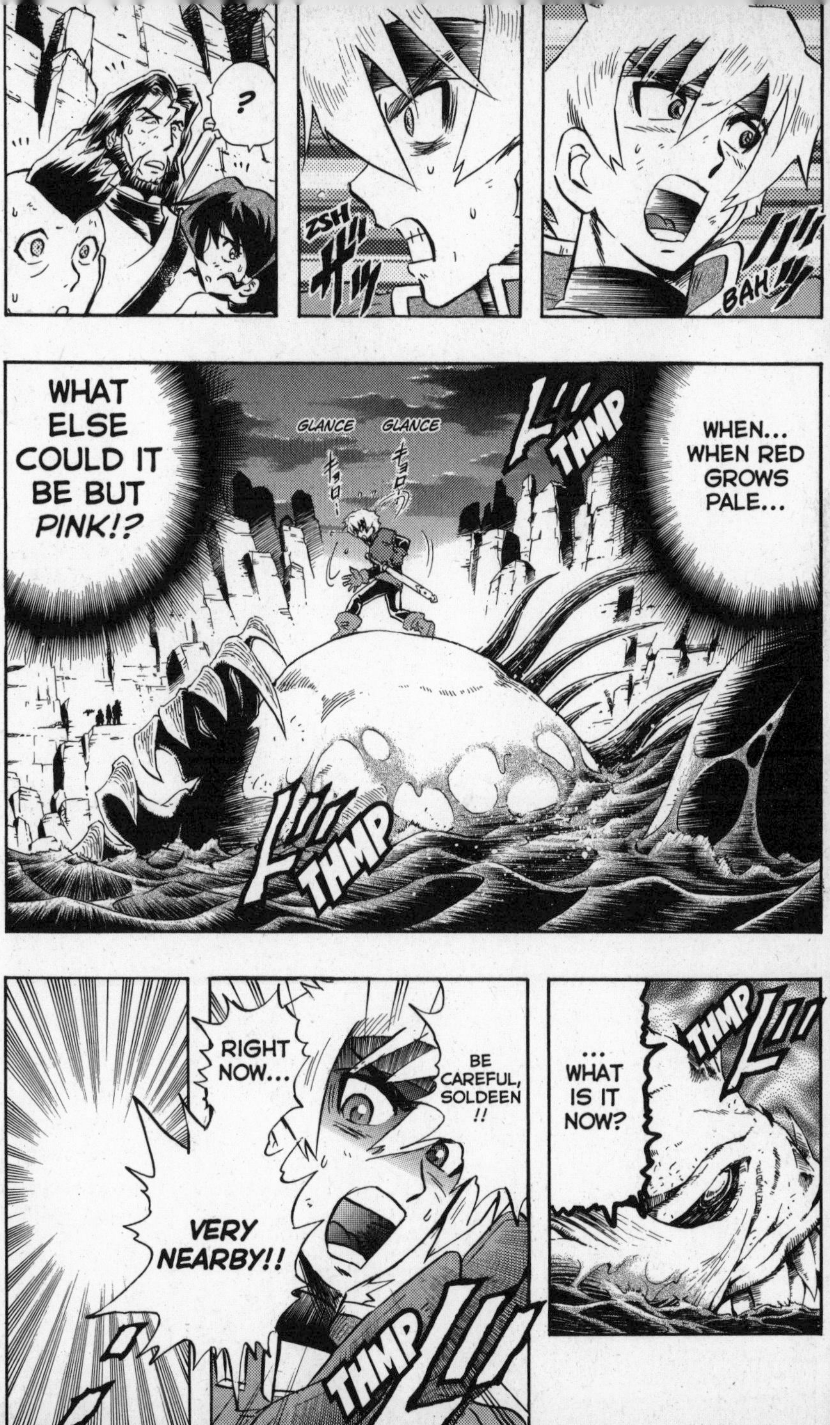
BAH!!
ZSH
?
WHEN... WHEN RED GROWS PALE...
THMP
GLANCE
GLANCE
WHAT ELSE COULD IT BE BUT PINK!?
THMP
THMP
... WHAT IS IT NOW?
BE CAREFUL, SOLDEEN!!
RIGHT NOW...
VERY NEARBY!!
THMP

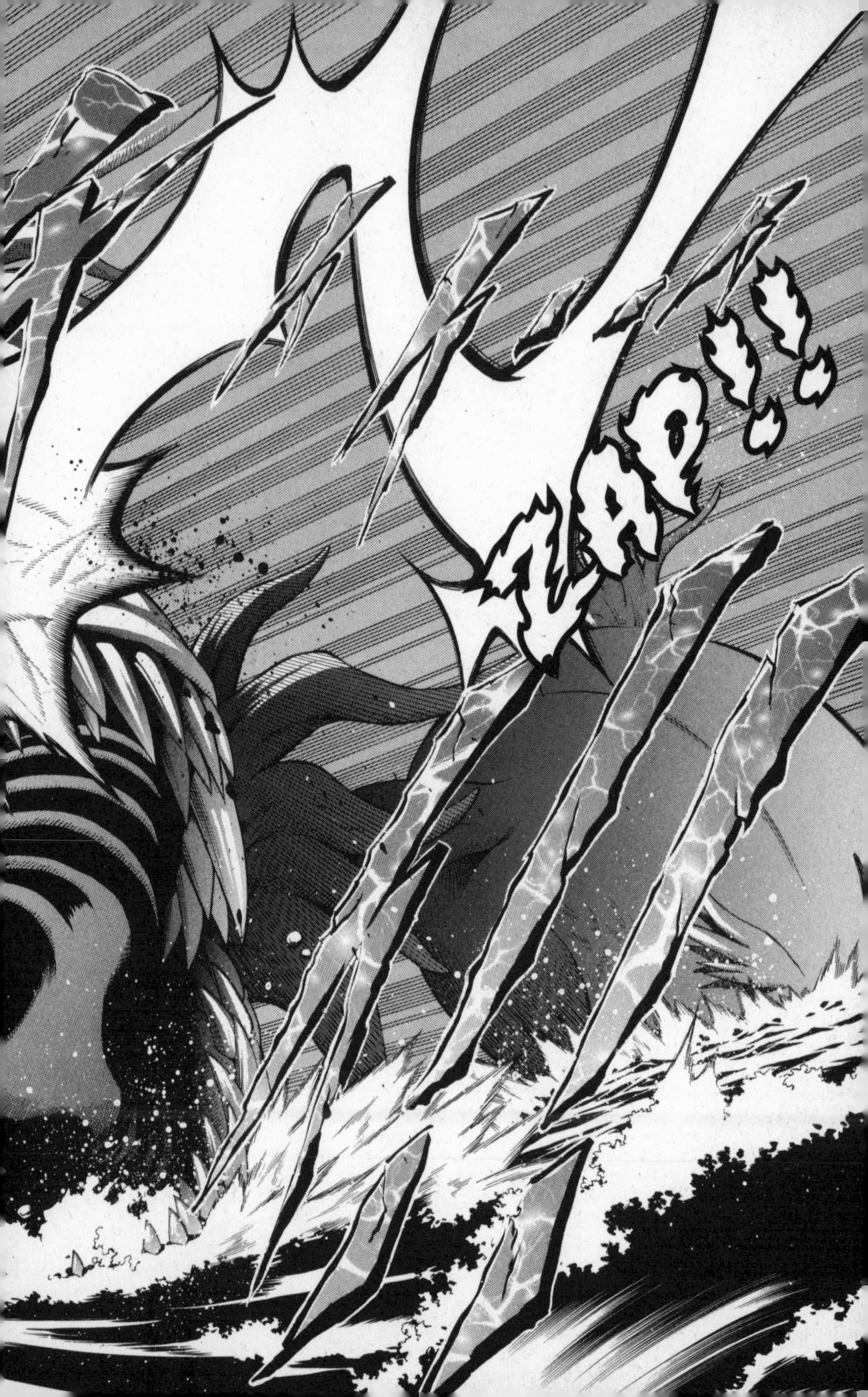
ZAP!!

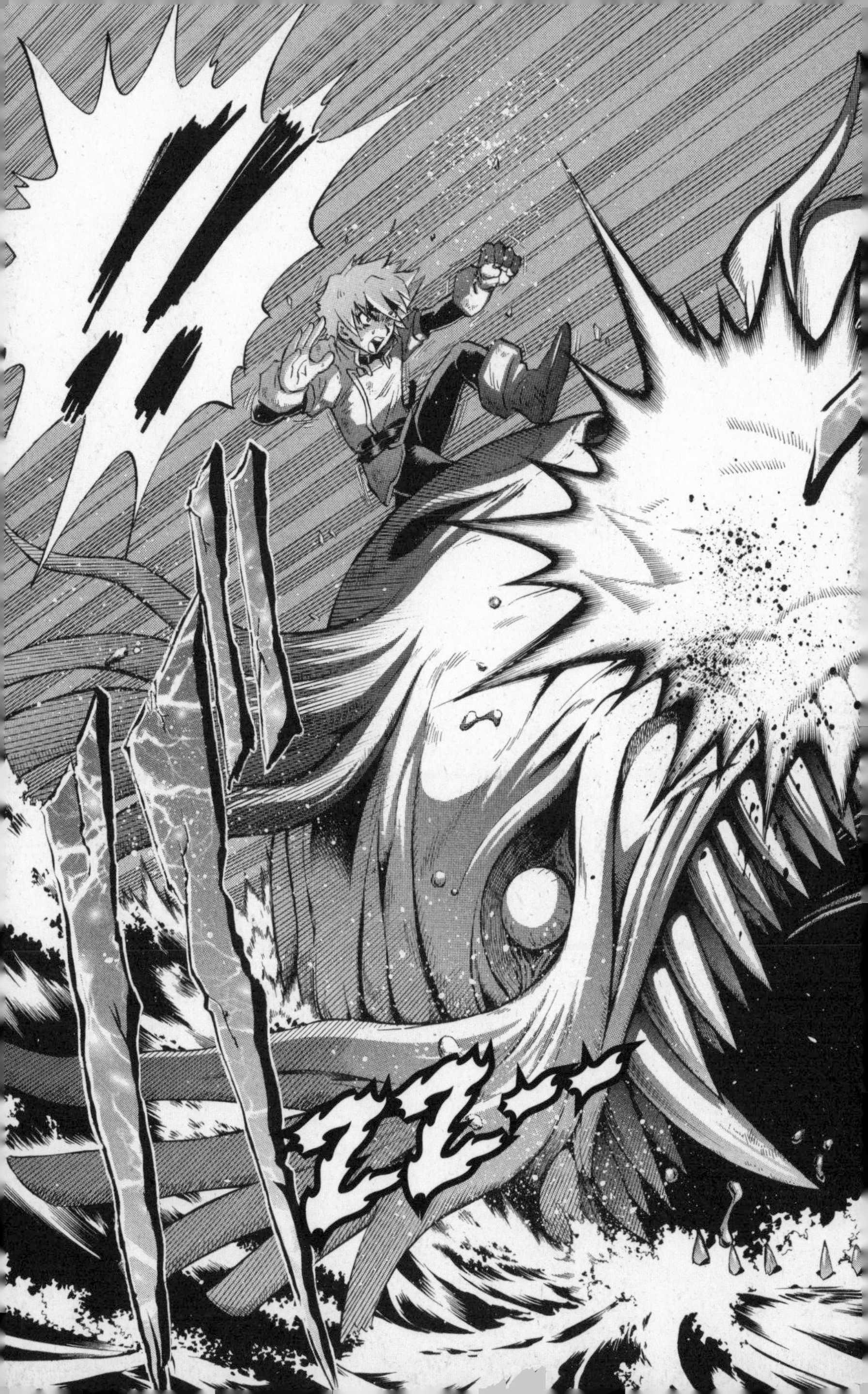

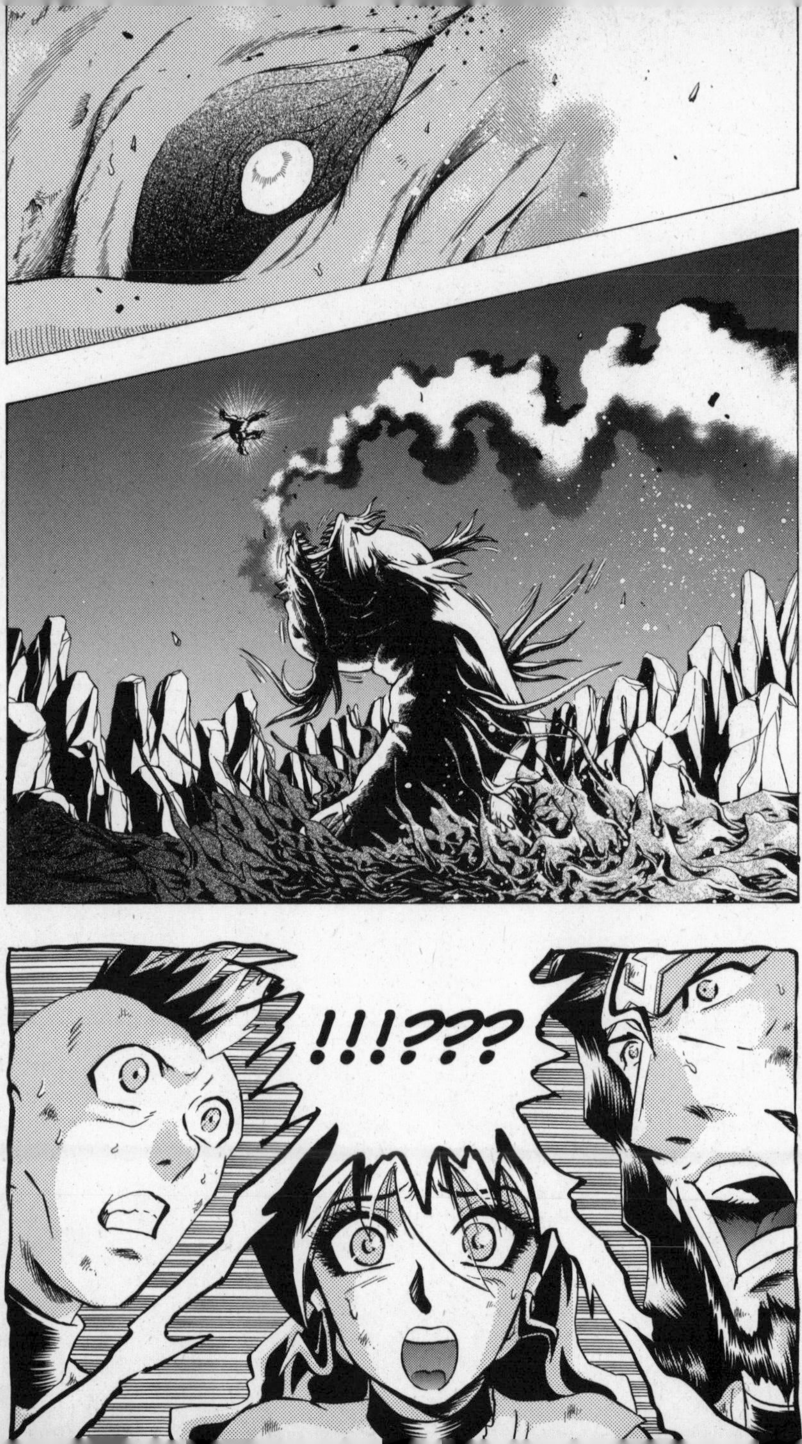
!!!???

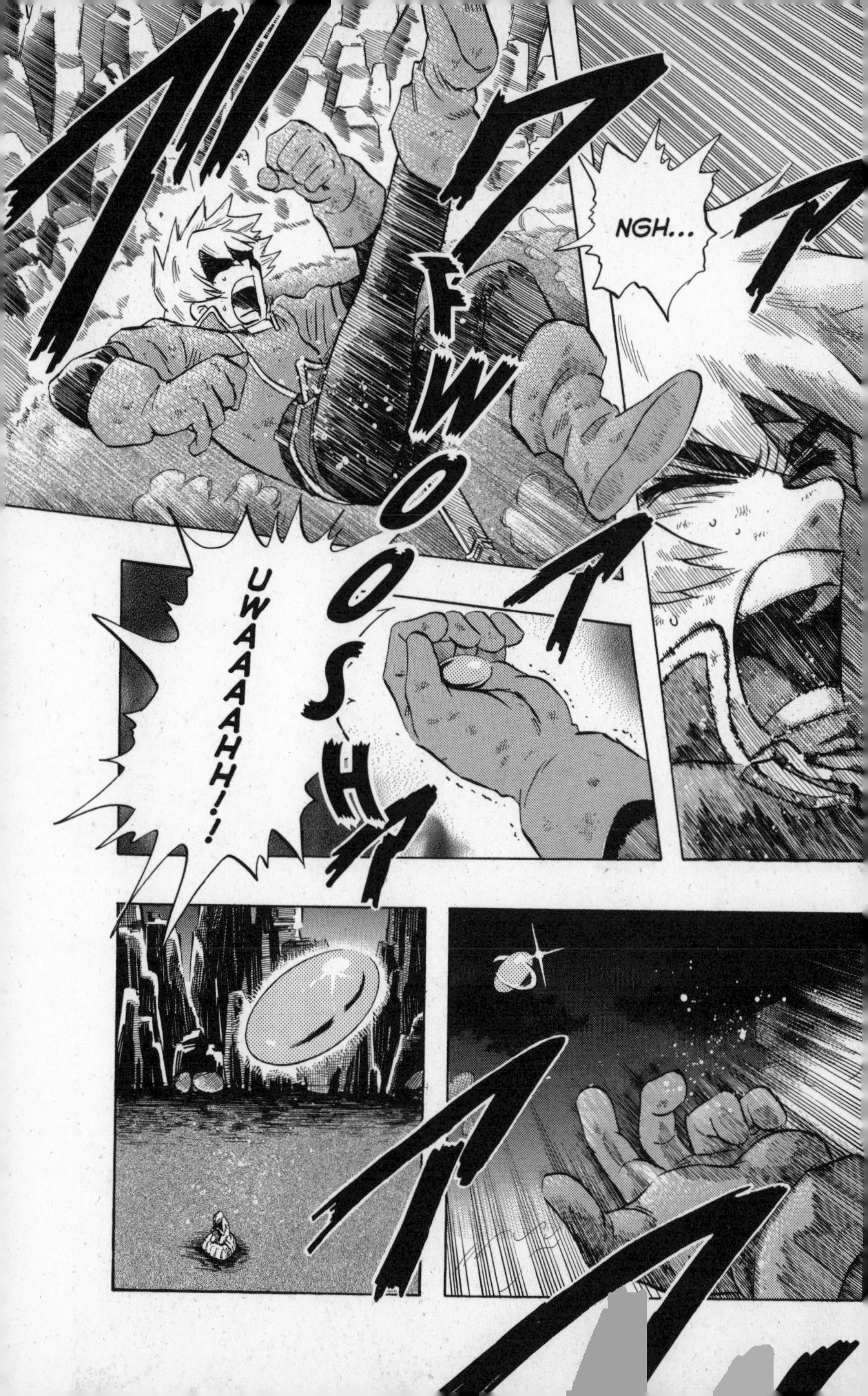
NGH...
FWOOOSH
UWAAAAAHH!!

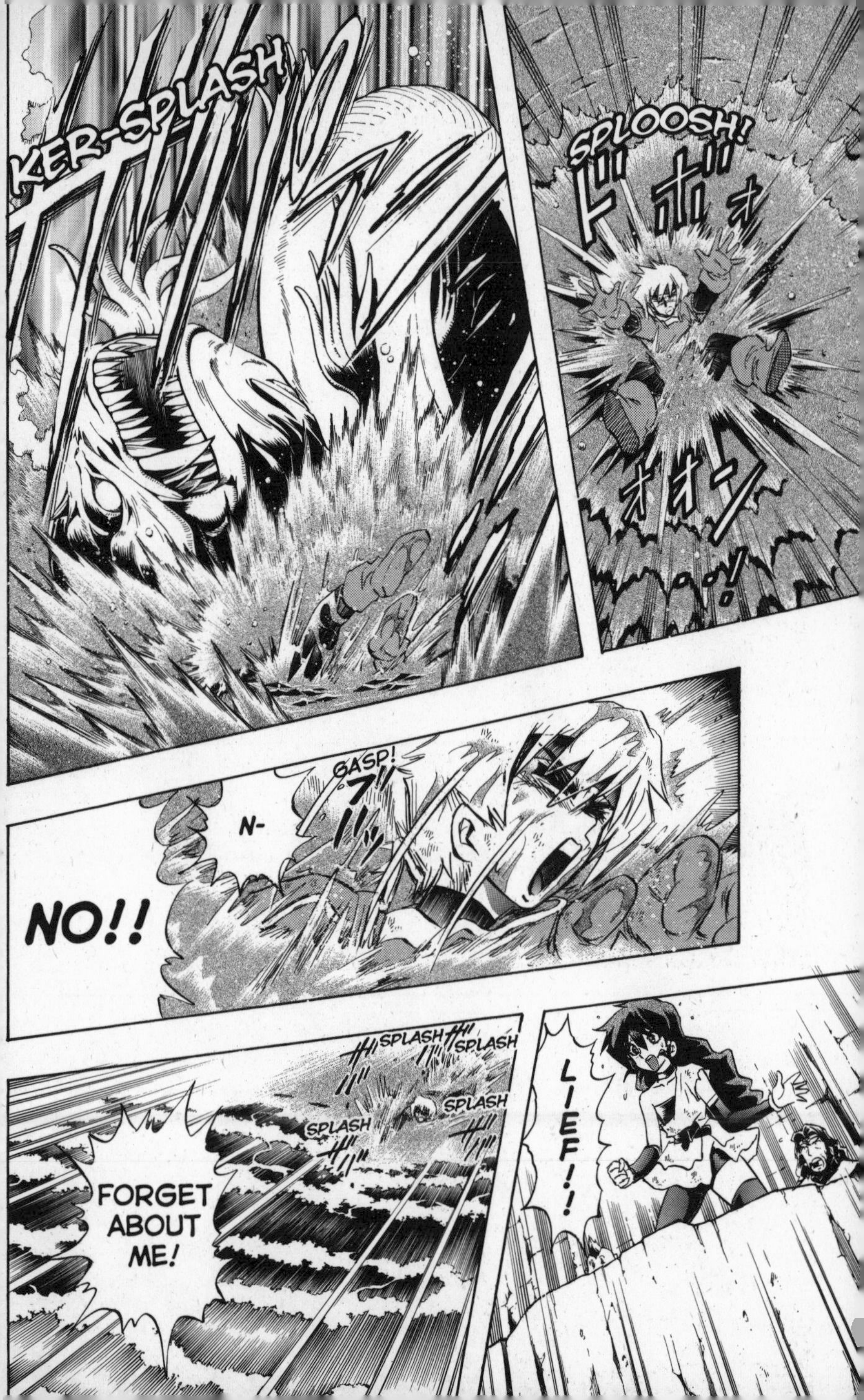
SPLOOSH!
ドボォ
オオーン
KER-SPLASH
GASP!
N-
NO!!
LIEF!!
SPLASH
SPLASH
SPLASH
SPLASH
FORGET ABOUT ME!

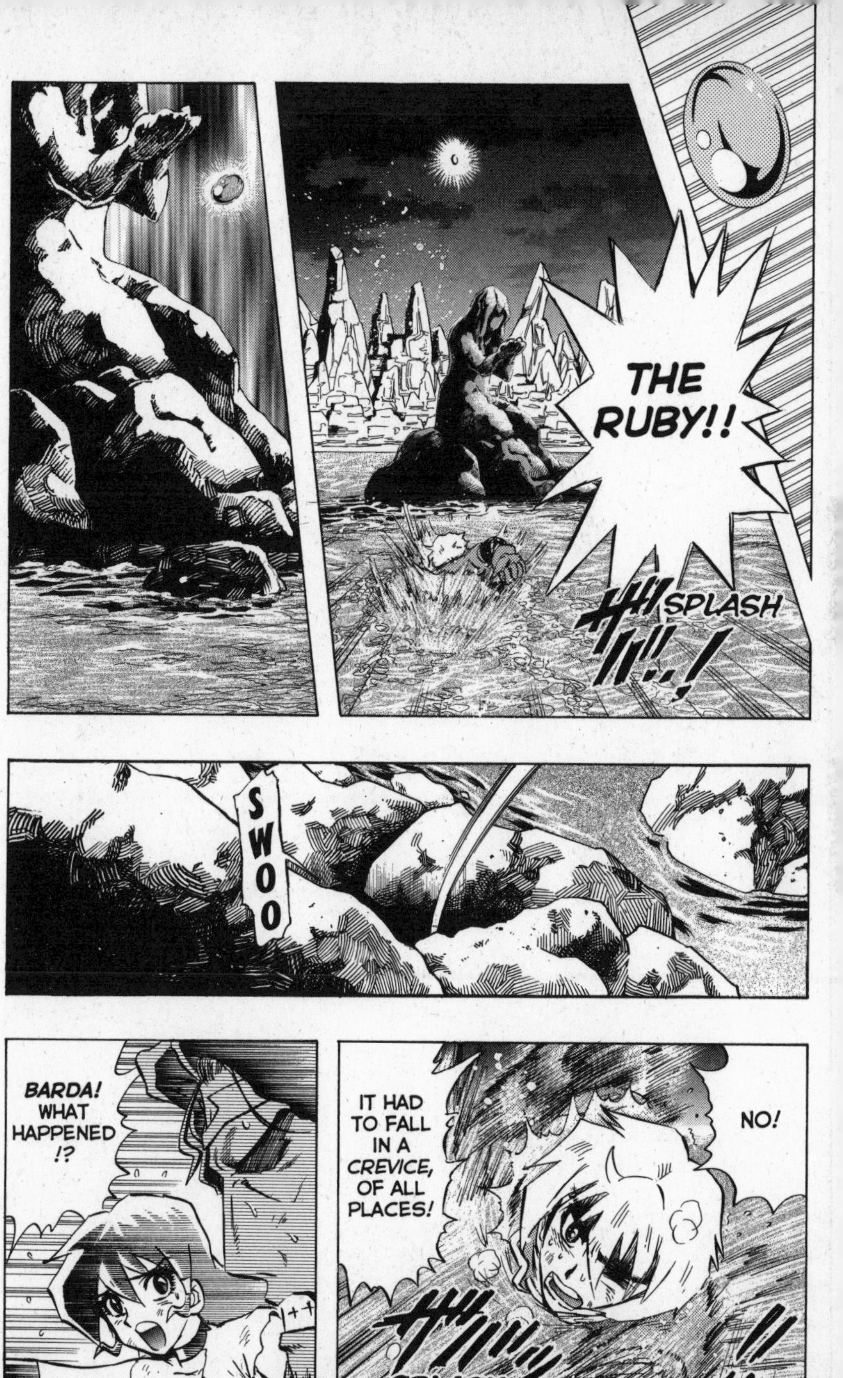
THE RUBY!!
SPLASH
SWOO
NO!
IT HAD TO FALL IN A *CREVICE*, OF ALL PLACES!
SPLASH
BARDA! WHAT HAPPENED!?

BUT WHATEVER IT WAS...

I DON'T KNOW!!

...IT WAS CLEARLY AIMING FOR SOLDEEN!

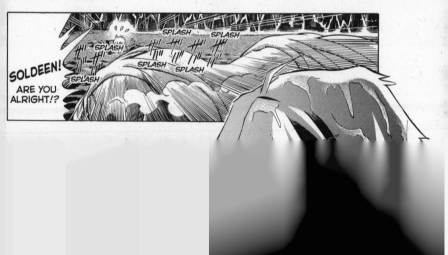

SPLASH SPLASH SPLASH SPLASH SPLASH SPLASH SPLASH

SOLDEEN! ARE YOU ALRIGHT!?

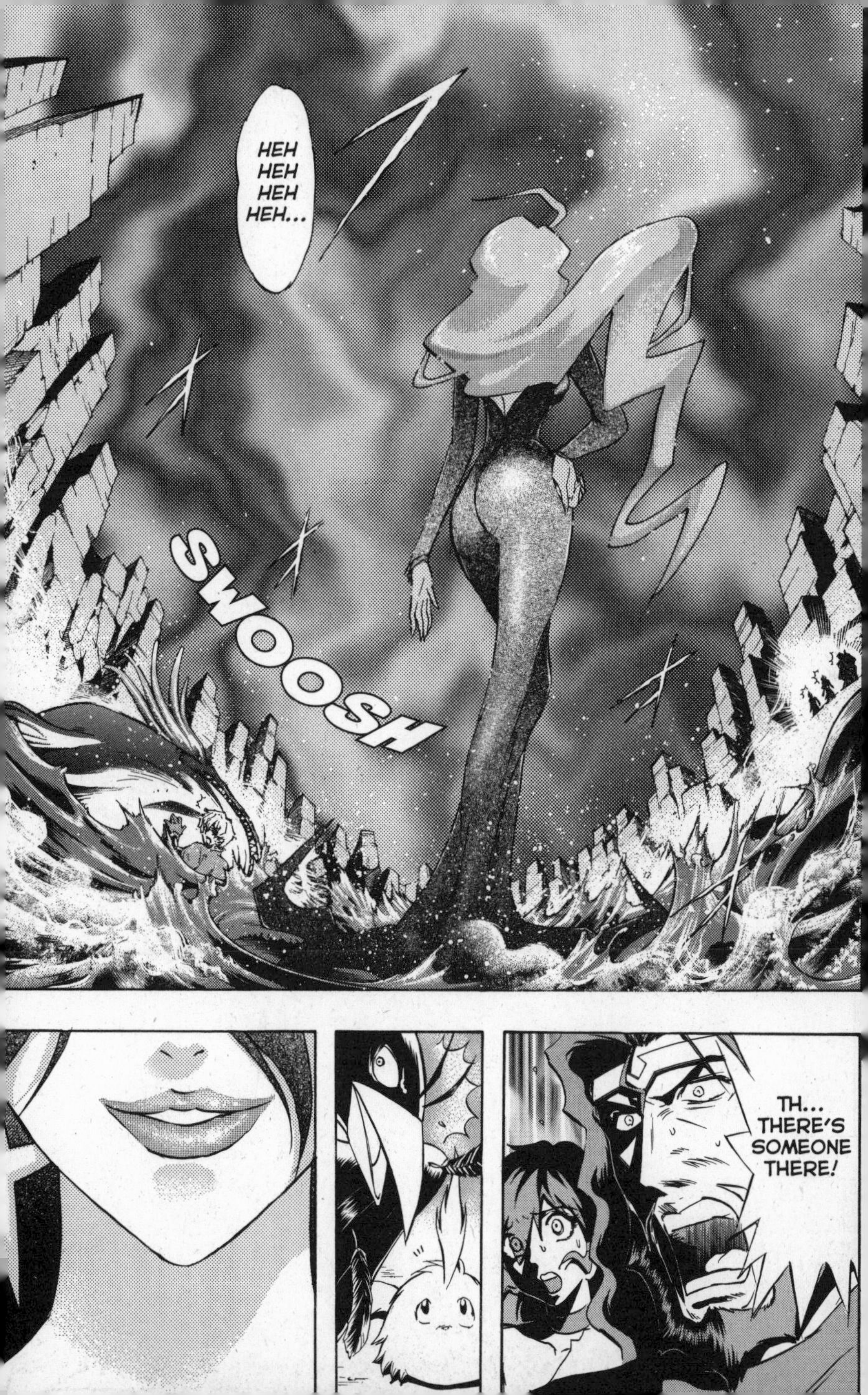
HEH HEH HEH HEH...
SWOOSH
TH... THERE'S SOMEONE THERE!

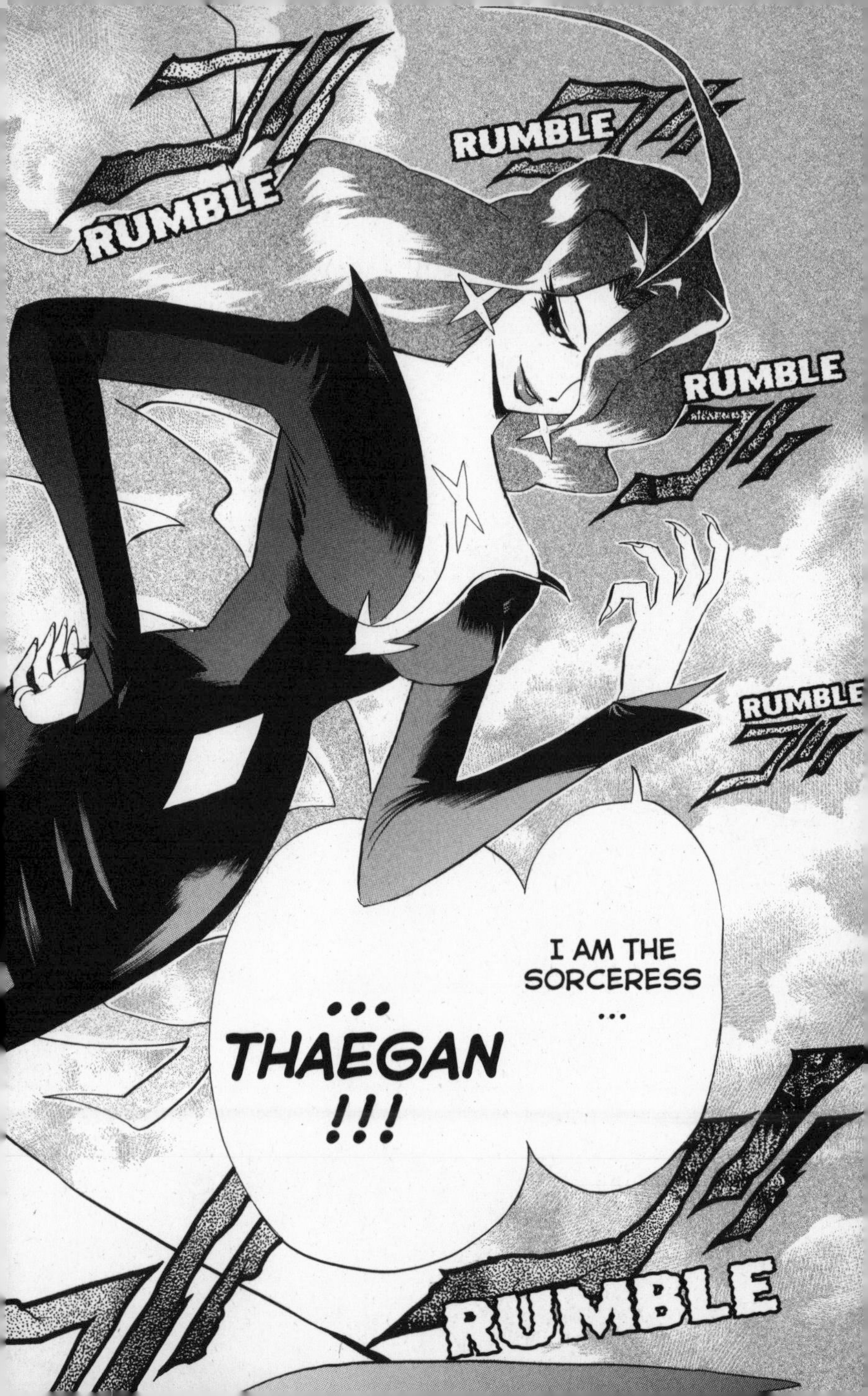
RUMBLE
RUMBLE
RUMBLE
RUMBLE
I AM THE SORCERESS ...
... THAEGAN !!!
RUMBLE

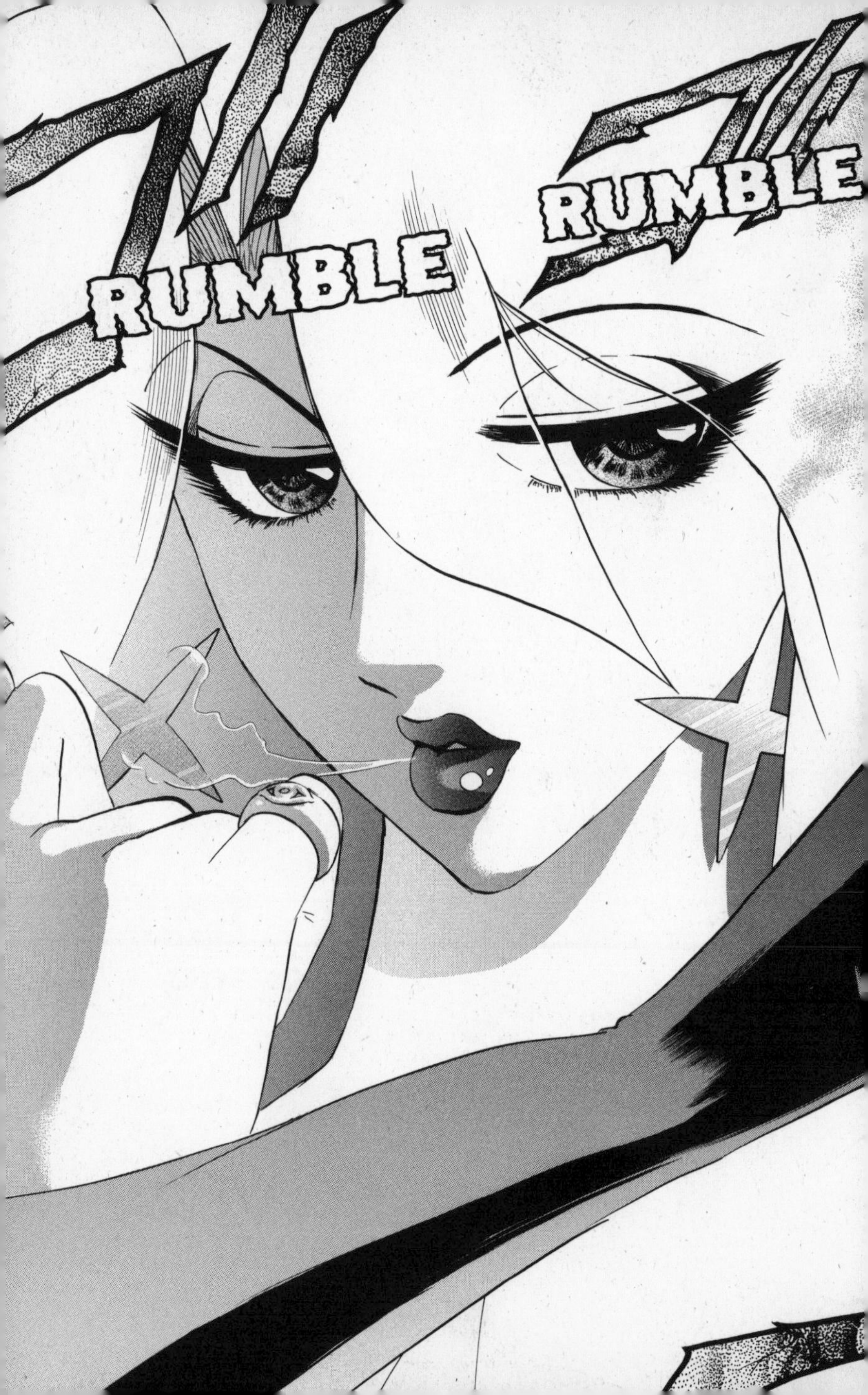
RUMBLE
RUMBLE

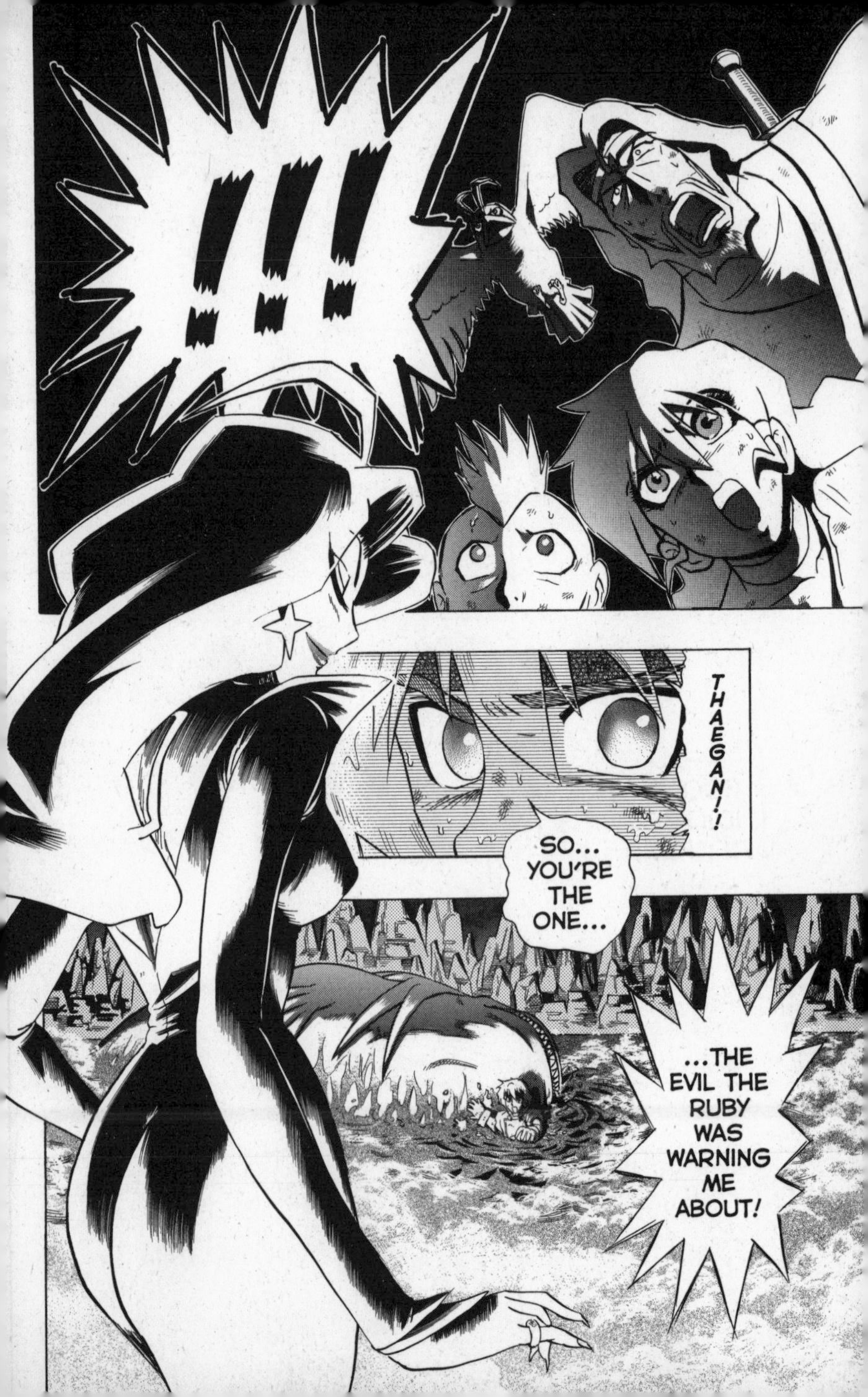
!!!
THAEGAN!!
SO... YOU'RE THE ONE...
...THE EVIL THE RUBY WAS WARNING ME ABOUT!

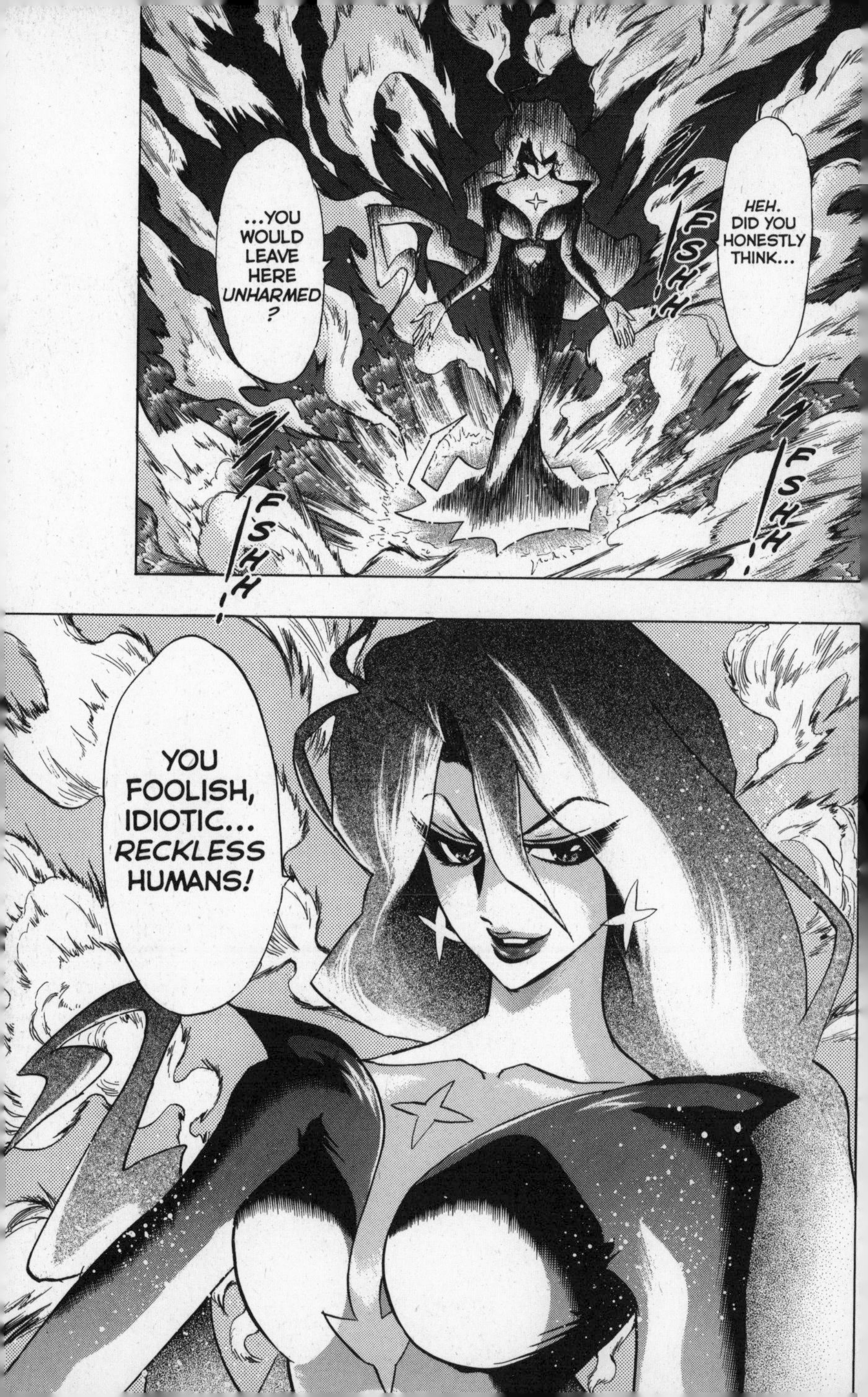
HEH. DID YOU HONESTLY THINK...
FSHH!
...YOU WOULD LEAVE HERE UNHARMED?
FSHH!
FSHH!
YOU FOOLISH, IDIOTIC... RECKLESS HUMANS!

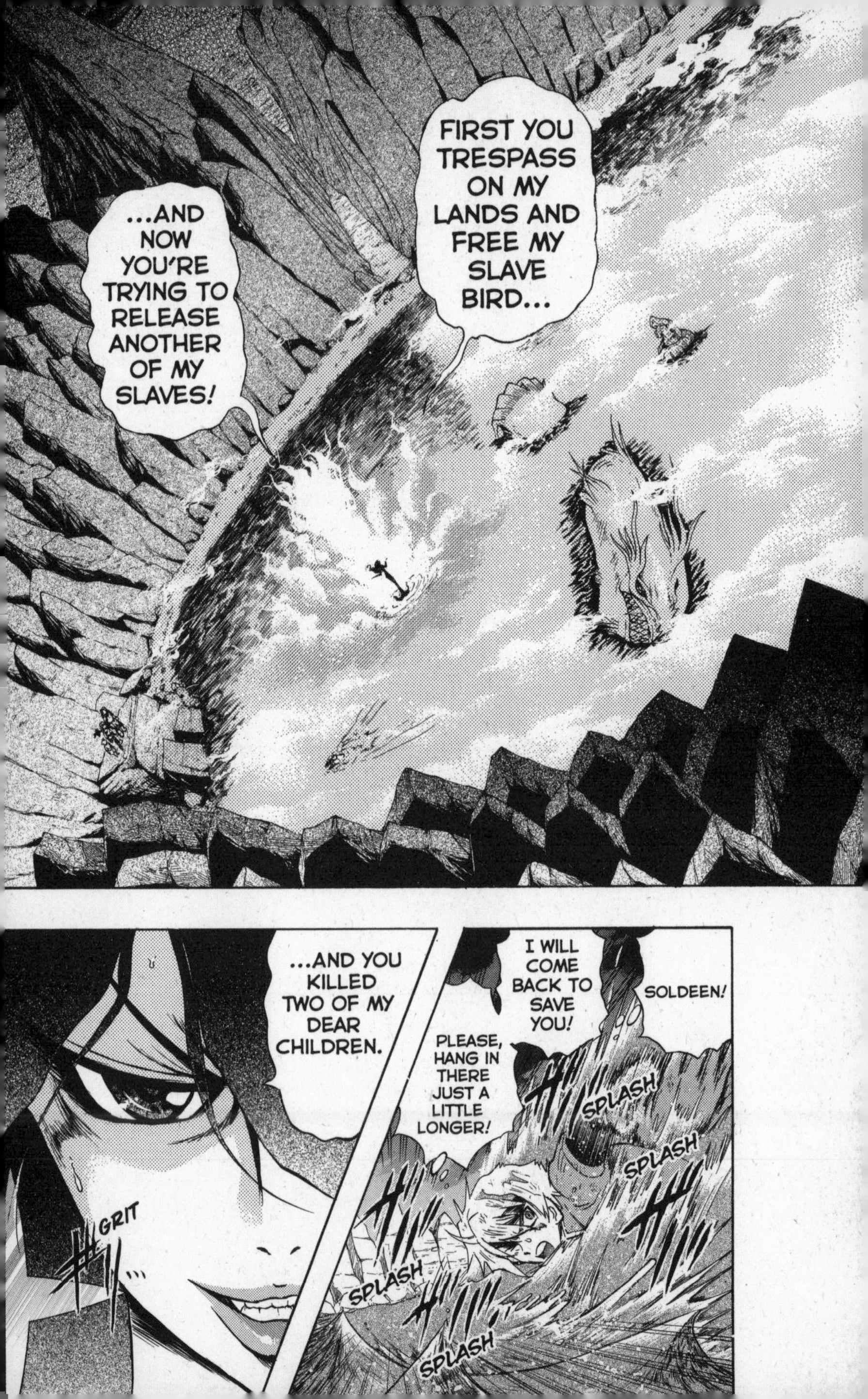
FIRST YOU TRESPASS ON MY LANDS AND FREE MY SLAVE BIRD...
...AND NOW YOU'RE TRYING TO RELEASE ANOTHER OF MY SLAVES!
SOLDEEN!
I WILL COME BACK TO SAVE YOU!
PLEASE, HANG IN THERE JUST A LITTLE LONGER!
SPLASH
SPLASH
SPLASH
SPLASH
...AND YOU KILLED TWO OF MY DEAR CHILDREN.
GRIT
...

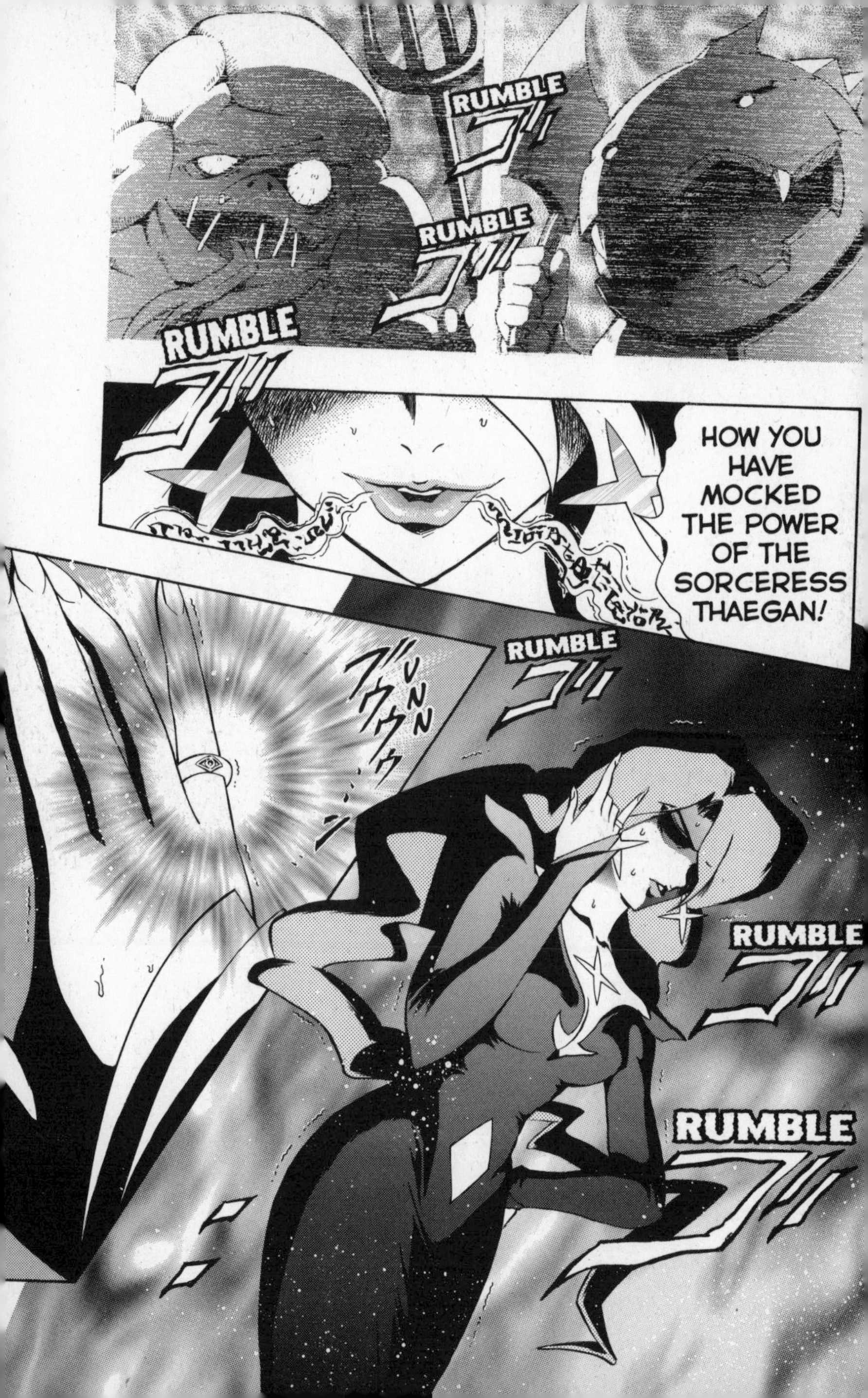
RUMBLE
RUMBLE
RUMBLE
RUMBLE
HOW YOU HAVE MOCKED THE POWER OF THE SORCERESS THAEGAN!
RUMBLE
UNN
RUMBLE
RUMBLE

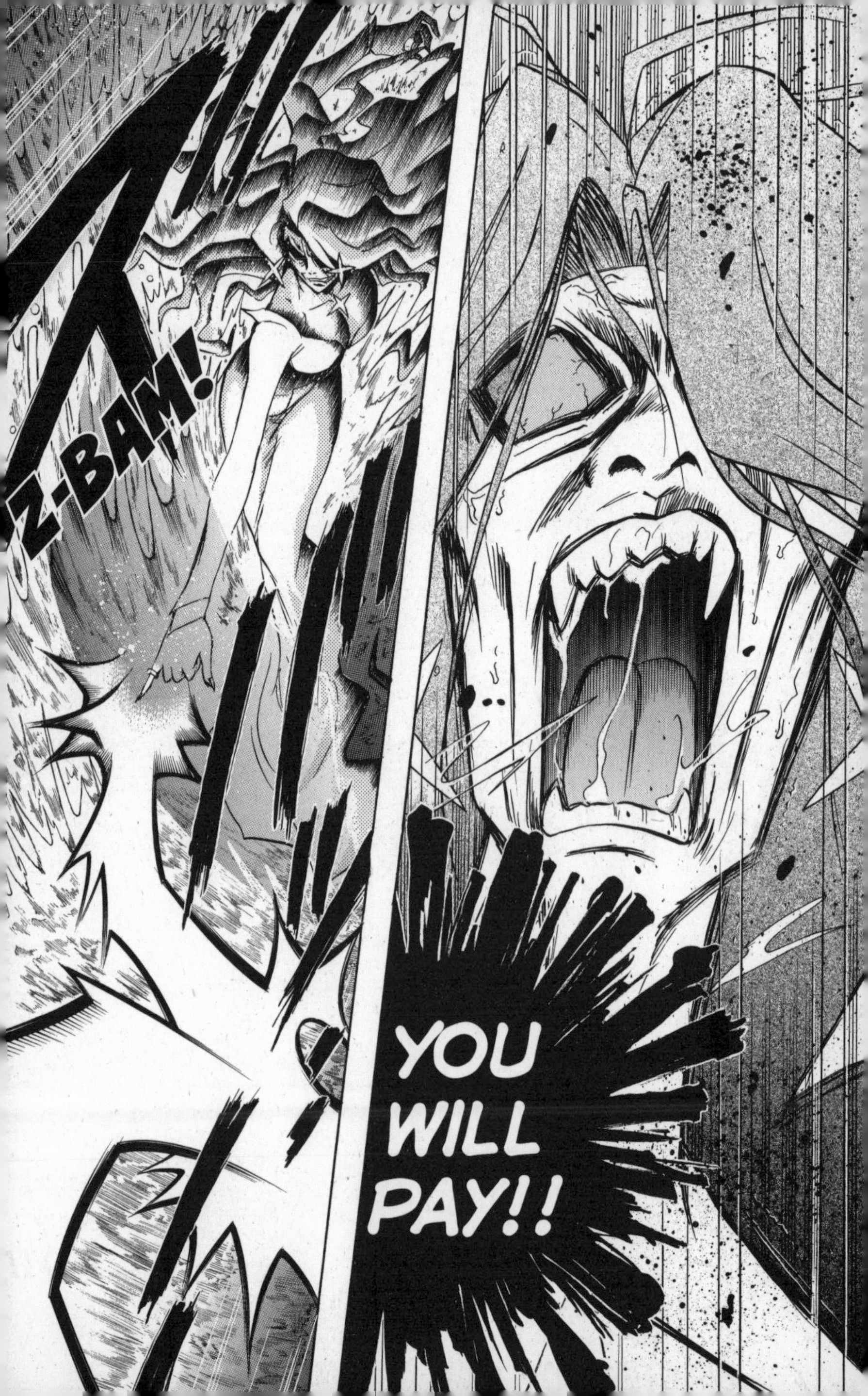
YOU WILL PAY!!
Z-BAM!

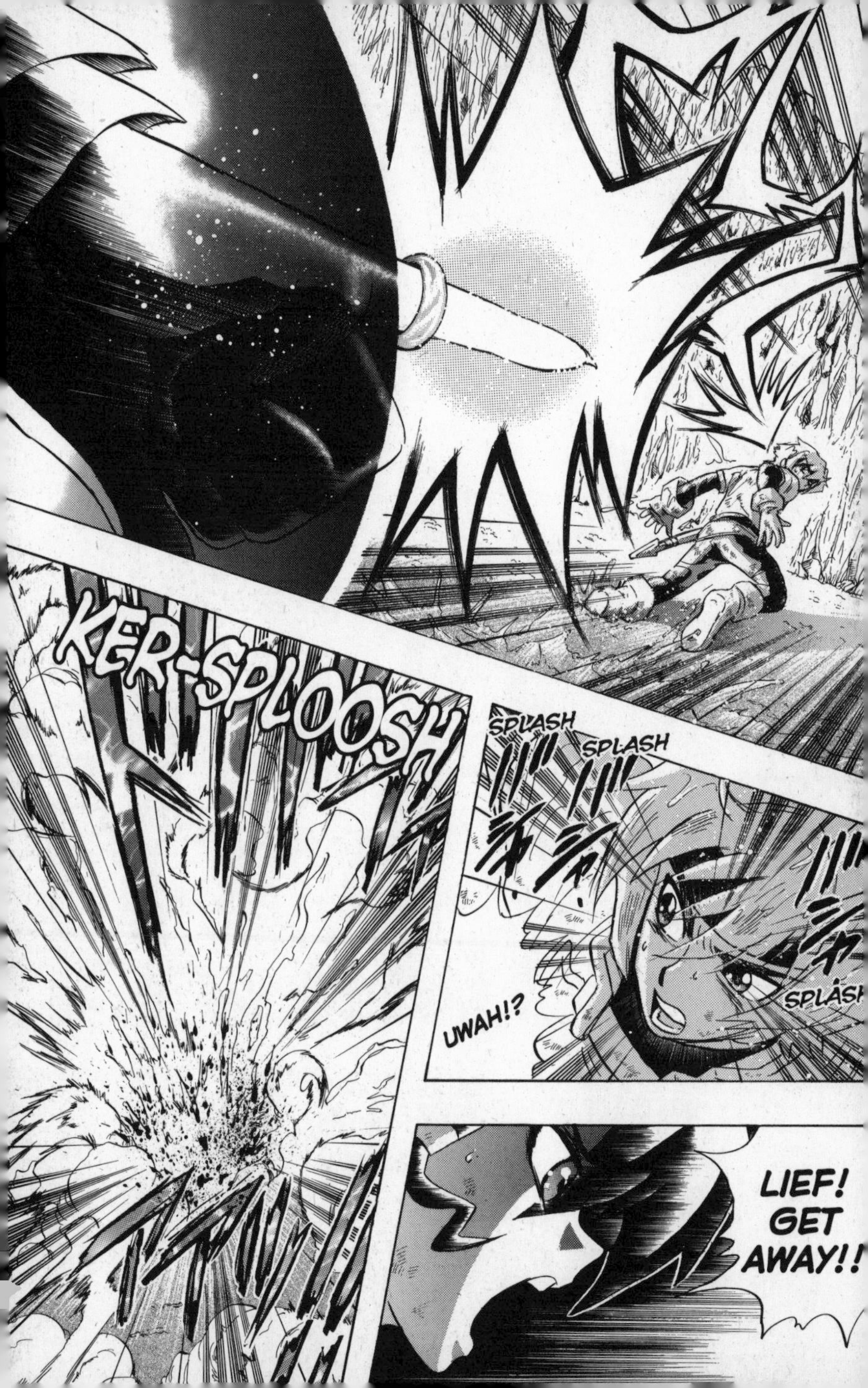
SPLASH
SPLASH
UWAH!?
SPLASH
KER-SPLOOSH
LIEF! GET AWAY!!

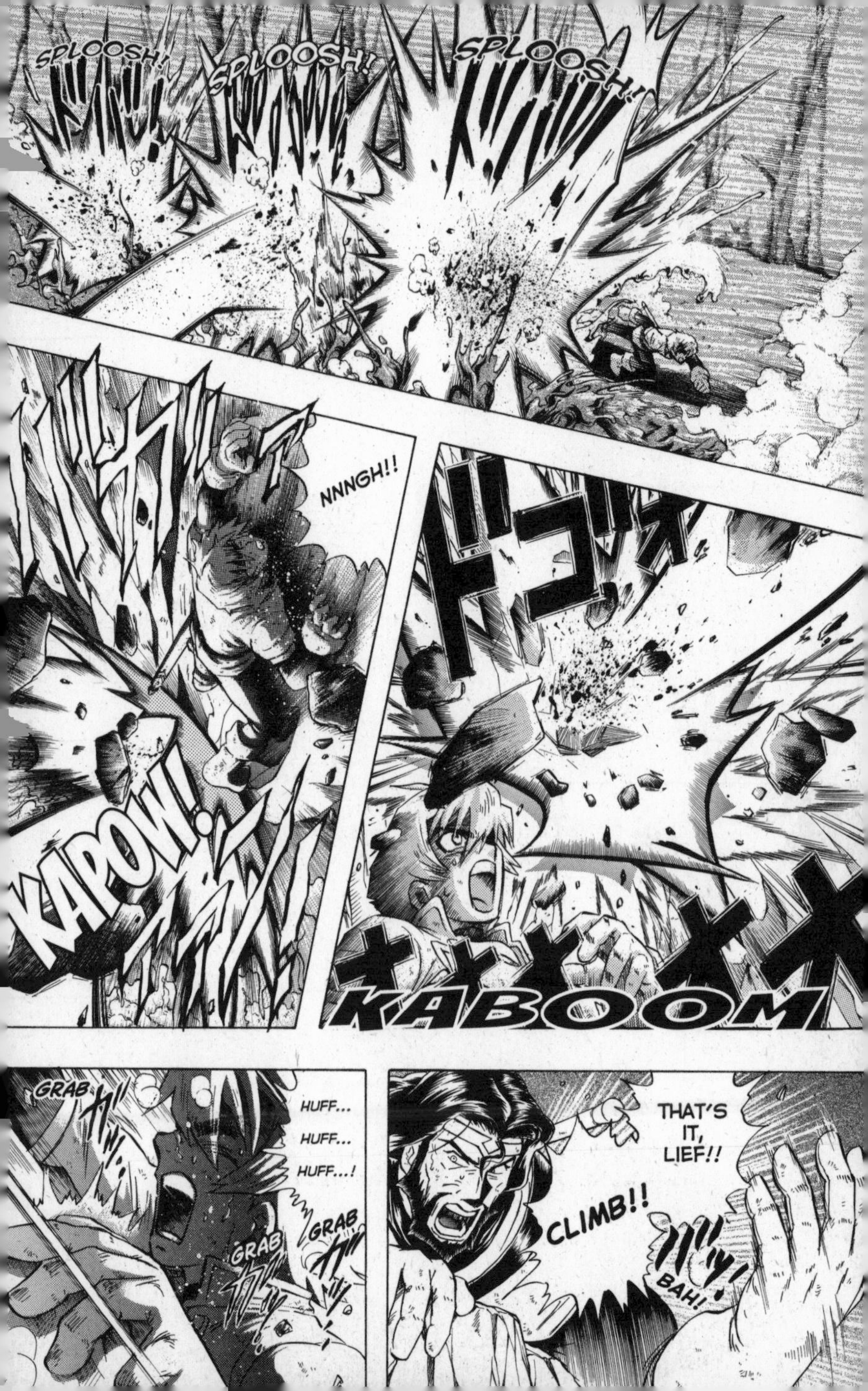
SPLOOSH!
SPLOOSH!
SPLOOSH!
KABOOM
NNNGH!!
KAPOW!!
THAT'S IT, LIEF!!
CLIMB!!
BAH!
GRAB
HUFF...
HUFF...
HUFF...!
GRAB
GRAB

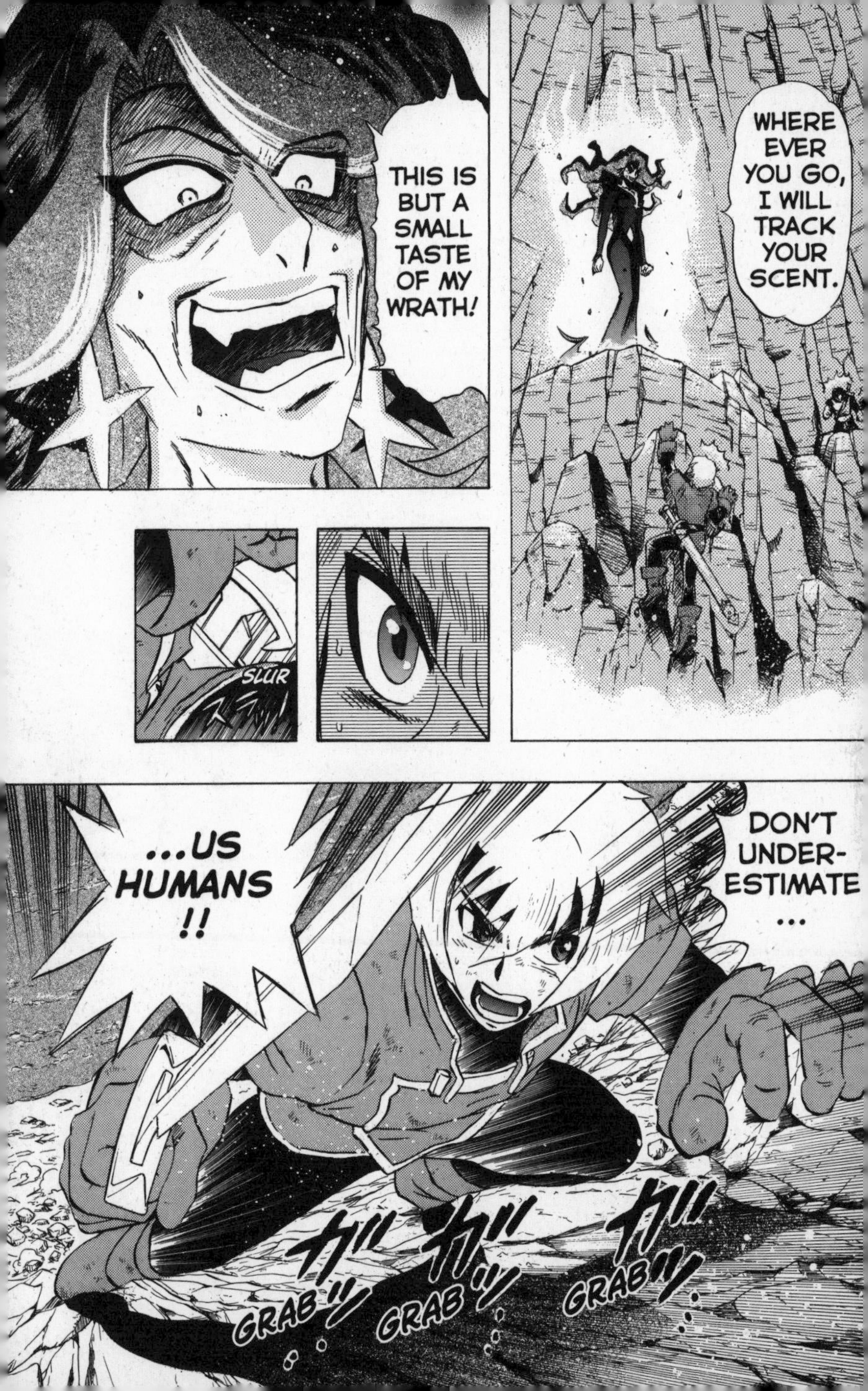
WHERE EVER YOU GO, I WILL TRACK YOUR SCENT.
THIS IS BUT A SMALL TASTE OF MY WRATH!
SLUR
DON'T UNDER-ESTIMATE ...
...US HUMANS !!
GRAB!!
GRAB!!
GRAB!!

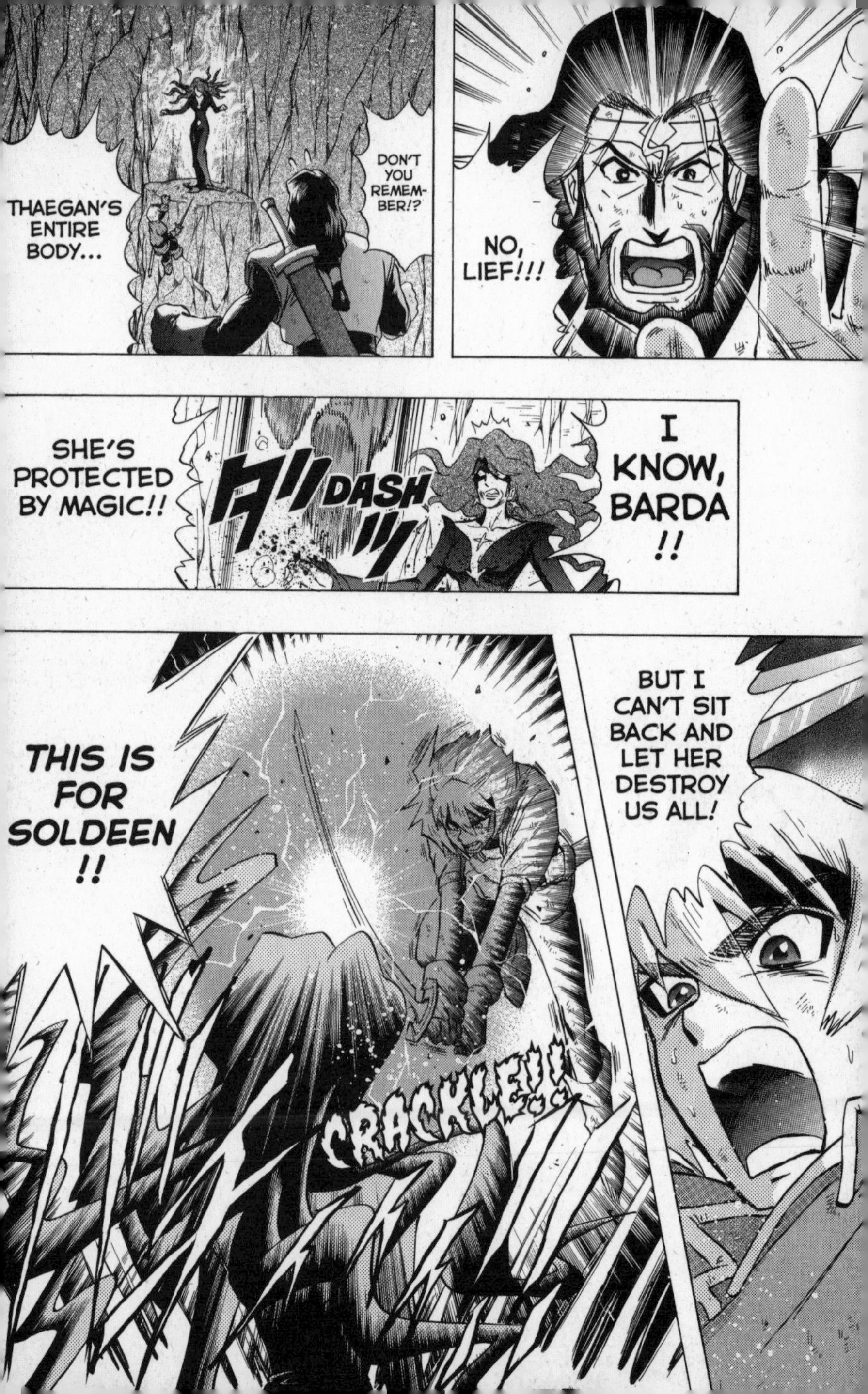
NO, LIEF!!!
DON'T YOU REMEMBER!?
THAEGAN'S ENTIRE BODY...
I KNOW, BARDA!!
DASH
SHE'S PROTECTED BY MAGIC!!
BUT I CAN'T SIT BACK AND LET HER DESTROY US ALL!
THIS IS FOR SOLDEEN!!
CRACKLE!!

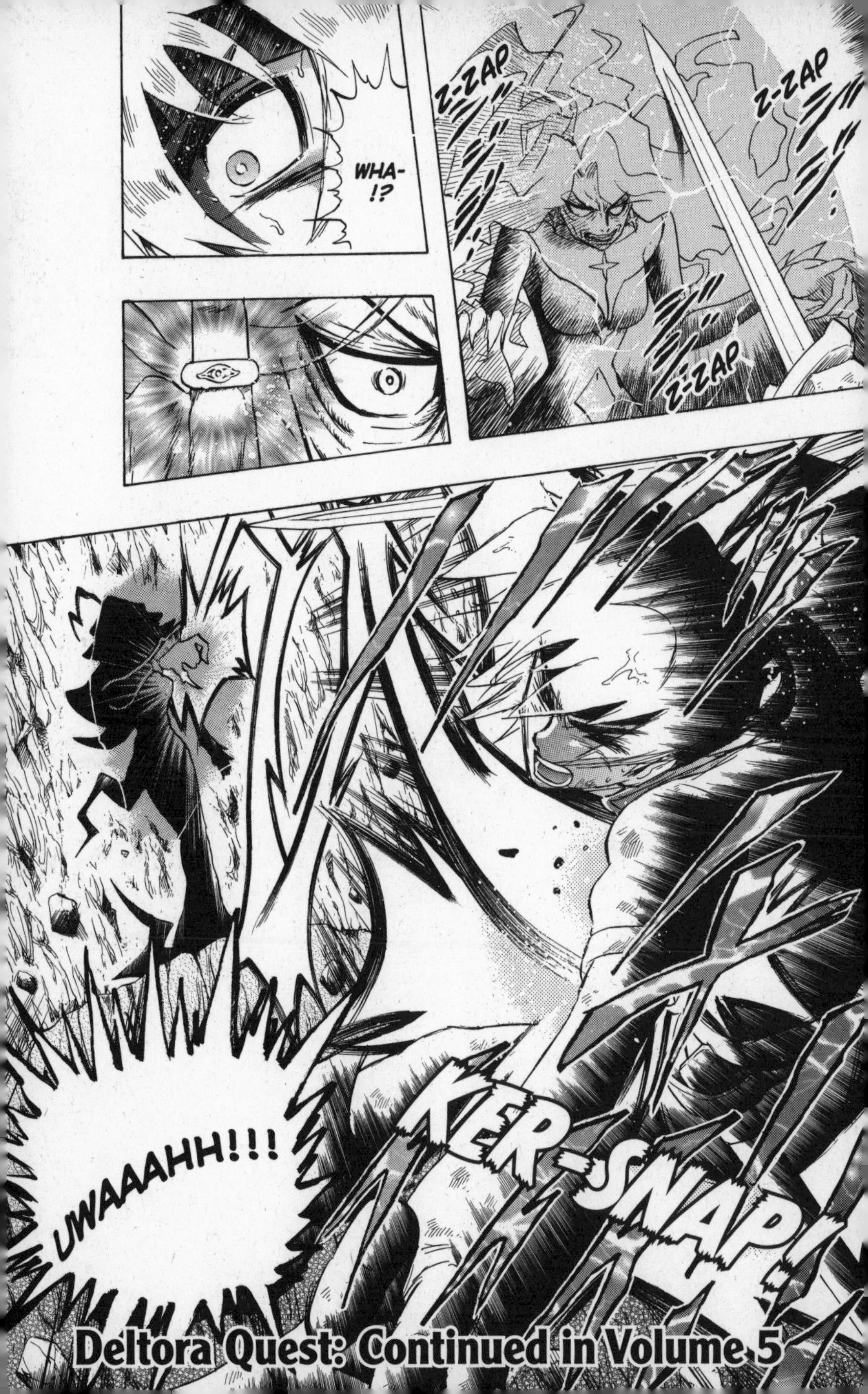
Z-ZAP
Z-ZAP
Z-ZAP
WHA-!?
KER-SNAP!
UWAAAHH!!!
Deltora Quest: Continued in Volume 5

Deltora Quest MONSTER GUIDE

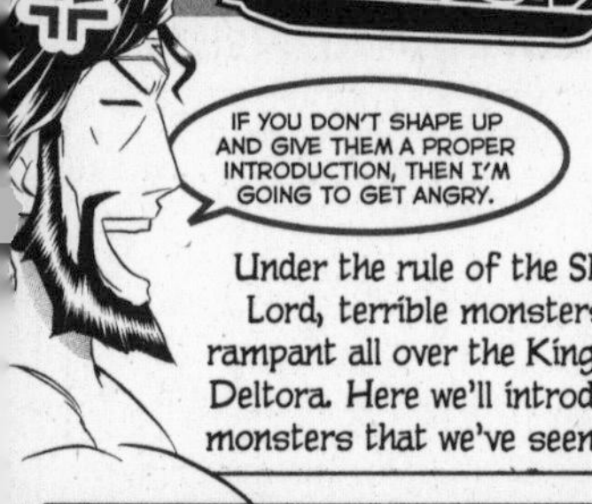
IF YOU DON'T SHAPE UP AND GIVE THEM A PROPER INTRODUCTION, THEN I'M GOING TO GET ANGRY.

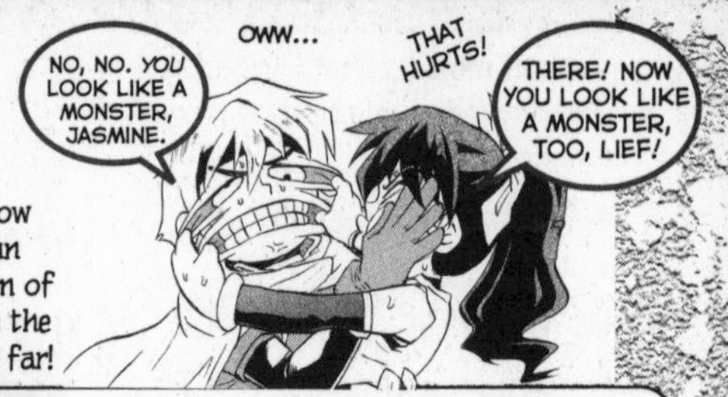
THERE! NOW YOU LOOK LIKE A MONSTER, TOO, LIEF!
THAT HURTS!
OWW...
NO, NO. *YOU* LOOK LIKE A MONSTER, JASMINE.

Under the rule of the Shadow Lord, terrible monsters run rampant all over the Kingdom of Deltora. Here we'll introduce the monsters that we've seen so far!

No. 1 The Monster Disguised as an Old Man

Appeared: The City of Del

A monster who disguised himself as an old man and wandered Del to settle his score with Jarred's father. He shows himself to Jarred after Jarred's escape from the palace, but is defeated with a single crushing blow.

➡ A former soldier of the Shadow Lord's army, he showed his monster form in the battle with Jarred's father.

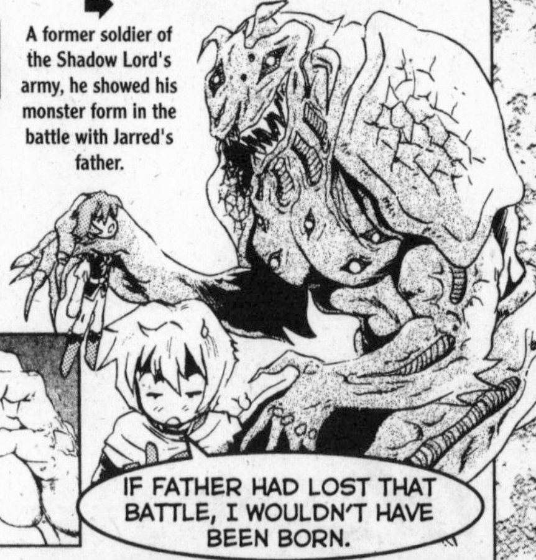
IF FATHER HAD LOST THAT BATTLE, I WOULDN'T HAVE BEEN BORN.

➡ Watch out for attacks from his long, sharp claws. The claws extend when he attacks.

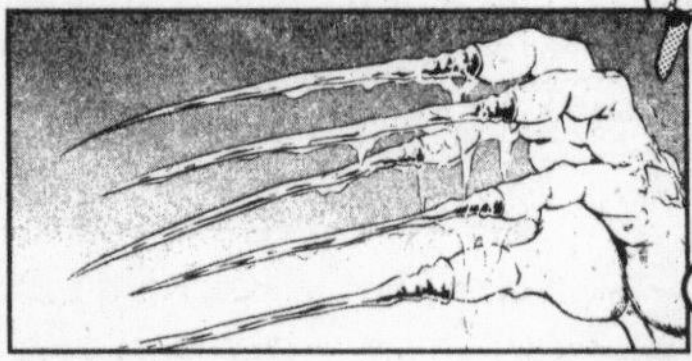

No. 2 Ak-Baba

Appeared: All over Deltora

Giant monster birds that serve the Shadow Lord and feed on dead flesh. It is said that during the reign of King Endon, seven Ak-Baba attacked the palace of Del, each stealing away one of the Seven Gems.

Under the Shadow Lord's orders, they attacked the palace of Del and stole the Seven Gems.

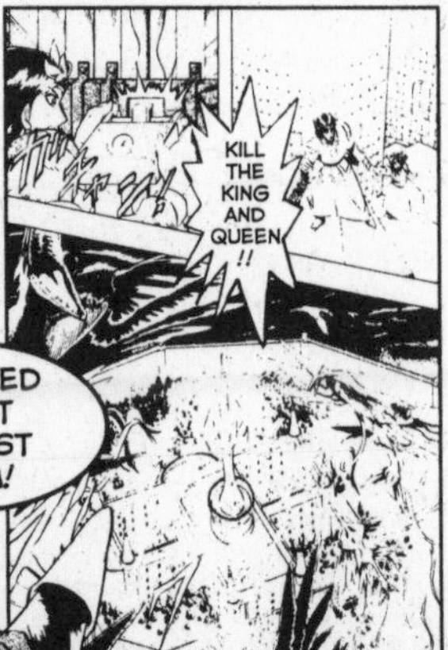
KILL THE KING AND QUEEN!!

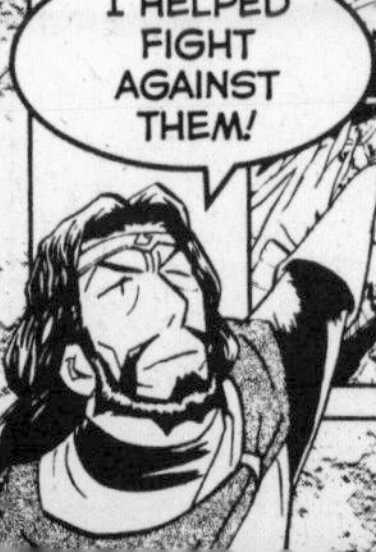
I HELPED FIGHT AGAINST THEM!

➡ Their large beaks are strong enough to break through the castle walls.

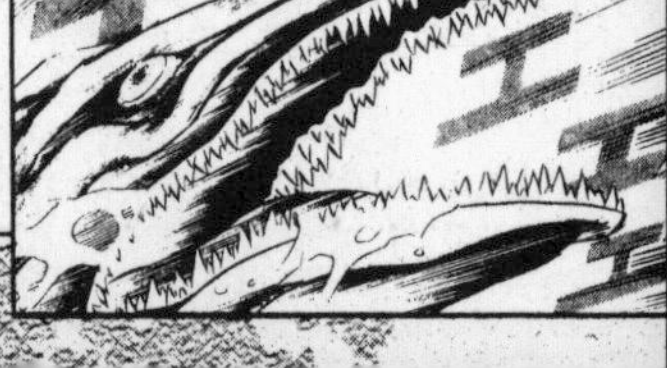

No. 3 Wenn
Appeared: The Forests of Silence

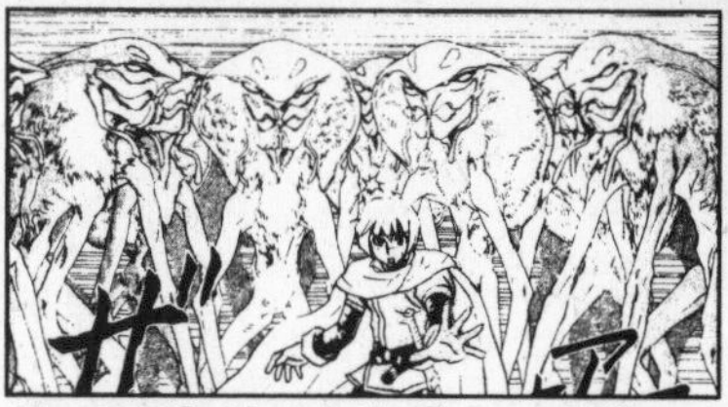

Monsters that lurk in the Forests of Silence, and along the path leading to the forests. They paralyze all passersby with their poison and offer them as live prey to the Wennbar, surviving off of the bits and pieces it leaves behind.

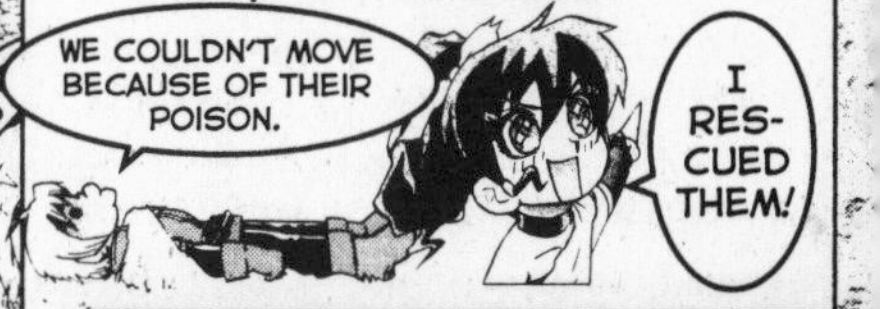
I RESCUED THEM!
WE COULDN'T MOVE BECAUSE OF THEIR POISON.

No. 4 Wennbar
Appeared: The Forests of Silence

A giant monster that lives off of the prey paralyzed by the Wenn. It can stretch its neck at will, so escaping to the treetops does not guarantee safety.

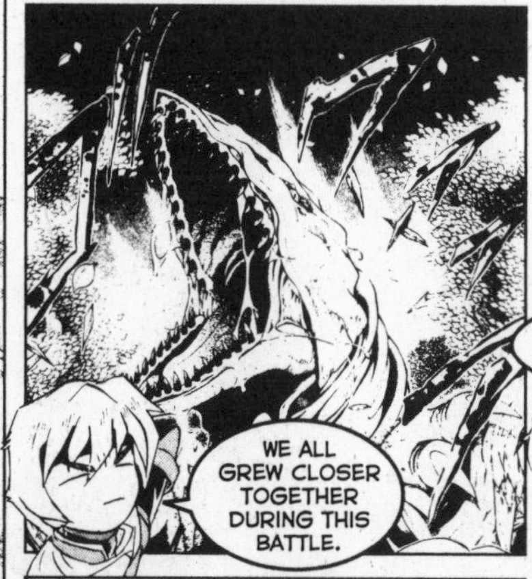
WE ALL GREW CLOSER TOGETHER DURING THIS BATTLE.

No. 5 The Golden Knight Gorl
Appeared: The Forests of Silence

A giant knight who guards the Lilies of Life in the Forests of Silence; in his past, he killed his own brothers so that he might gain eternal life. Thanks to Jasmine's strategy, he was crushed under a giant tree and lost his life.

The body inside the armor had already wasted away, so attacking gaps in the armor had no effect. ➡

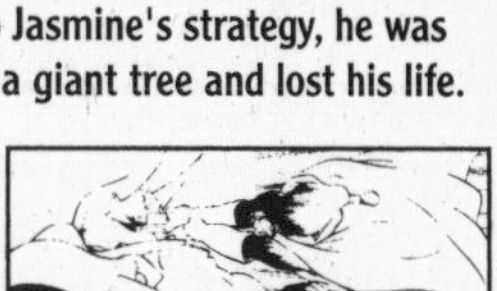
A POSSESSED MAN LIKE YOU WOULDN'T UNDERSTAND!!

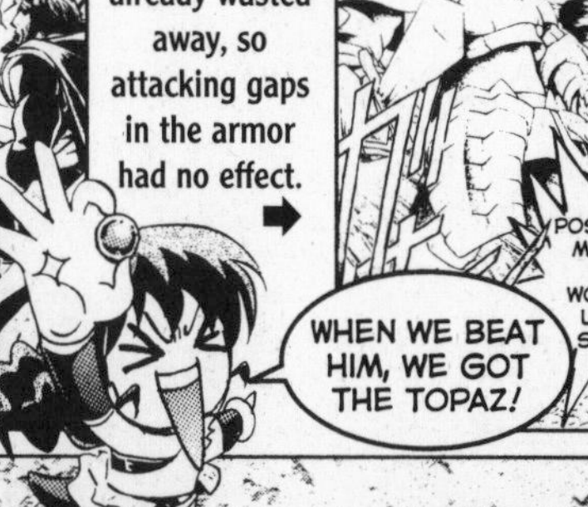
WHEN WE BEAT HIM, WE GOT THE TOPAZ!

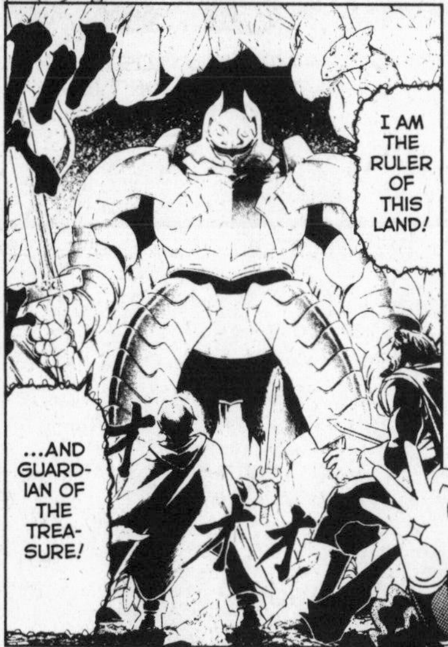
I AM THE RULER OF THIS LAND!
...AND GUARDIAN OF THE TREASURE!

No. 6 The Giant at the Gorge
Appeared: At the gorge

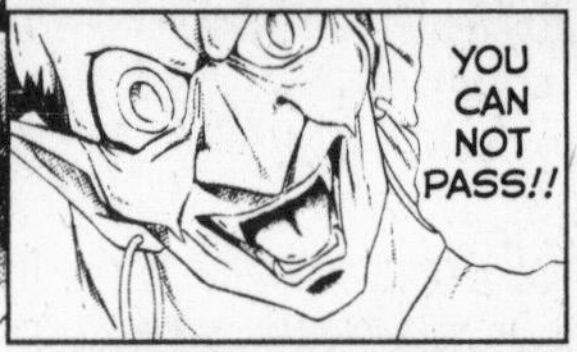
YOU CAN NOT PASS!!

Formerly a big bird, Thaegan's curse transformed him into a giant.

The guardian of the suspension bridge over the gorge on the way to the Lake of Tears. He asks travelers to answer his riddles, and only those who answer correctly are allowed to cross the bridge. All who answer incorrectly face the giant's sword.

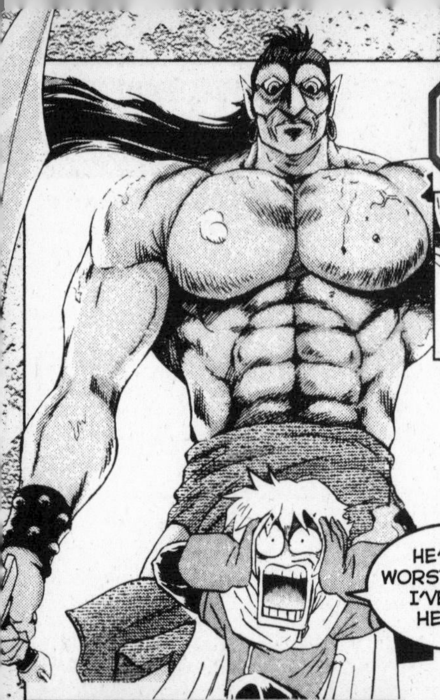

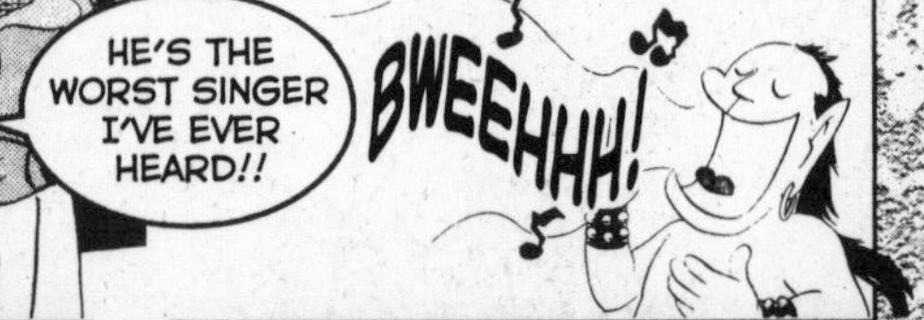
BWEEHHH!
HE'S THE WORST SINGER I'VE EVER HEARD!!

No. 7 Jin and Jod
Appeared: At the Quicksand Swamp

Thaegan's children; Jod is the older brother, and Jin is his younger sister. Disguised as humans, they lived by the quicksand swamp, attacking visitors and eating all who fell into the quicksand.

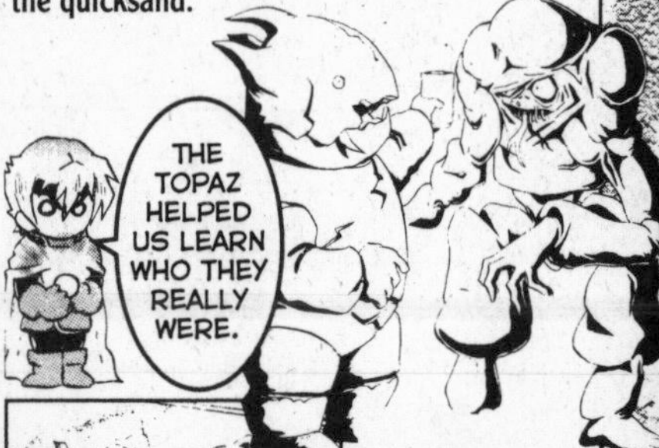
THE TOPAZ HELPED US LEARN WHO THEY REALLY WERE.

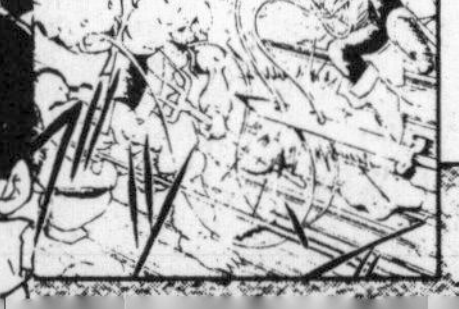

Jin and Jod can merge into one. Their long tongues serve as weapons.

No. 8 Soldeen
Appeared: The Lake of Tears

A giant aquatic monster that dwells in the Lake of Tears. He can freely move each of the spines that grow all over his body. Sometimes, his eyes look very sad.

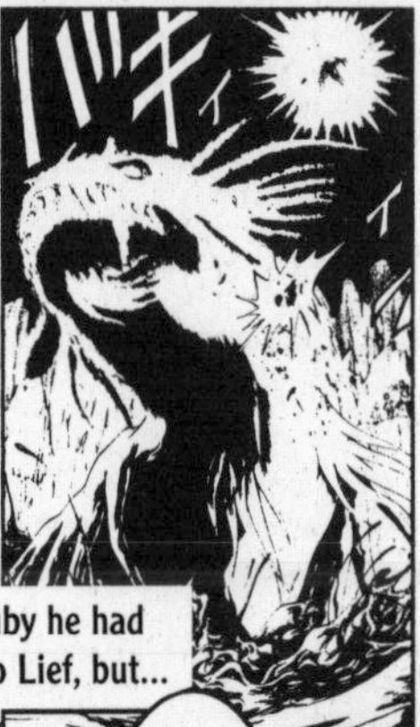

He gives the ruby he had been guarding to Lief, but...

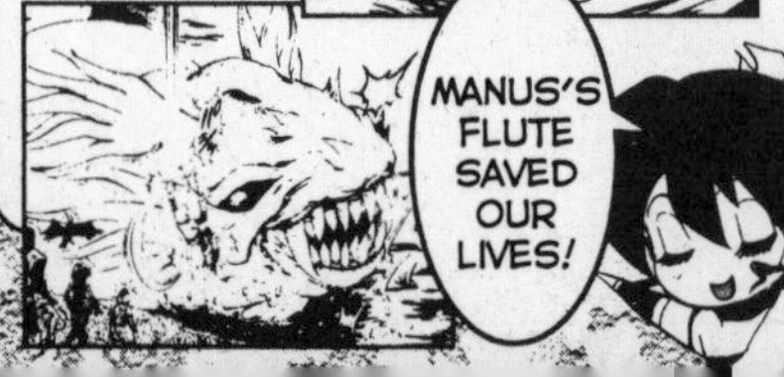
MANUS'S FLUTE SAVED OUR LIVES!

TOMARE!

[STOP!]

You are going the wrong way!

Manga is a completely different type of reading experience.

To start at the *beginning*, go to the *end*!

That's right! Authentic manga is read the traditional Japanese way— from right to left, exactly the *opposite* of how American books are read. It's easy to follow: Just go to the other end of the book, and read each page—and each panel—from the right side to the left side, starting at the top right. Now you're experiencing manga as it was meant to be.

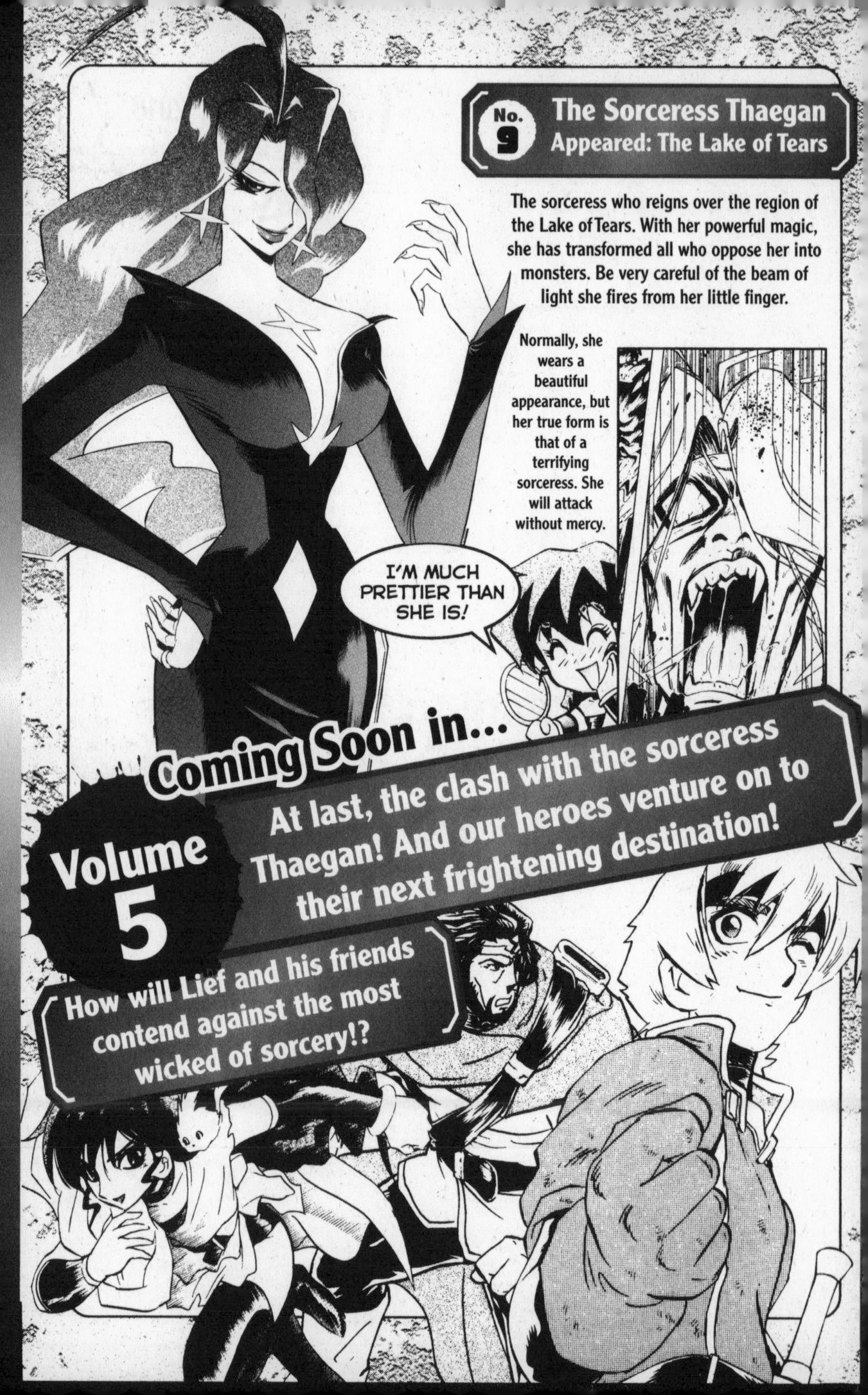
No. 9
The Sorceress Thaegan
Appeared: The Lake of Tears
The sorceress who reigns over the region of the Lake of Tears. With her powerful magic, she has transformed all who oppose her into monsters. Be very careful of the beam of light she fires from her little finger.
Normally, she wears a beautiful appearance, but her true form is that of a terrifying sorceress. She will attack without mercy.
I'M MUCH PRETTIER THAN SHE IS!
Coming Soon in...
Volume 5
At last, the clash with the sorceress Thaegan! And our heroes venture on to their next frightening destination!
How will Lief and his friends contend against the most wicked of sorcery!?